D1683292

USING THE "NARCOTRAFICO" THREAT TO BUILD PUBLIC ADMINISTRATION CAPACITY BETWEEN THE US AND MEXICO

American Society for Public Administration
Book Series on Public Administration & Public Policy

David H. Rosenbloom, Ph.D.
Editor-in-Chief

Mission: Throughout its history, ASPA has sought to be true to its founding principles of promoting scholarship and professionalism within the public service. The ASPA Book Series on Public Administration and Public Policy publishes books that increase national and international interest for public administration and which discuss practical or cutting edge topics in engaging ways of interest to practitioners, policy makers, and those concerned with bringing scholarship to the practice of public administration.

RECENT PUBLICATIONS

Using the "Narcotrafico" Threat to Build Public Administration Capacity between the US and Mexico
by Donald E. Klingner and Roberto Moreno Espinosa

Environmental Policymaking and Stakeholder Collaboration: Theory and Practice
by Shannon K. Orr

Organizational Assessment and Improvement in the Public Sector Workbook
by Kathleen M. Immordino

Challenges in City Management: A Case Study Approach
by Becky J. Starnes

Local Economic Development and the Environment: Finding Common Ground
by Susan M. Opp and Jeffery L. Osgood, Jr.

Case Studies in Disaster Response and Emergency Management
by Nicolas A. Valcik and Paul E. Tracy

Debating Public Administration: Management Challenges, Choices, and Opportunities
by Robert F. Durant and Jennifer R.S. Durant

Effective Non-Profit Management: Context, Concepts, and Competencies
by Shamima Ahmed

CRC Press
Taylor & Francis Group

JL
1231
.U755
2014

American Society for Public Administration
Series in Public Administration and Public Policy

USING THE "NARCOTRAFICO" THREAT TO BUILD PUBLIC ADMINISTRATION CAPACITY BETWEEN THE US AND MEXICO

Edited by
Donald E. Klingner • Roberto Moreno Espinosa

CRC Press
Taylor & Francis Group
Boca Raton London New York

CRC Press is an imprint of the
Taylor & Francis Group, an **informa** business

CRC Press
Taylor & Francis Group
6000 Broken Sound Parkway NW, Suite 300
Boca Raton, FL 33487-2742

© 2014 by Taylor & Francis Group, LLC
CRC Press is an imprint of Taylor & Francis Group, an Informa business

No claim to original U.S. Government works

Printed on acid-free paper
Version Date: 20131217

International Standard Book Number-13: 978-1-4665-7109-9 (Hardback)

This book contains information obtained from authentic and highly regarded sources. Reasonable efforts have been made to publish reliable data and information, but the author and publisher cannot assume responsibility for the validity of all materials or the consequences of their use. The authors and publishers have attempted to trace the copyright holders of all material reproduced in this publication and apologize to copyright holders if permission to publish in this form has not been obtained. If any copyright material has not been acknowledged please write and let us know so we may rectify in any future reprint.

Except as permitted under U.S. Copyright Law, no part of this book may be reprinted, reproduced, transmitted, or utilized in any form by any electronic, mechanical, or other means, now known or hereafter invented, including photocopying, microfilming, and recording, or in any information storage or retrieval system, without written permission from the publishers.

For permission to photocopy or use material electronically from this work, please access www.copyright.com (http://www.copyright.com/) or contact the Copyright Clearance Center, Inc. (CCC), 222 Rosewood Drive, Danvers, MA 01923, 978-750-8400. CCC is a not-for-profit organization that provides licenses and registration for a variety of users. For organizations that have been granted a photocopy license by the CCC, a separate system of payment has been arranged.

Trademark Notice: Product or corporate names may be trademarks or registered trademarks, and are used only for identification and explanation without intent to infringe.

Library of Congress Cataloging-in-Publication Data

Using the "narcotrafico" threat to build public administration capacity between the US and Mexico / editors: Donald E. Klingner, Roberto Moreno Espinosa.
 pages cm. -- (ASPA series in public administration and public policy) Includes bibliographical references and index.
 ISBN 978-1-4665-7109-9 (hardback)
 1. Public administration--Mexico. 2. Public institutions--Mexico. 3. Mexico--Politics and government--21st century. 4. Drug traffic--Government policy--Mexico. 5. Drug traffic--Government policy--United States. 6. Drug traffic--Mexican-American Border Region. 7. Narco-terrorism--Mexico. 8. United States--Foreign relations--Mexico. 9. Mexico--Foreign relations--United States. I. Klingner, Donald E., author, editor of compilation. II. Moreno Espinosa, Roberto, author, editor of compilation.

JL1231.U755 2014
353.1'30972--dc23   2013048806

Visit the Taylor & Francis Web site at
http://www.taylorandfrancis.com

and the CRC Press Web site at
http://www.crcpress.com

To Janette Klingner, the love of my life, who several years ago suggested I write something together with Roberto Moreno.

Contents

Preface ix
Acknowledgments xi
Editors xiii
Contributors xv

1   The "Perfect Storm": Drug Trafficking in the Mexico–U.S. Trans-Border Region as an Unrecognized Opportunity to Strengthen Public Administration 1
DONALD E. KLINGNER

2   Drug Trafficking and Public Administration: A Natural Relationship and a Global Problem.......................................17
DENIS PROULX

3   Regional Development, Education, and Trans-Border Governance: Toward the Creation of a True Economic and Social Community 35
ANGÉLICA PÉREZ ORDAZ

4   Looks of Fear: A Reflection of Violence and Crime in Mexico.............47
JOSÉ LUIS CISNEROS

5   A High-Risk Profession: Risks and Costs for Mexican Democracy of Journalists in the Middle of the War against Drug Trafficking.......61
JOSÉ ANTONIO ROSIQUE CAÑAS AND GLORIA ROSIQUE CEDILLO

6   The Military in the Homeland: Comparing the United States and Mexico 79
KURT A. JOHNSON AND MICHAEL A. NOLL

7   Institutional Capacity and National Security Policy in Mexico: From Formalism to Realism 97
MARIO A. RIVERA AND SOFIA ALEJANDRA SOLIS COBOS

| 8 | Critically Low Hispanic College Graduation Rates and a Clear Absence of Hispanic High-Level Administrators in Arizona, California, and Texas 119
RAMONA ORTEGA-LISTON AND RAJADE M. BERRY-JAMES |
|---|---|
| 9 | The Frontier of Knowledge: Between Life and Death 141
ADRIANA PLASENCIA DIAZ |
| 10 | How Cartel Violence Is Affecting Cross-Border Collaboration 163
ESPIRIDION ("AL") BORREGO |
| 11 | The U.S.–Mexico Border in the Making of Bilateral Policy............... 179
OSCAR MAURICIO COVARRUBIAS |
| 12 | Civil Service: A Critical Feature of Stability for Reducing Corruption in a Country Such as Mexico? 193
DAVID ARELLANO GAULT AND ENRIQUE CABRERO MENDOZA |
| 13 | Latin American States and the Imperatives of Unfinished Modernity: State Crisis and Public Security in Mexico 209
MIGUEL MORENO PLATA |
| 14 | Publicness and Governance...223
RICARDO UVALLE BERRONES |
| 15 | Analysis, Conclusions, and Final Considerations 239
ROBERTO MORENO ESPINOSA |

Index 253

Preface

A binational publishing project is a complex, unpredictable, and exciting undertaking. First, we had to choose a topic or problem that would interest those involved. Second, we had to select a team of authors who are experts on various aspects of this topic and then depend completely on their willingness and ability to complete their contributed chapters in spite of other personal and professional commitments. Third, we had to select publishing houses that would support this project and allow simultaneous publication in Spanish and English. Fourth, we had to work with 20 contributing authors on the many logistical issues involved in compiling, editing, and translating their chapters. In doing all this, we built on almost 20 years of collegiality and friendship to shape a shared editorial perspective on the drug trafficking crisis.

We are indebted to many people without whom this book would not have been possible. First, we would like to thank Dr. Ricardo Paredes Solorio, director of the School of Management at the Benemérita Universidad Autónoma de Puebla (BUAP) and other sponsors of the seminar on "The Agenda of Government in Mexico: Challenges and Prospects for Democracy," which took place in March 2012, from which the idea for this book originated. Over the course of this conference, we came to understand that many issues the Mexican government confronts are related to the "drug wars" between the United States and Mexico. These involve complex "intermestic" policy issues—transnational criminal organizations (TCOs), border security, economic development, and migratory policy—that neither the United States nor Mexico can resolve alone. Because of this, and despite their many negative consequences and the threat they pose to both countries, they nonetheless represent an unrecognized opportunity to improve public administration across our shared border. Hopefully, this book will be of interest to those in both countries who study and practice public administration and to those members of the general public who are interested in building governance capacity in the border area between the United States and Mexico. Because public administrators and institutions in both countries view problems from different perspectives and propose different strategies, we include the perspectives of Mexican, U.S., and Canadian authors. Because each country has a predominant language, and because language and culture are keys to comparative public administration research, we have published the book in English and Spanish. Hopefully, our approach will model the approach required to achieve the book's objective.

Second, we would like to thank the authors who contributed to this book: David Arellano Gault, RaJade M. Berry-James, Espiridion ("Al") Borrego, Enrique Cabrero Mendoza, José Luis Cisneros, Oscar Mauricio Covarrubias, Kurt A. Johnson, Miguel Moreno Plata, Michael A. Noll, Ramona Ortega-Liston, Angélica Pérez Ordaz, Adriana Plasencia Diaz, Denis Proulx, Mario Rivera, José Antonio Rosique Cañas, Gloria Rosique Cedillo, Sofia Alejandra Solis Cobos, and Ricardo Uvalle Berrones. Without their expertise and their willingness to collaborate with us by contributing expertly written chapters on a range of politically sensitive public policy and management issues in the United States and Mexico, this book could not have been written.

Third, we appreciate the unflagging and responsive support offered by our editor Lara Zoble, and are grateful to Taylor & Francis for granting us Spanish language publication rights.

Donald E. Klingner
Littleton, CO

Roberto Moreno Espinosa
Amecameca, Mexico

Acknowledgments

I would like to thank my friend and colleague Dr. Roberto Moreno Espinosa. When we first met as members of the Binational Consortium for U.S.–Mexico Public Administration Education in 1996, he was professor and director of postgraduate programs in the faculty of social and political sciences at the National Autonomous University of Mexico (UNAM). Since then, he has become a professor–investigator (level 2) in Mexico's national evaluation system (SNI) sponsored by CONACyT (Consejo Nacional de Ciencia y Technologia). Through shared conference presentations, workshops, seminars, and summer intensive courses at UNAM and UAEM (Autonomous University of the State of Mexico), he has helped me increase my knowledge of Mexico and Mexicans. Our collaborative efforts continue and intensify, including his participation on several panels at annual ASPA (American Society for Public Administration) conferences in the United States. Without his trust and support, this book would not have been written. I am indebted to many Mexican colleagues and friends—students, practitioners, and researchers, including those at the UNAM, the UAEM, the Center for Research and Teaching in Economics (CIDE), the University Anáhuac Xalapa (UAX), and other Mexican institutions of higher education, and the leaders of the National Institute of Public Administration (INAP), including IAPEM (Institute for Public Administration of the State of Mexico) and other state institutes of public administration. I'd like to express my appreciation to Marshall Kaplan for creating and the U.S. Department of State for funding the Binational Consortium for Public Administration Education (1996–2003), where many of us met and began working together. Without their help, I would understand very little about this complex and extraordinary country, which I love in the sense that the philosopher Wallace Stegner expressed so perfectly: "I had never been to this place before, but everything I learned about it told me who I am." Francisco A. Gonzalez, University of Colorado Colorado Springs, located many of the research materials needed to document this book, and help translate some chapters from one language to the other. Faustino Pino showed me the El Paso he grew up in and the one he returned to in retirement, and shared his dream of a border that connects rather than divides our two countries.

Donald E. Klingner

This is an appropriate opportunity to express my appreciation for Donald E. Klingner, who is a distinguished professor in the School of Public Affairs at the University of Colorado, Colorado Springs and a former president of the ASPA. The work he has done in Latin America provides ample evidence of his academic and professional commitment to the development of public administration globally. This includes visits to almost every country in Central and South America and Mexico for conferences, summer courses, and training seminars, consulting, advising, and mentoring. I have shared many of these visits with him. While coordinating the graduate program in public administration in the Faculty of Social and Political Sciences at UNAM, I promoted his summer courses there, as well as several other intensive courses and training seminars with the UAEM and IAPEM.

Roberto Moreno Espinosa

Editors

Donald E. Klingner, PhD in public administration from the University of Southern California, is a distinguished professor in the School of Public Affairs at the University of Colorado, Colorado Springs, a Fellow of the National Academy of Public Administration (NAPA), and past president of ASPA. He is the coauthor of *Public Personnel Management* (Sixth Edition, 2010), published in English, Spanish, and Chinese. He has been a Fulbright Senior Scholar (Central America, 1994), a visiting professor at UNAM, Mexico (1999–2003), and a consultant to the United Nations, the World Bank, and the Inter-American Development Bank on public management capacity building. He was a faculty member at IUPUI (1974–1980) and Florida International University (1980–2001), and worked for the U.S. Civil Service Commission (1968–1973). Email: donald.klingner@gmail.com

Roberto Moreno Espinosa, PhD in public administration from UNAM and a postdoctoral fellow at the University of New Mexico, has been a member of the Inter-American Development Bank's Advisory Council on Civil Society Representation in Mexico (2001–2009) and graduate coordinator of public administration at UNAM (1996–2008). He is the author of five books and numerous articles and essays, and has been a visiting professor at 20 Mexican and seven international universities. He is a member of the National System of Researchers (SNI), Level 2; chairman of the Board of the International Academy of Political and Administrative Sciences and Future Studies, AC, and professor at the Autonomous University of the State of Mexico (AUEM), Amecameca Campus. Email: rmorenoespinosa@yahoo.com.mx

Contributors

Ricardo Uvalle Berrones, PhD in public administration from UNAM, is a coordinator of the Center for Studies in Public Administration at UNAM. He is the author of 14 books and editor of seven more, author of over 30 book chapters and almost 100 articles published in national and international journals. He is a member (Level 3) of the National Research System established by CONACyT. Email: ricardo_uvalle@yahoo.com.mx

RaJade M. Berry-James, PhD, is an associate professor in the Department of Public Administration at North Carolina State University. Her research and teaching interests in public administration focus on social equity, program evaluation, and research methods. Dr. Berry-James serves on the editorial board of the *Journal of Public Management and Social Policy* and the *Journal of Public Affairs Education*. Her research has appeared in the *Journal of Black Political Research*, *Public Performance and Management Review*, *International Journal of Public Administration*, *International Journal of Humanities*, *Journal of Public Budgeting, Accounting and Financial Management,* and *Journal of Public Management and Social Policy*. She is a past recipient of *The Donald S. Stone Service Award* from ASPA and current chair (2012–2014) of NASPAA's Commission on Peer Review and Accreditation (COPRA). Email: rmberryj@ncsu.edu

Espiridion ("Al") Borrego, PhD in public administration from the University of Southern California, is an associate professor in the Department of Security Studies and Public Affairs at the University of Texas–Pan American. He was a member of President Obama's transition team. He has been a senior consultant and lead business partner at Alignment Strategies, Inc. (ALS). He served as the assistant secretary for Veterans' Employment and Training, U.S. Department of Labor. He was the dean of the School of Business and Public Administration, University of Alaska Southeast and an associate professor of public administration. He was a presidential management intern at NASA, Office of the Comptroller, and a Ford Foundation Fellow. Email: alborrego@utpa.edu

José Antonio Rosique Cañas is a PhD scholar in political and social sciences from UNAM and a postdoctorate in public affairs from The University of New Mexico and a Diploma in Public Organizations from Harvard University. He is a professor-research and was coordinator of graduate studies at the Autonomous Metropolitan University (Xochimilco) in Mexico City. He is a member of the National Research System established by Mexico's National Council for Science and Technology (CONACyT), and has written four books and numerous articles on urban and metropolitan issues. He has served as a consultant to several governmental organizations, as an editorial board member of three journals, and a visiting researcher at six universities in France, Spain, and the United States. Email: arosique@correo.xoc.uam.mx

Gloria Rosique Cedillo is a PhD scholar in information from the Complutense University of Madrid, MBA and communications studies from the University Carlos III (Madrid). She is the author of nearly 30 research papers and several national and international conference presentations. Her main areas of research are: university educational content and methodology (EHEA), associations of viewers in Spain, France, and Mexico, content and users of television, media groups, and journalism. Research stays in the CEMTI of Paris-Sorbonne University 8, University IHEAL Paris III-Sorbonne Nouvelle, and a postdoctoral fellow at the Metropolitan Autonomous University (UAM-X) in Mexico City. Since 2010, she has been a professor in the Department of Journalism and Audiovisual Communication at the University Carlos III of Madrid. Email: grosique@hum.uc3 m.es

José Luis Cisneros, PhD in sociology, is a research professor (National Researcher Level I) at the Universidad Autónoma Metropolitana in Xochimilco (Mexico City). He is a research area member in education, culture, and social processes. He also has a master's in criminology; specialization in forensic anthropology; and diplomas in addictions and anthropology of violence. His research areas include violence, crime, and prisons. Email: cisneros.joseluis@gmail.com

Sofia Alejandra Solis Cobos, MPA from the University of New Mexico and a law degree from Universidad del Valle de Mexico, is a corporate attorney in Mexico City with significant experience in the public safety and insurance sectors. In the private sector, she has implemented measures to combat money laundering, designed policies for customer identification and verification, and drafted and implemented codes of conduct. She worked as secretary of the Board of ING Mexico, Comercial America Insurance and their subsidiaries. In the public sector, she worked in the offices of the Attorney General, Public Security, and the Legal and Governmental Affairs Office of Tlahuac Political District, specializing in electoral crimes. Email: sascobos@hotmail.com

Oscar Mauricio Covarrubias is a PhD scholar in political science (specializing in public administration) from UNAM, postgraduate studies in educational planning, administration, and research at Mexico's National Institute for Public Administration (INAP) in 2009, and postdoctoral studies in government and public policy at the University of New Mexico (Albuquerque). He currently serves as vice president of the Academy of Political-Administrative Sciences and Future Studies (IAPAS). Email: mauricio.covarrubias@iapas.mx

Adriana Plasencia Diaz is a PhD scholar in political and social sciences (with honors) from UNAM, and postdoctoral studies at the Autonomous Metropolitan University (Mexico City). She has combined academic activities in institutions such as UNAM and the INAP with administrative responsibilities in the Ministry of Social Development and the Ministry of Public Education. She has also served as a project consultant on innovations in public administration and education. She is the author of books on *Public Management: Theoretical and Conceptual Foundations* (1994) and *The Federalization of Basic Education in Mexico: A Work in Progress* (2010), as well as of articles on transparency, education, and public administration. Email: adrianaplasencia@hotmail.com

David Arellano Gault, PhD in public administration from the University of Colorado, is a professor at the Center for Teaching and Research in Economics (CIDE) in Mexico; coeditor of *Organization Studies*, and an editorial board member of the *Journal of Public Administration Research and Theory*, the *American Review of Public Administration*, and *Gestión y Política Pública* (Mexico). His recent publications include: "Bringing Public Organization and Organizing Back in Organization Studies" (with Demortain, Rouillard, and Thoenig, February 2013), "The Evaluation of Performance in the Mexican Federal Government: A Study of the Monitoring Agencies' Modernization Process" (*Public Administration Review*, 2013), and *Can We Reduce Corruption in Mexico? Limits and Possibilities of the Instruments at Our Disposal* (CIDE, 2012). Email: david.arellano@cide.edu

Kurt A. Johnson is a corporate alliances executive with Colorado Technical University, part of Career Education Corporation. Mr. Johnson was most recently the director of the Center for Homeland Security (CHS) at the University of Colorado at Colorado Springs, where he led the Center's growing domestic and international homeland defense and homeland security education and training programs at all levels of government and in the private sector. Mr. Johnson retired from the U.S. Navy in 2008 with the rank of Captain (O-6). During his 24-year career, he served worldwide primarily as an advisor to U.S. military commanders. His final assignment was as the senior legal advisor to the Commander of NORAD and U.S. Northern Command from 2005 to 2008. Mr. Johnson earned his JD from the University of Wisconsin, and his LL.M from the University of Virginia. Email: kjohnson2@ctuonline.edu

Enrique Cabrero Mendoza, PhD in management sciences from the HEC School in France, is a general director of Mexico's Science and Technology National Council (CONACyT). He has been a visiting professor at L'École Normale Supérieure in France, at the University of Birmingham in Great Britain, and at the University of Barcelona in Spain, among other universities of excellence. Dr. Cabrero is the author of more than 25 books and has published more than one hundred papers and chapters internationally. His main topics of interest are public policy analysis, decentralization, federalism, city governments, competition, and science and technology public policy. He is member of the Mexican Academy of Science, participates in many editorial and academic Boards, and has been consultant at different international organizations. He was a tenured professor at the Center of Economics Research and Teaching (CIDE) and from 2004 to 2012 he directed the Center. Email: ecabrero@conacyt.mx

Michael A. Noll retired in 2010 from the Senior Executive Service after almost nine years as the director of Intelligence (J2) for North American Aerospace Defense Command, U.S. Northern Command and director of Joint Intelligence Operations Center North. Mr. Noll retired from the U.S. Navy in 2004 with the rank of Captain (O-6). Over a period of 28 years, he served at sea and ashore in the European, Central, and Pacific Command areas. In addition to his time in the U.S. Navy, Mr. Noll served twice as an exchange officer with the UK's Royal Navy. Mr. Noll is now an adjunct research professor and graduate-level instructor for the University of Colorado at Colorado Springs. He teaches courses on intelligence and on border security. Email: kalmnoll@comcast.net

Angélica Pérez Ordaz is a PhD scholar in political and social science (specialization in public administration) from UNAM with a postdoctoral fellowship in Milan, Italy (2009–2010) that focused on the application of information and communications technologies (ICTs) to undergraduate programs at UNAM. She is currently a professor of sciences and humanities at UNAM, and a founding member of the Academy of Management and Political Science Future Studies (IAPAS). E-mail: angelica.perez@cch.unam.mx.

Ramona Ortega-Liston is an associate professor at the University of Akron, Department of Public Administration & Urban Studies (PAUS). She teaches introduction to public administration, ethics in public service, leadership and decision-making, strategic management, comparative public administration, and the Washington, DC Summer Seminar for MPA students. She earned a doctorate from Arizona State University (1998); master's from Harvard University (1981); and a BS (*magna cum laude*) from Arizona State University (1976). She was director of the Unaccompanied Minors Shelter Care Program (UMSCP), a nonprofit organization. For exemplary service and leadership of the UMSCP, she was recognized by the U.S. Office of the Inspector General for creating a model shelter for illegal minors. Her current research focus is on Hispanic political efficacy. She has published articles on the variables influencing careers of Mexican Americans in public service. Email: ramona3@uakron.edu

Miguel Moreno Plata, PhD in environmental law from the University of Alicante and master in public administration from UNAM, is a research professor of the Academy of Political Science and Urban Management at the Autonomous University of Mexico City. He is a visiting professor in the Master of Environmental Law and Management Research and Development Center of the State of Michoacán and the Master of Civil Law at Lasalle University, and a member of the National Research System of CONACYT (Level I). In 2011, he won first place in the contest "crisis and disaster management" organized by the Latin American Center for Development Administration (CLAD). He is the author of several books and articles on sustainability, environment, climate change, public policy, risk management, and governance. Email: morenoplata@hotmail.com

Denis Proulx, PhD from Laval University (Quebec), is a professor at the National School of Public Administration (ENAP) at the University of Quebec. He has 36 years of experience in teaching and research on themes linked to public management, intercultural management, NGOs, and organizational assessment and change. He has published widely, made numerous conference presentations and lectured in over 45 countries throughout the world. He has worked extensively throughout Canada, the United States, and Latin America, directing projects in Mexico, Peru, Colombia, and Argentina. Email: denis.proulx@enap.ca

Mario A. Rivera, PhD, is Regents' Professor of Public Administration in the School of Public Administration at the University of New Mexico. He has consulted extensively with public and nonprofit agencies on performance management, program evaluation, accountability in the United States and in Mexico, Central and South America, and West Africa, including the U.S. Agency for International Development, U.S. Department of Labor, and New Mexico State Legislature. As a trainer and evaluator for the Inter-American Development Bank and Associates in Rural Development (ending in 2001), Dr. Rivera worked with the Supreme Court, Ministry of Justice, National Police, and five other cabinet-level justice-sector agencies of El Salvador in strengthening their strategic planning and performance management capabilities. He is a senior associate editor of *The Innovation Journal* (Canada) and an editorial board member of the *Journal of Public Affairs Education, Policy and Management Review, Journal of Business and Public Affairs, Problems and Perspectives in Management, Scholarship on the Assessment of Learning, The Journal of Information and Operations Management*, and *Revista de Gestión Pública* (Chile). Email: marivera@unm.edu

Chapter 1

The "Perfect Storm"
Drug Trafficking in the Mexico–U.S. Trans-Border Region as an Unrecognized Opportunity to Strengthen Public Administration

Donald E. Klingner

Contents

Preface 1
A History of Drug Trafficking and Public Policy in Mexico and the United States......3
The Complexity of Relations between Mexico and the United States.....................6
The "Perfect Storm": An Unrecognized Opportunity to Build Governance
Capacity..8
The Organization of This Book 13
References 14

Preface

It is easy to see the impact of the "drug wars" on everyday life in Mexico. The media are full of sensational accounts of abductions, assaults, and murders in cities along the U.S. border such as Juarez, Nuevo Laredo, and Nogales, and in others that are located on major north–south trafficking corridors along the Caribbean and Pacific coasts, such as Veracruz and Culiacán (Vulliamy 2010). In areas known as major drug-trafficking routes, highway checkpoints are guarded by truckloads of soldiers masked to reduce the risk of reprisals against their families by the drug cartels and billboards threaten those convicted of kidnapping with 70 years in prison. Even in areas that remain relatively safe, people are concerned about the threat drug trafficking and related violence poses to Mexico's traditional values, sense of community, and family structure.

Drug-related violence in Mexico became commonplace beginning in 2005, and increased dramatically between 2008 and 2012 (Shirk 2010; Stratfor 2012a) despite—and perhaps also because of—massive efforts of the U.S. and Mexican government to stop drug trafficking. It is concentrated in a few key states critical to the drug trade such as Chihuahua, Durango, Guerrero, and Sinaloa (Stratfor 2011). In Mexico, it poses a disproportionate threat to civil servants, police, and women under 18. Officials and citizens in the trans-border area fear that cross-border drug trafficking and violence will spill over into the United States (Stratfor 2012a,b).

Being an American public administrator who works closely with counterparts in Mexico doesn't help either. At least until recently, most Mexicans considered themselves innocent bystanders in the "drug wars," hostages to insatiable U.S. demand for cocaine, marijuana, methamphetamine, and other drugs. Now, even as indisputable evidence of Mexicans' active participation in the drug trade continues to emerge and as its fundamental negative effects on Mexican society are irrefutable, revelations confirm the U.S. government's active complicity (or even guilt) in arms trafficking and money laundering, albeit as unanticipated negative consequences of its efforts to combat transnational criminal organizations (TCOs). For example, the ATFE (U.S. Bureau of Alcohol, Tobacco, Firearms, and Explosives) initiated a program (called "Fast and Furious") designed to track the flow of illegal weapons to the Mexican cartels that resulted in the release of hundreds of firearms in Mexico, many of which have been subsequently used against that country's citizens. A similar operation by the DEA (U.S. Drug Enforcement Agency) was designed to allow agents to trace the flow and laundering of drug money (Realuyo 2012). Understandably, Mexicans are both deeply troubled by the "perfect storm" and aghast at U.S. complicity—witting or unwitting—in the violence, corruption, and social disruption it has produced in their own country.

This chapter will (1) review the recent history of drug trafficking in Mexico and policies of Mexico and the United States against it, (2) put this history and public policy within the complex historical context of the relationship between these two countries, (3) suggest why this "perfect storm" represents an opportunity too important to waste to build governance capacity on both sides of the border, (4) propose some steps for doing so, and (5) present this book's organization.

A History of Drug Trafficking and Public Policy in Mexico and the United States

Mexican marijuana has been imported into the United States for over a century. This flow of contraband increased during the 1930s after the U.S. government outlawed marijuana and other drugs, using the same criminal organizations that had smuggled alcohol into the United States during the 1920s, when alcohol was also a prohibited drug in the United States. The flow of drugs from Mexico to the United States accelerated after World War II as organized crime spread from the East Coast to Las Vegas, and TCOs used trafficking routes through Mexico to reach expanding West Coast markets.

The advent of the "war on drugs" and the creation of the DEA (U.S. Drug Enforcement Agency) in 1971 greatly intensified U.S. efforts to control drug production and distribution. These initially focused on the production and shipment of cocaine from Colombia through the Caribbean and South Florida. The success of these efforts, coupled with continued demand for drugs in the United States, led to the development of alternative smuggling routes through Central America and Mexico into Texas, New Mexico, Arizona, and California. Coincidentally, the growth of major drug trafficking operations in Mexico was aided by fundamental economic developments in the trans-border area during the 1990s. First, Mexico experienced a period of intense economic development, integration, and trade with the United States. The same factors that drove legitimate economic interests—and the new global economy in general—also benefited TCOs and other elements of the illegal economy (Astorga Almanza 2010). The approval of NAFTA (the North American Free Trade Agreement) in 1994 generated a "gray market" along the entire U.S.–Mexico border, and especially between Mexican "gateway" cities such as Monterrey, Nuevo Laredo, Reynosa, Ciudad Juarez, Ensenada, and Tijuana. Mexican residing in the United States had traditionally made road trips back to Mexico over Christmas and Easter holidays, bringing toys, electronics, small appliances and other U.S. goods for family and friends there. Enterprising Mexican businessmen expanded this trade, selling goods from cities such as San Antonio, El Paso, and San Diego in formal and informal markets throughout Mexico. This cross-border traffic included everyone from small-scale traders with goods in suitcases or shopping bags to large-scale TCOs using cars, trucks, and shipping containers. Smugglers also used planes, submarines, and sophisticated tunnels equipped with rail tracks, lights, and ventilation systems. Viewed from this perspective, current TCO operations are a logical extension of the social and economic networks that have historically existed throughout the border area between the United States and Mexico, albeit driven by profits and augmented by criminal practices (coercion, extortion, and violence) (Sandoval 2012). These historical trends—legitimate and illegitimate—have led to what may be called a "perfect storm"—the flow of drugs north and the flow of firearms and money south across the heretofore largely open 2000 mile border between the United States and Mexico.

Matt Wuerker (June 29, 2011). Politico.com

Once the Cold War ended in 1989 with the collapse of the former Soviet Union, drug trafficking and international terrorism came to be viewed by U.S. policy makers as the greatest threats to U.S. national security (Valeriano and Powers 2010). After the terrorist attacks of September 11, 2001, the security of its southern border became the highest priority of U.S. foreign policy toward Mexico (Kleiman 2011). The United States has sought to close its border with Mexico in order to shield against possible terrorist attacks and combat TCOs' involvement in drug trafficking and organized crime. Within Mexico, at least beginning with the administration of President Felipe Calderón (2006–2012), other foreign policy goals also became subordinate to these objectives.

The Merida Initiative (2007) was promoted in both the United States and Mexico as a mechanism for cooperation to achieve common goals—a Mexican government better positioned to combat TCOs and thus abler to provide greater stability and security in that country, and fewer drugs entering the United States as a result (Benítez Mahaut 2011; Chabat 2010a,b; Ribando Seelke and Beittel 2009; Velázquez and Schiavon 2009; Rodríguez and Kuri Meyer 2011). It did not fundamentally alter relations between Mexico and the United States. However, it was based on similar perceptions, ideas, and concerns about the drug between the governments of the United States and Mexico, created greater opportunities to build bilateral cooperation (Chabat 2010c), and added new elements to the bilateral relationship (Bonner 2012).

However, underlying factors have undermined the positive effects of short-term agreements intended to enhance border security and combat TCOs. Despite widespread expectations of change for the better, the Obama administration has shown more signs of continuity than of change in its policy toward Mexico. The many stakeholders that contribute to the process of decision making on common issues have impeded President Obama's ability to make changes in the two countries' fundamental binational agenda (Velázquez 2011).

The relationship between Mexico and the United States is complex because it has historically included cooperation, conflict, intervention, invasion, and conquest. The United States has always tried to project its own goals and interests onto its southern neighbor. When the two countries' interests agree and their views on common problems seem similar, they have cooperated. When these differ, it has heavy-handedly intervened in Mexican politics and sometimes invaded Mexico to secure its own national objectives. Historically, the most important of these have been border control, trade and financial liberalization, territorial expansion, and containment of communism. Currently, they focus on border control as an adjunct to national security, joint drug interdiction, and joint economic development.

From a Mexican perspective, the "drug wars" constitute an unwelcome distraction from that country's perpetual problems of poverty, economic development, and global competitiveness. Mexico's economy is now growing rapidly, to the point where it once more merits comparison with that of Brazil. This growth, combined with the demographic "bonus" resulting from its rapidly declining birth rate and coupled with continued emigration and urbanization, has positioned Mexico to take its place among the world's largest economies. Unfortunately, the "war on drugs" has reduced international tourism, impeded the expansion of democratic practices and institutions, encouraged corruption and impunity, and complicated the professionalization of the judiciary. At a conceptual level, the "perfect storm" represents a "vicious circle" that is the contemporary expression of three intersecting and debilitating tendencies in Mexico's traditional political culture: (1) the weakness of local government compared to national government, (2) the frequent subordination of civil government to the armed forces, and (3) the weakness of civil society compared to the two absolutes of authoritarian government and drug trafficking (Oyarvide Morales 2011; Lindau 2011). Drug trafficking and the "war on drugs" reveal endemic historical tendencies since pre-Hispanic times toward violence, authoritarianism, and centralization (Klingner 2000; Klingner and Arellano Gault 2006). The use of the Mexican military against TCOs reveals the lack of trust in the state and local governments responsible for civilian public safety. It reflects the weakness of community-based values and organizations, and perpetuates the fatalism and cynicism that have long been part of Mexican political culture (Rubio 2011). Applying the Merida Initiative in areas of endemic poverty and inequality, "… criminalizes the fight for social justice and other social activity, reinforces open war against drug cartels and justifies the widespread use of violent means to fight them, while making possible abuses, fighting in public spaces and the violation of the population's human rights by the military and police forces" (Chabat 2010c, p. 6).

Nor is it possible to evaluate the effects of TCOs and the "drug wars" in Mexico without viewing them as part of the endless global war against drug trafficking. The prohibition of drugs in the United States and the consolidation under U.S. leadership of a global regimen of international control are directly linked to the emergence of Latin American countries as producers, exporters, and distributors of narcotics (Serrano 2010). In 2009, the DEA estimated that TCOs' drug trafficking in Mexico and Colombia contributed between $17 billion and $38 billion a year in gross wholesale drug sales in the United States. In comparison, Google's revenue worldwide in 2009 was $23.6 billion (Kellner and Pipitone 2010). As Ignacio Pichardo Pagaza dryly noted (2009) in discussing Mexico's role in drug trafficking with the United States, "There's supply and there's demand."

The Complexity of Relations between Mexico and the United States

History provides the symbols and confirms the myths countries use to define themselves. In this regard, U.S. history, at least as it is commonly understood and taught in the United States, confirms a deep prejudice against that country's extensive historical roots in Spain and Latin America. Long before the British landed at Jamestown (1607) and Plymouth Rock (1620), the Spanish colonized Florida and "New Spain," creating flourishing outposts of empire in St. Augustine, Santa Fe, and along the California coast. Long before the Lewis and Clark expedition (1803–1805), Spanish explorers such as Hernando de Soto traveled up the Mississippi River from Florida, created the Santa Fe Trail from New Mexico to Colorado, and built the Kings Highway ("el Camino Real") to connect a chain of missions along the California coast.

Thus, the United States is not only an Anglophile nation of former British colonies, but also a Hispanic country that was a significant part of Spain's colonial empire in the New World for 300 years. What is now the southwestern U.S. (Texas, Arizona, New Mexico, California, and Southern Colorado) constituted the northern half of Mexico from its independence in 1821 until the United States conquered Texas in 1836 and the rest of this region in the War of 1848 (Hurtado 2012).

Because of this complex history, Mexico and the United States have a "special relationship" characterized by intense and complicated patterns of conflict and cooperation, and increasing political, economic, social, and cultural interdependence on a range of domestic and international (i.e., "intermestic") issues (Velázquez 2011). Each country has tended to define their relationship in ways that have proven difficult to break because of historical trends and events (Selee 2005). Within the United States, perceptions of Mexico tend to reflect the negative impact of Mexican immigration—legal and illegal—on our systems of education, public health, and criminal justice. While conservatives accept that immigration of young workers is needed to sustain U.S. economic growth, they also support tighter controls to keep out those who might take away jobs from native-born Americans, and to reduce the perceived negative effects of "unassimilated" immigrants on U.S. culture, language, and values.

Because U.S. views on Mexico focus on its fear of "illegal" immigrants, few Americans know much about how Mexicans see them, or why. For example, they don't know that:

- Mexicans generally believe that Americans are prejudiced against them and their country. The United States is the largest trading partner of Mexico, and Mexico is our third largest trading partner (after China and Canada). But despite this close economic interdependence, U.S. policy toward Mexico seems to oscillate between two extremes, neglect and intervention, in ways that are reactionary and myopic. The inability of the United States to deal honestly and openly with its economy's demand for Mexican workers is considered hypocritical. Mexicans regard the border fence as a particularly blatant expression of U.S. prejudice: given that all of the 9/11/2001 terrorists entered the United States from Canada, what does the U.S. national security objective justify the fencing of the border between the United States and Mexico? The 2012 Presidential campaign was characterized not by any serious consideration of immigration reform, but instead by a contest among the Republican candidates over who had the strongest policy position in favor of tighter border security and deportation of "illegal" immigrants. While demographic realities—by 2050, a majority of the U.S. population will be of Hispanic origin—may result in immigration reform, they are less likely to cause substantive changes in U.S. attitudes toward Mexico or toward Mexicans.
- Mexicans have always moved back and forth across the river called the Rio Grande in the United States and the Rio Bravo in Mexico. Historically, people have always moved due to comparative economic conditions. The Mexican economy has grown three times faster than the U.S. economy since 2007. Therefore, despite assertions to the contrary by conservative U.S. politicians, the net flow of immigrants (legal or illegal) has been from the United States to Mexico, and the net flow of remittance money has been from Mexico to the United States, sent by Mexicans to support relatives in the United States until job opportunities improve in that country. Unfortunately, and in contrast to the treaties underlying the European Union, NAFTA (1994) covers only the movement of goods within Canada, Mexico, and the United States, not people.
- Mexicans see migration to the United States from a viewpoint based on their own economic and social interests. The wall, border security, and the costs and risks associated with treatment of human beings at the hands of border crossing "guides" and others who benefit from human trafficking lead many to stay in Mexico. However, many villages in the Mexican countryside have been depopulated by the migration of working age adults to Mexican and U.S. cities in search of work. This threatens established systems of agriculture, rural education, village governance, land use, and economic development (Rodriguez 2012), and erodes the sense of place that has traditional defined Mexican society.
- Mexico has always had a love–hate relationship with the United States. Mexicans generally admire the United States for its infrastructure, economic opportunities, and relatively open social and political structures. They

generally dislike the United States because of its wealth, its imperialistic economic and political tendencies, and its ingrained prejudices against them and their country. A century ago, Mexican President Porfirio Diaz expressed a saying more recently attributed to Carlos Fuentes: "Poor Mexico, so far from God and so close to the United States."

The "Perfect Storm": An Unrecognized Opportunity to Build Governance Capacity

Despite this history of negative perceptions, conditions, and events, the "perfect storm" represents an unrecognized opportunity to build closer and stronger long-term linkages between Mexico and the United States. Once we accept that a crisis this serious is too good to waste, we can begin to think about how to use the drug trafficking, violence, and instability it has generated to build governance capacity and public administration on both sides of our shared border.

Despite some U.S. prognostications, Mexico will not become a "failed state"—it has the capacity to provide basic services, hold free and fair elections, and to exercise civilian control over the armed forces (Nava 2011). Current events in both countries make it increasingly likely that the United States will accept Mexico as a permanent strategic partner rather than as an unwanted or neglected neighbor, and that Mexico will accept the United States as a permanent strategic partner rather than as a source of uncertainty, economic domination, or post-colonial intervention.

If this is to happen, each country must recognize its areas of domestic policy weakness and focus on reducing their negative impact on the other. For the United States, this starts with viewing Mexican migration to the United States from a Mexican perspective, and in the context of the U.S.'s historical prejudice against Mexico and Mexicans. Then, the United States might shift the way it frames gun control by viewing it primarily as a public health concern rather than as a legal issue based on Constitutional rights under the Second Amendment. Finally, the United States should rethink its 75-year-old policy on possession and use of "soft" drugs such as marijuana. Instead of an outright ban, Americans might consider imposing consequences for their dangerous uses, and substitute community-based treatment programs for legal sanctions through the criminal justice system.

For Mexico, this requires facing corruption as a domestic policy issue that impedes economic development and increases the cynicism and the risks associated with efforts to professionalize public administration, particularly in public security agencies and municipal government. Under current conditions, Mexican police officers and municipal officials do not have good choices when drug traffickers force them to choose between accepting large bribes or death, either their own or of family members. Next, it means combatting over-centralization by making constitutional changes that enhance the power of mayors and municipal managers, and to diminish over-reliance on an authoritarian national government. This implies a related shift in political culture so that Mexicans see themselves as citizens rather than subjects, and thus responsible for changing conditions rather than being passive victims of them.

As each country works to improve its internal policy landscape in the ways outlined above, both countries should work together to focus on strengthening their long-term relationship. Mexico and the United States have long squandered opportunities for constructive dialogue and cooperation along their common border. The costs have been enormous—not only tens of billions of dollars in economic losses, but a general feeling that the border is "broken" or dysfunctional. However, there are some hopeful signs. To carry out its campaign against organized crime, the government of Mexico has moved beyond the reflexive and excessive concern for sovereignty and frustrated binational collaboration in law enforcement (Smith 2012). Meanwhile, a new administration in Washington has committed itself to comprehensive immigration reform and has recognized that the United States shares responsibility for drug trafficking and weapons. Both governments seem more willing to replace nationalist finger-pointing with a twenty-first century approach to border management that benefits both parties (BGC 2009, Binational Task Force on the United States–Mexico Border 2009). In the long run, this means finishing the dream of NAFTA by expanding it to include the legal movement of people as well as goods. It is only by envisioning a trinational economic entity (the United States, Mexico, and Canada) that North America will have a chance to compete successfully with China and the European Union in the world of the future.

Together, both governments must articulate a shared vision of the frontier that promises tangible and substantial benefits to both countries (BCG 2009). Within this strong and broad vision of binational cooperation, border management involves six key "intermestic" policy areas: (1) public safety and security, (2) facilitation of legitimate trade and transit, (3) economic development, (4) water management, (5) environmental protection, and (6) migration. For each subject area, Mexico and the United States should work together to expose the challenges involved and offer data-based recommendations that address them.

The first element of this vision is a model of binational law enforcement where officials from parallel, professionalized agencies work together as a matter of course. The second is a coherent economic strategy for the border region, based on the acceleration of legitimate trade, the easing of restrictions imposed by the federal government on border communities, and the development of existing institutions with greater authority. The third component is the intelligent management of all natural resources that both countries share. The fourth is a binational comprehensive legal migration solution. Together, these steps can transform border management from a source of contention and frustration in a model of cooperation in addressing common challenges (BGC 2009, Binational Task Force on the United States–Mexico Border 2009).

As with any long-term foreign policy initiative, this one will require a series of incremental legislative or administrative actions by each country. It is recommended that some changes be implemented immediately:

- The United States should officially recognize that, with respect to migration, Mexico is unique and treatment of Mexican migration requires a set of policies adapted to the situation.
- Mexico and the United States should establish a joint commission of economists, demographers, and prominent business and labor leaders to discuss the job market complementarity produced by long-term demographic trends and economic integration; the Commission should report to the President and Congress of each country. If a joint commission is not possible, separate parallel commissions with the same charge should be established and work together.
- Both governments should jointly develop a plan for managing future flows of migrants (both temporary and permanent) to take into account the demographic and labor market realities in both countries. This plan should address the possibility of fraud by recruiters and ensure that labor rights are fully protected.
- The United States should use existing laws to investigate and sanction employers who hire undocumented workers, initially focusing on those who hire large numbers of undocumented workers or rely on undocumented workers as a critical part of their business model.
- The United States should develop a reliable electronic verification system for resident workers, and encourage business entrepreneurs to use it.
- The United States should simplify the existing categories of visas for foreign migrants, the establishment of which will be required under a reformed immigration system.
- The United States should begin to strengthen and modernize the Immigration and Customs Enforcement agency (ICE) now, so that it is ready to handle comprehensive immigration reform when it comes to pass (BGC 2009, Binational Task Force on the United States–Mexico Border 2009).

Once these changes are implemented, others should be made within the next three years (Conferencia de Gobernadores Fronterizos 2009):

- The United States should adopt policies to address both the situation of undocumented Mexicans living in the country and future legal flows of migrants from Mexico. The level of future legal flows should be flexible, reflecting economic conditions and the demand for labor. Once these reforms are in place, Mexico must actively prevent unauthorized migration to the north by ensuring that persons who enter the United States from Mexico do at certain crossing points and with the requisite documents. The United States must provide sufficient consular staff and ICE personnel to

accommodate the increased workload that will accompany the inevitable high demand for new visas.
- The United States should develop a plan for full integration into American society of those granted permanent residence as a result of comprehensive immigration reform.
- Given that much of the current drug trafficking and migration of undocumented persons through Mexico and into the United States is caused by historic discrimination against Central Americans and indigenous populations in Chiapas and Oaxaca, Mexico should adopt policies that discourage migration by promoting broad-based economic development, focusing on these indigenous areas in and along the Guatemalan border (BGC 2009; Binational Task Force on the United States–Mexico Border 2009; Rodriguez 2012).

Policy innovations will also need to include the "war on drugs." There are three possible strategies available to manage drug abuse and deal with drug trafficking networks along the Mexico—U.S. border: complicity, confrontation, or a change in the paradigm of regulation of drug use, each of which has inevitable negative effects (Astorga Almanza and Shirk 2010; Kilmer et al. 2010). Currently, we focus on the second strategy, with mixed effects. The United States and Mexico have both made considerable progress in attacking TCOs' economic power by restricting their operating environment and increasing their cost of doing business. Intensified efforts to disclose and combat money laundering against both sides of the border have required sustained political commitment, the increased institutionalization of cooperative bilateral measures and mechanisms, and increased strategic communications to stigmatize TCOs and money laundering with the general public (Realuyo 2012). However, the general failure of the global "war on drugs" in the face of continued demand, particularly in the United States and other developed countries, means that legalization and alternative policy options—like treating drug abuse as a public health rather than criminal justice issue—will need to be considered.

Universities and other academic institutions can help by cooperating in three ways:

- *Strategic Research Exchanges.* Higher education institutions in the United States and Mexico should maintain and improve their linkages through exchanges of visiting scholars, reciprocal scholarships and joint degree programs. For several years, under the direction of Juan de Dios Pineda, Cheo Torres and former President David Schmidly, the University of New Mexico has developed strategic relationships with Mexico and Latin America through the LAT-Net program. This program includes postdoctoral exchanges of teachers, researchers, and co-sponsored conferences (http://www.unm.edu/solai~/). In the United States, the Fulbright-Garcia Robles program (http://us.fulbrightonline.org/program_country.html?id=70) has for years provided funding to U.S. citizens studying in Mexico. In Mexico, CONACYT (the National Council of Science and Technology) sponsors programs and scholarships for international cooperation (http://www.conacyt.gob.mx/CooperacionInetrnacional/Paginas/default.aspx). Finally, the American Council on Education (ACE) and the Henry Luce Foundation funded eight programs that allow U.S. universities, including the University of Colorado at Colorado Springs, strategically combining international research and national diversity of students (http://www.acenet.edu/content/NavigationMenu/ProgramsServices/cii/current/gap/index.htm). Unfortunately for this type of exchange, at least among students, some universities in the United States (such as the University of Texas) have banned student travel to Mexico given the warning announced by the Department of Foreign Affairs of that country in response to the increasing violence in the states of Baja California, Chihuahua, Coahuila, Nuevo Leon, Sonora, and Tamaulipas (Boulard 2010).

- *Education through Professional Associations.* Professional associations build the administrative capacity of organizations and individuals by increasing individual and organizational competencies. In the United States, they include the American Management Association (AMA—with a not-for-profit and public sector), the American Society for Public Administration (ASPA), the American Planning Association (APA), the Association for Public Policy and Management (APPAM), the American Political Science Association (APSA) with a Public Administration Section, the Association for Research on Nonprofit Organizations and Volunteer Agencies (ARNOVA), the International City/County Management Association (ICMA), and the International Public Management Association for Human Resources (IPMA-HR). In Mexico, the National Institute of Public Administration (INAP) and its 31 affiliates statewide offer free courses, options for distance learning, and academic degree programs (http://www.inap.org.mx).

- *The ASPA Good Governance Website.* The American Society for Public Administration (ASPA) has carried out a comprehensive strategy since 2006. For 18 months, the purpose of the International Chapter of ASPA has been to provide a home for ASPA members outside as well as within the United States, to develop a website aimed at the practice of "global governance," and provide opportunities for ASPA members of all nations to unite together to improve professional practice of public administration worldwide. These efforts have resulted in the creation of a global good governance Internet portal. Through this portal, professionals from around the world can share information about promising innovative "smart practices" worldwide. The website (http://www.aspaonline.org/global/index.html) is an interactive website designed to promote good governance in a global community of practice in public administration, including in new democracies and developing countries. It was developed over the last nine months in collaboration with the Section on Public Management Practice (SPMP), which offers a wide range of best practice content via e-articles, comments, book reviews, interviews, blogs, podcasts, videos, forums, and wikis; and opens opportunities for practitioners, researchers, students, trainers, and consultants (among others) to work together in virtual as well as physical networks. The Good Governance website is an important service for ASPA members worldwide. It links the ASPA International Chapter, the Section on Public Management Practice, and other communities of interest that apply ideas and experiences to develop and share "smart practice" solutions to the pressing problems that hinder the advancement of professional public administration and public service worldwide.

The guiding principle is to include a growing network of participants (countries, national government agencies, organizations, and individuals) in the global exchange of ideas and knowledge to improve governance and government performance. If ASPA can do this through its SPMP and the International Chapter, it will reinforce its position as the main U.S. professional association responsible for and capable of mobilizing global resources to support professional public administration and public service. This is, after all, nothing but the current iteration of the goals shared by the founders of ASPA in 1939.

The Organization of This Book

This book comprises 15 chapters written by 20 authors. The first and last chapters are its introduction and conclusion, each was written by one of the book's coeditors. In between are 13 chapters on various aspects of the drug trafficking crisis and its antecedents and effects in both countries, particularly in the border area between Mexico and the United States. In Chapter 2, Denis Proulx describes the history of the global drug trade and its general effects on public administration. In Chapter 3, Angelina Perez Ordaz describes general geographic and demographic conditions in the border area, and defends the importance of education in building a regional community. In Chapter 4, Jose Luis Cisneros describes the harrowing effects of drug-related violence on Mexican society. In Chapter 5, José Antonio Rosique Cañas and Gloria Rosique Cedillo describe the dangers of the drug wars for Mexican journalists. In Chapters 6 and 7, two sets of authors (Kurt Johnson and Michael A. Noll, and Mario Rivera and Sofia Solis) discuss the role of the respective roles of military forces in border security and the war on drugs. In Chapters 8 and 9, Ramona Ortega-Liston and RaJade Berry-James discuss education and employment of Hispanics in the United States; and Adriana Plasencia Diaz describes educational systems and outcomes in Mexico. In Chapter 10, Espiridion ("Al") Borrego gives specific examples of how the drug wars have affected cross-border inter-agency cooperation. In Chapter 11, Mauricio Covarrubias outlines a general model for why and how governments can work together to resolve trans-border policy issues. In Chapters 12 through

14, Mexican authors (David Arellano and Enrique Cabrero, Miguel Moreno Plata, and Ricardo Uvalle Berrones) discuss specific problems in Mexican public administration, including corruption, a lack of administrative capacity and inadequate governance. Because the contributing authors cover different topics from different viewpoints, they do not always agree. As coeditors, Roberto Moreno and I consider this normal and desirable, a reflection of complex historical realities in relations between our two countries.

References

Astorga Almanza, L. and D. Shirk. January 2010. *Drug Trafficking Organizations and Counter Drug Strategies in the U.S.–Mexican Context.* San Diego, CA: Evolving Democracy, Center for US—Mexican Studies, University of California at San Diego. Available online: http://www.escholarship.org/uc/item/8j647429. Accessed May 24, 2012.

Benítez Mahaut, R. March 2011. México, Centroamérica y Estados Unidos: Migración e inseguridad, in *Migración y Seguridad: Nuevo Desafío en México.* DF: Ediciones de Lirio, pp. 179–192.

Binational Task Force on the United States-Mexico Border. 2009. *Managing the United States–Mexico Border: Cooperative Solutions to Common Problems.* San Diego, CA: Pacific Council on International Policy, y Consejo Mexicano para Asuntos Internacionales, A.C. [COMEXI]. Available online: http://www.pacificcouncil.org/interior.aspx?pageID=Studies&subID=3&itemID=47.

Bonner, R. May/June 2012. The Cartel crackdown. *Foreign Affairs 93*, 3:12–16.

Boulard, G. September 16, 2010. Mexican drug war threatens U.S. college study-abroad programs. *Diverse Issues in Higher Education 27*, 16:9.

Chabat, J. January 2010a. *La Iniciativa Mérida y la relación México-Estados Unidos: En Busca de la Confianza Perdida.* México: CIDE (Centro de Investigaciones y Docencia Económicas), Documento de Trabajo #195.

Chabat, J. January 2010b. *La Respuesta del Gobierno Calderón entre el Desafío del Narcotráfico: Entre lo Malo y lo Peor.* México: CIDE (Centro de Investigaciones y Docencia Económicas), Documento de Trabajo #196.

Chabat, J. December 2010c. *Combating Drugs in Mexico under Calderon: The Inevitable War.* México: CIDE (Centro de Investigaciones y Docencia Económicas), Documento de Trabajo #205.

Conferencia de Gobernadores Fronterizos. 2009. *Strategic Guidelines for the Competitive and Sustainable Development of the U.S.–Mexico Transborder Region.* Washington, DC: Woodrow Wilson International Center for Scholars, y El Colegio de la Frontera Norte.

Hurtado, A. 2012. *Herbert Eugene Bolton: Historian of the American Borderlands.* Berkeley, CA: University of California Press.

Kellner, T. and F. Pipitone. Spring 2010. Inside Mexico's drug war. *World Policy Journal* Boston: MIT Press, 29–37.

Kilmer, B., J. Calkins, B. Bond, and P. Reuter. 2010. *Reducing Drug Trafficking Violence and Revenues in Mexico: Would Legalizing Marijuana in California Help?* Santa Monica, CA: The Rand Corporation, International Programs and Drug Policy Research Center.

Kleiman, M. September/October 2011. Surgical strikes in the drug wars. *Foreign Affairs 90*, 5:89–101.
Klingner, D. December 2000. Implementing new public management reforms in Mexico today. *American Review of Public Administration 30*, 4 (articles by D. Arellano Gault, E. Cabrero Mendoza and P. Romero Lankao).
Klingner, D. and D. Arellano Gault. Summer 2006. La Ley de Servicio Profesional de Carrera en México: Gobernanza, cultura política y reforma administrativa. *Servicio Profesional de Carrera 3*, 5:55–82.
Lindau, J. 2011. The drug war's impact on executive power, judicial reform and federalism in Mexico. *Political Science Quarterly 126*, 2:177–2010.
Meyer Rodríguez, J. A. and O. O. Kuri Vidal. 2011. Agenda mediática y narcotráfico en la relación binacional México—Estados Unidos. *XXIII Encuentro Nacional AMIC* 2011, Pachuca, Hidalgo—Memoria Mesa Comunicación Política.
Morales Oyarvide, C. July/August/September 2011. La guerra contra el narcotráfico en México: Debilidad del estado, orden local y fracaso de una estrategia. *Aposta: Revista de Ciencias Sociales*, No. 50, pp. 1–35. Available online at: http://www.apostadigital.com/revistav3/hemeroteca/oyarvide.pdf. Accessed August 5, 2013.
Nava, J. May/June 2011. México: Estado frágil o democracia emergente? *Military Review*, pp. 68–78.
Pichardo Pagaza, I. March 8, 2009. Inaugural address, Annual Conference of the American Society for Public Administration (ASPA), Miami, Florida.
Realuyo, C. 2012. *It's All about the Money: Advancing Anti Money-Laundering Efforts in the U.S. and Mexico to Combat Transnational Organized Crime*. Washington, DC: The Woodrow Wilson International Center for Scholars: Mexico Institute.
Ribando Seelke, C. and J. Beittel. 2009. *Merida Initiative for Mexico and Central America: Funding and Policy Issues*. Washington, DC: Congressional Research Service, Report 7-5700.
Rodriguez, O. July 13, 2012. More Central Americans take risky trip north. *The Denver Post*, p. 15A.
Rubio, L. (2011). *Perspectives on the Americas: Decentralization and its Consequences*. Miami: University of Miami, Center for Hemispheric Policy.
Sandoval, E. January-April 2012. Economía de la fayuca y del narcotráfico en el noreste de México: Extorsiones, contubernios y solidaridades en las economías transfronterizas. *Desacatos 38*, 43–60.
Selee, A. 2005. *Perceptions and Misperceptions in U.S.–México Relations*. Washington, DC: Woodrow Wilson Center for International Scholars, Mexico Institute.
Serrano, M. 2010. El problema del narcotráfico en México: Una perspectiva Latinoamericana, Gustavo Vega and Blanca Torres (Eds.) Los *grandes problemas de México XII: Relaciones Internacionales*. México: El Colegio de México.
Shirk, D. January 2010. *Drug Violence in Mexico: Data and Analysis from 2001–2009*. San Diego: Trans-Border Institute, University of San Diego.
Smith, M. July 13, 2012. Reason for hope in Mexico. *The Denver Post*, p. 21A.
Stratfor. October 28, 2011. *Mexico's Areas of Cartel Influence and Smuggling Routes*. Austin, TX: Stratfor. Available online at: http://www.stratfor.com/
Stratfor. January 24, 2012a. *Mexico's Drug Cartels*. Austin, TX: Stratfor. Available online at: http://www.stratfor.com/
Stratfor. April 16, 2012b. *Mexico's Criminal Cartels*. Austin, TX: Stratfor. Available online at: http://www.stratfor.com/

Velázquez, R. November 2011. La política exterior de Estados Unidos hacia México bajo la administración de Barack Obama: Cambios y continuidades. México: CIDE (Centro de Investigaciones y Docencia Económicas), Documento de Trabajo #211.

Velázquez, R. and J. Schiavon. July 2009. La Iniciativa Mérida en el marco de la relación México-Estados Unidos. México: CIDE (Centro de Investigaciones y Docencia Económicas), Documento de Trabajo #186.

Valeriano, B. and M. Powers. 2010. United States–Mexico: The convergence of public policy views in the post 9/11 world. *Policy Studies Journal 38,* 4:745–775.

Vulliamy, Ed. December 27, 2010. As Juárez falls. *The Nation*, pp. 39–44.

Chapter 2

Drug Trafficking and Public Administration
A Natural Relationship and a Global Problem

Denis Proulx

Contents

Introduction	18
Global Drug Markets: Operation and Evolution	20
From Mexico to Central America and West Africa: Market Evolution	21
West Africa	21
Brazil	22
Colombia	23
FARC and AUC	25
Public Administration	27
Drug Victims and Collateral Victims	28
Other Issues	29
Conclusion for Mexico	31
References	32

Introduction

The violence occurring today in Mexico is a result of drug trafficking in Colombia and Brazil, which in turn relates to situations in Bolivia, Peru, and other countries in the region. Drug markets adapt to state-imposed obstacles that are designed to limit consumption. Trafficking is extremely profitable and promotes the use of dirty money for many purposes; traffickers use it to protect their businesses and markets and to maintain their peace and security.

States can be producer states, transit states, or consumer states. Producer and transit states tend to become consumers too, which then come to dominate the producers. Drug trafficking is a dynamic market in which the players may exchange roles when governments attack them or impose business limitations and other obstacles; traffickers are quick to adapt by changing methods, productivity, distribution systems, and products. The most significant profits are made where the drugs are consumed: only 5% of Afghan opium profits go to farmers, traders, and insurgents, while 70% of cocaine profits go to consumer countries (Costa, 2010).

Developed countries follow a similar pattern (Costa, 2010). Organized crime generates more than $300 billion a year from drug trafficking alone (UNODC, 2012). Some of this money is generated in rogue jurisdictions and unregulated economic sectors, but much of it is at large in the global economy. Traffickers need to control these cash flows (through real estate, tourism, entertainment, and gambling facilities) and informal money must be controlled. What is at stake for the various players, in terms of their interests and constraints?

Drug trafficking is first and foremost an economic activity that depends on strategies to dominate the market while avoiding public interventions that could limit business growth. It is extremely profitable but illegal. Traffickers must find a way to use the huge amounts of money they earn while avoiding having their business restricted or closed down by the authorities, going to jail or being killed. They need to look respectable to avoid being investigated, and they have to find businesses to invest in so that they can legitimize or launder their earnings.

Any economic activity that encourages spending, provides official financial documents, and gives respectability is good. Earning money is secondary but often comes with time, because investing really can be profitable in all senses. Food industries, services—anything from owning a car-wash to a private university—is a good investment. Traffickers diversify their activities and often end up at the head of large groups of companies and thus controlling the main supply networks (Araujo, 2001).

Public administration (PA) involves laws, law enforcement, financial regulations, and policing. It collides with the drug trade because traffickers need politicians and civil servants who are gullible, cooperative, or prepared to turn a blind eye at just the right moment. Corruption, threats, or even physical suppression are not the only methods used: being agreeable and friendly with naïve people can create cozy relationships with the authorities, and is much simpler than entering directly into corruption. Most individuals are slow to believe they are being manipulated, managed, or organized by people with hidden interests. Being a good citizen, giving money to charities and providing the region with jobs are effective ways of being accepted, and this way traffickers avoid police or politicians looking too deeply into what they are doing while they continue to access markets and profits.

Drug trafficking often thrives on the weakness of governance. In Colombia, trafficking has been a serious obstacle to decentralization because stronger governments are more capable of resisting traffickers (Gutiérrez Sanín et al., 2010; Serrano et al., 2011). From the trafficker's point of view, Geffray (2001a,b) presents this approach as a technique for hiding their business or, if this is impossible, limiting the ability of state officials to apply the law. The objective is to convince officials to withdraw their charges against traffickers while keeping their jobs. If these officials lose their jobs, the traffickers' problem begins anew. The usual process is offering money, benefits, or specific services the officials desire and, if this does not work, threatening them, including with death: "Sell us your land, or we'll negotiate with your widow" (Ballvé, 2011).

In many cases, civil servants are badly paid. Making ends meet is difficult, so the temptation is great when faced with the money and contacts that traffickers can offer them. The other method traffickers use is to gain public respectability as good contributors to society, sports, or the economy and then gain the support of gullible civil servants. In Latin America, Asia, and North America, traffickers contribute to electoral campaigns, which give them political contacts and enable them to influence society to their benefit.

An Italian policeman working on mafia crime said on Canadian television* that Canada and the Nordic countries were perfect places for criminals because of softer criminal laws and the presumption that "we are honest people and crime is for someone else." Citizens are unaware of the situation, he said, while criminals take advantage of these "soft laws" to operate freely. These situations also affect the political legitimacy of the states affected by trafficking (Geffray, 2001a). While a positive public perception of the state and its politicians affects the legitimacy of the state, the money that trafficking provides may also allow some politicians to improve their image and increase their legitimacy among citizens.

Schiray (2001) notes that in regions where state institutions have less control and capacity to intervene, there is deeper interpenetration between official economic activities and trafficking activities, with people engaged in illegal commerce taking a dominant position in economic life and even in local politics. This has been particularly obvious in some Amazonian states in Brazil. When public institutions exert little control, entire mid-size cities may develop or decay depending on the presence, shifting, or withdrawal of drug trafficking. Profit redistribution also supports large sectors of the regional economy and local public enterprise.

---

* "Enquête". Radio Canada television, Oct. 4, 2012.

In Brazil, a federal parliamentary commission of investigation (CPI) on drug trafficking implicated 800 persons (Schiray, 2001), mainly white collar workers including federal deputies and elected personnel from various states, but few people from Rio de Janeiro or Sao Paolo, and no economic or political VIPs. In Brazilian Amazonia, not only is the state ill-equipped to provide public control, but some of its representatives are themselves associated with criminal organizations. They may eventually control these for their own profit and resort to using their legal monopoly on violent repression for their private interests.

Global Drug Markets: Operation and Evolution

From a market point of view, Peru, Bolivia, Pakistan, Afghanistan, and Myanmar are the most significant "drug economies." While drug distribution may also be significant in Brazil, Mexico, and China, and even Colombia, trafficking is only a marginal part of their overall economies.

According to a 2012 report by the United Nations Office on Drugs and Crime, 230 million people, or 5% of the world's adult population, are estimated to have used an illicit drug in 2010, while those who have a drug problem account for 27 million (0.6% of world population). Land surface used for cultivating coca has fallen by 18% since 2007 and 33% since 2000. But the report does not provide data on the productivity increases for these plants, and cocaine has seen "a decline in production but no fall in global consumption" (UNODC, 2012, p. 35). If consumption and prices are stable while surfaces are smaller, there must be an increase in productivity.

Many authors have written on government incapacity to control the illegal drug market, arguing that efforts are huge but ultimately useless, and that in consequence drugs should be legalized (Becker et al., 2006; Alexandre, 2009; Inkster and Comolli 2012a,b,c,d). Some consider that results of control efforts are positive, at least partly (Preston IV, 2004). Most recognize the tragic effect trafficking has especially on the Andean countries, Mexico, and Afghanistan, destabilizing them and compromising their future.

Few addicts stop taking drugs because of price increases; they don't even consider reducing their consumption (Costa, 2010). While long-term measures on drugs have some success, such as the decrease of the annual prevalence of cocaine use in North America from 1.9% to 1.6% between 2009 and 2010 (UNODC, 2012), producers faced with decreased consumption tend to open new markets elsewhere, resulting in new gang wars such as those in Mexico or Central America as the global market expands.

For traffickers, their control of the market in the countries where the drug is important is a determining issue. Early on, when drug trafficking penetrates a country, a production phenomenon occurs in which producers and traffickers need other traffickers to manage their distribution. This happens when severe restrictions in the country of production force traffickers to find transit partners who can make the necessary contacts in a country with a "softer" legal environment. Subsequently, the transit partner becomes the leader and begins to dictate what happens.

At the micro level, ordinary producers do not earn a lot of money and are mostly poor farmers trying to increase their income. Eradication officers often focus their efforts on these farmers, but it is the groups to whom they sell who earn more money. They too have the same problems: they fear the law that does not allow them to pursue their business, the police who can send them to jail, and other traffickers who can steal their protected markets and spend their dirty money. This is where PA becomes part of the portrait.

From Mexico to Central America and West Africa: Market Evolution

In 1972, Turkey prohibited the export of opium to the United States, creating a window of opportunity for Mexican traffickers. Within three years, they had secured 80% of the U.S. heroin market, up from a 15% share. The United States and Mexico later decided to embark on a joint operation to eradicate the opium poppy. Operation Condor exposed the level of corruption of Mexican forces and several high-profile arrests were made among police ranks. Even though the Mexican state had portrayed itself as willing to cooperate with Washington on counter-narcotics, it was clear by the mid-1980s that traffickers were ready to take their activities to the next level (Inkster and Comolli, 2012e). When government forces attack traffickers, they move to other areas in what has been termed the "cockroach effect." Following drug fighting in Mexico, cartels developed in Guatemala, Salvador, Honduras, and Nicaragua, where local criminals and *maras* (gangs) play an active role (Inkster and Comolli, 2012). Now, the Mexican drug mafia is seeking to "inherit" the drug routes once organized by notorious Colombian crime syndicates, run by traffickers who are now behind bars (El Espectador, 2012).

West Africa

West Africa (mainly Nigeria) once supplied heroin to the United States (Inkster and Comolli, 2012). Later it became a hub for sending marijuana to the United Kingdom. Pressure from European navies on transit from South America forced South American traffickers to turn to West Africa for alternative routes. Thus shipments from Colombia and Venezuela have been seized in Guinea Bissau and Ghana, where poverty, corruption, and weak governance provide the perfect situation for traffickers. Some of these states now have drug-centered economies, with few other economic sectors left. Their dilemma is illustrated by the double standards they demonstrate in their fight against corruption. In Liberia and

Sierra Leone, the percentage of young people using drugs is extremely high: 65% of Sierra Leone's street children use cannabis, 6.8% use cocaine, and 5.6% use heroin (UNODC, 2012, p. 17).

The huge amount of money made from drug trafficking is a constant danger for weak institutions, making them dependent on drug money and traffickers, and mortgaging their future. Governance becomes weak and informal as it adapts to traffickers' money-laundering needs (Gutierrez Sanin et al., 2010; Inkster and Comolli, 2012e). Gutiérrez Sanín et al. as well as Inkster and Comolli also note that these elements play a direct role when traffickers choose locations for drug cultivation (opium or coca). Weak countries become choice territory because criminals can easily take control of government, making them and their populations collateral victims of the severer drug prohibitions in destination countries.

Brazil

One drug trader became the reigning monarch of a Brazilian city of 20,000 near the Tarauacá River in less than 10 years (Araujo, 2001). He owned dozens of businesses, including three air-taxi planes, a soft drinks business, river barges, a coffee roasting plant, gas stations, cattle farms, warehouses, a bar, and a catering business. Around 1980, Bolivian traffickers had set up their laboratories in the State of Beni. Brazilians provided the chemicals and Bolivians paid them with cocaine, which helped the Brazilians start their own business. One trafficker developed close relations with politicians and VIP civil servants (Geffray, 2001b). His associates were the governor's pilot and a federal deputy who were prospecting markets in Brazil and Europe and managing private investments and drug transits through Latin America. When this trafficker was arrested by federal police in 1985, state deputies signed petitions denouncing police violence and harassment toward him while collectively standing as guarantors of his honorability. He was judged and acquitted in 1987 and his trafficking increased. He denied all political accusations. His fellow deputy-trafficker was judged and condemned. Another Brazilian man started buying coffee to launder his trafficking money (Geffray, 2001b). He bought over the market price and sold under it. Competition rapidly disappeared, bought up by his straw men or bankrupted. He played a central role in negotiating between producers, merchants, and the national market and his firm became the state's biggest coffee buyer. Producers from other states came selling to him. Nobody understood how he managed his business so successfully. Considering the regions poor soil and expensive transportation, politicians, civil servants, and even World Bank local employees called it "Rondônia's miracle." Local coffee producers never complained about prices or asked for the state's help. Fearing local merchant elites, this trafficker engaged in politics at local and state levels in order to control potential damage from them. He was generous with many people, and hence very popular. He gave poor children toys and chocolate, provided soft drinks to charities and gifts to politicians. Elites, politicians, and civil servants love respectable people.

Now Brazil is fighting hard against drug producers (Lyons, 2012). The government crosses frontiers to fight traffickers, sending soldiers to Peru to fight in tandem with the Peruvian army, placing up to 10,000 soldiers at critical smuggling points. They have two drones and plan to buy 12 more. They are signing cooperation treaties with their neighbors; the federal police are increasing the number of agents by 30%. Nonetheless, these resources are limited when compared to what is used in Colombia. After the United States, Brazil is the second largest world market for cocaine, with 1 million users. According to Lyons, former president Cardoso does not believe this war against trafficking is useful: traffickers can always build new laboratories elsewhere and the millions spent will be lost, while in the meantime many people will die.

Colombia

Colombia is an important case because of its past importance in the drug market and the social consequences of drug trafficking on its economy and politics. Unlike other countries so deeply involved with drug trafficking, however, the situation seems to be improving. How did Colombia get into such a situation, where drug production and trafficking mixed with social unrest led to violence, kidnapping, guerillas, and paramilitaries?

As Braudel (1985) explains, external conflicts contribute to the founding of nations and promote the development of governments. Conflicts demonstrate the need for a state presence and subsequently its obligation to react to events that threaten its autonomy and independence. Conflicts make citizens realize they have common traits, which builds up nationhood. Perhaps it was guerilla conflicts in Colombia that forced the creation of a modern state, obliging government to negotiate with different groups inside the country that had historically been left out. Political violence in Colombia existed before drugs appeared (Dufort, 2007), particularly during the period known as *La Violencia* (1948–1960). Many editorials in Colombian newspapers claim that these conflicts emerged because the State was virtually absent in many regions. "Colombia's national political project has been thwarted in large measure by a deficient presence, and in some cases absence, of the state apparatus in much of what is sovereign territory" (Mason, 2005, p. 5; Murillo and Valdivieso, 2002).

The traditional industries were bananas and coffee. Violence was worse in banana-producing regions: multinational enterprises ruled with violence, had union leaders killed, and created frustration and social and economic unrest. The banana companies could do whatever they wanted and the state turned a blind eye. This provoked social unrest, facilitating the emergence of leftist groups and later giving support to revolutionary movements. In coffee production sectors, there was less violence: people worked in cooperatives, allowing better income distribution and wealth.

Colombia consists of three different countries (González, 2008). First, several strong cities including the capital: Bogota, Cali, Medellin, Barranquilla, Cartagena, and others; second, Amazonian forests, barely accessible even today; and third the Atlantic and Pacific coasts. Initially the cities were colonized and the rest of the country was left apart. Later other zones were colonized, first the mountains and finally the forest. There has been some frustration in these regions directed toward the center and this is where guerillas and coca production appeared, in the absence of a permanent state presence. Violence mainly stayed in the peripheral regions until the 1980s, when guerillas started to move from the periphery to the center. That provoked a military effort to defend the center and a paramilitary effort to defend the Caribbean coast. Colombia shifted from being a small-time player in the drug world, producing coca leaves and paste, to taking a leading role in production and trafficking (Pécaut, 2002). Mass coca production requires state absence and Colombia, with its disorder and violence, weak central authority, lack of security, and of human rights protection (Mason, 2005) was the perfect candidate. Guerillas filled up the empty space.

In this situation, corruption rapidly grows. It appears in the courts, the police, and general legal matters. It flows into construction, commerce, and agriculture. It helps finance political parties, even if politicians condemn it. If the law cannot catch criminals, they are free to do what they want and their business can grow. To be effective, sanctions need a fast reacting state, which was not the case. As authors F. González and C. Esteban Posada explain, "The administration of justice suffers from congestion so that laws are not correctly applied" (2001, p. 56).

Market conditions determined Colombia's role in drug production. Its first operations were mostly selling chemical products to Peru to produce cocaine, and then transforming coca base from Peru and Bolivia to cocaine in laboratories. Later traffickers realized it was simpler to produce the coca leaf at home in remote uncontrolled places and then market it themselves. Producers in one country need help from providers in another, and then these become producers themselves (if possible) and later on traffickers. Colombia had no tradition of coca cultivation but became the center for cocaine—until it needed Mexico's help. Colombia's national government was slow to react to trafficking and the extradition treaty it signed with the United States in 1987 produced massive violence, in particular when drug lord Pablo Escobar and the Medellin cartel directly challenged the State. The Medellin cartel lost, but its defeat gave birth to numerous smaller groups who resumed the fight for trafficking.

It is difficult to separate data on the legal and illegal economies in Colombia because they overlap: illegal crops are hidden inside legal ones; illegal money is invested in formal and legal activities (Leiteritz et al., 2009). Illegal activities are also intertwined with the armed conflict. We met people working in palm oil plantations who explained that the crop was an attempt to grow something other than coca. It looked encouraging, but Leiteritz et al. point out that growing palm oil required population displacement enforced by paramilitaries with waves of massacres and homicides to terrorize the population. Trafficking fuelled the conflict between leftist and right-wing guerillas and kept these groups alive and active.

FARC and AUC

Fuerzas Armadas Revolucionarias de Colombia (FARC) was a revolutionary Maoist group whose members began as opponents of coca cultivation. Then it started levying a 15% tax in the areas it controlled, began its own coca production and then moved into full trafficking business. Its earnings were around US$140 million in 2002, allowing it to finance an army of up to 16,000 combatants (Inkster and Comolli, 2012d). In recent years, the Colombian government has fought them and significantly reduced their troops and their territory. The government says FARC now produces 70% of Colombian cocaine (Inkster and Camolli, 2012a,b,c,d). In 2012, Colombia's defense minister evaluated FARC's earnings at between US$2.4 and 3.5 billion annually, based on a 50% share, with membership evaluated at more than 8000 (El Tiempo, Oct. 30, 2012).

In reaction to FARC, rural producers and local elites organized the *Autodefensas Unidas de Colombia* (AUC) to fight back. They soon became even more violent and also involved in the cocaine trade, financing most of their activities through trafficking. Farmers in Cordoba Department told us how they had to leave their farms when visited by the AUC. They were offered a fraction of the value of their land but had no choice but to sell and never received an official deed of sale. AUC was demobilized in 2006 but many citizens complain that while the top leaders were sent for trial to the United States, the important players reintegrated into civilian life, most low-level militias stayed in illegal business. "Would you prefer to go back to earning 100,000 pesos (US$50) working on a farm," people asked us, "or earn US$1,000 being an outlaw?"

In October 2012, FARC resumed negotiations with the government, but both parties went on fighting during the discussions. The Colombian government refused a cease-fire to avoid giving FARC a break during which it would arm itself anew, as it has done in the past. With the military offensive, FARC suffered important losses but the Colombian government had no success against the *Bloque Sur*, a FARC group that opposes negotiations and stays in a remote region that produces 70% of FARC's cocaine.

As for AUC, it has become more and more involved in elections (Acemoglu et al., 2009). In 2002, it influenced the vote, changed voting patterns, and directly influenced who had the right to be candidate. When authorities seized AUC boss Jorge 40's computer, they discovered traces of more than 500 murders and incriminating links with politicians.

Links between politicians and paramilitaries are deep and widespread (Acemoglu et al., 2009). In 2009, one-third of Colombian legislators were found to have links with paramilitaries while both the 2002 and 2006 elections were rigged. The AUC made random death threats if the "right" candidate did not win. In some places, they picked two candidates and let the people vote freely for a third. Not playing by their rules meant death for candidates. Although they were also guilty of political interference, FARC were less active, probably because of their lack of interest in democracy.

Colombian defense budgets show a disproportion with the country's extreme poverty and social problems. Colombia has lost about 2–3% of GDP per year over 30 years, and without this disproportionate defense spending the national economy would be "between 75% and 125% larger than it currently is" (Inkster and Comolli, 2012, p. 24). Drug trafficking now accounts for 1.5–2% of GDP, down from the 8% peak during the profitable years of the Medellin cartel.

We can conclude that drug trafficking provided FARC with lots of money so that it was able to survive. FARC action forced the reaction of right wing paramilitary guerillas that were even more violent than FARC. Both these obliged the Colombian state to react through military spending to defend itself. This spending affected the whole population. It is explained in part in the following paragraphs.

The financial resources cocaine gave access to—including money indirectly earned through diverted public funds—were central to developing and maintaining insurgents' activities, making violence a permanent fact of national life (Eaton and Kurtenbach, as cited in Baumeister, 2007). Cocaine has cost Colombia thousands of lives, economic development, social investments, and functioning social systems. It has produced a chronic form of civil war.

What else could Colombia have done with the money it has invested in fighting trafficking and violent armed groups? Cocaine has fueled this battle, but Colombia was far from a healthy democracy before cocaine arrived from Peru and Bolivia. The Santos government must manage its huge security problem while considering that the level of spending on this general problem is undermining the national economy, despite American help (Plan Colombia). During the conflict, Colombia has changed from a rural to an urban population in a few years. The drug trade and political violence fueled the displacement of about 4 million *campesinos* in Colombia (Ballvé, 2011) from 1997 to 2011. This displacement was extremely violent and the expropriated lands are used for trafficking and money laundering by narcoparamilitaries (Ballvé, 2011). The Colombian government estimates that 25,000 people are killed each year in the conflict (*El Tiempo*, October 2012).

There is now a plan for land restitution: In the first ruling (Oct. 2012), the Supreme Court ordered the return of approximately 160 acres of land to 14 Mampujan families in one of the most affected regions. Twelve years ago, up to 150 soldiers from an AUC paramilitary group had allegedly forced 338 households to leave (Verdadabierta, 2012).

Since 2000, urban violence in Colombia has been decreasing in spite of drug trafficking. Has the violence been sent somewhere else—that is, Mexico? We have no specific data on this phenomenon, but the question is interesting. Can violence related to drug trafficking be stopped in one place without emerging elsewhere?*

Public Administration

Criminal economies are based on the existence of infiltrated PA networks and the threat or use of violence when corruption does not work (Fabre, 2001). Drug trafficking needs weak states with a reduced or limited public administrative capacity and ill-controlled, remote territories. It generates escalating violence, constant danger, and people being killed. Local populations start developing addiction problems, social and health problems.

Although public agencies and administrators are responsible for enforcing prohibition, it has proved unproductive and costly. Historically, drug prohibition was developed under pressure from American and English churches (Alexandre, 2009); just as alcohol prohibition was inspired by temperance movements and experiences in China, associating it with a fight against evil. PA cannot avoid the drug trafficking question; it is at the center of the phenomenon. Drug traffickers need to deal with public administrators; and while public administrators would rather forget about them, they cannot. Because a country's PA is the national body responsible for exerting control over traffickers, it is in constant danger from them.

Drug traffic induces violence that affects the public and provokes constant social unrest. It also fuels long-lasting inside wars, and fighting these wars has proven extremely expensive financially, socially, and economically. Wars on drugs leave entire populations in the middle of a battle between traffickers and their own governments. In addition, because the temptations of corruption are so great, many governments lose their respectability and their population's confidence and trust.

Not fighting drug traffic has also been disastrous in the past, resulting in the death of hundreds of thousands of addicts. But fighting it has been worse, with hundreds of thousands of innocent people dead. We have seen how the markets evolve; drug traffic avoids controls in one place by moving to another, while benefiting from all the facilities globalization offers the world (Varese, 2012), such as unregulated financial transactions and easy travel. Economic tendencies press for

---

* Thousands of politicians, particularly mayors have been killed by rebels in Colombia. This is documented by *El Tiempo* (http://www.eltiempo.com/archivo/documento/CMS-6826807), BBC (http://news.bbc.co.uk/hi/spanish/latin_america/newsid_3173000/3173010.stm), and the Colombian news chain, Caracol (http://www.caracol.com.co/noticias/actualidad/veinticinco-alcaldes-asesinados-en-colombia-en-los-dos-ultimos-anos/20000426/nota/22683.aspx). The present situation in Mexico is equally uninspiring (www.fenamm.org.mx/site/index.php?).

less government and less public control, but opening the economy provides new opportunities for everyone involved in trafficking and makes it harder for debt-ridden governments. Traffickers just diversify their business from money laundering to cybercrime, terrorism, or arms dealing (Costa, 2010). States have fewer options for fighting them.

Drug Victims and Collateral Victims

Drugs produce numerous victims and no society can tolerate this. Thus, there are two issues at stake. The first is about deciding if governments should continue to fight traffickers as they do now, investing billions of dollars in producer countries and accepting the high rate of people who die, or are hurt, or suffer from economic, politic, and social domination and violence.

Uprimny Yepes et al. (2012, pp. 28, 30–34) show how, in Latin America, drug sentences are extremely long. They are longer than murder sentences in many countries, with the worst case being Bolivia. Sentences have lengthened significantly each decade since 1960 and particularly in Colombia, Peru, and Mexico since 1990, where the rates of incarceration were already extreme. Sending more people to jail overloads the prisons, and the price is very high. WOLA (Washington Office on Latin America) shows on its website an interview with a single mother of three who has spent 14 years in jail for attempting to traffic 750 grams of coca paste that would have allowed her to earn $125. When her sentence is up she will not recognize her youngest daughter who was two when she was arrested.

Costa (2010) writes that the main objective must be to reduce the demand for drugs through control, or else reduce the monopoly on the drug supply through legalization: if criminals are motivated by profit, he adds, that is where one should primarily act. He believes there are health and economic arguments for both these approaches, but that more should be invested in prevention and treatment than in law enforcement. President Santos (2012, p. 4) of Colombia commented on the criminalization of consumers in an interview in journal *El Tiempo*: "If my son becomes a drug addict, I would prefer seeing him go to a hospital than to a jail."

Becker et al. (2006) writes that because the market demand for drugs is inelastic (addicts do not stop buying when the product gets more expensive), trying to curb consumption will only increase the social cost of enforcement efforts. According to Alexandre (2009) and to Santos (2012), prohibition does not work and fails to punish the people involved in trafficking. Alexandre asserts that economists' studies conclude in large part that drug prohibition laws are not only ineffective but costly. In the past few years, in spite of drug prohibition efforts, narcotics have killed twice as many people in Russia as did the invasion of Afghanistan (Costa, 2010).

Other Issues

Violence is diminishing in Colombia: in 2012 it is half what it was in 2002, or down to 1986 levels (*El Tiempo*, Dec. 2012). But growers do not want coca to be legalized (Hernández Mora, 2012, p. 19). These growers have very small farms, generally one or sometimes two hectares, and grow just enough coca to pay for food and little more. Now they are paid $150 per kilo, down from $1000 per kilo 12 years ago. They fear the guerillas who fight against coca eradication (cocaine is FARC's main income) and also the people who work in eradication, who ask them to go on planting because if there is no more coca to eradicate, they will lose their jobs. Growers say that legalizing coca would be legalizing vice and immorality. Hernández Mora says that FARC makes the farmers work for them, forcing them to plant mines to protect their fields and using them as fighters when there is an attack against them.

President Santos (2012) of Colombia has criticized his country's drug strategy: "How can we say to a Colombian farmer it is illegal to cultivate marijuana, so that he has to eradicate the crop or go to jail, when American consumers can legally smoke it?" (even if only under certain conditions in certain states). He adds that the war on drugs has been a total failure, while unintended consequences are numerous and devastating. His position is that the government should further analyze and evaluate the situation. The current Colombian drug laws and policies are useless and extremely expensive from a financial and social point of view. Former presidents Cardoso (Brazil), Gaviria (Colombia), and Zedillo (Mexico) have suggested regulating drugs, not legalizing them.

Maybe a solution can be found if policy makers in the affected countries can agree that the current situation is no longer acceptable. Agreeing to this means seeking a solution other than just sending people to jail, when we know that prisons are the perfect place to become a criminal. Portugal was the first country to decriminalize drug possession for personal use and was so successful that Spain and Italy followed suit.

This report has made the following observations: drug production is a small business for many producers but this production is used by others to make big profits. Drug-producing regions are places that have common characteristics such as large areas of unoccupied land, poor security, and weak PA. Drug production generates much violence because it has become a way of survival for criminal groups such as FARC and paramilitaries in Colombia and *Sendero Luminoso* in Peru (whom many fear are making a comeback). Any approach to solving the problem of drug trafficking must take into consideration the violence that now surrounds drug trafficking in Mexico but also still in Colombia and other countries. Fighting drug consumption using arguments about individual morals makes sense only if we consider that in countries that produce and traffic drugs the violence and unrest may have economic and social causes, and that these are moral questions too.

Drug consumers in America and in other OECD countries bear some personal responsibility for becoming addicts. Can we say the same for the small farmers in Colombia, Peru, or Brazil who suffer the predations of the guerillas who make a living from drug trafficking? Can we say the same for the thousands of victims in these countries and in Mexico who are caught in the crossfire between traffickers? Do the young Africans or Afghans who are press-ganged into this system for market reasons have the same freedom as Western consumers to harm themselves?

On the one hand there are the negative consequences of drug addiction, such as family disintegration, health and work problems, and on the other, there is crime, violence, corruption, and death caused by the production and marketing of narcotics. PA is concerned with the first group of people involved in drugs as a social and health issue, and with the second group as a social, health, and economic issue for people whether they personally are involved in drugs or not, plus the budgetary problems related to fighting drugs and particularly the misdirection of public funds toward military programs instead of health programs.

If we are studying the moral question of drug consumption, we have to consider all elements of the problem, including the loss of quality of life of the thousands who suffer not from drug consumption but from trafficking. That should include people who have gone to jail for long periods, whose lives are destroyed, and who become tougher criminals. In Portugal, after decriminalization of drug possession, not only did drug consumption drop but the number of addicts registered in rehab clinics tripled from 1999 to 2008.

Some former presidents of Latin America are pleading for drug decriminalization and a present one (Perez Molina of Guatemala) for legalization. President Santos' position in favor of decriminalization is particularly interesting and politically courageous, considering the billion dollars Colombia is receiving from the US Government for *Plan Colombia*.

The violent situation we observe in Mexico has its roots in the past where tolerance for drug trafficking (Astorga, 2001) was common among politicians. Now it seems that traffickers have become independent from their political friends and increased the violence. With a broader vision, we can sense that fighting trafficking is a lost game: as we have seen, the situation in Mexico spread from Colombia and from other countries. Maybe what we see now in Mexico will later be common in West Africa where some states already depend on drug trafficking to survive economically.

We have also seen that PA can be the most important obstacle to the trafficking business and that hence the drug lords must actively control it when possible. The smaller a country's PA is, the easier it is to control. Public agencies may create laws, implement these laws, and put pressure on the army or police to restrain traffickers, but this is expensive and generates secondary problems. When governments fumigate crops with herbicides, for example, they punish poor individual producers more than anyone else in the chain.

Unfortunately, the trafficking problem has been approached in most countries from an individual moral and social point of view, overemphasizing addicts' health problems and according to them more human value than the collateral and systemic victims of the trafficking itself. We need now to take a holistic view and look at the problem in a more comprehensive way that includes the global effect of the policies Western societies have been applying for decades without success.

Conclusion for Mexico

Mexico inherited trafficking violence because of its proximity to the US market. In 1917, the federal government (Carranza) prohibited opium sale, while the governors of states such as Cantú were promoting it despite the law. Trafficking was used for paying troops, buying arms, and PA (Astorga, 2001). Relations between traffickers, politicians, and the state have continued along these lines. What is new now is that the drug traffickers have detached themselves from the politicians' support in Mexico: they need it less than they did before (Astorga), partly because they can fight the state directly with their arms, according to their own rules. Powerful traffickers do not have moral obligations or constraints: they feel free to kill or kidnap people, which has a strong impact on the level of violence in society. When Pablo Escobar was denied the right to associate himself with established political parties, he entered into a cycle of high-level violence ending with his own violent death.

Can Mexico get rid of *narcoviolence,* and if so, how? Mexican proximity to North American markets cannot be changed, and the US–Mexican level of economic exchange facilitates all commercial transactions, including trafficking. There cannot be sanctions or restrictions on Mexican exports to the United States because economic exchange between the two countries is already too extensive.

One solution is to fight violence with violence, putting emphasis on the army, on intelligence and direct armed confrontation: this approach is one of the main causes for the escalating level of violence. Fighting FARC and paramilitary guerillas has been a relative success only in Colombia, where violence has been reduced. Another solution is trying to cut the traffickers' revenues by controlling traffic through PA. That is what was done with alcohol in America at the end of the prohibition era. This means decriminalizing possession and legalizing distribution, while controlling production and distribution. It also means directly challenging those at the origin of drug prohibition, especially Protestant churches and their individualistic morality.

Fighting drug trafficking has a cost that few countries are ready to pay. Raising taxes to increase army and police presence is unpopular everywhere, particularly in the United States. Data on the long-term effects of lifting the prohibition are not available, but Portugal and the end of the prohibition era in North America give us some clues. Drug trafficking must be accepted and analyzed as a market issue, with supply and demand, and with the obligation to constantly find new consumers for the available products. Drug traffickers are very rich people who have problems spending their money, while governments have the opposite problem.

Mexico is paying a high price for prohibition in terms of violence, loss of quality of life, social unrest, and this situation is not improving. It cannot improve until something radical happens at the level of all the stakeholders, both in production and marketing and at the consumer end of the business.

References

Acemoglu, D., Robinson, J. A. and Santos, R. J. 2009. *The Monopoly of Violence: Evidence from Colombia.* MIT, Department of Economics, Working Paper 09-30. Nov 30, 2009.

Alexandre, M. 2009. Sex, drugs, rock and roll and moral dirigisme: Toward a reformation of drug and prostitution regulations. *UMKC Law Review*, 78 (1), 101–137. Electronic copy available at: http://ssrn.com/abstract=1512062.

Araujo, R. 2001. Trafic de drogues, économies illicites et société en Amazonie occidentale, *Revue internationale des sciences sociales,* 3 (169), 493–499. DOI : 10.3917/riss.169.0493. Available Online at: http://www.cairn.info/revue-internationale-des-sciences-sociales-2001-3-page-493.htm.

Astorga, L. 2001. Les limites de la politique antidrogue au Mexique, *Revue internationale des sciences sociales,* 3 (169), 469–476. DOI: 10.3917/riss.169.0469. Available Online at: http://www.cairn.info/revue-internationale-des-sciences-sociales-2001-3-page-469.htm.

Ballvé, T. 2011. *Territory by Dispossession: Decentralization, Statehood, and the Narco Land-Grab in Colombia.* Paper presented at the International Conference on Global Land Grabbing. 6-8 April 2011. Organized by the Land Deals Politics Initiative (LDPI) in collaboration with the Journal of Peasant Studies and hosted by the Future Agricultures Consortium at the Institute of Development Studies, University of Sussex.

Baumeister, R. 2007. *Resistance during the armed conflict in the Chocó, Colombia.* Master's thesis. Political Science and Master's in Development and International Cooperation, Department of Social Sciences and Philosophy, University of Jyväskylä, Finland, August 2007.

Becker, G. S., Murphy, K. M. and Grossman, M. 2006. The market for illegal goods: The case of drugs. *Journal of Political Economy,* 2006, 114 (1). University of Chicago.

Braudel, F. 1985. *La dynamique du capitalisme.* Paris: Champs, Flammarion.

Costa, A. M. 2010. The economics of crime: A discipline to be invented and a Nobel Prize to be awarded. *Journal of Policy Modeling*, 32(5), September–October 2010, 648–661. United Nations Office of Drugs and Crime (UNODC), Vienna International Center, PO Box 500, A 1400 Vienna, Austria.

Dufort, P. 2007. Paramilitarisme et scandale de la parapolitique en Colombie. *La Chronique des Amériques* Octobre 2007 (17) http://risal.collectifs.net/IMG/pdf/COL97.pdf.

El Espectador (Friday, October 12, 2012). The Mexican drug mafia seeks to "inherit" drug routes once organized by notorious Colombian crime syndicate "Los Rastrojos." *El Espectador.* Available online at: http://www.elespectador.com/noticias/judicial/articulo-379512-mafia-mexicana-quiere-quedarse-rutas-colombianas-de-coca. Consulted October 12, 2012.

El Tiempo. December 7, 2012. Bogotá. [Colombian national newspaper].

El Tiempo. Caitlin Trent 2012. Supreme Court calls on authorities to control crime in south-Colombia. Sept. 27, 2012.
Fabre, G. 2001. État, corruption et criminalisation en Chine, *Revue internationale des sciences sociales,* 3 169, 501–508. DOI: 10.3917/riss.169.0501. Available Online at: http://www.cairn.info/revue-internationale-des-sciences-sociales-2001-3-page-501.htm.
Geffray, C. 2001a. Introduction: Trafic de drogues et état. *Revue internationale des sciences sociales,* 2001/3 (169), 485–492.
Geffray, C. 2001b. Brésil: Le trafic de drogues dans l'État fédéré du Rondônia, *Revue internationale des sciences sociales,* 2001/3 169, 485–492.
González, F. and Esteban Posada, C. 2001. Criminalidad, Violencia y Gasto Público en Defensa, Justicia y Seguridad. Bogotá: *Revista de Economía Institucional,* No. 4, Primer Semestre, 2001. P. 78–102. Online [consulted September 23, 2012]: http://www.scielo.org.co/pdf/rei/v3n4/v3n4a5.pdf.
González, G. F. E. (ed.) 2008. *Hacia la reconstrucción del país: Desarrollo, Política y Territorio en regiones afectadas por el conflicto armado.* Bogotá DC: ©CINEP-ODECOFI.
Gutiérrez Sanin, F., Barberena, V., Garay Salamanca, L. J. and Ospina, J. M. 2010. *25 Años de la Descentralización en Colombia.* Bogotá: Konrad Adenauer Stiftung.
Hernández Mora, S. P. 19 *El Tiempo,* December 6, 2012.
Inkster, N. and Comolli, V. 2012a. *Drug, Insecurity and the Failed State.* "Introduction", Adelphi Series. http://dx.doi.org/10.1080/19445571.2012.677267.
Inkster, N. and Comolli, V. 2012b. Chapter 1. The evolution of the International drugs trade. http://dx.doi.org/10.1080/19445571.2012.677270.
Inkster, N. and Comolli, V. 2012c. Chapter 2. Prohibition. http://dx.doi.org/10.1080/19445571.2012.677275.
Inkster, N. and Comolli, V. 2012d. Chapter 3. The producer states. http://dx.doi.org/10.1080/19445571.2012.677277.
Inkster, N. and Comolli, V. 2012e. Chapter 4. The transit regions. http://dx.doi.org/10.1080/19445571.2012.677278.
Inkster, N. and Comolli, V. 2012f. Chapter 5. Alternatives to prohibition. http://dx.doi.org/10.1080/19445571.2012.677284.
Inkster, N. and Comolli, V. 2012g. Chapter 6. Conclusion. http://dx.doi.org/10.1080/19445571.2012.677285.
Leiteritz, R., Nasi, C. and Rettberg, A. 2009. Para desvincular los recursos naturales del conflicto armado en Colombia Recomendaciones para formuladores de política y activistas. *Colombia Internacional,* 70, July–December 2009:215–229.
Lyons, J. 2012. Brazil reaches across border to battle source of cocaine. *Wall Street Journal.*
Mason, A. C. 2005. Constructing authority alternatives on the periphery: Vignettes from Colombia. *International Political Science Review,* 26 (1), 37–54.
Murillo, G. and Valdivieso, Y. 2002. El escalonamiento de la crisis política colombiana. WP núm. 201. Institut de Ciències Polítiques i Socials Barcelona, 2002. Online: http://ddd.uab.cat/pub/worpap/2002/hdl_2072_1261/ICPS201.txt.
Pécaut, D. Trafic de drogue et violence en Colombie, *Cultures & Conflits* [Online], Mafia, drogue et politique, online December 31, 2002, Consulted September 2, 2012. URL:/index117.html.
Posada Carbó, E. 2006. Las elecciones presidenciales en Colombia. Área: América Latina—ARI N° 61/2006 Fecha 24/05/2006. Real Instituto Elcano.
Preston IV, C. P. 2004. *Drugs and Conflict in Colombia: A Policy Framework Analysis of Plan Colombia.* Major Paper submitted to the Faculty of the Virginia Polytechnic Institute

and State University in partial fulfillment of the requirements for the degree of Master in Public and International Affairs. December 2, 2004. Blacksburg, Virginia.

Salama, P. 2008. Informe sobre la violencia en América latina. *Revista de Economía Institucional*, 10(18), primer semestre/2008, 81–102. Electronic copy available at: http://ssrn.com/abstract=1174382.

Santos, J. M. 2012. Interview in *El Tiempo*, December 7, 2012. Bogota.

Schiray, M. 2001. Introduction: Trafic de drogues, organisations criminelles et politiques publiques de contrôle. ERES | *Revue internationale des sciences sociales*, 2001/3 (169) 389–396.

Serrano, C. and Acosta, P. 2011. El proceso de descentralización en Colombia. Proyecto gobernanza subnacional para el desarrollo territorial en los Andes. *RIMISP*. Enero 2011. Centro Latinoamericano para el desarrollo rural.

United Nations Office of Drugs and Crime (UNODC). 2012. *Report* Vienna International Center, PO Box 500, A 1400 Vienna, Austria.

Uprimny Yepes, R., Guzman, D. E. and Parra Norato, J. 2012. La adicción punitiva. La desproporción de leyes de drogas en America latina. CEDD. (Research Consortium on Drugs and the Law). Research supported by Transnational Institute (TNI) and WOLA. Website consulted Dec. 2012.

Varese, F. 2012. How mafias take advantage of globalization. *The British Journal of Criminology*, 52 (2), 235–253.

Verdadabierta. 2012. Internet consulted October 30, 2012: http://www.verdadabierta.com/component/content/article/158-captura-de-rentas-publicas/4267-el-drama-de-los-desplazados-de-mampujan.

Chapter 3

Regional Development, Education, and Trans-Border Governance
Toward the Creation of a True Economic and Social Community

Angélica Pérez Ordaz

Contents

Introduction 36
The Meaning of the Border: Demographic Trends, Economic Imperatives 37
A Shared Opportunity for Economic Development and Public Education
Policy in the Trans-Border Region 39
Conclusion 43
References 44

> The best way for two neighbors to approach each other is through mutual understanding.*
>
> **Daniel Cosio Villegas**

---

* Taken from Krauze (2003, p. 14).

Introduction

The United States Mexico border region is a shared space with peculiar features and common dynamics that transcend both countries' geopolitical boundaries. In this shared space, education has become a critical element in the context of a more globalized economy where better-trained citizens can respond more proactively and effectively to the challenges and opportunities created by greater global economic integration. Education is one of the main engines of economic growth and social development, promoting productivity and competitiveness of any region or country.

Around the world, it is essential that countries move toward the creation of true economic and social communities that transcend nationalism, xenophobia, and ethnic conflicts marked by intolerance, religious fundamentalism, and other mechanisms of exclusion. Education can become the key instrument for understanding these problems and providing solutions to them. Only education can provide every citizen with the essential elements needed to understand and act in society, to change as the world changes, not as a reactive adaptation to the present but in anticipation of the future. It is a vital element to facilitate first the engagement and then the integration into society of all citizens excluded from the benefits of development. Education leads to individual creativity and improves participation in the social, economic, cultural, and political life of communities. And apart from its economic value for society education is also a basic human right. It is not enough to ensure a certain level of education for all citizens, or to consider it as a process that ends at a certain age. Since no nation can aspire to competitiveness without exploiting the potential of the most precious resource (i.e., human capital), public authorities should promote education that will last a lifetime (Urzúa et al., 1995).

The second half of the twentieth century witnessed the rebuilding of educational systems around the world as the result of the underlying social, economic, political, and cultural transformations that followed the end of the 1970s, marked by the demise of the welfare state and the end of an era of unprecedented prosperity (Pérez Ordaz 2009). The development of science and technology transformed all countries, bringing new forms of social organization, increased economic competition, and greater differentiation between rich and poor countries, a new world map, and a new international order with capitalism established as the dominant economic system. After the fall of the Berlin Wall and the collapse of the former Soviet Union at the end of the 1980s, the United States became the world's major country due to its economic, political, and military power as well as its cultural influence. This has mainly been due to the human capital that has been the engine of its economy (Schiller, 2008), from its establishment as an independent nation to its history of large-scale immigration that characterizes it as one of the ethnically most diverse and multicultural nations of the world.

This new global order is driven by the diffusion and adoption of new knowledge and innovative technologies of information and communications technologies (ICTs), biotechnology, and nanotechnology. These in turn drive the demand for increasingly globalized educational models open to evaluation and modification. The strengthening of economic ties among the three biggest countries of North America (i.e., Mexico, Canada, and the United States) resulted in the creation of the North American Free Trade Agreement (NAFTA) in 1994. This marked the beginning of trade liberalization, strengthening regionalization, and highlighting Mexico's greater social, economic, and political interdependence with these two countries.

The Meaning of the Border: Demographic Trends, Economic Imperatives

Mexico and the United States share one of the most extensive and dynamic borders in the world. It is 3185 km long, geographically varied, characterized by heterogeneous cultures, attitudes, and traditions, and affected by unparalleled economic and social development issues. Approximately 15 million people live in this region, over half of them in Mexico. The population is primarily located in 30 sister cities, so called because they are located in pairs on opposite sides of the border. The adjacent states are Baja California, Sonora, Chihuahua, Coahuila, Nuevo Leon, and Tamaulipas in Mexico, and California, Arizona, New Mexico, and Texas in the United States.

The border is a geopolitical boundary, and in recent years a physical boundary as well, marked by a fence and by increasingly militarized border security. Yet the border is also a meeting place characterized by intense communication, interaction, and movement of people, goods, and services. It is thus the region where obstacles and opportunities for people on both sides of the border are concentrated, and a flash point where disagreements over how to regulate these interactions have historically played themselves out (Rincones, 2004; Zamora, 2008: 5; Jáuregui Díaz and Avila Sánchez, 2007).

Mexico–US border area, showing "sister states" and "sister cities"

Mexico experienced high population growth through the 1980s, at which time economic development and urbanization slowed its birth rate. So despite the fact that Mexico's infant mortality rate is decreasing and life expectancy is increasing, it now has a large cohort of employment-aged (18–64) workers, a "demographic bonus" available to support economic development. By contrast, the US birth rate has steadily declined since the post-World War II "baby boom" (1946–1965) (Smead, 2000). The number of people aged 45–64 increased to 81.5 million between 2000 and 2010. The number of people over 65 years of age grew more rapidly than any other demographic group to 41.2 million, 13.1% of the total population (IndexMundi, 2013). The US Social Security Administration estimated that over the next 20 years, 10,000 people will file retirement applications every day. According to data from the US Bureau of the Census, the population aged 65 or over is projected to grow from 38.7 million in 2008 to 88.5 million by 2050; those over 85 will increase from 5.4 to 19 million.

These demographic shifts have profound economic implications for the United States. The Bureau of Labor Statistics projects a decline in the available labor force, increased demands on the Social Security system, increased pressure on government budgets, and increased need for immigrant labor to reduce the gap between supply and demand. The number of people registered in Medicare (a universal health insurance program financed by the federal government and available to retirees at age 65) will balloon from 47 million in 2010 to 80 million by 2030. In addition, the number of Social Security system beneficiaries (i.e., those receiving a federal government-financed defined benefit pension available at a starting age between 62 and 67) will increase from 44 to 73 million over the next 20 years. Currently, both programs cost 8.4% of gross domestic product (GDP); by 2030 this is estimated to increase to 11.2% (IndexMundi, 2013).

The imbalance between increasing number of retirees and the decreasing number of working-age adults, coupled with higher-than-average rates of inflation for federal- and state-supported health programs for low-income persons (Medicaid) and Medicare, will raise the US budget deficit to stratospheric levels. At the same time, the slower growth in the number of workers will require an increase in productivity per worker. The US Bureau of Labor Statistics estimates that of the 15 occupations predicted to grow at least twice as fast as the national average (13%), 10 will require at least an associate degree (equivalent to a post-secondary technical degree in Mexico). In 2005, four of these high-skill occupations had a higher concentration of immigrant workers than did the US labor force in general: medical science (46%), computer engineering (35%), data management (21%), and high education teaching and administration (20%) (Gonzales, 2009, p. 14). Among many sectors, the main areas predicted to have a large number of vacancies are the automotive and pharmaceutical industries, mechanical, aerospace, and chemical engineering. These vacancies will be extremely difficult to fill, since the US education and vocational training systems are currently unable to produce enough qualified workers in these fields to meet the expected demand.

Because fewer native-born workers are available to enter the labor market, the United States needs skilled immigrants to sustain economic growth and development, particularly in high-tech fields such as aeronautics, biotechnology, and information technology (Fiscal Policy Institute, 2009). Immigrants accounted for 49% of the total growth of the labor force between 1996 and 2000, 60% between 2000 and 2004 (Gonzales, 2009, p. 14). Foreign workers are currently responsible for 20% of economic output in the 25 largest urban areas of the country. Coincidentally, immigrants also represent 20% of the population in these metropolitan areas, so they contribute to the economy in a proportion equal to their percentage of the population. In this perspective, it is easy to understand why immigration and growth (Fiscal Policy Institute, 2009) are strongly connected. For example, in Miami immigrants account for 37% of the population and 38% of GDP; in Los Angeles, they represent 35% of the population and contribute 34% of GDP; and in San Diego, 23% of both population and GDP.

Hispanics constitute almost half (46%) of the immigrant population in these same 25 largest metropolitan areas of the United States, including San Francisco, Washington, Dallas, Philadelphia, and Chicago (Schiller, 2008). Most live in states along the southern border of the United States: California,[*] Florida,[†] and Texas[‡] together comprise about 13% of US territory and have about 15 million people over age 65. Hispanics are employed in a wide range of jobs, and their economic contribution is significant because they are more likely to be of working age than those born in the United States. Twenty-four percent of immigrants in these 25 urban areas are in professional or management positions. Another 25% work in sales, administrative, or technical jobs. While economic data are not available on undocumented workers, their economic contribution is significant, but for obvious reasons is not included in these figures.

A Shared Opportunity for Economic Development and Public Education Policy in the Trans-Border Region

These demographic contrasts, plus the greater degree of economic interdependence between the two countries, are exerting powerful pressures on the governments of both countries to provide complementary, coordinated, and inclusive public

---

[*] California has 38 million people and covers an area of 410,000 km². It is the most populous state in the United States and the third largest after Alaska and Texas (The Official Portal of the State of California).

[†] In 2010, Florida's population was more than 18.8 million, is the fourth most populous in the country (The Official Portal of the State of Florida).

[‡] With an area of 696,241 km² and a population of 24.7 million, Texas is the second largest and second most populous state in the United States. It is bordered on the south by the States of Tamaulipas, Nuevo Leon, Coahuila, and Chihuahua in Mexico (The Official Portal of the State of Texas).

policies than respond in a timely and efficient manner to trans-border policy issues. Notwithstanding these demographic and economic imperatives, however, various US states have created or increased barriers to immigrants' educational access. To prevent this, a more global, comprehensive, and inclusive binational public education policy is needed. Democratizing educational access generally—and in particular by young people in the border area—will allow the United States to have access to a potential source of highly skilled workers, productive contributors prepared to take on the challenges in the collective future of both countries.

In states such as New Mexico and Texas that allow undocumented students to compete for financial aid to continue post-secondary studies, results have been positive. The number of undocumented students has not significantly increased, nor has educational funding decreased. Such measures tend to increase school revenues and attract enrollment by students who would otherwise not attend college (Gonzales, 2009, p. 23). With the emergence of an economic and social "common market" in the border area, the label of "undocumented student" will no longer be applied. Their increased participation in post-secondary education, and their increased importance to the economy and the community as tax-paying citizens, will justify increased investment in primary and secondary schools.

Given the contrasting demographic conditions in the United States and Mexico, the growing demand for qualified labor in the United States and the supply of surplus available labor in Mexico has created tensions in the border area. This situation can only be resolved by the US approval of migration policies that open its border to immigrant workers, legalize the presence of undocumented immigrants, and encourage access to education. This will lay the foundations for the construction of a true economic and social community in the border region based on a common purpose and intended to benefit both countries. It is estimated that each worker with higher education, in the course of their working life will, be paid more than 1 million dollars in Taxes (Maciel, 2011, p. 44).

Addressing the shortage of skilled workers by building a common economic and social area between the member countries of NAFTA Mexico, Canada, and the United States would be a first step to increase the size of the US workforce. At the same time, crafting common educational objectives and policies would strengthen the cultural interaction and the economic and social dynamism of people, goods, and services needed to deal with the challenges of an aging population in the United States and Canada, and expand opportunities for immigrants from Mexico and other countries in Latin America. In the long run, it would expand opportunities for trilateral cooperation in consolidating the three largest countries of North America into a geostrategic block capable of competing with the European Union, China, and other economic powerhouses.

Achieving a goal of this magnitude requires putting an end to the waste of human lives and capital represented by current US immigration policies. Approval of the "Dream Act" would help the United States meet its growing demand for trained workers and fulfill the promise of an increasingly heterogeneous US society

(Gonzales, 2009, p. 2). Immigrants have long been the cornerstone of US development. Now is the time to help them—and the United States' long-term prospects—by giving them the same opportunities as previous generations of immigrants. Creating a border between the United States and Mexico that encourages regional economic, cultural, and social development would expand the richness of the United States. It would also mean a step toward diminishing the internal boundaries against Hispanics in the United States, moving beyond a vision based primarily on economic development to a human-centered vision that accepts freedom of movement, and changes in residency and citizenship, as fundamental individual rights.

The need for social and political mobility in the border area also implies rights for the people who live there: access to education, health care, and employment opportunity under conditions of social, political, and economic equality. By promoting employment, improving the conditions of life and work, providing adequate social services and fostering cultural and linguistic dialog, we can reduce exclusion, develop human resources and maintain economic competitiveness, the functioning of the common market, and the harmonization of social systems.

In this context, education takes on a key role for human development. High levels of education are associated with increased access to resources and to their best use, and with more generation and conservation of human capital. Access to knowledge is crucial if people are to add value to their lives. At the same time, it increases labor productivity, incorporates technological innovation, and strengthens economic competitiveness. Because it is the key to individual development and economic competitiveness, education is a mechanism for social mobility. Because education contributes to greater social equity, providing adequate programs is an unavoidable ethical challenge for governments that profess interest in promoting human development in the society. Education is a right of all and for all, and should be granted to people based on equality of opportunity and directed toward the maximum expansion of people's cognitive and emotional capabilities, as a tool that allows them to develop, integrate themselves into, and give back to the society where they belong (Pérez Ordaz, 2009; Castells, 1999).

How is this to be done? Beyond a doubt, we need to increase teachers' qualifications through pre-service and in-service training, and to support their work in the classroom with effective administration and other resources. Education should be viewed not only as the means by which we provide potential workers with the skills needed to perform more technically demanding jobs, but also as the way we prepare them to contribute as citizens who are members of a democratic society. This means giving students the skills they need to think for themselves, learn on their own, and to—as we noted earlier—help create the society they and their children will live in, rather than merely keeping up with changing job competencies (see Castells, 1999, 63). For this to happen, governments must promote higher education, which is the area where knowledge is generated and applied. If in the short-term governments are able through their educational systems to offer access to quality learning opportunities, the end result will be the construction of a more just and more humane society (Pérez Ordaz, 2009).

Public education systems are the institutions responsible for building an inclusive society of qualified workers and citizens. They are the open space for the training that is conducive to lifelong learning, providing an optimal range of options and the ability to enter and exit easily, as well as opportunities for social mobility and individual realization in order to form citizens who actively participate in society and are open to the world, within a framework of justice, human rights, sustainable development, democracy, and peace (UNESCO, 1998, p. 4) is in sense, a cohesive and comprehensive education policy across Mexico, Canada, and the United States would help consolidate shared interests, and bring about the cultural transformation of the North American community. The formation of a common economic and social area will contribute to the development of quality education by encouraging cooperation between member states through the diffusion of languages and cultures, greater mobility of students and teachers, and greater transferability of educational credits and academic degrees. Greater cooperation between educational institutions, the exchange of information, and experience on common concerns through education and training systems that include both traditional and distance education will lay the foundation for an educational system in the border region that can effectively train workers to enter the labor market, and then retrain them as demanded by the increasing or evolving skill requirements of new positions.

The educational reform agenda should aim for greater inclusion, improved quality, and more flexible academic and administrative structures that would encourage curricular reform and the creation of better options for accreditation and certification at local and regional levels. It is necessary that young people acquire the capacities, skills, and competences that form the foundation for work in the global information- and knowledge-based society and at the same time allow them to create the bonds of self-confidence and community that are essential to building equitable and participative interactions among the citizens and countries of the world.

Developing a knowledge-based society that can compete effectively in the global economy requires an educational system that drives societal learning and knowledge management by understanding and taking advantage of the "knowledge spiral" (i.e., the interactive and mutually supportive relationship between education, research, and innovation). As a key component of the "knowledge spiral," education helps promote growth and job creation. It is also related to improved governance. Since participative governance requires social equality, it is essential to be aware of the economic and social impact of education and training policies, strengthen measures to ensure sustainable financing, correct socio-economic disadvantages by making equitable access, participation and outcomes a priority, and provide teachers with professional preparation and continuing development.

We need to adopt a long-term perspective on educational policy that not only gives workers entering or reentering the labor market the competencies they need to compete in global, regional, and local labor markets, but also that builds civil society by inculcating values, culture, and the ability to adapt to changing conditions in society. This means that education, whether traditional or distance-based, becomes a physical or virtual space for learning that meets social needs by promoting a shared vision of the fundamental ethical and civic values required to foster lifelong learning, creativity, and innovation.

The current education trend is oriented toward the creation of flexible models for lifelong learning that enables people to meet the economic and social challenges implied by the knowledge society and empowers citizens so that they are able to move seamlessly between work and learning environments, and from one region or one country to another to maximize their skills and qualifications. Within the framework of the knowledge society and the new global economy, the educational policy of NAFTA member states must be targeted to maintain competitiveness not only in each country, but with other regions and countries of the world.

A well-rounded education means developing students' intellectual, cultural, ethical, and social capacities. We want that students have the logical, critical thinking, and creative skills they need for the knowledge society. Working requires the ability to add value to multicultural and multilingual work teams. This requires building skills in interpersonal communication, coordination, and problem solving. These can best be achieved by innovative teaching and learning strategies that consciously design educational systems to model the autonomy, creativity, diversity, flexibility, adaptability, and innovation that the contemporary workplace requires. Education is a lever toward economic development and sustainable economic growth, and an instrument for building a more inclusive society with higher levels of collective welfare. This implies that a key responsibility of government is the creation of an environment where education, culture, and knowledge can become core elements of an innovative economy and a just society. It requires that we all work together to first imagine and then build a coordinated educational system that can help our countries fulfill the potential of NAFTA by expanding it to include greater mobility of workers as well as of goods and services.

Conclusion

Ultimately, development is for people. Things do not give quality to life if they do not transform those who produce and use them. Techniques do not improve existence if those who employ them are not masters of their destiny. Power does not improve people if it is not exercised to serve them. The critical point is human improvement; it is being, not having. Therefore, no nation can advance beyond the point of its educational development (Solana Morales, 1982, p. 289).

It is urgent that we rethink, from a geostrategic point of view, the foundations of our education, science, and technology policies. Taken together, they can comprise an engine for development (Del Val, 2011). While it is true that the border area between Mexico and the United States has been marked by economic, social, and cultural asymmetries, it is equally true that the border today represents an opportunity for both countries. It is essential to take advantage of this proximity to build a true economic and social community where public education policy contributes to a "virtuous circle" that can counteract the "vicious circle" (i.e., the "perfect storm") represented by drug trafficking, and the resultant gridlock over migration, border security, and other policy areas. A "virtuous circle" comprising coordinated national policies to encourage regional economic and social development in the border area will improve conditions and the quality of life for the population on both sides of the border, strengthen the social fabric, and perhaps even improve relations between the two countries.

In the past, relations between Mexico and the United States have been varied between friendship and conflict depending on the extent to which each country perceived its policy interests as being compatible or incompatible with those of the other. They were "good neighbors" in 1928 through 1952 due to their alliance during World War II and their economic interdependence. They were more "distant neighbors" during the Cold War because of the tensions created by their having adopted different international policies. They became "associated neighbors in 1994 with the signing of the NAFTA accord" (Krauze, 2003, p. 12). It's time they became "good neighbors" so they can construct a common economic and social community that benefits both countries, building on shared educational objectives that strengthen the presence and leadership of North America at the global level. As the co-signers of NAFTA, Canada, Mexico, and the United States constitute as a true economic community. They share a responsibility for working cohesively to achieve economic and social progress marked by balanced and sustainable development of a physical and psychological space that allows and encourages free movement of persons, goods, services, and capital within the border region.

References

Castells, M. 1999. *La Era de la Información*. México: Siglo XXI.
Del Val, E. 2011. Educación superior, ciencia y tecnología en México: Tendencias, retos y prospectivas. *Nueva Época, 87* (National Autonomous University of México). Available online at: http://www.revistadelauniversidad.unam.mx/8711/delval/87delval02.html. Accessed December 1, 2012.
Fiscal Policy Institute. 2009. *Immigrants and the Economy Contribution of Immigrant Workers to the Country's 25 Largest Metropolitan Areas with a Focus on the Five Largest Metro Areas in the East*. New York: Fiscal Policy Institute. Available online at: http://www.fiscalpolicy.org/ImmigrantsIn25MetroAreas_20091130.pdf. Accessed January 25, 2013.
Gacel Ávila, J. July–September, 2000. La dimensión internacional de las universidades mexicanas. *Revista de la Educación Superior*, XXIX (3), 115. México: ANUIES.
Gonzales, R. G. 2009. *Young Lives on Hold: The College Dreams of Undocumented Students*. New York: College Board. Available online at: http://advocacy.collegeboard.org/sites/default/files/young-lives-on-hold-college-board.pdf. Accessed February 12, 2012.

Indexmundi. 2013. *Perfil de Población 2012*. Available online at: http://www.indexmundi.com/es/estados_unidos/poblacion_perfil.html. Accessed February 1, 2013.

Jáuregui Díaz, J. A. and Ávila Sánchez, M. J. 2007. Estados Unidos, lugar de destino para los migrantes chiapanecos. *Migraciones internacionales*, 4(1), 5–38. Recuperado en 19 de diciembre de 2013, de http://www.scielo.org.mx/scielo.php?script=sci_arttext&pid=S1665-89062007000100001&lng=es&tlng=es.

Krauze, E. 2003. Historia de vecindad. *Letras Libres*, No. 53. México: Letras libres, 12–14.

Maciel, A. 2011. La generación que se va. *Revista Proceso No. 1785*, 43–45.

Pérez Ordaz, A. 2009. Hacia dónde avanzar? Tendencias de la educación en el mundo. *Revista Eutopía. Segunda Época*, 3(9) Ene-Mar. México, Dirección General del Colegio de Ciencias y Humanidades. Universidad Nacional Autónoma de México.

Rincones, R. 2004. La frontera México-Estados Unidos: Elementos básicos para su comprensión. *Revista Araucaria*, 5 (11). Spain: University of Seville.

Schiller, T. 2008. Slowly growing older: Demographic trends in the third district states. *Philadelphia. Business Review*, Q4, 21–28. Available online at: http://www.philadelphiafed.org/research-and-data/publications/business-review/2008/q4/brq408_growing-slowly-getting-older.pdf. Accessed January 15, 2013.

Smead, H. 2000. *Don't Trust Anyone Over Thirty: The First Four Decades of the Baby Boom*. Available online at: http://www.howardsmeadcom/boom.htm. Accessed December 18, 2013.

Solana Morales, F. 1982. *Tan Lejos como Llegue la Educación*. México: Fondo de Cultura Económica.

The Official Portal of the State of California. Available online at: http://www.ca.gov/. Accessed December 18, 2013.

The Official Portal of the State of Florida. Available online at: http://www.myflorida.com/taxonomy/government/. Accessed December 18, 2013.

The Official Portal of the State of Texas. Available online at: http://www.tdi.texas.gov/. Accessed December 18, 2013.

UNESCO. 1998. *Declaración mundial sobre la educación superior en el Siglo XXI: visión y acción. Marco de acción prioritaria para el cambio y el desarrollo de la educación superior*. París. UNESCO.

Urzúa, R., M. de Puelles y J. I. Torreblanca. 1995. *La Educación Como Factor de Desarrollo*. Argentina. Organización de Estados Iberoamericanos.

Zamora Canizales, F. October 2008. Complementariedad e interdependencia comercial en la frontera México-Estados Unidos. *Revista CESUN-Universidad*, 1(2). México. Escuela de Negocios CESUN-Universidad. Available online at: http://www.cesununiversidad.aplicacionesweb.us/revistaCESUN/Complementareidad-Zamora%20Canizales.pdf. Accessed December 2, 2012.

Chapter 4

Looks of Fear
A Reflection of Violence and Crime in Mexico

José Luis Cisneros

Contents

Introduction 47
Violence as Discourse 48
Violence as an Instrument of Control and Dominance 53
Scenarios of Violence 56
Conclusion 58
References 58

Introduction

These lines begin a reflection on the effects of violent death. This topic, particularly the phenomenon and significance of extreme violence in Mexico, emerged as a result of the so-called war on drugs, which has intensified enormously in recent years. This violence is not only the result of common crimes, but also includes murders, kidnappings, and confrontations caused by the escalating conflict between organized crime (drug gangs) and government efforts to contain them. The fight against drug trafficking has exposed us to forms of violence intended to provoke terror and induce fear in the population, like torture, decapitation, and dismemberment. I have been studying violence in all its forms for some time. This includes not only its objective, formal aspect as the outcome of conflict between criminals and citizens or between drug traffickers and the authorities, or even its more abstract definition as a result of the conflict between good and evil. In this chapter, I am trying to portray the violence as a more complex social phenomenon and to demonstrate that certain forms of violence are in fact weapons or a form of symbolic discourse intended to strike terror in the citizenry.

In the context of this research, I have needed to act in ways that run intuitively counter to the very considerations that led me into it, in that publicizing the results of this research forces me to rely on graphic, disturbing images of violence in order to explain its social significance and thus justify why it must be viewed differently. If I am to do this, as Paola Ovalle (2010) says, people must be forced to stop and look at what they do not want to see, to see these scenes of terror and explain media use of death as deliberate instruments of terror aimed at breaking the will of the people to demand justice. The images used in this chapter were obtained primarily from *Diario Milenio* (the *Millennium Journal*), the magazine *Proceso* (*Process*), and from online blogs and web posts.

Violence as Discourse

In the aftermath of the current government's fight against drug trafficking networks, a firestorm of violence has spread more and more strongly throughout many of our countries cities, giving rise to unrelenting complaints and protests. This increased violence has not only shaped the public's perception of crime, but has also caused profound changes in how we define and organize urban spaces by creating gated communities and segregated residential areas. It has changed how citizens behave, creating distrust, changing how people behave together, disrupting physical and mental health by increasing stress and mental illness, and bringing about a profound deterioration in Mexicans' quality of life (Puerta Henao, 2008).

These effects are the general outcome of a range of local, regional, and national scenarios where violence is sometimes viewed not only as a result of the struggle of one group against the other, but also as a social mechanism of persecution and cleansing directed against specific groups in the population, both by the drug traffickers themselves and by the military and other national security forces acting against them. This type of violence must be viewed as a form of domination exercised as a control mechanism, both the institutions responsible for the fight against drug trafficking, the warring groups of drug traffickers, or the paramilitary groups that sometimes act as mercenaries for sale to the highest bidder. Under these circumstances, violence creates what may be termed as "geography of crime," expressed by type and degree and with respect to both victims and perpetrators, that has defined domestic order and the dynamics of relationships between members of communities.

Viewed as a control instrument, violence can be expressed a very wide and complex range of manifestations. One, usually described as virtuous and public spirited, is used by the State and its public institutions to enforce behavioral norms as part of a social contract among citizens. The other, the opposite, is employed by those termed the "enemies of society" who undermine legal authority due to their bad habits and addiction to drugs or money, or to violence and conflict. It is beyond the scope of this chapter to discuss these two archetypes, but I need to describe them briefly in order to contextualize my conclusions, and to explain the image many Mexicans have of the effect of violence and death.

I want to go beyond a pathological analysis of violent behaviors *per se* in order to understand their general effects on social relations. In this manner, I hope to explain violence not only as an individual problem, but as the outcomes of social conflict between competing interests of groups, subjects, and actors. As you can notice, the following map describes the geography of violence, by zones and cumulative number of violent murders in 2011, which also shows the number of low public forces fighting in the containment of organized crime (Figure 4.1).

Since violence is a social control mechanism, we must also be aware of the effects of extreme violence on Mexican's socialization and networks of interaction. What is the intent of publicizing these macabre and chilling images of bodies first desecrated and then exhibited in disputed territories where violence has been imposed as an interminable conflict without resolution? The effects of this violence have been devastating, and it has spawned a market for new forms of illegality. The profusion of

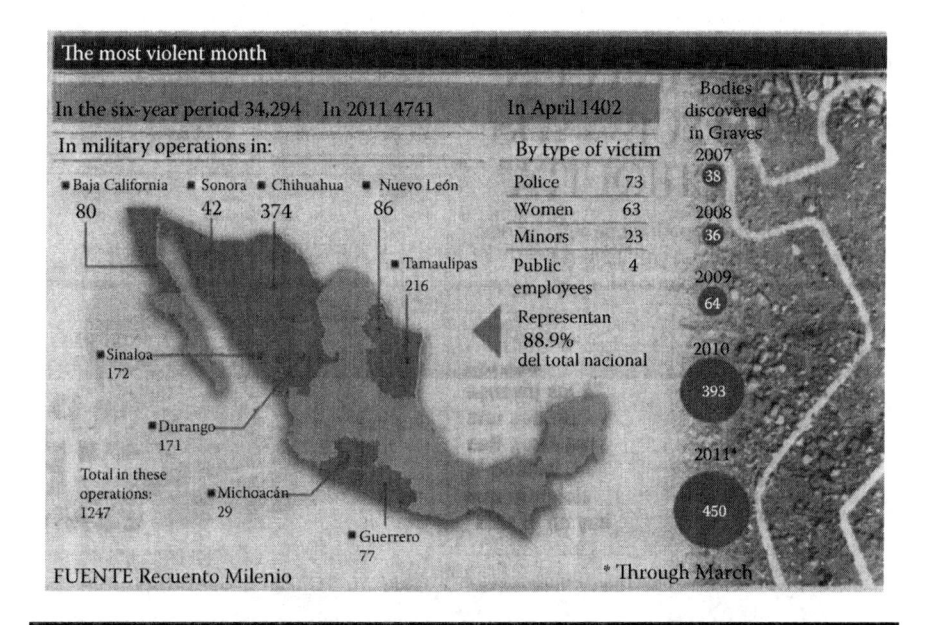

Figure 4.1 Geography of violence. (Adapted from Diario Milenio Available online at: http://www.milenio.com/buscador/?text=el+mes+mas+violento+abril+2011. Accessed June 10, 2012.)

images has created a new class of offenders who will do anything for prestige, money, respect, and power (Carrion, 2003). These are young people aged between 15 and 35 years, who constitute a seemingly inexhaustible supply of operatives for cartel networks. They are actors in a macabre national theater of violence, and contributors to the high human cost of conflict between groups fighting for territorial control.

Explaining this phenomenon requires that we take a brief and circumspect tour of the outer limits of violence. The objective is not to sensationalize violence by showing graphic images of thousands of victims, nor to titillate viewers by putting the victims' private pain and horror on public display but raise awareness and create empathy so that readers may understand the pain, join the cry for justice for those killed and buried in unmarked graves, and fight to build a more just society. This violence, rooted in the discontent that has fueled the economic crisis we have endured over the last decade and the repeated cycles of violence we have undergone, has had a significant impact on our population by increasing the general sense of terror, fear, and hatred. This structural violence is the outcome of social relationships based on constant force and the abuse of power, and seeks to keep control over those groups that grew under his shade and now resist strongly through repeated waves of violence. Figure 4.2, in outline, may show conceptual categories of our analysis and its importance in the everyday life of our society.

As many scholars and other commentators have noted, the Mexican government has a history of authoritarianism and violence. The national government began by modifying the legal system and implementing a strategy of violence to contain violence. That is, ostensibly to enforce the rule of law, the Mexican government began to exercise power in a way that dragged citizens back into the kinds of excesses and abuses that had not been experienced in recent generations. This struggle also served to highlight underlying weaknesses in Mexican society—the lack of

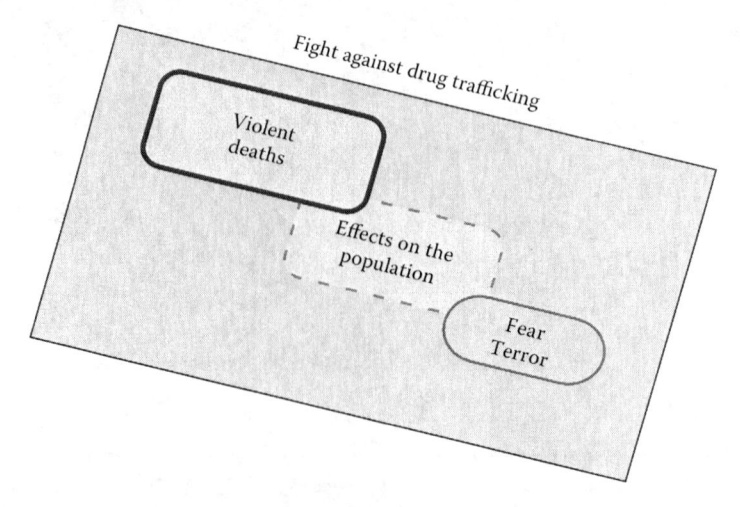

Figure 4.2 Conceptual categories.

authority and institutional capacity, and the rule of impunity and corruption. We are forced to respond to violence, but find it impossible to act without confronting our own feelings about our history, feelings that play themselves out every day as we fear one another as a potential enemy (Osorio Enrique, 2011).

This fear of violence has not only become an instrument of social control, but it has also led to the growth of a "fear industry" among a population gripped by fear and fueled by violent images of bloodshed, persecution, and detention. Mexicans have come to see themselves as potential victims. An example we can show, on the next picture, which shows how the federal government uses propaganda, showing tasks performed in the fight against drug trafficking and the supports that daily to report the number of arrests and deaths in clashes with organized crime (Figure 4.3).

This idea is reinforced by political rhetoric that insists on stigmatizing others as enemies, in order to encourage people to collaborate by informing authorities of their whereabouts to enable their capture and detention. This negative image of "the other" is supported by a cooperative media that reinforces the negative attributes of drug traffickers, assassins, drug dealers, kidnappers, and anyone else to control political discourse and maintain state security. Newspapers play an essential role. Inflammatory headlines and graphic images emphasize atrocities committed by these groups; in some cases the State earns support for arrests; in others, heightened fear justifies the exercise of violence to contain the social deviance caused by organized crime.

There are ready examples of how government authority and sensationalist journalism combine to project the fight against drug traffickers as a national

Figure 4.3 Federal government propaganda. (Adapted from propaganda spread in the mass media by the federal government.)

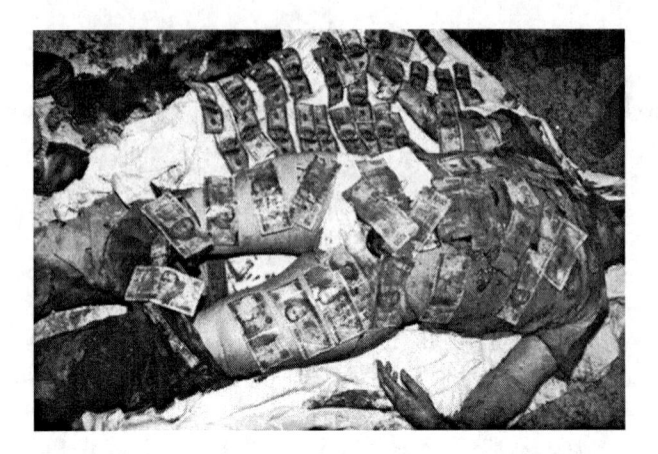

Figure 4.4 Staged execution of drug trafficker Arturo Beltran Leyva.

"morality play." One was the staged detention of Edgar Valdez Villarreal (aka "The Barbie,") or the arrest of Edgar Jimenez Lugo (aka "The Ponchis"). The most spectacular case was arguably the staged execution of Arturo Beltran Leyva, whose nude body was shown upholstered in bloody pesos and dollars (Figure 4.4).

This display of images is part of a deliberate State strategy of violence that makes each arrest a scene of heroism and glamor, somewhat in the style of those bad Almada Brothers movies.* But by themselves, even these repeated scenes are not sufficient to explain the violence that has existed for years in such areas as Ciudad Juarez, Michoacán, Guerrero, and Veracruz. The only explanation is this violence is deeply embedded in the social fabric of the community, experienced every day as part of life itself, and reinforced with images that unfortunately repel us less as we become more inured to them. It is through images like this that the State sends a message to drug traffickers and in passing to society as a whole. The underlying message (i.e., "the State exterminates") is also one that can lead to human rights abuses.

With such actions and augmented by the use of national agencies and the military, the State has contributed to the escalation of violence, which it justifies by emphasizing the need to impose order and liberate our country from the evil of drugs and from what it terms the "enemies of Mexico." But it is the members of these law enforcement and military institutions who use this violence as a pretext to commit illegal detentions, disappearances, and killings, and to produce false positives in the "war on drugs."

---

* The Almada brothers are famous in Mexican cinema as actors, directors, and producers of action and revenge movies with bad sets and scripts. They were considered droll and "campy" during the 1970s when Mexican cinema seemed to produce nothing else.

Violence as an Instrument of Control and Dominance

The practice of violence is not new in Mexican history. In fact, it is an old companion that has played an essential role in our evolution as a society. If anything, we must admit that as a people we are characterized by the practice of violence. The great social upheavals that formed the Mexican State have been told and retold in hundreds of violent and macabre stories (e.g., the hangings and beheadings that were common in the era of the Cristeros[*]).

It is not my intent to justify this history of violence, but rather to point out that violence was often used to subdue villagers because there seemed to be no effective alternative, or because it is seen as justifiable by those who exercised it. Violence was an accepted strategy to capture the inhabitants of a region not only because it was imposed by blood and fear, but also because it offered some measure of security against other groups fighting for territory, or against criminal gangs and kidnappers (Figure 4.5),

> They killed my son! I can't tell you my name, but they killed him.... The lady wove many fine words out of thin air. I live in Poanas ... by the village of La Ochoa. Two days ago the Zetas took my son ... took him to make him a gunman ... I tell you, my kid didn't want to

Figure 4.5 Execution in Durango. (Adapted from *Diario Milenio*, March 14, 2011 on http://www.milenio.com/)

---

[*] The time of the Cristeros, also known as Cristero War, which was an armed conflict in Mexico that lasted from 1926 to 1929. This period was characterized not only by the struggle between the government of Plutarco Elias Calles and secular militia, but also by extreme manifestations of violence between these groups.

do this, because they tortured him, they dressed him up as a girl and then machine-gunned him. I hope *El Chapo's* [Joaquín Guzmán Loera] people listen and come help us.

A few days before, in a place there called The Cave of the Bad Ones, right next to Calabazal, Zacatecas, the narcos had taken several children from their homes. A guy I know, who watched like a hawk, told me the children were offered a thousand dollars a day in exchange for working as hit-men. He told me they drugged them, beat them, and even forced them to masturbate. In the end, sixteen clung to the good, and they put them up against the wall and killed them. They put all the children in skirts and painted their lips, supposedly to teach them a lesson because they were cowards.

Almazán, 2011

Under these circumstances, we can see how the demand for security reaches a point at which, in the absence of a strong state that supports the rule of law, violence is employed as a strategy. This is especially true since many Mexicans know very well that our rights are precarious, and therefore we feel deeply vulnerable to violence exercised by organized criminals, and structural violence exercised by the authorities (i.e., unjustified arrests, kidnappings, disappearances, and detentions) and perpetuated by corruption and institutional neglect.

We live under a constant threat that makes us deeply afraid of this excessive violence, a violence that is disseminated in many ways, among them the images broadcast by the media and the accounts of deaths. Diffused in secret by word of mouth, these constitute a hidden transcript that chronicles the pain and suffering caused by the unstoppable social hemorrhaging represented by violent deaths. This discourse about violence reveals the flagrant impunity that stifles the country and reinforces terror. The authorities ignore it, but it perpetuates a strong and constant image of fear and terror in our everyday lives.

Those who use the threat of violence as a social control mechanism understand this imagery. Because this discourse is a resource that allows them to subdue and subordinate the population, its practices are real, and they open a gap that allows the construction of fear.

> The mess in the capital began because the "M"s split up. M-11 to M-18 didn't want Chapo Guzman as their boss. So they didn't care about subjecting their fellow Mexicans to kidnapping, extortion, wholesale murder, and burial in pits next to the damned Zetas.
>
> Let me tell you, I just followed orders ..., to pick up this guy, cut this other guy's head off, or skin that bastard. Do you know how to skin someone quickly? You boil oil, spray it on the guy, bathe him in salt, and in ten minutes, you scrape his skin off with a phone card and it falls right off. Keeping track, I think that of every ten we picked up,

Figure 4.6 Mutilated corpse.

we only let one go. But as I was saying, M-11 to M-18 had been Zetas, and one's past is never forgotten. They believed they were the hottest shits, and stirred up the city. Now not so much, but then they did what they wanted because they bought all the police, nearly all federal police, much of the military and a whole shitload of officials. That's why so many of them are going around sheltering them, because they are all in bed together. I even remember that when we went to the taibol dances all those bastards were escorting us. There were times they helped us make people disappear. (Figure 4.6)

But I'd say … El Chapo's guys in Durango told him to tell M-11 to calm down and calm down the others, that the anger was against the Zetas. But the mothers earned them. So "The Anthrax" arrived in Sinaloa where they still are around, to clean out the traitors. That's why they killed a bunch of cops (thirty-three so far). So the matazonas are in prison, although the government says no more than two have died, because it does it's not convenient for them to say sixty. Nor have they said anything about Jonas, the biggest bastard of all the "M" assassins. They killed him. That dude was twenty years old and was relocated. … I remember one day he had a bet with "M" to see who was wilder. Each had to cut what he wanted on a dude who was standing. Alive, right? And after Jonah won, the "M" fainted. But, hey, so as not to mess them both up, "The Anthrax" came in the saying, "Fuck all the "M"s." Some already called a truce and pray it will work with the "New People." The remaining "M"s didn't hesitate to kill them. I say they should hurry up because the Zetas already control all the cities close to the capital cities. And this is going to make them even bigger bastards.

Almazán, 2011

We observe that when a group is actively involved in violence of an area, it becomes a job provider that recruits by threats and force, and even becomes a regulator and an intermediary in resolving tensions in the community tensions, to the point where it monitors not only its own employees but also regulates the daily lives of all it touches. For an example, we have the case of Michoacán drug family called the "Knights Templar," who punished husbands who were abusive or unfaithful, unfulfilled, and infidels. These are violent practices that intermediate by imposing oversight, punishment, and authority, thereby gaining control of community activities and establishing relations with public officials. Through these community interventions involving the use of violence as power, they create cracks in social structures through cruel and brutal acts. They seek to impose their authority and autonomy in the struggle to control social space.

Scenarios of Violence

The scenario of violence shown by the spread of macabre images unleashes looks of fear that evoke an array of narratives. These images represent a cruel and unpleasant reality that is part of human nature. They signify forgetfulness in the fight for peace and justice. They are images of desolation that cast doubt on our concept of what it means to be human.

These scenes are broadcast daily, even in the face of agreements established to prevent the counterproductive coverage of violence by the media (Acuerdo para la Cobertura Informativa de la Violencia, 2011). These images make us aware of others' pain and suffering, limits of human suffering, forcing us to be aware of cruelty, despair, and desolation, to the extent that their effects are burned indelibly into our memories.

The terrible thing about all this is that the media have made us accustomed to these images that are imposed as a common part of real life, justifying their appearance as a fraction of a problem that not only concerns but also intimidates us. These images tell a story that is repugnant and horrible, that alters our identity, overturns order, which goes beyond the bounds of sense (Ovalle, 2010) and thus feeds the black hole that already holds hundreds of dead in a nameless grave. Those who do this are as mentally dead as the others, those who seem not to be human and who don't deserve any kind of recognition, or rather, whom no one wants to admit recognizing for fear of being involved with the others.

Under this idea, the content of the images puts us on a scale of something less than human, which involves both the victims and the perpetrators. This is why the information and images disseminated by the media are associated with organized criminal violence as if it were exclusively a drug trafficking problem. Furthermore, it takes advantage of the context of executions and body counts to convey messages of terror, both to the opposing combatants and to the population in general. Like other forms of systemic violence, it is terror territorialized as control, which acts or is intended to act upon all the groups involved. Thus, every act of violence inflicted on the bodies of the victims makes them messengers of terror. Everybody who has been marked, dismembered, burned, decapitated, or skinned serves to increase the general feeling of terror, both between opposing group and among populations caught by uncertainty and surprise. The bodies are in effect extensions of or substitutes for the geographical territories the enemy cannot attack or control, are thus also messengers of deterritorialization (Lair, 2003). Thus, we can say that violence has become an agent that adds a sort of order to, in which both the State and the media have become part of a chain of instrumental of violence (Ovalle, 2010). As violence becomes theater and violent death becomes ritualized, both violence and death come to represent a series of symbols from which to extract a web of meanings that express the excesses of life and different ways to die.

These are then images that show us death, and with it a mummified message that has as its objective to brand an indelible image on the memory of enemies and spectators alike. These are images that paralyze daily life by fear and terror and also images that show violence practiced for its own sake, because cruelty is characterized by violence for the sake of violence, in consequence of which intended explanations characterize this as absolute violence (Sofsky, 2006).

Hence, violence finds its own sense of enjoyment, even when it passes the bounds of excess. Look at some pictures and find different faces, some young adult men and other women. Let us fix our attention on their faces, the expression of the faces, in their eyelids, the proportion of his mouth and nose, the mummified looks of their eyes, when it is possible to observe through their injuries. In their mouths can be noted expressions of anguish and fear, but even so, nothing one can see allows us to comprehend the suffering of the experienced. What remains is their stoicism and composure in the face of intentional and dehumanizing violence that seeks to dehumanize them by removing its identity. To transmit a message of exacerbated terror, it is not enough to simply read about death (Lair, 2003: 95).

Some are images of tortured bodies that show us the face-to-face relationship between victim and victimizer. The bodies show evidence repeated violence combined with a desire to inflict suffering. The objective is not only to eliminate the person, but to possess and destroy them morally. These images represent the limits of physical existence under pressure, some with hands and feet tied, others blindfolded with tape. The postures of bodies and hands covered with dirt and gunpowder, or by the ravages of death, or those bodies so tormented that they are beyond recognition, represent unspeakable acts (Blair, 2005). The pain, horror, suffering, and fear caused by these images of dismembered and beheaded bodies are therefore images that express contempt for human life, acts that intimidate and promote a feeling of terror that destroys the social fabric in order to dramatize death and make the deformed and mutilated bodies deconstructed acts of symbolic communication (Lair, 2003).

They are images whose experience confront us an inexpressible view of the unspeakable, the sinister, and the unthinkable. They allow us to realize that for the moment are driving on dark roads. Only by reconstructing the image and finding our limits will we be able to understand the possibility of pain and death as a result of the magnitude of the violence and the spectacle offered by the abandoned and unburied bodies, because the intention is to terrorize and humiliate the other. This violence dehumanizes us, and seeks to erase all traces of human identity through anonymity of the victim. Its goal is to make their horrible experiences visible, and thus lead us to the boundary of what it means to be human (Imbert, 1994).

Conclusion

There is no doubt that the "drug wars"—both the fights for money and territory among the criminal organizations and the government's crackdown against them—have increased violence in Mexico. But the media is also indirectly responsible for maintaining the public's sense of insecurity by filling newspapers and television news stories with sensational accounts and grotesque photos of meaningless acts of violence. This may improve their ratings; but it also plays into the hands of other interests in society—like the private security industry—that benefits from enhanced fear of violence.

In the face of direct challenges to its authority by drug cartels, the state can reduce the general level of violence and insecurity by enforcing the law and maintaining its position as the only entity authorized to use violence to protect public security. Along with this strategy to contain violence should do this not only by containing violence in support of its role as the sole entity exercising legitimate violence in support of public security. This will restore public confidence and trust in the institutions responsible for administering and enforcing the law. At the same time, the nonstop portrayal of violence in the media also contributes to a generalized fear, which undermines public security and confidence. This requires that the media work with the government to build control mechanisms that curtail the dissemination of violent images. This is not censorship, but rather telling the truth while being responsive to the need for the ethical and sensitive handling of information.

References

Acuerdo para la Cobertura Informativa de la Violencia. 2011. Available online at: http://spanish.christianpost.com/articulo/20110325/medios-de-comunicacion-firman-acuerdo-sobre-cobertura-de-violencia/Accessed August 1, 2013.

Almazán, A. 2011. *Carta desde Durango*. Rev. El gato Pardo. Available at: http://www.gatopardo.com/ReportajesGP.php?R=94

Blair, E. 2005. *Muertes Violentas. La Teatralización del Exceso*. (Colección de Antropología) Universidad de Antioquia, Colombia.

Carrion, M. F. 2003. *La Violencia Urbana y sus Nuevos Escenarios.* ENLACE, FLACSO, Ecuador. Available at: http://www.flacso.org.ec/portal/paginas/informacion-institucional.5

Imbert, G. 1994. *Los Escenarios de la Violencia.* Icaria, Argentina.

Lair, E. June 2003. Reflexione acerca del terror en los escenarios de Guerra interna. *Revista de Estudios Sociales, 15.* Universidad de los Andes, Colombia. Available at: http://redalyc.uaemex.mx/redalyc/pdf/815/Resumenes/81501507_Resumen_1.pdf

Osorio Enrique, D. 2011. *País de Muertos. Crónicas contra la Impunidad.* Debate, México.

Ovalle, P. 2010. Imágenes abyectas e invisibilidad de las víctimas. Narrativas visuales de la violencia en México. *El Cotidiano, 164.* UAM-A, México.

Puerta Henao, C. M. 2008. Discurso político y violencia en Colombia o como se construye un enemigo 1949–1980. *Rev. Estudios de Derecho.* Facultad de Derecho y Ciencias Políticas. Universidad de Antioquia, Colombia. Available at: http://aprendeenlinea.udea.edu.co/revistas/index.php/red/article/viewFile/849/742

Sofsky, W. 2006. *Tratado sobre la Violencia.* Abada editores, España.

Chapter 5

A High-Risk Profession
Risks and Costs for Mexican Democracy of Journalists in the Middle of the War against Drug Trafficking

José Antonio Rosique Cañas and
Gloria Rosique Cedillo

Contents

Introduction 61
The Socio-Economic Context of Journalism in Mexico 65
Journalism under Attack 67
Protecting Journalists and Journalism in Mexico 72
Reflections and Final Recommendations 74
References 75

Introduction

Journalism in Mexico has become a high-risk profession. With 137 journalists killed and 14 missing since the start of the "drug wars" there, Mexico has become the Latin American country with the most crimes against journalists (Rodríguez Olvera, 2011). Between 2000 and 2011, the National Commission of Human Rights (CNDH. Mexico) reported 74 murders of journalists in Mexico (cited in Meneses, 2012); consequently, some international organizations placed it as the second most dangerous country to practice journalism (Meneses, 2012). They have become endangered observers of drug trafficking crimes when retaliation threatens their disappearance or murder. This reduces freedom of expression and freedom of the press, and threatens citizens' right to be informed. Historically, journalists have performed their jobs under pressure, and have thus been dependent on the interests of the media. In Mexico, over the past decade, members of this profession have faced great risks in order to do their jobs in the midst of a war against drug trafficking.

There are laws on the books that guarantee freedom of the press and the public's right to information. Article 6 of the Mexican Constitution discusses the "right to information" and commits the State to providing it (Title I, Chapter 1. Individual guarantees. Art. 6); and Article 7 refers to the Law of Printing, which covers freedom of the press (Title I, Chapter 1. Individual guarantees. Art. 7). However, these laws are not effectively enforced, and have not been updated to deal with widespread attacks on journalists and journalism in the "drug wars."

The National Commission of Human Rights (Mexico) states that an attack on a journalist or on a communicator in the practice of his work is equivalent to attacking the society and its right to be informed, to know, communicate, and make free decisions, autonomous and informed (National Commission of Human Rights, 2010). Given the lack of security for journalists who investigate organized crime, the principles that sustain journalism—primarily the responsibility to make the truth public (Kovach, 2001)—remain at risk. Exercising freedom of expression and the right to inform, as well as the citizen's right to receive information have become increasingly dangerous in an environment where violence and impunity reign.

The consequences of this impunity make it clear that the rule of law is an indispensable pillar to enforce and protect the principles of the journalism: responsibility, independence, and freedom. Thus, we must ask some questions that allow us to consider the context of "war" in the way that the journalist works.

- How has organized crime been able to penetrate the institutions of justice (e.g., public ministries, the police, courts, and prisons) designed to guarantee the rule of law?
- Why did the government make the controversial decision in 2006 to use the armed forces in the war against organized crime?
- Why, after six years of confrontations and so many deaths on both sides, has this war "not subsided" in intensity and at moments becomes more cruel and out of control?
- How can we expect journalism in Mexico to become a viable profession when the president himself doubts the capacity of civil institutions to secure justice?
- How can journalists fulfil their duty to inform the public under "wartime" conditions where the army is abusing the civilian population and journalists' only recourse is to ask the Supreme Court of Justice to have soldiers tried in civil courts?

- What is happening to the social fabric of these rural communities and cities where these groups operate with impunity and where police, judges, and prisons are unable stop them?

Organized crime is characterized by two conditions: a level of planning and the joint participation and coordinated of several individuals, in entities created to obtain and accumulate economic profits by mainly illegal means. Criminal organizations ensure their survival, operation, and protection through the use of violence and corruption (De la Corte Ibáñez, 2010). Organized crime emerges in States unable to provide the population with basic goods and services, or to protect and maintain order in the national territory. In a situation where the failed economy is characterized by high unemployment and a large informal economy, organized crime serves as an alternative provider of scarce goods and services, and of risky but well-paid employment. The failure of political institutions promotes criminality:

> There is no stage more conducive to delinquency that where the juridical order does not receive the support of a justice system and sufficiently powerful security agencies. For this reason, is perfectly logical that the countries or zones characterised by the ineffective application of laws and control over illegal behavior become the focus of attraction for organised crime.
>
> **Albanese, 2000, p. 409**

Durkheim (1928) developed the concept of anomie to explain the relation between insecurity, violence, and the underlying elements that encourage the breakdown of the social equilibrium. He states that social conflicts are generated in contexts where there is a gap between structural changes and social regulation. Building on this theory, Merton (1987) identified the conflict between cultural goals and the social norms needed in order to reach them. In a society dominated by material values, this conflict generates tension and unrest, often accompanied by frustration, resentment, and disregard for established norms by which success is supposed to be achieved. In Mexico, given endemic poverty, continued economic crises, and the lack of developmental opportunities, many young people choose the easier immoral route and become a part of organized crime. Also, organized crime is more prevalent in countries afflicted with generalized corruption involving citizens, businesses, and political parties. Where the tendency toward corruption already exists, it encourages the formation of criminal organizations to enforce it (De la Corte Ibáñez, 2010). There are many networks of recruitment, from the lowest to the highest levels of politics and government.

The existence of a strong social demand of products or services constitutes the primary risk factor for the emergence of organized criminality (Albanese, 2000, p. 409). In this case, the current conflict between the State and organized crime in Mexico has been aggravated by continued demand for drugs in the United States.

Given the added factors of socioeconomic exploitation of Mexican immigrants and the availability of firearms in that country, drug trafficking represents a "perfect storm" that has overwhelmed Mexican institutions and exposed their inability to maintain social structures and norms. It may be seen as the current version of an ironic comment by ex-President Porfirio Diaz coined a sentence that is deeply embedded in Mexican popular culture: "Poor Mexico! So close to the United States and so far away from God" (Gulevich, 2013).

Violence is part of the equation because criminal law represents the crystallization of social norms, and strong States are characterized by a collective sense of what types and levels of violence are acceptable and allowable (Durkheim, 1967). However, when the State loses the ability to enforce rights, violence comes to represent a conflict between a "state within the state," or organized crime versus the State and its citizens, as happened in Colombia in the 1990s. Under these conditions, organized criminals use physical and psychological violence through threat, intimidation, and extortion, despite the fact that these acts are outside the norm and oppose constitutional rights. This violence can be seen as

> An act of strength on the part of institutions, groups or individuals, or other groups or individuals with an instrumental purpose, to obtain something from those who suffer from the use of strength, and/or with the express purpose of expressing the power and the convictions of the executor of strength.
>
> **González, 1998**

Such situations are characterized by conflict between opposite political interests: government seeks to preserve social norms and institutions, and criminal organizations seek to destroy these norms and institutions to achieve their own ends (González, 1998). If such conflicts are viewed as a normal part of societal change theory (Durkheim, 1967; Dahrendorf, 1990), history is the major driver in the conflict because it changes social structures. Today in Mexico, change through the use of violence is provoking transformations that affect journalism and society. Those who accept the Hobbesian notion that good institutions are all that stands between civilized and barbaric societies would conclude that Mexico is having problems constructing the good institutions that it requires. Yet given US involvement in the underlying conditions that promote drug trafficking, Mexicans are also quite sensitive to US criticism on the matter. Several years ago, Mexican President Vicente Fox requested the resignation of a US ambassador who had claimed that Mexico was a "failed state," and added insult to injury by adding that "Mexico was the backyard of the United States" (Carbot, 2003).

One element of government is the State's ability to monopolize violence as the exercise of legitimate authority or the force of law. But when the government is feeble, it creates a power vacuum that can be filled by organized crime. This means that State authority, defined as the monopoly of the power in a country, is replaced in lawless areas by drug dealing, money laundering, and criminal organizations' threatened or actual control over prisons, police, and judges. Organized crime is born from a power vacuum and occupies the place of the State with use of violence and terror; this does not prosper in stable democracies with strong institutions and a healthy civil society.

This sociological model of the relationship between history, social conditions, organized crime, and violence helps us see why Mexico now faces one of the most important challenges in its history. After a lengthy transition to national stability (1930–1976) followed by a series of economic and political crises (1976–2006), journalism is now threatened, and the country's fledgling democracy is at risk.

The Socio-Economic Context of Journalism in Mexico

Mexico is the fifth largest country in the Americas after Canada, the United States, Brazil, and Argentina (from Instituto Nacional de Estadística y Geografía [INEGI], as cited in *The Economist*, 2012). Currently, Mexico has more than 112 million inhabitants, of which 48.9 million are poor and 18 million live in extreme poverty, mostly in 59 metropolitan zones of the country (INEGI, 2010). Though unemployment in Mexico is the lowest of all OECD countries (4.9%), much of the economy is informal. Presently, 14 million employees are in this labor category (*The Economist*, 2012), which translates into low income and high instability.

The national homicide rate tripled between 2005 and 2011, increasing from 8 to 24 murders per hundred thousand inhabitants; of every 100 crimes committed, only 25 are reported and only 2 are taken to trial (INEGI, 2012). Between 2000 and August 2011, 74 journalists were murdered: the majority of these cases remain unsolved though the investigations are still open (Meneses, 2012). Regarding the prison system and the penal code, according to a report from the National Commission of Human Rights, 46% of common law prisoners have not received sentences (Meneses, 2012). Not surprisingly, this leads to mistrust and a low expectation that the authorities will be able to carry out their duties effectively (Televisa, 2006).

In annual surveys of perceptions of corruption conducted by Transparency International, Mexico was rated below the minimum passing mark (Table 5.1).

According to data compiled by the US Federal Bureau of Investigation (FBI), the drastic increase of kidnappings in 2011 of family members living in the United States by Mexican organized crime cartels has led these Mexican families to ask for help from the American authorities to free family members that have been kidnapped in this country (Gómora, 2012).

Arguably, Mexico is a country whose inhabitants have lost confidence in its institutions because of injustices, impunity, corruption, and governmental indifference. This contributes to an increasing "vicious circle" that increases the problems a journalist confronts in his daily routine. In the most affected zones, this means

Table 5.1 Perceptions Index of Corruption (IPC): 2010 Data

Rank	Country	IPC Score
4	Sweden	9.3
14	Germany	8.0
22	Chile	7.2
24	The United States	7.1
25	France	7.0
31	Spain	6.2
73	Brazil	3.8
100	**Mexico**	**3.0**
100	Argentina	3.0
172	Venezuela	1.9

Source: Developed by the authors based on information obtained from Transparency International, 2012. A country's IPC ranking indicates the degree of perceived corruption in the public sector, ranging from 10 (no corruption) to 0 (corruption).

more crimes against journalists, and greater threats to freedom of press and of expression (Peces Barba, 1995).

The first notable act of violence in modern Mexican journalism was the murder of Manuel Buendía in 1984. Over the 26 years, he wrote the column "Private Network" at the newspaper *The Excélsior*, a column which was reproduced by another 60 newspapers, his main subjects were about the presence of the CIA in Mexico, the extreme right, drug traffickers, and the corruption in high power circles implicated in drug trafficking. Considering his influence in journalistic circles and his unsparing treatment of these subjects, it's easy to see why he was murdered.

Although a certain level of violence has always characterized Mexican society, it increased markedly in 2006 when President Felipe Calderón decided to put the army in the streets to confront drug trafficking. At this point, it also began to affect journalism as a profession because the politics of control in the fight against the drug trafficking in Mexico and the United States generated a violent reaction on the part of the organized crime. From then through 2011, 35,000 murders have been reported; some of police officers and drug traffickers, but many more of youngsters, children, and journalists (Actu, 2012). Kidnappings also increased significantly from 325 in 2005 to 595 a year later, and 384% from 2005 to 2011 (El Informador, 2012). According to the National System of Public Security (SNSP), "this was the effect of the decision of a strategy of direct confrontation with organised crime" (El

Informador, 2012). Viewed as a problem of national security, this violence challenges the authorities because increased crime means increased popular insecurity caused by increased crime, and is a consequence of the internal struggle among Mexican cartels for territorial control of drug markets and distribution routes, which in turn duplicates the level of violence and insecurity.

Nor can we ignore the effects of geography on organized crime. Mexico's climate and topography make much of it (e.g., the State of Durango) ideally suited for marijuana and poppy production. Drugs can be easily transported along remote border footpaths to other states like Sinaloa and Chihuahua. Mexico's location between producers of drugs in South America and consumers in the United States combined with its 3326 km border with that country—one of the longest in the world, shared by the states of Baja California North, Sonora, Chihuahua, Coahuila, and Nuevo León, makes it an ideal location for the trafficking of all types (De la Corte Ibáñez, 2010). Historically, the Mexican border has been used as a drug trafficking route to satisfy the demand of the American market. Colombia, Peru, and Bolivia are the top three global exporters of this drug; the United States is the world's major consumer; and Mexico's northern border, its Pacific ports, the Mexican Gulf, and the Caribbean are the main drug transport routes. Ultimately, the current level of violence with respect to organized crime is a shared responsibility with the United States. That country is the number one consumer of drugs in the world and also one of the main arms producers. According to the data contributed by the Procuraduría General de la República (PGR), between December of 2005 and January of 2009, the authorities successfully confiscated more than 31,000 firearms, 93% of which originated in the United States (Barrón, 2012). It is not surprising then, that the cities most affected by organized crime are recognized on a worldwide level as the most violent, and at the same time are caught up in deaths and the disappearances of journalists (Table 5.2).

The five Mexican cities on this list are in the tier of states bordering the United States, and along major Pacific- and Gulf trafficking routes. Institute Studies Citizen Insecurity (ICESI) estimates that Mexico, with Colombia, Russia, and Brazil, also has one of the highest indexes of kidnappings in the world (Televisa, 2006).

Figure 5.3 reports the number of Mexican journalists who have been murdered or "disappeared" from 1983 to 2011. From January to mid-June 2012, an additional six journalists were killed and one reported missing in the States of Veracruz (3), Cuernavaca, Morelos, Ciudad Obregón, Sonora, Nuevo León, and Saltillo (El Universal, 2012) (Figure 5.1).

Journalism under Attack

Because organized criminals use violence yet seek anonymity, the violence they use tends to evade all news, or at least it does not appear to be deliberate (De la Corte Ibáñez, 2010). Thus, they seek to silence journalists and the media. The potential for cartel violence against the media and journalists comes into existence the moment

Table 5.2 The Ten Most Violent Cities in the World (2011)

Rank	City and Population	Country/State
1	San Pedro Sula	Honduras
2	*Ciudad Juárez: 1,332,131	Mexico/Chihuahua
3	Maceió	Brazil
4	*Acapulco 789,971	Mexico/Guerrero
5	Distrito Central	Honduras
6	Caracas	Venezuela
7	*Torreón: 639,629	Mexico/Coahuila
8	*Chihuahua: 819,543	Mexico/Chihuahua
9	*Durango: 582,267	Mexico/Durango
10	Belém	Brazil

Source: Developed by the authors based on data obtained from Cable News Network Mexico (CNN) 2012. *5 de las 10 ciudades más violentas del mundo están en México.* Accessed April 4, 2012 at: http://mexico.cnn.com/nacional/2012/01/13/5-de-las-10-ciudades-mas-violentas-del-mundo-estan-en-mexico.

Note: One thing that stands out is that in the annual Balance of the 2011 for the 10 most dangerous places to practice journalism, done by the organization of Reporters Without Borders, the State of Veracrúz, Mexico appears as one of the riskier cities to practice journalism (Reporters Without Borders, 2011). The cities marked with asterisks (i.e., 5 of the top 10) are all in Mexico.

that information about crime and drug trafficking is published. Given the high rate of murders, kidnappings and disappearances, and the demonstrated inability of public agencies and institutions to prevent it, it is not surprising that government agencies and media managers have opted for the minimum possible coverage of violence. This self-censorship has contributed to the general spread of misinformation. A study by the Foundation of Investigative Journalism (MEPI) analyzed coverage of crime and drug trafficking by 11 local newspapers over a six-month period in 2010, and compared them with statistics of executions and editorial testimony in the same affected cities. It concluded that these newspapers had published only 10% or less of the true record of events (MEPI, 2010). This retreat to superficial journalism occurs most often in the zones most affected by organized crime, where the media have implicitly decided against divulging any information related to the activities of organized crime—not even official Army bulletins (Hernández Ramírez, 2011). In many of Mexico's most violent cities, current journalism consists only of press releases. In the absence of investigative reporting or editorial pressure, only superficial journalism remains.

[Map of Mexico showing states and cities with reported murders and disappearances of journalists]

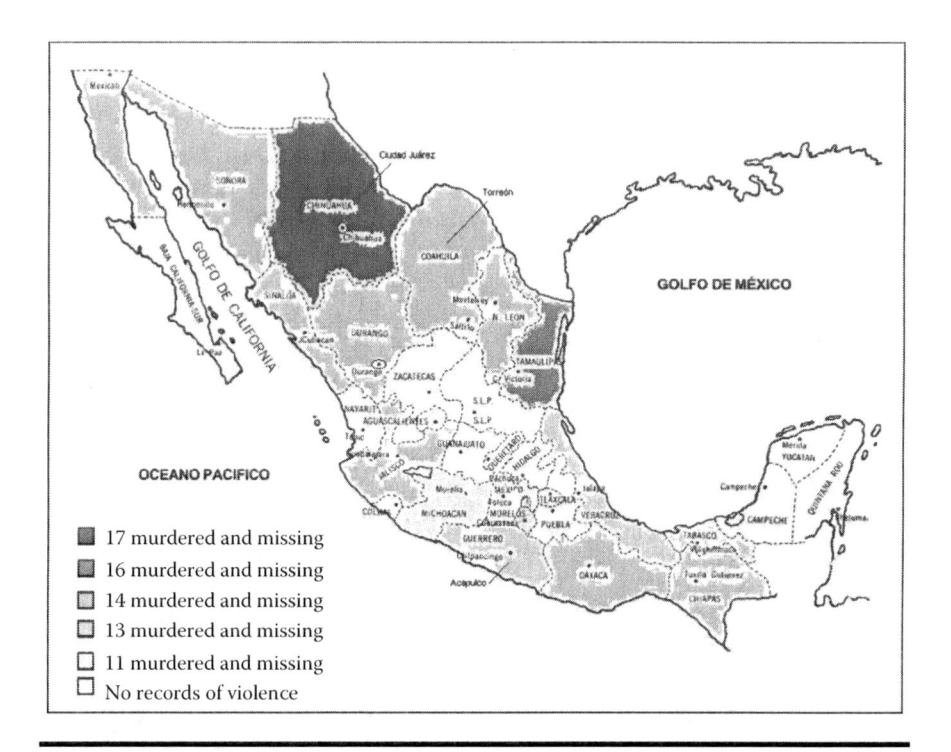

- 17 murdered and missing
- 16 murdered and missing
- 14 murdered and missing
- 13 murdered and missing
- 11 murdered and missing
- No records of violence

Figure 5.1 States and mexican cities that have reported murders and disappearances of journalists (1983–2011). (Developed by the authors based on the information collected in the web page from the Latin American Federation of Journalists [FELAP] 2011. *Informe actualizado sobre la situación del periodismo en México al tercer trimestre de 2011.* Accessed April 2, 2012 at: http://www.actualidadesmexico.mx/2011/11/informe-actualizado-sobre-la-situacion-del-periodismo-en-mexico-al-tercer-trimestre-de-2011/.)

Journalists who cover subjects related to public security are faced with a growing dilemma between publishing or not publishing information related to organized crime, for fear of retaliation (Hernández Ramírez, 2011):

> … in some areas of the country, violence has reached such a level and groups of drug traffickers have such power that publishing almost anything on them becomes an accusation, a kind of betrayal in their eyes, of what are their illicit activities; the pointing of names, places, activities and authorities possibly involved, has gone back to being uncomfortable information; they are, in many places, almost the true authority.
>
> **Daniel Moreno cited in Article 19, 2012**

According to Jorge Zepeda, the infiltration of drug trafficking networks into the media is also an important element in their aggressive retaliation against journalists, who must always guard against the very real possibility that their news agency coworkers are on the pad for the cartels (Rodríguez Olvera, 2011). Consequently, through violence, threats, manipulation of reporters, and infiltration in the newsrooms, the drug cartels are deciding what can be said about them and the events related to their actions (Hernández Ramírez, 2011).

Without a doubt, insecurity and the government's inability to guarantee their right to practice their profession have caused self-censoring of journalists and the media. Therefore, freedom of the press is increasingly limited and subordinate to external powers that seek to control information in their own interests. Villanueva states: "the freedoms of expression and information and their relative rights constitute ideal instruments to preserve the rule of law and favor democratic practices, because they generate counterweights in the face of the application of power" (as cited in Morgan, 2000). Table 5.3 shows the number of journalists affected by the violence, as well as the most dangerous states to practice the profession.

The Mexican States with the highest indexes of violence are located in the far north (i.e., Tamaulipas and Chihuahua) and—given that port cities generally are strategic locations for the development of criminal activities (Finckenauer and Voronin, 2001)—along the coast (i.e., Veracrúz and Guerrero). The data reflected in Table 5.3 coincide with a study on the most violent cities in the world, done by the Citizen Council for Public Security and Penal Justice. This study indicates that three of the 10 most violent cities in the world are in Mexico (Citizen Council for Public Security and Penal Justice, 2012). Likewise, another investigation reveals that the 23 Mexican entities that have been most affected by the organized crime are: Guerrero, Morelos, Baja California, Coahuila, Veracrúz, Michoacán, New León, Jalisco, Chihuahua, Durango, Tamaulipas, Sinaloa, State of Mexico, San Luis Potosí, Zacatecas, Colima, Nayarit, Mexico City, Aguascalientes, Oaxaca, Sonora, Chiapas, and Quintana Roo (Flores, 2013).

These data also allow us to make a correlation between the states that report greater indexes of violence and extortion on a general level, and those that report a greater number of murders and disappearances of journalists, contextualizing the scene in which they practice their profession and the risks which come along with it. Of the total number of people killed and missing in the period comprised of 1983–2011, 128 worked in diverse digital media, printed media (press and magazines), on the radio and in television, carrying out their functions in the journalistic field that go from the newspaper editor, deputy director of a newspaper, all the way to technical personnel, for example: chief editor of a newspaper of correspondents, journalists and ex-correspondents, founders of magazines, columnists, article writers, reporters, photographers, TV and radio presenters, assistants, and technicians. The majority of those killed or missing were attacked while carrying out their journalistic duties. Journalist Lydia Cacho notes (cited in Article 19, 2012): "the majority of the journalists threatened or pursued were

Table 5.3 Dead and Missing/Kidnapped Persons, by State and Journalistic Function (1983–2011)

State and Population (in Millions)	Function	Murdered	Missing or Kidnapped	Total
Tamaulipas: 3.2	Journalists	16		16
Chihuahua: 3.5	Journalists	13		17
	Cameraman	1		
	Photographer	1		
	Newsboy	1		
	Friend	1		
México (State): 15.0	Journalists	8		9
	Others	1		
Durango: 1.6	Journalists	4		6
	Newsboy	1		
	Auxiliary	1		
Veracruz: 7.7	Journalists	11	3	14
Guerrero: 3.3	Journalists	13	1	14
Tabasco: 2.2	Journalists	1	1	2
Baja California Norte: 3.1	Journalists	2		4
	Newsboy	1		
	Photographer	1		
Sinaloa: 6.8	Journalists	8	1	13
	Others	3		
	Son	1		
Guadalajara: 7.3	Journalists	2		2
Coahuila: 2.8	Journalists	3	1	6
	Technical staff	1		
	Cameraman	1		
Chiapas: 4.8	Journalists	3		3
Michoacán: 4.3	Journalists	7	4	11
Oaxaca: 3.9	Journalists	7		7

continued

Table 5.3 (continued) Dead and Missing/Kidnapped Persons, by State and Journalistic Function (1983–2011)

State and Population (in Millions)	Function	Murdered	Missing or Kidnapped	Total
Sonora: 2.7	Journalists Others	4 1	1	6
Monterrey: 4.7	Journalists Assistant of presenter	2 1	1 1	5
México City: 8.9	Journalists	11		11
Morelos: 1.8	Journalists	4		4
Unidentified		1		1
Total		137	14	151

Source: Authors' elaboration based on the information of the Instituto Nacional de Estadística y Geografía (INEGI) 2010. Censo de Población y vivienda 2010. México INEGI. Accessed April 5, 2012 at: http://www.inegi.org.mx/sistemas/mexicocifras/default.aspx?src=487&e=9.

in the process of investigating a high-level public servant at the moment they suffered the attacks." According to the Committee for the Protection of Journalists (CPJ), 90% of these crimes around the world remain unpunished; this is due to the fear of retaliation that organized crime can generate (CNDH, 2013). Since 2000, the National Commission on Human Rights (CNDH) has noted 65 journalist homicides, of which only 10 (16%) have resulted in prosecution and sentencing (CNDH, 2010, p.4). As its President Plascencia Villanueva affirms,

> It is not a problem of penalties but a lack of institutional efficiency, of executing without adjusting to the reality and above all else, that the criminals are not detained and therefore they continue killing, abusing and violating the rights of the people.
>
> **Milenio, 2010**

Protecting Journalists and Journalism in Mexico

In 1991, the CNDH created a "Special Program for Journalists," given the extent to which this profession was considered vulnerable due to the history of aggression and violation of their rights. Six years later, they expanded this program to integrate and give continuity to complaints received, helping to make sure that the authorities became more sensitive to the importance of journalists, and focusing attention on individuals, the media, and civil organizations for responding to these cases (CNDH, 2013). In 2006, they also created the position of "Special District Attorney to Deal with Crimes Committed against the Freedom of Expression" (FEADLE) (National Center of Social Communication [CENCOS], 2010), a unique entity at an international level, with the competency to manage, coordinate, and supervise the investigation and prosecution of crimes committed against national or foreign journalists inside Mexico. However, violence has continued to increase in spite of these measures: 155 cases were reported in 2010 compared with 172 in 2011. In addition, this organization's budget has been reduced by 72.4% since 2006, from $2.3 million to $637,000 pesos (Article 19, 2010).

A year later, the Council of the Commission on Human Rights of the Federal District (Mexico City) (CDHDF) created the "Court Reporter of Freedom of Expression and Attention to Defenders of Human Rights," intended to promote respect for the day-to-day work of journalists and defenders (Commission on Human Rights of the Federal District CDHDF, 2007). In 2010, this same organization created a "Guide to implement precautionary measures in order to benefit journalists and communicators in Mexico," with the goal of helping journalists and media in the coverage and treatment of subjects related to organized crime (CNDH, 2010). In June 2012, President Felipe Calderón signed an executive order for the protection of defenders of human rights and federalization of the crimes committed against journalists. The document establishes protective measures such as evacuation, temporary relocation, personal security escorts, property protection, and other measures to safeguard life, integrity, and freedom for journalists. The law also establishes cooperation between national and state authorities to implement measures that protect people at risk (Notimex, 2012).

Nonetheless, given that institutions have been overtaken by violence linked to organized crime, and because these measures have not been effective at guaranteeing the security of citizens or journalists, other community-based national and international organizations have sought to reinforce the official fight against violence suffered by this profession (e.g., The "Forum of Journalists," the "Inter-American Press Society" [SIP], the "International Press Federation" [FIP], the "National Center for Social Communication," "Reporters Without Borders," the "Citizen Network," the "New Foundation for Latin American Journalism," the "Mexican Association for the Right to Information," the "Federation of Associations of Mexican Journalists," "CENCOS," and "Article 19" [Freedom of expression, 2013]).

After the "Meeting of Border Editors" in 2005, the directors of Mexican newspapers agreed upon common actions to protest against the murders and attacks against journalists (Inter American Press Society [SIP], 2005). In the "Statement of Hermosillo," they demanded that the authorities publicize crimes committed against journalists, and advocated training and education of journalists and editors via specialized seminars in how to cover high-risk subjects (SIP, 2005). They organized public education campaigns against impunity in cases involving journalists, and formed a special team of reporters to more deeply investigate murders and other attacks on journalists. On August 4, the first "Protocol of Security for Journalists High Risk Situations" was born in Chihuahua (Belt Ibérica, 2010).

In sum, a diverse group of independently funded civic organizations have headed a modest but viable campaign of training and dialogue between the affected, the authorities, and the employers of the journalism (Meneses, 2012). These initiatives speak to the necessity of safeguarding civil rights in Mexican journalism. This subject is of great concern to governments and civil organizations, both national and international, considering that other Latin American countries can find themselves in a similar situation.

Reflections and Final Recommendations

This increased violence against journalists and the journalistic profession stems from a tradition of tolerance toward crime, exacerbated by the fragility of the State and its institutions, and derived from underlying factors such as poverty, impunity, and corruption. In the face of these conditions, the above efforts are not enough. More effective efforts will require institutional change. Reporters Without Borders (RSF) states that real change in countries like Mexico and Honduras will require fundamental reform of police and the judiciary operation of the judicial and police organizations (EFE Agency, 2012). Given that the transition to violence occurred very quickly and institutional adaptation has been very slow, public responses must also be more proactive, notes Gustavo Lizárraga Reyes, a journalist from the newspaper *El Debate* in Mazatlán, Sinaloa (Lizárraga cited in Article 19, 2012). Until this happens, journalists will at best remain caught in the middle of the violence that ensues when both organized crime and the State want to win citizens' hearts and minds. At worst, they become targets (Rachel Levil cited in Article 19, 2012) by serving as war reporters in a conflict without uniforms or other means of identifying the groups in conflict, a conflict without clear territorial boundaries, a conflict not only over territory but also over control of information.

Although this conflict most directly affects freedom of press and the coverage of information by the journalists and of the media, media policy has traditionally been controlled by other stakeholders (i.e., political parties and "Televisa") (Trejo Delarbe, 2009).

Given the current atmosphere of pessimism caused by societal violence and its journalistic repercussions, and considering the continued high consumption of drugs in the United States that drives both the violence caused by organized crime and its profit motive, it is appropriate to question whether the new government (2012–2018) will be able to develop policy initiatives to address this threat. These political decisions, and in particular a reevaluation of the effectiveness of the Calderon administration's strategy of using the armed forces against organized crime, could reduce the violence and thus the risks for professional journalists. The confrontation that pits the military against organized crime is counterproductive because its unintended negative consequences such as the violation of civil rights and the undermining of police and the judiciary pose a threat to on-going governance reforms, particularly as the military presence covers a larger amount of territory over a longer period of time.

Under these circumstances, the Mexican government must continue its efforts to provide journalists with the protection they need to do their jobs. It is not alone. Given that, in 2012, Brazil reported six murders of journalists, Honduras four, Bolivia two, Colombia one, Argentina one, and Mexico eight (Carmona, 2012), this problem extends throughout Latin America, international entities must continue to pressure Latin American governments to adopt effective policies.

Media directors must take self-protective and preventative measures to safeguard the security of their journalists by implementing collective security agreements and training journalists in better ways to cover drug trafficking. For example, the "Practical Guide of Reporters" from RSF suggests alternative methods of data collection (e.g., the use of databases) that do not expose journalists to risk. These techniques are not commonly used in Mexican journalism (Meneses, 2012). The two national media companies, Televisa and Azteca TV, should put aside their traditional rivalries in favor of more collaborative reporting. The objective of all of this is to guarantee Mexicans' right to information and freedom of expression in order to confront the threat of organized crime (Universidad Iberoamericana, 2006).

To speak meaningfully about "journalism," it is first necessary to advance in democracy, in human rights, in the reconstruction of institutions. This problem will only be resolved by the joint efforts of the citizens, the media directors, and national and international entities, all led by governmental actions aimed at finding solutions to this predicament.

Only in this way will there be a possibility to elevate journalism to a critical and independent status, separated from the agendas and of political interests, of the parties and any power that it looks for to oppress the journalistic exercise, to the detriment of the freedom of expression, of the right to information and democracy. As Kovach notes, journalism and democracy were born together, they will either prosper together, or they will die together (Kovach, 2001).

References

Actu, Ch. 2012. *El tráfico de drogas en México*. Accessed April 14, 2012 at: http://www.alertaperiodistica.com.mx/noticias/el-trafico-de-drogas-en-mexico/.
Albanese, J.S. 2000. The causes of organized crime: Do criminals organize around opportunities for crime or do criminal opportunities create new offenders? *Journal of Contemporary Criminal Justice*, 16, 408–423.
Article 19 2010. Informe 2010: La violencia en México y el Derecho a la Información. Accessed May 13, 2012 at: http://www.articulo19.org/portal/index.php?option=com_content

&view=article&id=112:informe-2010-qla-violencia-en-mexico-y-el-derecho-a-la info rmacionq&catid=12:anticensura&Itemid=49.

Article 19 2012. *Silencio forzado*. Documental audiovisual. Available at: http://www.youtube.com/watch?v=7D7aoPqznxM.

Barrón Cruz, M. G. 2012. *El tráfico de armas hacia México*. Accessed May 10, 2012 at: http://digital.inacipe.gob.mx/post/16771679772/el-trafico-de-armas-hacia-mexico.

Belt Ibérica 2010. *Presentan protocolo de seguridad para periodistas en alto riesgo*. Accessed July 29, 2013 at: http://www.belt.es/noticiasmdb/home2_noticias.asp?id=10198.

Cable News Network México [CNN]. 2012. *5 de las 10 ciudades más violentas del mundo están en México*. Accessed April 4, 2012 at: http://mexico.cnn.com/nacional/2012/01/13/5-de-las-10-ciudades-mas-violentas-del-mundo-estan-en-mexico.

Carbot, A. 2003. *Aguilar Zínser, crónica de una remoción anunciada*. Accessed July 30, 2013 at: http://esp.mexico.org/lapalabra/una/13448/aguilar-zinser-cronica-de-una-remocion-anunciada.

Carmona, E. 2012. Latinoamérica: 21 periodistas asesinados en lo que va de 2012. Accessed April 14, 2012 at: http://www.cubasi.cu/index.php?option=com_k2&view=item&id=6342:latinoamerica-21-periodistas-asesinados-y-uno-desaparecido-en-lo-que-va-de-2012&Itemid=17.

Citizen Council for Public Security and Penal Justice. 2012. *Ránking de las 50 ciudades más violentas del mundo 2012*. Accessed April 14, 2012 at: http://www.seguridadjusticiaypaz.org.mx/biblioteca/finish/5-prensa/163-san-pedro-sula-otra-vez-primer-lugar-mundial-acapulco-el-segundo/0.

Commission on Human Rights of the Federal District. CDHDF 2007. *Anuncia CDHDF nombramientos en su cuerpo directivo*. Accessed June 18, 2013 at: http://portaldic10.cdhdf.org.mx/index.php?id=bol16107.

Dahrendorf, R. 1990. *The Modern Social Conflict: An Essay of the Politics of Liberty*, California: University of California Press.

De la Corte Ibáñez, L. and Jiménez-Salinas Framis, A. 2010. *Crimen.org. Evolución y claves de la delincuencia organizada*. Madrid: Ariel.

Durkheim, E. 1928. *El Suicidio: Estudio de Sociología*. Madrid: Reus.

Durkheim, E. 1967. *De la División del Trabajo Social*. Buenos Aires: Shapire.

EFE Agency. 2012. *RSF urge a Honduras a crear un mecanismo para la protección de periodistas*. Obtenido el 16 de agosto de 2012 de: http://www.latribuna.hn/2012/08/16/rsf-urge-a-honduras-a-crear-un-mecanismo-para-la-proteccion-de-periodistas/.

El Informador. 2012. *Secuestros se duplican en tres años en México*. Accessed May 10, 2012 at: *El Informador*: http://www.informador.com.mx/mexico/2011/265958/6/secuestros-se-duplican-en-tres-anos-en-mexico.htm.

El Universal. 2012. *Cronología periodistas asesinados en 2012*. Accessed June 14, 2012 at: *El Universal*. http://www.eluniversal.com.mx/notas/853557.html.

Finckenauer, J.O. and Y.A. Voronin. 2001. *The Threat of Russian Organized Crime*. Washington, DC: US Department of Justice.

Flores, N. 2013. *Los 89 cárteles que arrasan México*. Accessed July 31, 2013 at: http://contralinea.info/archivo-revista/index.php/2013/06/02/los-89-carteles-arrasan-mexico/.

Freedom of expression. 2013. *Campaña permanente de protección a periodistas en México*. Accessed July 28, 2013 at: http://www.libertad-expresion.org.mx/quienes-somos/.

Gómora, D. 2012. *Narcos mexicanos piden ayuda al FBI*. Accessed May 15, 2012, at: *El Universal*: http://www.eluniversal.com.mx/notas/833804.html.

González, L. A. and Villacorta, C. E. 1998. Aproximación teórica a la violencia. Accessed May 15, 2012 at: http://www.uca.edu.sv/publica/eca/599art4.html.
Gulevich, V. 2013. *México: tan lejos de Dios y tan cerca de Estados Unidos.* Accessed August 2, 2012, at: http://www.nodo50.org/ceprid/spip.php?article 1596.
Hernández Ramírez, M. H. 2011. Periodismo y violencia: Hacia un debate necesario [Versión electrónica]. *Revista Mexicana de Comunicación,* n° 28. Accessed April 12, 2012 at: http://mexicanadecomunicacion.com.mx/rmc/2011/02/28/periodismo-y-violencia-hacia-un-debate-necesario/#axzz1tF4nsKUR.
Instituto Nacional de Estadística y Geografía [INEGI]. 2010. Censo de Población y vivienda 2010. México: INEGI. Accessed April 5, 2012 at: http://www.inegi.org.mx/sistemas/mexicocifras/default.aspx?src=487&e=9.
Instituto Nacional de Estadística y Geografía [INEGI]. 2012. Censo de Población y vivienda 2012. México: INEGI. Accessed May 31, 2012 at: http://www.inegi.org.mx/inegi/contenidos/espanol/prensa/Boletines/Boletin/Comunicados/Especiales/2013/julio/comunica9.pdf.
Inter-American Press Society. SIP 2005. *Editores mexicanos se unen para combatir la violencia.* Accessed July 31, 2013 at: http://www.sipiapa.org/editores-mexicanos-se-unen-para-combatir-la-violencia/.
Kovach, B. 2001. *The Elements of Journalism.* New York: Crown.
Latin American Federation of Journalists [FELAP] 2011. *Informe actualizado sobre la situación del periodismo en México al tercer trimestre de 2011.* Accessed April 2, 2012 at: http://www.actualidadesmexico.mx/2011/11/informe-actualizado-sobre-la-situacion-del-periodismo-en-mexico-al-tercer-trimestre-de-2011/.
Meneses, M. E. 2012. Medios, violencia y gobernanza. [Versión electrónica]. *Revista Mexicana de Comunicación,* n° 18. Accessed May 14, 2012 at: http://mexicanadecomunicacion.com.mx/rmc/2012/01/18/medios-violencia-y-gobernanza/.
MEPI. Foundation of Investigative Journalism 2010. *México: La nueva espiral del silencio.* Accessed July 31, 2013 at: http://www.fundacionmepi.org/index.php?%20option=com_content&view=article&id=102:me%20xico-la-nueva-espiral-delsilencio&catid%20=50:investigaciones&Itemid=68.
Merton, R. K. 1987. *Teoría y estructura sociales.* México: Fondo de Cultura Económica.
Milenio. 2010. *Impunidad, uno de los principales problemas de México.* Accessed May 9, 2012 at: http://www.milenio.com/cdb/doc/noticias2011/c9bf3233bdc19a11f955b9c851681ef.
Morgan Franco, R. C. February–April 2000. Deben legislarse los medios de comunicación *Razón y Palabra,* 17. Accessed May 13, 2012 at: http://www.razonypalabra.org.mx/anteriores/n17/17rmorgan.html.
National Center of Social Communication. CENCOS 2010. *Nueva Fiscalía Especial conocerá de los delitos contra la libertad de expresión.* Accessed July 30, 2013 at: http://www.libertad-expresion.org.mx/noticias/nueva-fiscalia-especial-conocera-de-los-delitos-contra-la-libertad-de-expresion/.
National Commission of Human Rights. CNDH 2010. *Guía Para Implementar Medidas Cautelares en Beneficio de Periodistas y Comunicadores en México.* México: CNDH. Accessed May 12, 2012 at: http://www.cdhezac.org.mx/pdfbiblio/Guia_para_implementar_medidas_cautelares_en_beneficio_de_periodistas_y_comunicadores_en_Mexico.pdf.
National Commission of Human Rights. CNDH 2013. *Programa de Agravio a periodistas y defensores civiles.* Accessed June 25, 2013 at: http://www.cndh.org.mx/Programa_Agravio_Periodistas_Defensores_Civiles.

Notimex 2012. *Firma Calderón la ley de protección a defensores DH y periodistas*. Accessed September 30, 2012 at: http://www.radioformula.com.mx/notas.asp?Idn=251952.
Peces Barba, G. 1995. Ética, poder y derecho, *Cuadernos y Debates*, 54. Estudios Constitucionales.
Rodríguez Olvera, A. L. 2011. La violencia en México durante 2010: Informe de Article XIX y Cencos [Versión electrónica]. *Revista Mexicana de Comunicación*, 20. Accessed May 20, 2012 at: http://mexicanadecomunicacion.com.mx/rmc/2011/05/20/la-violencia-en-mexico-durante-2010-informe-de-article-xix-y-cencos/.
Televisa. 2006. *Diálogos por México*. México: Televisa. Accessed May 8, 2012 at: http://www.esmas.com/dialogospormexico/AgendadeDesarrollo/.
The Economist. 2012. *El desempleo en México*. Accessed April 12, 2012 at: http://eleconomista.com.mx/taxonomy/term/5980.
Transparency International 2012. Índice de Percepción de la Corrupción 2011. Accessed May 10, 2012 at: http://www.transparencia.org.es/indice%20de%20percepcion%202011/TABLA_SINT%C3%89TICA_DE_RESULTADOS_IPC_2011.pdf.
Trejo Delarbe, R. 2009. Mediocracia en la democracia. Medios, partidos y gobernabilidad en México. In Alcántara Sáez M. and Hernández Norzagaray, E. (Eds.), *México el nuevo escenario político ante el bicentenario*. Salamanca: Universidad de Salamanca.
Universidad Iberoamericana [UIA]. 2006. *Propuesta de Indicadores Para un Periodismo de Calidad*. México: Universidad Iberoamericana.

Chapter 6

The Military in the Homeland
Comparing the United States and Mexico

Kurt A. Johnson and Michael A. Noll

Contents

Overview 79
Law Enforcement or Defense of National Security? 81
Limitations on Use of the Military in the Homeland 83
SEDENA and SEMAR: Culture and Capabilities 84
Mexican Military Operations: Strategic and Tactical Challenges 86
Mexican Military Transformation: A Mixed Score Card 88
Intelligence and Counterintelligence: The Key Enablers 89
Human Rights: Treading Carefully 90
Border Control: A Federal Mission without Federal Troops 91
The US Military on the Border: How Big a Role? 93
The Military as Enabler: Options for Bolstering Governance in Lawless Zones 94

Overview

Any analysis of how to counter challenges to governance in the US–Mexico border region must necessarily include a study of the roles played by the two nation's military establishments. In both countries, the military represents arguably the most powerful institution within the federal government. In both countries, the military is the most respected institution within the federal government. Both countries have large military forces immediately available to the president, who is their commander-in-chief. Both the US and Mexican militaries are highly professional, with all-volunteer forces. There the similarities end.

The most obvious difference between the US and Mexican militaries is their relative size. While the United States has a population roughly three times that of Mexico, the US armed forces, at approximately 2.3 million, are almost 10 times the size of Mexico's, which number approximately 240,000. The disparity is even greater when it comes to funding. As a percentage of each county's GDP, the United States spends about eight times as much on its military as does Mexico (4% of GDP vs 5%).* The disparity in absolute terms is far larger. The relative size of the two militaries reflects differences in their missions. While both are charged with national defense, the US military has a global presence and frequently engages in foreign wars and other overseas contingencies. The Mexican military has an insular role that reflects the mindset of Mexicans when the Constitution of 1917 was drafted.

Not surprisingly, the US military is much more organizationally complex than Mexico's. The US military has four services within the Department of Defense and a fifth (the Coast Guard) in the Department of Homeland Security. It also has significant Reserve and National Guard forces, and a large civilian component. A vast military–industrial complex supports all this. Mexico has the Department of National Defense (or SEDENA), which is a unified Army and Air Force, and the Department of the Navy (or SEMAR), which is essentially a Coast Guard and a Marine Corps. Domestic military industries, while substantial, do not meet anywhere near all Mexican military equipment and support needs—imports are required. The Mexican Secretaries of National Defense and the Navy are active-duty four star officers who also rank as cabinet secretaries with direct access to the president. In the United States, the Chairman of the Joint Chiefs of Staff also has direct access to the president, but only as the senior military adviser.

Both the US and Mexican militaries have bases scattered throughout their countries. In the US case, there are also a number of overseas bases. Within the continental US, large military facilities are more common in the southern part of the country. There are three big bases on or very near the US–Mexico border: Fort Bliss in El Paso, Texas, Fort Huachuca on the Arizona–Sonora border, and the major Navy and Marine Corps bases in the San Diego, California area. The Mexican military has a number of garrisons on or near the US border, but its largest facilities are well to the south—near Mexico City (for the Army) and at Veracruz (in the case of the Navy).

In terms of the use of the military in the homeland, both nations' presidents have an attractive option to employ federal military forces in response to an internal

---

* Central Intelligence Agency. *CIA*. n.p., 2012. Web. <https://www.cia.gov/library/publications/the-world-factbook/>.

crisis. This attraction stems from a number of factors. First, as commander-in-chief, both countries' presidents can be assured of the responsiveness and loyalty of their respective armed forces. To deploy military forces sends a signal of decisiveness. It also sends a signal of reassurance, since both publics have a high regard for the competence of their military forces. Although US culture and tradition generally look skeptically on employment of military forces internally, the military is well-received in dealing with major crises such as Hurricane Katrina. Additionally, the military is largely self-sufficient and does not add to the burdens in a disaster area. Finally, both nations' militaries have equipment that is useful in a wide range of scenarios—transport aircraft, helicopters, fleets of trucks, amphibious ships, fully staffed hospitals, sophisticated portable communications capability, and so forth.

Law Enforcement or Defense of National Security?

From the US perspective, a threshold question in determining the proper role of the military in dealing with drug cartels and related border issues is whether those challenges fall into traditional law enforcement functions, or, at least under certain extreme circumstances, call for military defense of the nation. The answer is surprisingly complex.

Military performing a civil support mission in the homeland will never, by definition, be in charge of the operation. When it comes to the murky divide between criminal activity and threats to national security, however, it becomes far less clear whether the military should always remain in a civil support role or, under extreme circumstances, shift to a homeland defense role.

To illustrate this conundrum, it is useful to imagine a civil support/homeland defense continuum. At the left extreme of the continuum, a few drug cartel members cross into Texas with the intent of delivering a small quantity of drugs and eliminating a "snitch" working with US authorities. It is likely that most Americans would agree that these drug cartel members are the primary responsibility of civilian law enforcement agencies and not the military, although the civilian law enforcement agencies might request and use certain unique military assets in support of their efforts. At the right extreme of the continuum, it is conceivable that one or more drug cartels might attempt to establish the sort of violent semi-sovereignty in small towns or neighborhoods on the US side of the border that they routinely exercise in locales on the Mexican side. It is also possible that cartel gunmen might stage a significant cross-border raid aimed at eliminating rivals who have established themselves on the US side of the border. Americans might, at least temporarily, see the response to these scenarios as the responsibility of the military, with civilian agencies in support.

Because there is nothing in law that clearly articulates the tipping point between law enforcement and a military response, most who have studied this question agree that the tipping point would be determined in any given situation by the president, using his constitutional authority as commander-in-chief. The president's determination has considerable legal and operational consequences for use of the military in the homeland.

To the left of the tipping point, normally the Department of Homeland Security or the Department of Justice has the lead role for any federal response, and the Department of Defense operates in *support*, underpinned by several statutory authorities permitting certain limited military support to civilian law enforcement.* That assistance may include Department of Defense assets.

To the right of the tipping point, the Department of Defense has the lead role, operating under the president's constitutional commander-in-chief authority. NORAD (a combined US–Canadian air defense command) routinely operates in both countries' homeland to the right of the tipping point in the air domain. It is conceivable that maritime forces would operate to the right of the tipping point in certain situations, such as an offshore vessel launching cruise missile strikes against the homeland. It is also possible that the drug cartel threat could reach such a magnitude that a president would choose, at least in the short term, to respond with military force in the land domain.

In that situation, the military would likely operate in both a support and a lead role simultaneously in different parts of the homeland. The president could choose to give a portion of the military the lead in a certain discreet operation—defending critical infrastructure, for example—while leaving the rest of the military in its traditional civil support role for other threats around the country.

To the left of the tipping point, attackers would be treated as criminals and prosecuted under the criminal justice system, with Miranda rights, *habeas corpus*, rules of evidence, attorneys, trials, and jail sentences. To the right of the tipping point, attackers would be treated either as enemy combatants under the law of war,† or perhaps as "unlawful enemy combatants" similar to those imprisoned at Guantanamo Bay in the "global war on terrorism." The attackers would not be entitled to Miranda rights or *habeas corpus* at that end of the tipping point. They could be killed or captured and, if captured, could be held as prisoners until the end of the conflict.

Although the United States has not yet reached the "tipping point" with respect to the drug cartel threat, it is increasingly moving in that direction with respect to declaratory policies dealing with the threat of transnational organized crime to national security. For example, "[i]n January 2010, the United States Government

---

* 10 U.S.C. Chapter 18, Military Support for Civilian Law Enforcement Agencies (2006).
† U.S. DEP'T OF DEFENSE, DIR. 2311.01E, DOD LAW OF WAR PROGRAM (May 9, 2006, incorporating Change 1, Nov. 15, 2010) defines the Law of War as "[t]hat part of international law that regulates the conduct of armed hostilities. It is often called the 'law of armed conflict.'" and is based primarily on the Geneva Conventions of 1949 and their Additional Protocols. The International Committee of the Red Cross provides an excellent overview of the Geneva Conventions and their Additional Protocols at http://www.icrc.org/eng/war-and-law/treaties-customary-law/geneva-conventions/index.jsp

completed a comprehensive review of international organized crime—the first on this topic since 1995. Based on the review and subsequent reporting, the Administration has concluded that, in the intervening years, international—or transnational—organized crime has expanded dramatically in size, scope, and influence and that it poses a significant threat to national and international security."* Additionally, the US military currently conducts homeland defense-based counterintelligence operations along the Mexican border. The military serves as the single lead agency of the Federal Government for the detection and monitoring of aerial and maritime transit of illegal drugs into the United States, in support of counterdrug activities of federal, state, local, and foreign law enforcement agencies,† and there is an effort to expand its authority to the land domain.

Limitations on Use of the Military in the Homeland

However, the urge to send in the military is tempered by other factors. The southern US states suffered from military abuse during and after the Civil War. The Mexican people suffered at the hands of Mexican government troops during civil wars and in conjunction with their long and bloody revolution at the beginning of the twentieth century. Civil law and policies therefore limit the scope of military operations inside both countries.

Use of the military in a civil support role within the United States is limited by the Posse Comitatus Act‡ of 1878 which prohibits the direct, active participation of federal military forces to execute civilian law. Although the Act was enacted in response to the perceived misuse of Army troops in the South after the Civil War, there is a very good argument that its principles are rooted in the country's foundational documents. The Act provides: "Whoever, except in cases and under circumstances expressly authorized by the Constitution or Act of Congress, willfully uses any part of the Army or the Air Force as a posse comitatus or otherwise to execute the laws shall be fined under this title or imprisoned not more than two years, or both."

Although the statute applies only to the Army and Air Force, Department of Defense policy extends its prohibitions to the Navy and Marine Corps.§ The Act applies to the National Guard only when units are under federal command and control. When under the command and control of individual states, the National Guard may be used in a law enforcement role to perform such functions as pre-

---

* *Strategy to Combat Transnational Organized Crime: Addressing Converging Threats to National Security*, The White House, July 2011, p. 3.
† 10 U.S.C. 124 § 124 (2006).
‡ 18 U.S.C. § 1385 (2006).
§ U.S. DEP'T OF DEFENSE, DIR. 5525.5, DOD COOPERATION WITH CIVILIAN LAW ENFORCEMENT OFFICIALS (Jan. 15, 1986, incorporating Change 1 of Dec. 20, 1989, pursuant to 10 U.S.C. § 375).

venting looting after a natural disaster. The Act does not apply to the Coast Guard during peacetime when it is operating as part of the Department of Homeland Security, but does apply when it is operating as part of the Navy in time of war or pursuant to orders of the president.[*]

Mexican military operations in the homeland, at least in practice, are far less constrained. Article 89 of the Mexican Constitution empowers the president "[t]o dispose of the permanent armed forces, including the land army, the marine navy and the air force for *internal security* and exterior defense of the Federation" (emphasis added). Article 89 is theoretically tempered by Article 129 which states that "[n]o military authority may, in time of peace, perform any functions other than those that are directly connected with military affairs." Whether operations against the drug cartels are "directly connected with military affairs" or the province of traditional civilian police forces has been the subject of intense debate in Congress and the media. Additionally, Article 21[†] defines public security as the task of civil authorities.[‡]

In Mexico, the military is the tool of choice in a domestic emergency, in large part because domestic law enforcement agencies at the federal, state, and local levels are much weaker institutions. In Mexico, disaster response is a central military mission. In the United States, it is a growing but still peripheral, secondary task for the active-duty military. Stripping away political and bureaucratic considerations, one could call the US Department of Defense the Department of Foreign Wars, and Mexico's SEDENA and SEMAR the Departments of National Emergency Response. Those names would better reflect the two militaries' actual core functions.

SEDENA and SEMAR: Culture and Capabilities

Mexican armed forces are far more active in the struggle against the drug cartels than is the US military. It is therefore useful to look at SEDENA and SEMAR in some detail.

---

[*] 14 U.S.C. § 3 (2006).

[†] Article 21 states "The imposition of all penalties is an exclusive attribute of the judiciary. The prosecution of offenses pertains to the public prosecutor and to the judicial police, who shall be under the immediate command and authority of the public prosecutor. The punishment of violations of governmental and police regulations pertains to the administrative authorities, which punishment shall consist solely of imprisonment for a period not exceeding thirty-six hours or of a fine. Should the offender fail to pay the fine, it shall be substituted by a corresponding period of detention, which in no case may exceed fifteen days. If the offender is a day laborer or a workman, his punishment cannot consist of a fine exceeding the amount of his wages, for one week."

[‡] *See* Laura Carlsen, *Mexico's False Dilemma: Human Rights or Security,* 10 Nw. U. J. Int'l Hum. Rts. 146 (2012).

SEDENA—the Army and Air Force—is the most powerful security organization in Mexico. Its officer corps is drawn from the middle class and the troops represent a cross-section of the Mexican people. SEDENA is a product of the Mexican Revolution but, paradoxically, it is a naturally conservative institution. To a visitor, SEDENA personnel and facilities have the look and feel of a stereotypical Latin American military (albeit at the high end of that scale in terms of quality). SEDENA exists to defend the nation from foreign invasion, a mission which is extremely improbable. For decades, SEDENA officers spent their time planning to repel a US invasion. Now they are called upon to cooperate with their US military counterparts—a task which some embrace but about which others are ambivalent.

When SEDENA is ordered to deploy troops, this has been in response to some domestic emergency. They have a superb track record in dealing with natural disasters. Their history in responding to domestic unrest—be it during the immediate post-revolution period, the troubles of 1968, or with the Zapatista uprising in the 1990s—has been politically sensitive and (fairly or unfairly) problematic from a human rights perspective. It is therefore not surprising that SEDENA is a reluctant actor in the current effort to defeat the drug cartels. SEDENA leadership would very much prefer to hand this mission to the police, even though they realize that option isn't feasible in the near or mid-term. SEDENA's field operations against the narcotraffickers since 2006 have tended to be what amount to "shows of force." They do not typically seek contact with the drug traffickers, although soldiers essentially always win the firefights they engage in. SEDENA troops are trained and disciplined. Cartel gunmen are not.

The Mexican Air Force—very much the junior partner within SEDENA—has significant deficiencies in transport aviation. Mobility is a central concern in fighting the drug lords, be it at the operational level using C-130 aircraft to lift troops from bases in Central Mexico to hot spots in the north, or at the tactical level using helicopters to react to a local incident. Unfortunately, the Mexican Air Force's assets are barely adequate in number and too often in poor material condition. New helicopters provided by the United States to aid the fight against the cartels have been slow in coming and few in number.

Finally, there is the issue of the size of SEDENA versus the scope of the organized crime problem in Mexico. The total available number of troops (180,000), only a fraction of whom are deployed at any one time, simply are not enough to obtain a one-to-one force ratio with cartel manpower, much less the ten-to-one ratio recommended by counter-insurgency doctrine.

SEMAR, with almost 60,000 personnel, is much the smaller of the two Mexican military services. The Navy has an offshore defense and security mission. In practice, that has meant protecting the critical oil industry infrastructure in the Gulf of Campeche and interdicting criminal maritime operations. In terms of equipment, SEMAR has a mixture of aging ex-US warships of little combat value and modern domestically produced patrol vessels equivalent to US Coast Guard cutters. SEMAR has its own dedicated aviation assets.

As expected in a seagoing service, SEMAR has an internationalist outlook. They are not averse to working with foreign nations, to include the United States. Indeed, SEMAR has traditionally cooperated well with the US Coast Guard, another very effective small service. SEMAR has a "can-do" culture that is more easily adaptive to changing circumstances than SEDENA's. As the smaller of the two military services, SEMAR has an institutional wariness of being swallowed by SEDENA. Inter-service rivalry between the two is obvious. While SEDENA projects reluctance to take on the cartels, SEMAR comes across as eager to prove their worth to the president and the nation.

Mexican Military Operations: Strategic and Tactical Challenges

This was the situation in 2006 when substantial Mexican military forces were first committed against the drug cartels: "From the end of the PRI's political dominance of almost seven decades in every national activity, the takeover of an alternative way of governance headed by the PAN in 2000 weakened the status quo that had evolved between elected authorities, civil servants and criminal gangs (aka 'drug cartels'), challenging the legitimate rule of law in areas subject to either narcotics traffic, consumption or related illegal activities like money laundering, extortion, kidnapping, etc.

"The progressive deterioration of the police force and other security agencies with law enforcing authority helped develop a kind of parallel rule resembling local control by warlords in certain parts of our country, giving President Calderon little 'sea room' with respect to choice of which national forces could be used to fight in a struggle against illegal activity. The fight had to be taken to the criminal networks considering that civil liberties and human rights must be respected, the government would not grant exclusion areas, and there would not be any kind of bargaining with the criminal organizations."

The scene-setter above was written by Vice Admiral Carlos Ortega of SEMAR, an officer who has played a key role in military operations against the criminal networks. The critical decision, as Ortega points out, was to directly confront the cartels rather than seek some kind of bargain and accommodation. This policy marked a sharp break with the past. President Calderon was inaugurated on December 1, 2006. Eleven days later the first military-led counter-cartel action, Operation Michoacán, began with the deployment of 6000 SEDENA troops. It was a show of force intended to quell cartel-related violence. This set the pattern for the coming years. Violence would spiral out of control in some city or region. The federal government would respond by dispatching federal police and military forces. Violence would subside, but often only briefly. Then another hot spot would flare up, drawing the same response.

The strategic dilemma faced by the Mexican military stemmed from the nature of their opponent. Having organized, trained, and equipped themselves to fight conventional enemies, SEDENA and SEMAR now had to engage a nonstate threat, one made more complicated by the fact that there are multiple criminal networks active in Mexico. It was to be a fight against a hydra.

The criminal presence was pervasive then, and remains so now across northern Mexico, with other areas of high cartel activity along both coasts and dotting the remainder of the country. In the zones where the criminals are strongest, there is a climate of fear which distorts the lives of ordinary Mexicans. Local governments are weak or helpless in the face of blatant criminal activity. The effectiveness of state-level government is limited at best. The cartels maintain their dominance not just through fear but also through corruption. This problem is most clearly seen with local police forces, which have been transformed from entities that support governance to supine and untrustworthy organizations by means of the classic narcotrafficker's question of "silver or lead?" The insertion of federal police has been insufficient to turn this situation around. The federal police are too few in number and too immature organizationally to make a strategic difference in crime-ridden northern cities like Juarez and Reynosa.

Enter the military. But the cartels quickly found an effective counter to troop deployments: lie low for a while, reassess the circumstances, and then resume activity while avoiding contact with military forces. When contact is unavoidable, the drug lords write off their losses as the price of doing business. The federal government, for its part, looked for reductions in the number of drug-related murders as a metric for success. But often a drop in the local murder rate simply signaled a pause or worse—that one cartel had gained dominance over another and thus had less need for violence.

Given the size of the areas within which the criminal networks are active and the large population needing protection, there are never enough troops available. While there are generally local garrisons, most SEDENA and SEMAR forces must deploy into the hotspots. Deployments are relative short—three months is typical. This practice serves to reduce the stress on deploying units and also limits the opportunities for attempting to corrupt military members. However, it also means the military has little staying power in areas of high cartel activity. There isn't really time to get to know the terrain and the local people, to whom military leaders are mostly transient or anonymous. The military leadership has also sought to minimize casualties among the troops. In this they have succeeded, abetted by the cartel tactic of avoiding confrontations with the military. It is a sad fact that higher military casualties would indicate that the cartels were being harder-pressed. Another major challenge for military forces is operational security. While the troops themselves are not corrupt, cartel informants are everywhere—it might be the man who mows the grass inside a garrison, or the street vendor just outside the gate, or the local government official who attends a military planning session. Truly surprising a drug lord requires extraordinary security measures. Often, it mandates the use of tightly compartmented national-level special forces.

Mexican Military Transformation: A Mixed Score Card

The onset of large-scale military operations against the drug cartels brought with it a pressing need for SEDENA and SEMAR to transform themselves—to adapt to this very difficult operational environment. Instead of a force-on-force mindset, the military clearly needs to adopt a population-centric strategy, one close to but not the same as US counterinsurgency doctrine. The similarities between the US battles against insurgents and terrorists in Iraq and Afghanistan are many, but the differences are crucial. Unlike the US military in its two twenty-first century wars, Mexican forces are operating in their own homeland. The population caught in the middle of the conflict between cartels and between the government and the cartels is not some foreign people. They are the Mexican people.

In a conflict where the population is a Clausewitzian center of gravity, it follows that winning them over to your side is the keystone of victory. This reality leads to several implied task for military forces. First, the public is a major—and sometimes the best—source of intelligence on the enemy. Here, both SEDENA and SEMAR have done well. Despite the risks, local citizens have often shown they are willing to call in tips on criminal activity. The second implied task is what the US military calls Civil Affairs—direct humanitarian outreach to local communities. Here, the Mexican military has done very little. It will be interesting to see whether new emphasis on this issue following the election of President Peña Nieto will cause a change in the military attitude toward it. Another task for the military is to protect the population. This they have done, but only to the extent that military forces are in an endangered community on a sustained basis. Finally, a population-centric strategy requires the military to work with the entire range of civil authorities. Both Mexican services have significant reservations about the operational security risks attendant to this.

The effort to suppress the drug cartels mandates a joint and interagency approach. It also mandates close coordination with the US military and law enforcement agencies. Thus the Mexican military services, previously unaccustomed to working with outside entities and jealous of each other, have been forced into a double maze of organizations external to their own. Nonetheless, both services have taken on this task, each in its own way. SEDENA is a reluctant collaborator, wary of the Americans (although willing to accept aid in the form of new equipment and US military training). They often look down on Mexican agencies they see as less than competent and trustworthy. SEMAR has been a more willing player, albeit one that always holds closely to their own service's agenda and priorities.

Implied in the concept of military transformation is the intent to go all-out to defeat the opponent, even at the expense of long-held priorities and dearly held institutional imperatives. In this area, it seems the Mexican military is both looking over its shoulder and looking beyond the fight against the drug cartels. They fear retrospective political/legal retribution if they push the campaign against the cartels too hard. In any major and long-existing organization, there will be many who put their parochial interests and their future career advancement above the mission of the day.

Intelligence and Counterintelligence: The Key Enablers

Here is a Mexican view on the value of intelligence in countering transnational criminal networks: "When the Navy started its new support role combating organized crime, it had to start from scratch by learning from current, up to date practices and adapting its capabilities to the new mission. But to be effective, there was an ingredient still missing: *intelligence*." As Vice-Admiral Ortega, who has led SEMAR's intelligence organization since 2006, noted:

> Our experience has shown that the absolute single element of advantage has been the reduction of uncertainty when fighting a new enemy under abnormal conditions. This requires knowing the opponent and changing the operational paradigm, so that intelligence drives very complex operations in urban, densely populated areas.

It is important to acknowledge that the criminal networks held—and to a certain extent still hold—the intelligence advantage. This situation stems from their ability to apply the power of fear and corruption to any locale they need to control. Fear suppresses the flow of intelligence to the government. Corruption facilitates the flow of intelligence to the cartels. Added to this is the narcos' ability to easily buy the services of lookouts. They can saturate an area with these low-level clandestine observation and reporting posts—think of the gardener on a military base, the street vendor, or the corrupt policeman in his patrol car. All each one needs is a set of eyes and a cell phone.

But nation states have great powers of intelligence. The drug cartels have to face the combined intelligence capabilities of the United States and Mexico. Binational cooperation can be difficult, and concerns over sovereignty are always present, but both countries' leaders accept the need for intelligence cooperation. President Calderon characterized it as "technical" assistance by the United States to Mexico. It would appear that the PRI administration holds the same view. The US side brings to the table its global intelligence capabilities. The Mexican side brings to the table tactical ground intelligence obtained by military and federal police units, a superior understanding of terrain and populations, and the critical tips provided by citizen call-in reports. Ultimately, it falls mostly to the Mexican side to synthesize all the available intelligence and translate it into effective military or interagency operations. There is "actionable intelligence" and "action on intelligence." Both are needed.

The intelligence war will be won when the two national governments can overwhelm the initial advantage held by the cartels. Local populations must feel safe enough to be willing to report criminal activity—not perfectly safe, but safe enough. Corrupt officials must be found and ruthlessly rooted out. Cartel lookout networks must be suppressed or tactically deceived. Ultimately, intelligence units have to penetrate the cartels' inner circles. While a difficult task, this last is not impossible. Simply put, there is no honor among thieves. It is possible to act effectively even when not all these conditions have been met. Timely intelligence paired with good, tightly compartmented operational security can yield spectacular success against drug kingpins.

Human Rights: Treading Carefully

The human rights issue is a more pressing one for the Mexican military than the United States because Mexican forces are far more directly involved in the struggle against the drug cartels than are US military forces.

If the Mexican military is to pursue a population-centric strategy against the criminal networks, then it follows that they cannot afford to alienate the population. Under these conditions, a single serious failure with regard to human rights can destroy years of progress. Nor can the military assume to enjoy unquestioning support of local populations in every region. Some areas of high criminal activity—for example, Michoacán and the Sierra Madre Occidental region in northern Mexico—have long traditions of ambivalence toward the central government. At times in the past, military forces dispatched by Mexico City have been the enemy, not the friend, of local people. Conversely, drug lords and their principal lieutenants can be local authority figures who distribute welcome largess, protect otherwise helpless families and/or resolve local disputes. Thus, while in the main people welcome the presence of military forces as a source of protection, in some cases the criminals are figures of respect. Winning and keeping the support of the populace requires troops to display a high standard of conduct.

Reasonable minds differ on the true level of professionalism of Mexican military forces. While some perceive continually improving professionalism,* others perceive that the relatively free use of Mexican military forces against the cartels since President Calderon came to power in 2006 has come at a heavy price. "The federal government continues to define a semi-permanent role for the Armed Forces in the drug war, which in the absence of a declared state of emergency is difficult to justify. Moreover, the domestic role of the Armed Forces threatens civil liberties and individual human rights and constitutes an affront to the rule of law."†

---

* See, e.g., Philip Treglia, *Emerging Threat to America: Non-State Entities Fighting Fourth Generation Warfare in Mexico* (master's thesis, 2010). Retrieved from http://www.hsdl.org/?view&did=15958

† Id. at 147.

Military forces have the potential to commit human rights violations in a number of ways. Good training and strict discipline go far toward mitigating these hazards, but in any large military deployment some troops will commit crimes. At that point, justice must be done and it must be seen to be done. Understandably, SEDENA and SEMAR want to try military members accused of human rights violations by court martial. "The persistence of trying all cases related to military personnel in military tribunals, known as the *fuero militar* or military exemption from civil prosecution, inhibits legal and social accountability and in practice has led to a very low prosecution rate."* However, Mexico has a very active human rights movement and there is significant political pressure to try alleged military-related crimes in civil court. In a historic ruling, the Mexican Supreme Court held on July 6, 2011 that the armed forces must respect the decision of the Inter-American Commission on Human Rights (IACHR) that human rights cases involving members of the armed forces should be litigated before civilian authorities.† While some human rights groups might see this as a panacea, Mexico's criminal justice system is plagued with corruption and its criminal conviction rate hovers around 2%. Military justice is likely to be more swift and sure—with some important caveats. Courts-martial proceedings need to be as public and transparent as possible.

The US military justice system, by contrast, is transparent, public, and subject to civilian court review. What is more, the United States occasionally even tries high-profile military abuse cases in open civilian court. Military forces—be they active duty, reserve or National Guard—are employed in a support rather than lead role. This limits the likelihood they will commit human rights violations. Even if the US military becomes more directly involved in border security, they will probably be attached to Department of Homeland Security personnel who have law enforcement training and authorities. The main law enforcement element on the US–Mexico border is, of course, the US Customs and Border Protection (hereinafter "Border Patrol").

Border Control: A Federal Mission without Federal Troops

One of the most basic functions of a nation-state is defense of its territorial integrity, including patrol and enforcement of its land borders. To the extent that the US military has been used in recent years to support federal border control, it is therefore curious that National Guard troops have remained under the operational control of their respective state's governors and under the tactical control of the governor of the state in which they operate. This was the case under two

---

* Ibid.
† Human Rights Watch, *Mexico: Ruling Affirms Obligation for Military Justice Reform*, July 6, 2011.

different administrations, from 2006 to 2008 when more than 30,000 National Guardsmen participated in "Operation Jump Start" along the southwest border, and in 2010 when approximately 1200 National Guardsmen were deployed for a similar mission.

Part of the reason for this oddity is the fact that the United States has not yet reached the previously discussed "tipping point" in which military forces would switch from a support to law enforcement mode to a war-fighting national defense mode. National Guard troops are far better suited for this support to law enforcement mission because, as a general rule, they are trained in both law enforcement and war fighting, whereas federal troops are trained solely for the war fighting mission. Moreover, it is general consensus that Title 10 federal forces have been stretched thin after more than a decade of continuous operations in Iraq and Afghanistan. Post-9/11 Department of Defense policy seeks to reduce the operational stress on Title 10 forces by preferring Title 32 forces in the conduct of domestic counter-narcotics activities, and limiting Title 10 domestic operational support to short-term, nonrepetitive assistance.*

Additionally, National Guard troops may operate in any one of three statuses: Title 10, reporting to the president and paid with federal funds; Title 32, reporting to their state's governor, but paid with federal funds; or State Active Duty, reporting to the governor and paid with state funds. National Guard forces deployed along the border to support civil authorities have been placed in Title 32 status, which by definition makes the restrictions of the Posse Comitatus Act inapplicable to their operations. Therefore, although these troops have not yet been tasked with direct law enforcement functions, they are eligible to exercise that function if and when the sending and receiving state Governors so agree. National Guard forces are paid with federal funds when in Title 32 status because they are performing one of two functions. They are engaged either in "training or other duty" for a federal mission† (such as deployment to Iraq or Afghanistan) or a "homeland defense activity."‡ A reasonable argument could be made that border operations by Title 32 National Guard forces fall into the statutory definition of "homeland defense activity" as "an activity undertaken for the military protection of the territory or domestic population of the United States, or of infrastructure or other assets of the United States determined by the Secretary of Defense as being critical to national security, from a threat or aggression against the United States."§

---

* U.S. DEP'T OF DEFENSE, CJCSI 3710.01B, DOD COUNTERDRUG SUPPORT (Jan. 26, 2007). Incorporates similar guidance in DepSecDef memorandum, *Department Support to Domestic Law Enforcement Agencies Performing Counternarcotics Activities,* 02 October 2003.
† 32 U.S.C. 502(f).
‡ 32 U.S.C. 901 (2006).
§ Id. at Sec. 901.

The US Military on the Border: How Big a Role?

The US military—and specifically the US Army—is no stranger to the US–Mexico border region. The Army first arrived on the Rio Grande (or Rio Bravo del Norte, if you will) in the run-up to the US–Mexican War in the 1840s. They fought Comanche in Texas before the US Civil War and Apaches in Arizona after it. The US Army staged a major show of force on the border after the Civil War, during the endgame of the French occupation of Mexico. The Army crossed the border for a second time during the Mexican Revolution in pursuit of Pancho Villa after he had attacked a US garrison in New Mexico. The legacy of all this is a string of often very large military bases located near the border. However—and reflecting the overseas focus of the post-World War II Department of Defense—these bases have purposes that have nothing to do with border security or the threat posed by transnational criminal networks: as an air defense missile forces garrison, a weapons testing range, a military intelligence training school, a Marine Corps air station, a big Navy home port and the bases for a Marine Division and air wing. In one case—Fort Huachuca in Arizona—the military base lies on a major transit route for migrants and drug smuggling, yet this fact is seen as an internal garrison commander's concern rather than a mission for troops there.

As the struggle between the Mexican government and the narcos heated up after 2006, the military's joint combatant command whose area of interest encompasses North America, US Northern Command, stepped up its cooperation with counterparts in the Mexican military. When border violence spiked alarmingly, the Bush and Obama Administrations chose to use military forces to augment the Border Patrol. These were explicitly time-limited assignments, meant to allow the Border Patrol time to recruit and train an expanded cadre of agents. In each case, the Secretary of Defense chose to meet the border requirement with National Guard troops, gathered on an ad hoc basis from the pool of individual Guardsmen willing to volunteer for the duty. Restrictions imposed by National Guard leadership limited the utility of these personnel so that they were, in effect, just temporary extra manpower. Direct operations against illegal border activity continued to require Border Patrol agents with law enforcement training and credentials. The decision not to deploy active-duty forces grew out of the military's concern about overstretched regular forces, which were then heavily committed to wars in Iraq and Afghanistan.

In the United States, there is a strong preference that law enforcement agencies have the lead role in domestic security. But really the mindset in the United States isn't that much different from in Mexico: If the situation is bad enough, the military will be committed. Americans can afford a higher threshold for deploying major military forces because US law enforcement agencies at every level are more robust, and because the United States has the National Guard as a military option before sending in the regulars. Thus, the level of US military operations inside the homeland is a product of the level of perceived or actual threat. It would only take one major incident of narco-related violence on the US side of the border to prompt Washington to bring in major military units.

The Military as Enabler: Options for Bolstering Governance in Lawless Zones

Currently, the struggle against the drug cartels is stalemated. But US analysts characterize the stalemate as "dynamic." Violence exhibits a saw tooth pattern, rising and falling in various locales as inter-cartel fighting spikes, government forces react, and criminal networks are either suppressed or gain undisputed dominance. Overcoming the strategic stalemate and ending the saw tooth pattern will require sustained pressure on drug cartels at every level, top to bottom. While many in Mexico have reservations about the "kingpin strategy," it has worked in Colombia and elsewhere. But President Peña Nieto is also right in that lower-level criminal activity must be suppressed. The two approaches are not mutually exclusive. Pressuring low-level cartel activities can lead to the big fish. For SEDENA and SEMAR, this means developing their currently limited counter-network capabilities so that criminal organizations can be attacked simultaneously, at all levels and from all directions. The US military can help a great deal with this process, but only if the American side understands and respects the Mexican environment—political, legal, and cultural.

The desired end state for Mexican military forces is to hand off counter-crime responsibilities to Mexican police. The first step will be a hand off to the federal police. To that end, more must be done to strengthen federal police numbers and professionalism. President Peña Nieto has toyed with the idea of creating a Mexican paramilitary police service along the lines of the French Gendarmerie.*
There are other models for this in Italy (the Carabinieri) and in Spain (the Guardia Civil). But to get there quickly and with minimal bureaucratic/organizational turbulence would be a major challenge. An obvious shortcut would be to put this service under SEDENA, and to require SEDENA to transfer a large portion of Army and Air Force personnel and capabilities to the new paramilitary police. This is an attractive potential course of action. Ultimately, of course, even the role of federal police should diminish as state/local police forces resume their appropriate roles. Realistically, this step is far in the future. Military forces—in one form or another—will probably retain a central role in countering organized crime for a decade or more.

Government officials and nongovernmental organizations in both the United States and Mexico need to accept and support the role played by their respective

---

* Global Insider: New Presidents of France, Mexico Opt to Reset Ties, Oct. 25, 2012, *available at* http://www.worldpoliticsreview.com/trend-lines/12450/global-insider-new-presidents-in-france-mexico-opt-to-reset-ties

military forces in defeating the menace posed by transnational criminal networks. The scope and duration of that role should certainly be a focus for ongoing public debate. But military *capabilities* are clearly required. The key is to ensure oversight, accountability, and transparency in terms of the *intent* with which the capabilities are used. Governmental oversight mechanisms need to be real, not token, and not toothless. Accountability for misdeeds—and they will happen, given the circumstances and the number of troops involved—also needs to be real, not just a matter of punishing the occasional scapegoat. Finally and most critically, military activities associated with a domestic counter-crime mission must be transparent. The citizens of Mexico and the United States must know what their military forces are doing, how it is being done, and why the military operations are justified. None of this will come naturally to any government bureaucracy—military bureaucracies most definitely included. Consistent outside pressure will be required, particularly from the media and nongovernmental organizations.

Chapter 7

Institutional Capacity and National Security Policy in Mexico
From Formalism to Realism

Mario A. Rivera and Sofia Alejandra Solis Cobos

Contents

Introduction 97
Legal and Institutional Frameworks in Mexico: Formal Capacity 98
Analysis and Conclusions: What's Real? 111
References 115
Other Webpages Consulted 117

Introduction

Owing to the economic, political, and social decline that Mexico has undergone in the past several years, which translates into unemployment, judicial sector corruption, and a continual crisis of values in Mexican society, a climate of insecurity, illegality, and impunity has alarmingly taken hold, and become routine. This process of accelerated sociopolitical decomposition has markedly contributed to the redoubling of organized crime, which clearly undermines the stability, efficacy, and security of the Mexican State. Drug trafficking, while prototypical of the growing, systemic violence linked to organized crime, is itself a threat to national security, considering the entirety of drug production, drug traffic, drug dealing, drug addiction, drug consumption, and related money laundering. These play out across local, national, and international boundaries, tied to transnational criminal networks. It is important to note that the Mexican criminal organizations involved enjoy greater resources and manifest greater initiative than may be apparent, making use of communications and weapons technologies that are supposed to be exclusively available to the nation's armed forces. This affects national security because the enormous economic capacity of criminal organizations allows them to infiltrate public institutions and civil society, through corruption and intimidation.

This chapter is a general yet selective evaluation of these themes, on the basis of a systematic review and research synthesis of relevant published literature, with emphasis on official decrees and statutes emanating from the Mexican government that lay out the formal national security responsibilities of a host of national agencies. The study indicates, first, that conjoint efforts among the executive and other branches and institutions of government concerned with organized crime have not yielded outstanding results—rather, the country's national security has suffered an ever-growing and constant threat that could turn Mexico into a failed state, incapable of guaranteeing the most basic civil right of its citizenry, that of public safety. Beyond corruption, the crux of the problem is the inability of the state to effectively deploy its formal institutional capacities and resource endowments. We now proceed to a systematic review of pertinent literature, followed by substantive reflection on these sources.

Legal and Institutional Frameworks in Mexico: Formal Capacity

Of singular importance is Article 89 of the Political Constitution of the United States of Mexico, published in the *Official Gazette of the Federation* February 5, 1917 (as amended, most recently, on May 4, 2004). Pursuant to it, the faculties and responsibilities of the president are as follows: "Article VI. To protect national security, consistent with corresponding law, and to have resort to the entirety of the permanent Armed Forces, i.e., the Army, Navy, and Air Force, for the internal and external defense of the Federation."

Against this constitutional backdrop, Rojas Aravena (2007) proposes that the most tangible threat consists of the weakening of the economy, society, and institutions of government, challenges which in their persistence and synergy undermine the State's control over national territory. Combating this threat requires information-sharing strategies marked by much greater political transparency and accountability than have in fact been present, so that sovereign territorial control may be extended and lawlessness diminished. For his part, Villareal Gabriel (2009) maintains that in Mexico the Armed Forces have turned from their traditional engagement in national defense and disaster response toward a central role in the advancement of national security policy for the federal government, as well as for state governments irrespective of the ideological or political stance of their dominant parties. The Armed Forces therefore represent an exception to historical regime manifestations of impunity and inefficacy, as a truly developed institution with real capacities, at least if one analytically separates the armed forces from their political and administrative setting.

Correspondingly, organized crime has been considered a threat to national sovereignty and security, whether in previous presidencies or recent ones. Herrera (2009) sees a determination to confront the high incidence of entrenched lawlessness and insecurity, through mobilization of the Armed Forces against organized crime and especially narcotrafficking, as a defining commitment of the previous presidency. Becerra (2008) underscores this point, positing that the model chosen by President Calderón to wrest federal control over territory controlled by criminal/drug cartels was exemplified by the Michoacán Joint Operation, the first of the great military initiatives of his administration. This operation was launched on December 11, 2006, just 10 days after President Calderón took office, and it involved the deployment of 1500 Federal Police and 5000 military forces in the State of Michoacán (Moloeznik, 2007).

Consistent with Article 3 of the Law of National Security (*Ley de Seguridad Nacional*), published in the *Official Organ of the Federation* (Diario Oficial de la Federación) on January 31, 2005, "national security" is defined *as actions directly and immediately aimed at safeguarding the integrity, stability, and permanency of the Mexican State that promote.*

I. The protection of the Mexican nation from threats and risks facing the nation;
II. The preservation of national sovereignty and independence and territorial defense;
III. Maintenance of constitutional order and the strengthening of the democratic institutions of government;
IV. Maintenance of the integrity of all governmental and territorial components of the Federation as indicated in Article 43 of the Political Constitution of the United States and of Mexico (Constitución Política de los Estados Unidos Mexicanos);
V. The legitimate defense of the Mexican State from other States or actors subject to international law; and
VI. Preservation of democracy premised on the economic, social, and political development of the nation and its people.

Article 1 of the Law of National Security is specified in the *Diario Oficial de la Federación* of November 29, 2006, as the Regulation for the Coordination of Executive Actions Material to National Security (Coordinación de Acciones Ejecutivas en Materia de Seguridad Nacional), as follows (quoting): The current order declares as its objective: the establishment of policies, norms, criteria, systems, processes, and procedures consistent with which coordinating actions material to

National Security, reference Article 3, will be promoted. Article 3; The competencies established under article 3 of the Law of National Security, among other actionable articles of the Law, aim at the immediate and direct protection of the integrity, stability, and permanence of the Mexican State, as these constitute its National Security interests. This regulation establishes that the proposal of the Program for National Security (Programa para la Seguridad Nacional), to be formulated by the Technical Secretariat of the National Security Council (Secretaría Técnica al Consejo de Seguridad Nacional), will create the foundations for integral response to these priorities, using as points of departure fundamental political decision making, integration of strategic intelligence, promotion of public policies, emergency planning and response, and security and protective operations.

Federal public administration relies on several institutions officially related to the theme of national security. This is the case with the Government Secretariat (Secretaría de Gobernación), with a mission of contributing to Mexico's democratic governability and political development through good relations among the Federal Government, competencies of the Union, and every level of government so as to guarantee national security, harmonious coexistence, and the welfare of all Mexicans in a State of Law (Cisen, 2008). This Secretariat is a decentralized agency that incorporates the Center for Investigation and Security (Centro de Investigación y Seguridad, better known as *CISEN*), an "organ of civil intelligence at the service of the Mexican State whose purpose it is to generate strategic, tactical, and operational intelligence such as would allow for the preservation of the integrity, stability, and permanence of the State and the sustenance of governability and the strengthening of the State of Law" (CISEN, 2008).

The Secretariat's responsibilities and powers as an investigative agency include the following: 1. To generate and implement intelligence tasks such as studies of a strategic nature that would make it possible to anticipate risks and threats to National Security; 2. To propose measures for the prevention, dissuasion, contention, and deactivation of risks and threats to National Security; and 3. To propose to the National Security Council (CSN) means for corresponding mechanisms of international cooperation. The Secretariat's key responsibility is the proposal of means for the prevention, dissuasion, contention, and so on that would render national territory, sovereignty, national institutions, democratic governability, or the State of Law "vulnerable." According to the Law of National Security, risks and threats are defined by "activities related to espionage, sabotage, terrorism (including the financing of terror), rebellion, treason to the nation, genocide, illegal traffic of nuclear, chemical, and biological materials, conventional weapons of mass destruction, and acts against the safety of aviation and maritime navigation." Included are actions "tending to block or neutralize intelligence or counterintelligence activities, as well as actions impeding official responses to organized crime, and military or naval operations against the same." As to *risks to national security*, what the term officially references is "an internal or external condition generated by political, economic, or social situations [deriving from] nonstate actors …"

Notwithstanding the comprehensive quality of these definitions, the Law of National Security does not and cannot catalogue all risks to national security, since these do not lend themselves to exhaustive specification, manifested as they are in singular contingencies periodically facing the nation. As already suggested in this chapter, corruption and intimidation are very difficult to categorize adequately, even in expressly tailored laws or in formally designated organizations.

The National Security System is headed by the President of the Republic and consists of those agencies that comprise the National Security Council (CSN), public sector organizations assigned to it, and state and municipal authorities collaborating with the Federal Government to preserve National Security. The National Security Council itself is a deliberative body (headed by the president) whose constitutive aim is to establish and link policies and actions material to National Security, and for which the following subsidiary objectives obtain (closely paraphrasing from the official document Ley de Seguridad Nacional, *Diario Oficial de la Federación*, January 2005): Integration and coordination of efforts and measures meant to preserve National Security, of international cooperation programs oriented toward the establishment of general policies, assistance, and cooperation with regard to National Security, of efforts in the advancement of justice by any other branch of public administration accorded to the Council, and of linked efforts (through the Security Program) at program evaluation and performance- or results-based management.

Another federal institution with jurisdiction over Mexico's national security is the Defense Secretariat, better known as *SEDENA*. It concedes that traffic in drugs has become an internal threat to the life of the nation, so that combating it is of highest priority for the armed forces, although it also acknowledges it to be a problem with no short-term solution (Secretaría de la Defensa Nacional [reportes]). The mission and authority of this ministry of state are delineated under the Organic Law of the Army and Air Force of Mexico (*Ley Orgánica del Ejército y Fuerza Aérea Mexicanos*, Instituto de Investigaciones Júridicas, UNAM, 2013, p. 1), as follows:

Article 1:

I. To defend the integrity, independence, and sovereignty of the nation;
II. To guarantee internal public safety;
III. To assist the civil population in cases of public emergency/necessity;
IV. To carry out civic and public works in advancement of national progress; and
V. In cases of natural disaster to assist in the maintenance of public order, in aid of persons and property, and in the reconstruction of affected areas.

Article 2: These duties may be carried out by the Army and Air Force, by themselves or in concert with the Navy or with other Federal, State, or Municipal agencies, pursuant to orders or approvals of the President of the Republic in his exercise of constitutional responsibilities.

Article 17: The Secretary for National Defense is in turn responsible, "consistent with instructions from the President of the Republic ... for organizing, equipping, educating, training, readying, administering, and developing the terrestrial and airborne Armed Forces." The "Mexican Army and Air Force act in concert, as a single governmental entity, composed of: Combat Units, Service Units, Special Forces, Rural Defense Forces, and Military Education Establishments."

Another document with specific mention of the legal scope of the military as an institution is the Organic Law of Federal Public Administration (*Ley Orgánica de la Administración Pública Federal*), Second Title, Chapter II, Article 29, which ordains that the following responsibilities belong to the Secretary of National Defense:

> I. To organize, administer, and make ready the Army and Air Force. VI. To Plan, direct, and manage national mobilization in time of war; to formulate and carry out, in that event, plans and orders necessary for national defense, and to assess civil defense; VII. To construct and prepare the fortifications and every type of fortified military installation, as well as the administration and upkeep of barracks, hospitals, and other military establishments. XVI. To intervene in the granting of licenses for carrying firearms, with the aim of excluding firearms prohibited by law and those reserved for the exclusive use of the Army, Navy, and National guard, with the exception of those noted in section XVIII of article 30, as well as monitoring permits for the sale, transport, and warehousing of firearms, munitions, explosives, chemical agents, and strategic materials. XVII. To intervene in the importation and export of every type of firearm, munitions, explosives, chemical agents, and strategic material. IX. To provide any auxiliary services that may be required by the Army and Air Force, as well as civil agencies as provided for by the Federal Executive, and XX. Other functions expressly given to it by law and regulation.

Another ministry institutionally charged (since its creation in 2001) with responsibility for national security was the Federal Public Safety Secretariat (Secretaría de Seguridad Pública Federal). The Secretariat, though formally a part of the judiciary also an arm of the federal government with regard to fulfillment of its mission of preventing and fighting crime, had no less of a charge than "the prevention of crime and combating of delinquency, purposes consistent with the preservation of the integrity and patrimony of persons, of public peace and order, of crime, and by extension the Rule of Law, with professionalism and honesty, and zeal for the protection of human rights."

However, among the first actions taken by the successor Peña Nieto administration was to abolish this ministry, which had been troubled by charges of both malfeasance and ineptitude—leveled personally at its only incumbent Secretary during the Calderón sexenio, Genaro García Luna, who served from December 1, 2006 to November 30, 2012. This ministry of state was officially dismantled January 3, 2013 by legislative vote, following a proposal by the new president. Institutionally, it has been replaced as a superministry by the Government Secretariat (Secretaría de Gobernación), with Manuel Mondragón named Subsecretary of Public Security (or Safety), a move widely read as signaling greater direct presidential oversight over security matters as well as a repudiation of the Calderón era approach to these governmental functions. The reorganized subsecretariat inherits the functions of proposing congruent public safety and security policies to the President of the Republic. In a coordinated move, the Public Function Secretariat (Secretaría de la Función Pública), charged with fighting corruption within the Federal Public Administration, was also abolished and its functions subsumed under the Secretaría de Gobernación. (Numerous journalistic sources, January 2013, including http://noticierostelevisa.esmas.com/nacional/543610/desaparece-ssp-federal/ and http://www.debate.com.mx/eldebate/movil/Articulomovil.asp?IdArt=12830885&IdCat=6103).

The Federal Police has played a preponderant (and less controversial) role with regard to national security, counting as it does on the following authorities and duties (Secretaría de Seguridad Pública, *Programa Nacional de Seguridad Pública 2008–2012*):

> I. To pronounce and implement all measures necessary to ensure the prevention of crime, and the maintenance or reestablishment of public order and public safety, consistent with its institutional scope and reach; II. To organize and supervise lines of investigation such as would be necessary for the collection, analysis, study, and processing of information pertaining to the prevention and combating of crime, within appropriate institutional constraints; III. To organize and supervise lines of investigation necessary for the collection, analysis, study, and processing of information pertaining to crime and its prevention, in keeping with designated authorities and available resources; IV. To outline criteria and policies for the preparation of reports, data, and technical and operational assistance that may be required by Federal, State, Municipal, and Federal District governments, and by other countries, as may be deemed necessary for the prevention and combating of crime, directly or by means of coordination with these entities, as provided for in applicable federal law; and regulation; V. To provide for the planning, procurement, and institutional function of information collection, in the process ensuring that requisite information systems are established and deployed; IX. Premised on Secretary's prior approval, to authorize covert operations relying on undercover agents, for the purpose of crime control; X. To establish, with the Secretary's approval, remuneration necessary for investigative operations and their supervision; XI. To articulate the operative, normative, and functional facets of the institution consistent with its areas of formal competency;

XIII. To provide for legal representation of the institution within the ambit of police matters, as befits a decentralized administrative body (Órgano Administrativo Desconcentrado), in conformity with applicable legislation. XVIII. To participate, in accordance with applicable authorities and constraints, in negotiation of international treaties carried out by the Federal Executive with respect to crime prevention, as required; XXIII. To establish and implement crime control policies relative to public transit, federal roads and bridges, federal auto transport services, auxiliary services, and private transport when occurring within the public transportation infrastructure; XXVI. To authorize, subject to Secretarial approval, fiscal and programmatic control and evaluation systems for all entities comprising the ministry; XXXII. To approve manuals, protocols, and systemic and operational procedures of component entities; XXXIII. To delegate to any institutional entity or agency, by way of assignments of responsibility and authority, rank or material standing, the realization of juridical acts inherent in the powers given to the ministry by this article of law, and other legal sources.

The Federal Police is comprised of several divisions related to national security and narcotrafficking, as follows: the Intelligence Division, along with Investigative, Regional Security, Anti-Drug Divisions and the Federal Forces Division (División de Inteligencia, de Investigación, de Seguridad Regional, Antidrogas, and División de Fuerzas Federales). As to its relationship with the Organización Internacional de Policía Criminal International (the Criminal Police Organization, commonly known as *Interpol*), the intelligence division is bound to coordinate, as the Office of National Liaison Interpol-Mexico (Oficina de Enlace Nacional Interpol-México), with whatever agency may be designated by the National Central Interpol Office (Oficina Central Nacional de Interpol).

The final key ministry comprising the formal national security framework in Mexico is the Justice Ministry (Procuraduría General de la República, better known as the *PGR*, equivalent to the United States Department of Justice), whose mission it has been to contribute to the effort to ensure and secure a Democratic State of Law (or Democratic Rule of Law), and to preserve the unrestricted realization and fulfillment of the Political Constitution of the United States of Mexico, by means of the efficacious and efficient procurement (procuración) of justice, according to principles of legality, juridical certitude, and respect for human rights, in collaboration with the three branches of government and in service to society.

The legal framework that is controlling with regard to acts of the Justice Minister (Procurador General de la República, equivalent to Attorney General in the United States), of agents of the Public Ministry of the Federation (Ministerio Público de la Federación), Investigative Police, and its various "experts" are found in the National Political Constitution, in the Organic Law corresponding to the ministry

(Ley Orgánica de la Procuraduría General de la Republica), and related subsidiary regulations and executive orders (Boletín Conjunto, 2011). Among the PGR's responsibilities and attributions of authority are found the investigation of federal crimes, as well as consequent actions taken before Federal Tribunals (Tribunales de la Federación). Crimes against public health, including drug trafficking, are considered to fall under the category of federal crime, inasmuch as these continually affect the national security of the entire country.

As a ministry, the Procuraduría relies on coordinate strategies for combating narcotrafficking, to be implemented integrally, inter-institutionally, with the participation of federal agencies involved, with equal attention paid to the dynamics of supply and demand. Response comes by way of three lines of action: eradication of illicit cultivation, interception of drugs and their chemical precursors, and finally combat against organized crime (the typical drug cartel) and its coextensive criminal activities. In these efforts to combat delinquency, the Procuraduría General de la República relies on its Agencia Federal de Investigación or *AFI* (Federal Agency of Investigation, equivalent to the American Federal Bureau of Investigation), an institution charged with investigating and prosecuting those responsible for the commission of federal crimes and crimes which in their public impact affect national security or fall within the federal ambit. This agency's primary mission is to privilege the scientific investigation of crime so as to combat organized criminal delinquency by means of the specialized regional formation of police personnel, equipping them thereby to address the complexity of federal crimes, and to modify the crime-fighting model away from reactive policing.

The institutional systems and processes and organizational logic involved are designed on the premise of information-sharing in the fight against corruption, on clear definition of spans of control, on avoidance of duplication in chains of command, and on a hierarchical command structure for the sake of precision with regard to the ministry's mandates. It is maintained that "institutional capacity depends on the concentration and verticality of organizational authority and task structures." This reliance on concentration and centrality needs to be probed as far as its implications for combating narcotrafficking, one of the nation's most complex challenges (which may not be entirely amenable to such centralization of institutional capacity).

As the foregoing suggests, as pertains to national security, the Mexican State exhibits a comprehensive normative-institutional policy framework, with ample legal–judicial supports, and with operational logistics marked out at the highest conceptual levels. According to the *Bulletin* (*Boletín*) published by the Procuraduría, the Secretariat of Governance, Secretariat of Defense, Public Safety Secretariat, and the Naval Secretariat, January 2, 2012, there is a national *aspiration* for safe communities shared by millions of Mexicans and the Federal Government. To this end, large-scale national initiatives have aimed at strengthening institutions across the three branches of government, under a National Security Strategy (Estrategia

Nacional de Seguridad) which would prevent and sanction criminal acts as well as improve the legal and regulatory instrumentalities surrounding the prosecution of crime. This strategy has allowed for strengthened, more capable, federal forces, for historic numbers of apprehensions and arrests, in the process diminishing the capacities of criminal organizations. However, it appears that the citizenry persists in doubting the real efficacy of these touted attainments and accomplishments, as we will consider at the conclusion of this chapter.

From the first day of his administration, President Felipe Calderón demonstrated his desire to unleash all of the strength of the State against organized crime, which had shown, for its part, that it had the wherewithal to corrupt institutions, control territories, and render vulnerable the Rule of Law for the nation (Rodríguez Sánchez Lara, 2009). For this reason, the administration rolled out a Security Program, comprising an Integral Strategy for the Prevention and Confrontation of Crime (Estrategia Integral de Prevención del Delito y Combate a la Delincuencia), by which the Federal Executive has set out to restore faith in the viability of the State's national security function, on the basis of protection of and service to society, pursuant to the now familiar principles of legality, efficacy, professionalism, and honesty. These proposals, previously discussed, depend on the concerted realization of eight vectors or axes of action and corresponding functions of public policy determination, instrumentation, and deployment. Concertation of these (termed *coacción*, or joint action), the first programmatic axis ("eje"), is considered properly to be the function of the National Public Safety Council (Consejo Nacional de Seguridad Pública), along the following tangents: operational coordination, the interconnection and inter-operativity of information systems, evaluation and control of police internal affairs, police training and professional preparation, and the determination of performance indicators and measures. The integration of efforts by various federal police authorities is required thereby, eventuating in a value-added initiative, with command functions coordinated under the Federal Preventive Police (Policía Federal Preventiva, PFP), the AFI, immigration agents (INM), and customs inspection (CIFA). However, in evaluating whether the coordination and integration of various commands and policies do in fact obtain, one must return to the question of the relative impacts, in context, of institutional decentralization versus centralization.

This Program and Plan articulate the investigative and tactical/analytical specialties of the AFI: the territorial deployment and response capacity of the PFP; the control of migratory points and of immigration by the INM, as well as the inspection faculties of the CIFA. These attributes are supposed to confer efficacy to crime fighting by a unified police force. The plan's overarching strategy also comprehends the alignment of functional attributions, meant to apply to the coordination of federal entities, with due attention to the penal system, here with special emphasis on the carrying out of criminal sentences and monitoring of those who are duly convicted.

The second axis is police operations, which proactively and permanently anticipate division into two rubrics: (1) The territorial restoration of public spaces for communities and the restoration of minimum conditions of safety for them, and (2) the demarcation of operative logistics in confronting criminal organizations. Correspondingly, the following premises apply: in the territorial plan, the selection of cities with high criminal activity in which strategic concentrations of force would be required in order to maximize results and generate safety zones, allowing for the extension of enhanced safety conditions across adjacent populations, privileging attention to states that harbor the principal criminal organizations, with assignment of human and technical resources for the generation of operative intelligence and systematic and permanent instrumentation of crime-fighting action.

Serving as a third axis, this trans-territorial effort emphasizes the prevention of crime and citizen participation, transitioning away from a punitive and reactive model toward one entailing social engagement. This essentially preventative plan, proposed under the new, participatory model for public safety, turns on the realization of "civic connection" and protection of human rights, from the point of view of the victims of violence. It is based on "conjunctive" effort, to be undertaken in continual movement between the population at large and state authority.

A fourth axis corresponds to institutional development, which consists of various important initiatives: Professionalization (police education and training); the development of methodologies, protocols, systematic processes of operation, and the conduct of investigation by means of information collection, processing, analysis, and exploitation. All of these are acknowledged to require apt processes of personnel recruitment, selection, and integration, the vigilant participation of a committed citizenry, and consistent dependence on ethical values of public service.

The penal system acts as a fifth axis, as it propels intergovernmental policies via the National Public Safety System (Sistema Nacional de Seguridad Pública). The key here is to restore the capacity of penal institutions and detention centers for the authoritative control of adjudicated criminal populations of prisoners; to generate intelligence regarding criminality by means of an effective monitoring of inmates; and to eradicate corruption and criminal operations within prison walls. This theme points to the sixth axis, the fight against corruption, especially though not solely among police forces.

Technology is a seventh axis, aimed at effective inter-organizational coordination. To this end, Plataforma México (Platform Mexico) is an informatics infrastructure for public safety, an effort at creating a single national telecommunications network involving computation, command-and-control, and compatible operational communications.

Finally, performance accountability involving Civil Society is the eighth and ultimate axis, with the finality of governmental transparency and a culture of accountability. This defining emphasis in the national security sphere is considered more fully in the section that follows (see the source report at http://www.oas.org).

President Felipe Calderón and his Secretary for Public Safety together launched the previously described National Public Safety Program (Programa Nacional de Seguridad Pública 2008–2012, or PNSP), using Visión México 2030 as their point of departure, along with the National Development Plan (Plan Nacional de Desarrollo, PND), the Sectoral Public Safety Program (Programa Sectorial de Seguridad Pública, PSS, 2007–2012), the National Security, Justice, and Legality Accord (Acuerdo Nacional por la Seguridad, Justicia y la Legalidad, ANSJL), and the National Strategy for the Prevention of Crime and Combating of Delinquency (Estrategia Nacional de Prevención del Delito y Combate a la Delincuencia, ENPDyCD) as additional elements of cross-government integration. The program in its totality is intended to establish strategies, objectives, coordinating mechanisms, plans of action, and indicators and measures that guide the alignment of State capabilities and resources so as to make the fight against crime more effective.

The strategies, objectives, coordination mechanisms, and plans of action are as follows (Secretaría de Seguridad Pública. *Programa Nacional de Seguridad Pública 2008–2012*. www.ssp.gob.mx):

1. Inter-institutional coordination among the three branches of government.
2. Social participation in crime prevention, the evaluation of implemented action, and communication with and among authorities in charge of public safety.
3. The combating and sanctioning of crime and criminals by means of modernized and otherwise improved instruments to be employed in police operations.
4. Modernization of technological resources for crime prevention and crime fighting.
5. Generation of police intelligence by means of the integration and communication of crime data.
6. Implementation, across governmental branches, of the Police Career (Civil) Service (Servicio de Carrera Policial, SCP), along with necessary processes of personnel evaluation, and plans for professionalization and promotion in police careers.
7. The strengthening of the penitentiary or penal system as to its function of social reintegration.

A legal framework is established within the Political Constitution, in Article 21, the fifth and sixth paragraphs: "Public safety is a function and responsibility of the federation, the federal districts, the states and municipalities, in the respective competencies determined by the constitution. The performance of these police institutions would be managed by principles of legality, efficiency, professionalism and honesty." Proceeding further, "The federation, the federal district, the states, and the municipalities would coordinate according to these terms of law, in order to establish a national system of public safety" (all residing within the Organic Law of Federal Public Administration, the Federal Law Pertaining to the Responsibilities of Public Servants, and other legislation).

One can readily appreciate that the entirety of this institutional and legal plan with regard to National Security and Public Safety is ample, at least semantically well-constructed, complete and comprehensive. Nonetheless, this formal institutionalism is obviously insufficient in and of itself for the accomplishment of all these tasks, however well-articulated the statutes, regulations, and programs involved.

Even strategic planning is provided for, in the text of a mechanism for *Planeación Estratégica* with regard to national security, ensconced in the principles and postulates of Visión México 2030, the National Development Plan, and the National System for Democratic Planning (Sistema Nacional de Planeación Democrática, SNPD). The National Accord (ANSJL) is the most inclusive set of commitments and goals for the short- to medium-term strengthening of institutional capacities in the national security domain, part of a fundamental process of institutionalization called the "new institutionalism" (*nueva institucionalidad*). In its farthest reaches, this national scheme concerns itself with all kinds of violence, including spousal or domestic partner violence and sexual ("gender") violence.

One of the most important objectives of this entire legal–institutional framework is to directly combat pervasive crime in Mexico, and to consolidate the Rule of Law by means of effective coordination of (and shared responsibility across) the three branches of government. Such collaboration is the premise of the corresponding National Strategy (Estrategia Nacional de Prevención del Delito y Combate a la Delincuencia), part of the aforementioned National System (Sistema Nacional de Seguridad Pública). Prioritization of intergovernmental cooperation (which would seem to contradict the simultaneous emphasis on centralization and control) is a hallmark of the Calderón Presidency and of the presidential transition, since the impact of violence on states and municipalities cries out for conjoint efforts between local governments and federal jurisdictions—the Secretariats of National Defense (SEDENA), of the Navy (SEMAR), of the Procuraduría, Customs, Revenue, and every other agency previously noted. To repeat, coordination among federal agencies and between them and local governments is universally acknowledged to be essential for an effective response to crime, especially, narcotrafficking, while the further challenge is finding the right dynamic balance between centralization and decentralization, or between directive management and collaboration.

Considering these pronouncements, one would expect of these federal agencies direct and indirect coordination, and centralized and decentralized deployment, with the exercise of executive functions occurring across all levels of government, reinforced and intensified by the very process of intergovernmental implementation. Recently there has been a discussion on the part of President Enrique Peña Nieto of both this kind of coordinated action and of greater use of intelligence capacities, with the anticipation of greater agility in the political actions these require, nationally as well as internationally, for the sake of the previously noted national security objectives. These objectives require, foundationally, full normativity and legality, as exhaustively specified in law, statute, and *sui generis* programs.

In the interplay of formalism and realism, normativity and legality are tied in turn, and in practice, to transparency and accountability. Performance measurement and performance accountability would be traced by empirical data closely calibrated to the requirements of program evaluation, according to yet another declaration by the current Presidential administration at the beginning of its sexenio. Once again, a specific State organ has primary assignation for this performance-management initiative, namely the PNSP's Tracking and Evaluation System (Sistema de Seguimiento y Evaluación). This agency has as its mission the establishment of a well-grounded evaluation system, and the periodic provision of "objective, trustworthy, and timely information," as would be needed for decision-making, as well as for the definition of "privileged actions and strategies."

This "System," the just highlighted *Sistema de Seguimiento y Evaluación* (SSyE), is concerned with the following (Red de Monitoreo y Evaluación de América Latina y el Caribe, February 3, 2011, http://redlacme.org/profiles/blogs/innovacion-y-cambio):

1. Implementation of goals, indicators, and measures. Each of the indicators established under the larger Program will be subject to periodic follow-up, to ascertain their progress.
2. Results-based measurement and evaluation, again to determine progress. The viability of the Program's goals and objectives will be tested by actual results, with "optimality" sought through course-corrections as may be merited by these evaluative outcomes.

As to performance measures and program evaluation, the intent by definition is to establish baselines and corroboration of outcomes with regard to national security, and to ascertain whether there are significant discrepancies between stated objectives and actual results. The two basic functions which go to the question of governmental efficacy are (1) those of accessible, timely, and usable information and, building on it, (2) the evaluation of outcomes. Performance accountability is of course fundamental to transparency and objectivity, though itself subject to formalization. The goal is the opportune disclosure of results obtained in fact. What is becoming apparent, however, as consideration of national public opinion surveys will suggest in our conclusion, is that public participation in this regard will be essential if formal commitments are to become real attainments under this Program.

The national commitment represented by the National Security Program (Programa para la Seguridad Nacional) 2009–2012, which took as a point of departure Visión México 2030 and the National Development Plan (Plan Nacional de Desarrollo) 2007–2012, amounts to a formal institutional instrument that would guide administrative efforts to protect National Security to the benefit of the

Mexican State. This Program lays out a strategy founded on high-minded normative values reflecting the Federal Government's stated commitment to all Mexicans in support of their aspirations and hopes for a better life. Again, however, their participation in the assessment of actual accomplishments would be important to the credibility of the effort involved.

We started this analysis with the premise that what most threatens national security is organized crime, and in particular narcotrafficking and its associated violence. On the other hand, in order for there to be effective coordination and control of the structures of the National Security System (Sistema de Seguridad Nacional), the articulation of various component elements is key for concerted action in the substantive areas of decision-making, assessment, information and intelligence management, operational planning and execution, and evaluation of outcomes.

The key question, as we move in 2013 into the administration of President Peña Nieto, is to actualize the imposing aims articulated in all of the constitutive documents, plans, and programs presented here. Formal declarations and initiatives do not automatically translate themselves into real impact, even when the resources of the State have been impressively mobilized (as did President Calderón with the armed forces in the war against the cartels).

Analysis and Conclusions: What's Real?

Garcia González and Mendoza Chan (2008) refer to real advances in the struggle against organized crime, spanning a period from December 1, 2006 to July 31, 2008, revealing that the drug cartels were able to distribute almost 2000 doses of cocaine and marijuana every minute of the final 20 months of that period. At the same time, 1673 millions of doses of narcotics were seized by the government, or 1936 doses forfeited by the cartels each minute, on average. Due to escalating confiscations of marijuana alone, these criminal organizations have forfeited 238 million dollars in illicit earnings, according to the authors' estimates (based on secondary analysis of government-supplied data). (Garcia González and Mendoza Chan, 2008).

Contrasting studies suggesting different conclusions about governmental efficacy abound, as suggested previously with respect to the dismantling and reorganization of the federal Seguridad Pública and Función Pública (Public Safety/Security and Public Function) Secretariats. Collecting data from national sources, especially the National Institute of Statistics and Geography (Instituto Nacional de Estadística y Geografía), the National System of Public Safety (Sistema Nacional de Seguridad Pública), the justice ministry (Procuraduría General de Justicia), the General Information, Statistics, and Criminal Identification Directorate (Dirección General de Información, Estadística e Identificación Criminal), as well as data from international sources, such as the Encuesta Nacional de Crimen de las Naciones

Unidas (*UN Crime Survey*) and *PAHO* (Pan American Health Organization), Molzahn et al. (2012) present very negative findings as to the runaway manifestations of drug-related and nondrug-related violence:

- Violence has grown dramatically in Mexico, and in general in the hemisphere, over the last several years, adversely impacting commerce and, in particular, tourism. The murder rate in Mexico is high, 18 per 100,000 inhabitants, but lower than that of Honduras (82 per 100,000), El Salvador (66), Venezuela (49), Belize (41), Colombia (33), Bahamas (28), Brazil (22), and the U.S. Territory of Puerto Rico (26). However, the authors consider that there may be routine underreporting of these statistics in Mexico.
- More than 50,000 murders attributed to organized crime were recorded in Mexico from 2006 to the beginning of 2012, during President Felipe Calderón's sexenio, a well-documented total but one that likely underestimates the number of murders related to crime, including drug cartel crime.
- Criminal violence grew less sharply in 2011, but it managed to account for more than half of all homicides. The increment in criminal violence totaled 11% in all of 2011, much lower than the dramatic jumps in 2008 (141.9%), 2009 (40.6%), and 2010 (58.8%), but the absolute number of homicides attributed to criminal activity continued to grow. The decline in marginal rates of growth in murders from 2008 to 2011 probably owed to the spectacularly high rate of 2008, after which the course of these murders was bound to taper off.
- Such violence continues to be highly concentrated in geographic areas closely related to narcotrafficking, but it has also become generalized across the whole country, deepening the lack of public confidence in the system of national security, and intensifying the prevalent fear of insecurity.

A final evaluation of the problem here posed will turn on whether there really has been gain or loss in national security, particularly with reference to narcotrafficking and cartel-related violence, and whether the exceedingly formal legal/normative frameworks and largely centralized institutional mechanisms that correspond to these are equal to the task. Finally, it is essential to consider not only official data concerning criminality but also public perceptions about these issues; we will begin our concluding evaluative review with this last question.

As far as the Presidency of Felipe Calderón is concerned, numerous public opinion surveys have revealed that the general population has associated it with enormous increases in violence and insecurity, although these surveys also manifest a certain tentative and ambiguous recognition that his struggle against narcotrafficking and organized crime, especially the cartels, has been a serious one. And while these surveys suggest some positive movement in public opinion toward the nation's executive power, what appreciation there is for an uncompromising counterdrug campaign translates into more positive regard for the Federal Police and the Armed Forces rather than for the Presidency as such (Levy, 2009).

One such survey, administered in November 2012 by the Center for Research and Public Opinion (Centro de Estudios y de Opinión Pública, 2012), found the following: "Toward the end of the government of Felipe Calderón, the population indicated that it would remember this period for the rise in violence and insecurity (22%), as well as for engagement in combat with organized crime (18%)." This national survey also indicates, with regard to the national security theme, public appreciation for the detention of a number of narcotraffickers, expressed as a more positive attitude toward executive power, though as just qualified: "[Public attitudes improved in these ways] between January 2011 and October 2012, [such that public approval of the federal executive] went from 47 to 60 percent, [while specifically that for] the Federal Police rose to 49 percent, that of the Navy rose from 68 to 73 percent, and positive perception of the Army rose to 71 percent." These positive shifts notwithstanding, the ambiguity involved is obvious: Even though 67% of respondents voiced agreement with the way the Calderón government was combating narcotrafficking and organized crime, "… more than half believe that the effort has had little or no success (65 percent)." Finally, "a majority considers that the operational approaches taken by the President only have temporary effect and do not get to the bottom of the problem (72 percent)."

It is relevant to note that there has been not only national disapproval or misgiving about the sexenio of Felipe Calderón, but also international official criticism, in particular from the European Union, which has been patently displeased. According to Appel (2012), an EU document "estimates that the war against narcotrafficking had pernicious effects on the effort to fight inequality." Appel adds that "[Mexico's] social welfare policies have failed in proportion to the devastating impact on the Mexican social fabric wrought by the war on drugs during his sexenio."

Finally, an important survey published by the Mitofsky Consultancy (Consulta Mitofsky, 2012) concludes the following: "What is evident as a principal result is that the final approval rating of 53 percent is strictly a general one. Insecurity was the dominant issue during Calderón's government, not employment as he had posited during his campaign." The report concludes that "[f]rom 2010 to 2012, public preoccupation focuses on insecurity, not on drug addiction or drug trafficking, which we understand to mean that public discontent was focused on violence and not on the presence of drugs."

Consequently, the Mexican public sees two kinds of "insecurity": Insecurity with respect to violence and insecurity as pertains to the basic needs of the population. Although the Mexican people voice a certain appreciation for the zeal and commitment with which Calderón took on narcotrafficking in particular, it doubts the actual results obtained, and both indicators of insecurity rose significantly during his sexenio. Violence combined with uncertainty about the future, and about the possibility of providing for basic needs, is what predominates in Mexican public opinion in these connections.

Klingner (2012) concludes that "Mexico will not fail—if it has the capacity to provide for the basic needs of its population, to celebrate free and fair elections, and to exercise civilian control over the armed forces" (p. 6). Klingner goes on to say that, in Mexico, "it is essential that corruption be faced as a national scourge that impedes economic development and increases cynicism and the risks involved in having to choose between 'silver or lead' ('plata o plomo'). It means that [they face] a deleterious tendency toward centralization ... and the government's authoritarian attitude. What is required is that Mexicans think of themselves as owners of their society and government instead of as subjects of the State" (p. 7). Klingner's analysis brings together several analytical strands in this study: the primordial responsibility of the Mexican government for the welfare and well-being of its citizenry; the intimate connection between national security and public welfare; the importance of recovery of effective agency on the part of the citizenry and all levels of government, and by civil society, given the overweening centralism and authoritarianism that have in fact been manifest. In other words, the challenge for Mexico is much more complex, much more dimensional, than what one government, over-focused as it was on narcotrafficking and drug-related violence, had proposed.

The sheer distance evident between formal frameworks and reality, in the struggle for national security in Mexico, is both the problem posed and conclusion reached in this chapter. More than an issue of appearances versus actualities, it is an issue of excess formal capacity and insufficient effective capacity. The inevitable implication is that the former factor—excessive formalism—accounts to a considerable extent for the latter—inefficacy. Over-reliance on formalist bureaucratic and regulatory expressions of what is, essentially, *aspirational policy* makes for insufficient attention to the development of real capacity and effective action on the ground. It is also a matter of the inadequacy of strategies chosen and tactics implemented, concerns acknowledged by the new Mexican president.

The reality of divided government under the new administration (a well-known phenomenon in executive–legislative relations in the United States today) may have the indirect and salutary effect of limiting over-centralization (as well as its corollary, authoritarianism) in the current sexenio, while necessitating a much more consultative inter-branch approach to national security and public safety. The Peña Nieto administration has demonstrated its ability to work with the National Congress (Congreso de la Unión) in the most recent "ordinary legislative session" (*período ordinario de sesiones*) begun February 2013, in the aforementioned reorganization of the Secretaría de Seguridad Pública (now subsumed under the Secretaría de Gobernación) and the creation of a National Anti-Corruption Commission (Comisión Nacional Anticorrupción) to succeed the Secretaría de la Función Pública (numerous news reports, e.g., http://www.debate.com.mx/eldebate/movil/Articulomovil.asp?IdArt=12830885&IdCat=6103).

President Enrique Peña Nieto insists that he will attack insecurity, violence, and narcotrafficking with greater intelligence (literally, and with reference to much better use of the State's intelligence agencies). He will undertake this effort, he adds, more adroitly than was done in the past, with better coordination with neighboring countries, particularly the United States (while restoring Mexican control over the process of collaboration, instead of yielding as much as did his predecessor to the DEA, CIA, and so on). If these changes are obtained, Mexico will develop greater adaptive capacity and exercise greater initiative with regard to national security, broadly defined. Taking into account all that has been considered in this chapter, this may be just what the nation needs.

References

Appel, M. 2012. La ineficacia de las políticas sociales en Mexico. *Revista Proceso*, 16 November 2012. Available: http://www.proceso.com.mx/?p=325417.

Becerra, O. 2008. Fighting back: México declares war on drug cartels. *Jane's Intelligence Review*, April 1, 2008. Available: www.janes.com.

Boletín Conjunto, entre PGR, SEGOB, SEDENA, SEMAR y SSP. January 2, 2011, Available: http://www.pgr.gob.mx/prensa/2007/bol11/Ene/b00211.shtm.

Centro de estudios y de opinión pública, LXII Legislatura-Cámara de Diputados, Tendencias predominantes en estudio de opinión. November 2012. Available: www.diputados.gob.mx/cesop.

Centro de Investigación y Seguridad Nacional (CISEN—reportes). 2008. Available: www.cisen.gob.mx.

Constitución Política de los Estados Unidos Mexicanos. *Diario Oficial de la Federación el 5 de febrero de 1917 (última reforma aplicada 05/04/2004)*. Available: http://www.biblioteca.jus.gov.ar/Constitucion-MEXICO.pdf.

Consulta Mitofsky. 2012. *The Poll Reference*. Available: http://consulta.mx/web/index.php/estudios/evaluacion-gobierno/96-felipe-calderon-2.

García González, S. and A. F. Mendoza Chan 2008. Cronología de América del Norte (agosto-diciembre de 2008). *Norteamérica*, 4(1), January-June 2009. Available: http://journals.unam.mx/index.php/nam/article/viewFile/15439/14684.

González Turnbull, A. 2005. Reflexiones sobre la inseguridad en México. *Revista Razón y Palabra*. June–July 2004. Available: http://www.razonypalabra.org.mx/anteriores/n39/agonzalez.html.

Herrera, A. 2009. Apuntes en torno a las fuerzas armadas y el sector de la seguridad y la defensa en México: La Coyuntura Actual y los Escenarios Futuros. Available: http://www.resdal.org/jovenes/apuntes-ffaa-herrera.pdf.

Instituto de Investigaciones Júridicas. 2013. Información Jurídica, Legislación Federal (Vigente al 22 de julio de 2013). *Ley Orgánica del Ejército y Fuerza Aérea Mexicanos.* Biblioteca Jurídica Virtual, Universidad Nacional Autónoma de México (UNAM). Available: http://info4.juridicas.unam.mx/ijure/fed/228/default.htm?s=

Klingner, D. 2012. La perfecta tormenta del narcotráfico en la zona fronteriza de México y los Estados Unidos: una no reconocida oportunidad para fortalecer la capacidad de la Gobernanza, Paper presented at the *XVII CLAD Congress (Congreso Internacional del CLAD sobre la Reforma del Estado y de la Administración Pública)*, Cartagena, Colombia, November 1, 2012.

Levy, C. 2009. Crisis y retos de la política exterior de México: 2006–2012. *Revista Mexicana de Ciencias Políticas Sociales*, LI(205), January–April 2009, 119–141. Universidad Nacional Autónoma de México. Mexico. Available: http://redalyc.uaemex.mx/pdf/421/42112421007.pdf.

Ley de Seguridad Nacional. *Diario Oficial de la Federación*. 31 January 2005. Available: http://www.ordenjuridico.gob.mx/Federal/Combo/L-65.pdf.

Ley de Seguridad Nacional. *Diario Oficial de la Federación*. 29 November 2006. Available: http://www.ordenjuridico.gob.mx/Documentos/Federal/wo41147.pdf.

Moloeznik, M. 2007. Militarización de la Seguridad Pública, Autonomía de la Fuerzas Armadas e Imperativo de la Reforma Militar en México. *El Cotidiano*, November–December, 22(146), Universidad Autónoma Metropolitana. México, DF. Available: http://redalyc.uaemex.mx/pdf/325/32514612.pdf.

Molzahn, C., V. Ríos, and D. Shirk. 2012. Drug violence in Mexico: Data and analysis through 2011, Justice in Mexico Project of the Trans-Border Institute, Joan B. Kroc School of Peace Studies, University of San Diego, *March 2012 Special Report*, Available: www.sandiego.edu/tbi y el TBI Justice in Mexico Project (www.justiceinmexico.org).

Plan de Desarrollo. 2007–2012. Available: http://pnd.calderon.presidencia.gob.mx/eje1/defensa-de-la-soberania-y-de-la-integridad-del-territorio.html.

Procuraduría General de la República (reportes). Available: http://www.pgr.gob.mx.

Programa para la Seguridad Nacional (2009–2012, reportes). Available: http://www.cofemermir.gob.mx/uploadtests/18081.59.59.2.PROGRAMA%20PARA%20LA%20SEGURIDAD%20NACIONAL%202009%202012.pdf.

Red de Monitoreo y Evaluación de América Latina y el Caribe. 2011. Innovación y cambio paradigmático en el sistema de seguimiento y evaluación (M&E) de las políticas públicas: El caso del CONEVAL-México, febrero 3, 2011. Available: http://redlacme.org/profiles/blogs/innovacion-y-cambio.

Rodríguez Sánchez Lara, G. 2009. *Seguridad Nacional en México, Evaluación a dos años de gobierno del Presidente Calderón*. Available: http://www.fundacionpreciado.org.mx/biencomun/bc168/G_Rodriguez.pdf.

Rojas Aravena, F. 2007. Crimen y Violencia en las Américas FLACSO. Prepared for the *Inter-American Dialogue/Focal Meeting on Inter-American Institutions*, October 12, 2007. Available: http://www.thedialogue.org/PublicationFiles/Crime%20and%20Violence%20-%20Rojas.pdf.

Secretaría de la Defensa Nacional (reportes). Available:
http://www.sedena.gob.mx/index.php/conoce-la-sedena/mision.
http://www.sedena.gob.mx/index.php/conoce-la-sedena/atribuciones.
http://www.sedena.gob.mx/index.php/actividades/combate-al-narcotrafico/3272-marihuana.
http://www.sedena.gob.mx/index.php/actividades/combate-al-narcotrafico/3273-cocaina.

Secretaría de Seguridad Pública. March 7, 2007. *Estrategia Integral de Prevención del Delito y Combate a la Delincuencia*. Available online at: http://www.oas.org/dsp/documentos/politicas_publicas/mexico_estrategia.pdf.

Secretaría de Seguridad Pública. *Programa Nacional de Seguridad Pública 2008–2012*. Available: http://www.ssp.gob.mx/portalWebApp/ShowBinary?nodeId=/BEA%20Repository/414002//archivo.

Secretariado Ejecutivo del Sistema Nacional de Seguridad Publica (reportes). Available: http://www.secretariadoejecutivosnsp.gob.mx/.
Seguridad Nacional (reportes). Available: www.cisen.gob.mx/espanol/seg_seguridad_nal.htm.
Villareal, Gabriel M. 2009. Seguridad Nacional: Un concepto ampliado y complejo. Cámara de Diputados, LX Legislatura. July 2009. Available: http://www.diputados.gob.mx/cedia/sia/spe/SPE-ISS-13-09.pdf.

Other Webpages Consulted

http://www.juridicas.unam.mx/publica/librev/rev/rap/cont/98/pr/pr9.pdf
http://www.seguridadcondemocracia.org/oco-im/
http://mexico.cnn.com/mundo/2011/02/10/eu-la-capacidad-militar-de-mexico-es-insuficiente-contra-el-narcotrafico
http://sdpnoticias.com/nota/15757/Narco_mexicano_representa_amenaza_terrorista_EU
http://www.agenciaapp.com/home/lea-lo-relevante-en/politica/la-situacion-de-la-seguridad-nacional-en-mexico
http://www.vanguardia.com.mx/amenaza_del_narco,_equiparable_al_terrorismo:_eu-670697.html
http://www.fundacionpreciado.org.mx/biencomun/bc173/C_Castano.pdf
http://noticias.universia.net.mx/en-portada/noticia/2011/01/13/779512/guerra-contra-narco-soluciones-corto-plazo-expertos.html

Chapter 8

Critically Low Hispanic College Graduation Rates and a Clear Absence of Hispanic High-Level Administrators in Arizona, California, and Texas

Ramona Ortega-Liston and RaJade M. Berry-James

Contents

Introduction 120
Theoretical Underpinnings 121
A Review of Narcotics Trafficking Literature..124
Restating Research Questions in the Context of U.S.–Mexico
Drug Trafficking 126
    Educational Attainment by Hispanics..126
    Population and Employment Demographics for the State of Arizona...........127
    Population and Employment Demographics for the State of California 131
Return on Investment 132
    Importance of Early Career Challenges, Management Trainee Programs,
    Education, and Mentoring to Job Success 134

Mentoring Influences on Careers 135
Hispanics in Mentoring Relationships 135
Conclusions 136
Future Studies 137
References 138

Introduction

The war on drugs in the United States and Mexico affects the economy, import/export relations, socio-political climates, and the safety and welfare of Americans and Mexican nationals (Klingner, 2000; Ledwith, 2000; Klingner and Pallavicini Campos, 2002; Finckenauer et al., 2007; Duran-Martinez et al., 2010; Jeszeck, 2011; Bjelopera and Finklea, 2012; Luce, 2012; Molzahn et al., 2012). The war on drugs may also affect rapidly growing trade relations between the two countries. Luce (2012) reported that "Mexico is rapidly becoming as important to the US economy as China" (*Financial Times*). Differing headline perspectives indicate that crime has increased in border states (Fox News, 2010; Jeszeck, 2011), but contrasting media views suggest that there is a drop in the rate of illegal crossings and deaths from trying to cross unforgiving desert terrain (Wagner, 2010; Associated Press, 2013); however, no-one suggests that the war on drugs is over or should be discontinued. These important issues will be explored in some detail.

This chapter examines what the war on drugs means for Hispanics residing in border states. U.S. Census information and demographic statistics show that Latino/Hispanics are the largest ethnic group in the United States, with large numbers of them living in border states. Census demographics show that in 2011 Hispanics numbered 52 million, and they also have been the fastest growing, increasing by 3.1% since 2010. This population growth propelled the Latino population to 16.7% in 2011—up from 16.3% in 2010 (United States Census Bureau, 2012). Increases in the Latino population are due largely to the proximity of Mexico to the southern border of the United States. Arizona, California, and Texas are border states that are most impacted by border issues, including illegal immigration and drug trafficking—among many others. To combat border state issues such as drug trafficking and illegal immigration, the budget for the U.S. Border Patrol has increased from $262,647, in 1990, to $3,549,295 in 2011 (U.S. Border Patrol Statistics). The significant increase in the budget underscores the seriousness of issues confronting border states.

Clarification of Terminology:

- Latinos and Hispanics are terms used interchangeably to mean all Spanish-surnamed individuals or individuals who have been identified and categorized as "Hispanic" in U.S. Census and government reports (U.S. Census, 2012).

- Officials and managers (a single category) and professionals are the two top occupational categories in the Equal Employment Opportunity Commission's (EEOC) employment categories. Both categories are upper management and executive—decision-making positions.

Theoretical Underpinnings

Theoretical underpinnings for this chapter are representative bureaucracy, affirmative action, and cultural competence. The war on drugs suggests a need for a more representative bureaucracy, affirmative action, and cultural competence in border state governments—at state and local levels. The concept and practice of representative bureaucracy, originally introduced by Kingsley (1944), gaining prominence in the United States with Krislov's (1974) publication of *Representative Bureaucracy*, suggests that it makes common sense, and it is morally responsible, to proportionally staff public bureaucracies with people who reside in communities, and who look like the people they are serving.

Both Kingsley (1944) and Krislov (1974) suggested that public sector agencies, to be more representative of the people, must move toward a more representative bureaucracy throughout every public sector agency. The primary role and place of representative bureaucracy in any system of public service, according to Kingsley (1944), is that "Bureaucracies to be democratic must be representative of the groups they serve" (p. 305). Similarly, Krislov (1974) espoused the view that diverse social groups should have spokesmen and office holders in *administrative* (italics added) and political positions. He further articulated "A major task of governance is to gain support for policies. No matter how brilliantly conceived, no matter how artfully contrived, government action usually also requires societal support. And one of the oldest methods of securing such support is to draw a wide segment of society into the government to convey and to merchandise a policy ..." (1974, p. 330). If Latinos are not employed in decision-making, policy making, and program implementation, they cannot contribute to policy merchandizing.

Building on the foundation laid by Kingsley (1944), Krislov (1974) focused primarily on Blacks in American society. He argued cogently that how Americans solve the "problem of Black participation in power ..." (1974, p. 331) impacts American self-image—here and abroad. The same thoughtful consideration must be given to identifying and implementing proactive personnel hiring measures to include greater numbers of Latino/Hispanics in decision-making positions in border state cities and towns. These ideas also have been propounded by Kaufman (2012) who said, "One type of proposal for making administrative agencies more representative is traditional in character; situating spokesmen for the interest affected in strategic positions within the organizations" (p. 266). The concern for broader representation of diverse groups of people within state, local, and federal bureaucracies has been at the top of the national agenda for decades and continues today. Research specifically focusing on the under-representation of Mexican Americans in public sector employment can be found in the career advancement and affirmative action literature. In a survey distributed among city employees in Phoenix and Tucson, Arizona, Ortega (1999, 2001) concluded that Mexican Americans were under-represented in upper-management positions in two key border states.

Mosher (1968), too, suggested that fresh new ideas must emanate from employees who come from different levels of social strata, including specific ethnic groups affected and served by public service agencies. Fresh ideas, originating from freshly trained officials and local bureaucrats, also have been suggested by Serrano (2012) who believes that training and hiring new people with new ideas may help stamp out police and judicial corruption. More to the point of representative bureaucracy, Rhys et al. (2005) opine that organizations will perform better when the respective workforces reflect characteristics of constituent populations. In our view, bureaucracies having primary responsibilities for finding solutions to border problems require that these same bureaucracies hire people who are ready to offer fresh ideas, and fresh new solutions, to intractable problems.

Another approach to representative bureaucracy involves cultural competence. Representative bureaucracy, affirmative action, and cultural competence walk hand-in-hand. Public servants, if they are to address constituent issues, must be culturally competent to do so. In Ospina's view (1996), there are many benefits to having an ethnically and culturally diverse public service, including: ethical benefits, legal and public policy benefits, human resource (HR) management benefits, and organizational benefits, supporting the assertion that work force diversity makes good management sense all around (p. 444). Ospina's (1996) point-of-view is shared by Berry-James (2010) who suggests that "Managing diversity, like acquiring diversity, becomes a priority only when internal and external pressures for organizational change are evident. One of the assumptions of racism theory has been that ... organizations seek to hire minorities and women only when there has been a threat of a legal challenge" (p. 73). Border state governments should not wait until there has been a legal challenge to the under-representation of Latinos in public sector services.

The thesis of this chapter, therefore, is that in order to meet obligations imposed by theories of representative bureaucracy, affirmative action, and cultural competence we must educate and train greater numbers of Latino/Hispanics as administrative professionals. Failing to do so will mean that the United States will lack the administrative capacity to effectively, and representatively, fill important leadership and decision-making positions. It is becoming increasingly more important to representatively hire new employees in open positions in Immigration and Naturalization Services (INS), Border Patrol (BP), local police and sheriff's departments, and any of the myriad public agencies currently combatting illegal immigration and drug trafficking in border states.

If Latino/Hispanics are not trained in the efficient, effective, responsive, and responsible delivery of critically important public goods and services, how can we expect to tap into their perspectives and special knowledge of social and political challenges facing state and local governments, especially those faced by border states? As educators, we must teach Latino/Hispanics in professional data collection methods, effective approaches to engage in mutually beneficial negotiations, such as those needed to affect border state issues, including trade relations, illegal immigration, and drug trafficking—as well as the ethical delivery of public goods and services. To this end, Berry-James (2010) argues that, "For several years now, some racial/ethnic and gender groups with limited opportunities for educational and occupational mobility have significantly benefited from equal employment and affirmative action policies, programs and practices. One of the most profound benefits of affirmative action is that many educational institutions and organizations, while acting 'affirmatively' have created seemingly diverse environments that provide channels that expand educational and professional opportunities for racial/ethnic minorities and women, and over the long run, enhance social mobility for these groups as well" (p. 61). If we do not recruit and retain Latino/Hispanics in our colleges and universities, then the country loses the opportunity to add skilled, well-educated, administrators to meet the needs of public service agencies, and border states will lack the administrative capacity to solve problems.

One approach to solving diminished administrative capacity within state and federal government is to invest in human capital and measure the rate of return on investment (ROI). Over the past several decades, there has been a significant investment in the education and training of the public sector workforce. Similarly, public service agencies have implemented strategies to address the practical and social implications of training a diverse workforce. While it may be difficult to measure the exact return on diversity investment in the public sector, social benefits should positively correlate with performance and behavioral changes among affinity groups in the workforce. Yet, when examining human service agencies, Hyde and Hopkins (2004) found that management and staff were mostly White and women and often lacked a sustainable diversity management plan. Smith and Joseph (2010) point out that "it is expected that human capital investments would lead to higher returns in terms of organizational access, promotions, compensation, and equitable treatment" (p. 749). Yet, Smith and Joseph (2010) also note that "prior research has demonstrated that women and minorities do not get the same career return on their human capital investments as do majority group members with the same level of human capital investment" (p. 749).

Other areas of importance—affirmative action and the potential for administrative evil—must be included in our discussion. Both relate to theories of representative bureaucracy and ROI. Affirmative action, according to Klingner and Campos (2002) "… emerged to represent social equity through voluntary or court-mandated recruitment and selection practices. It was supported by the fundamental beliefs that a proportionately representative bureaucracy was essential for our government to function as a democracy …" (p. 351). Simply stated, democracy and the rule of law require that public service agencies be composed of a diverse group of employees—at all levels of the bureaucracy.

Diverse minority groups should not be found only at the bottom of the employment hierarchy. They should be found at upper levels where important decisions are made. Berry-James (2010) suggests that "Where an organization stands depends on its ability to attract and retain diverse employees to remain competitive and effective. Organizations that have difficulty attracting minorities and women through job announcements, job fairs, and word of mouth will also experience limited success in recruiting minorities and women into the organization. That said, organizations that experience problems in attracting and maintaining diversity will probably be unable to manage diversity as well" (p. 70). Recruiting, retaining, and promoting diverse employees from under-represented groups go to the heart of affirmative action policies and programs.

The second area that needs to be included in this discussion concerns administrative evil, a term coined by Adams and Balfour (2012), and is germane to discussions of representative bureaucracy. Adams and Balfour (2012) argue, "When administrative evil can be unmasked, no public servant should be able to rest easy with the notion that ethical behavior is defined by doing things the right way. Norms of legality, efficiency, and effectiveness—however 'professional' they may be—do not necessarily promote or protect the well-being of individuals, especially that of society's most vulnerable members, whose numbers are growing in the turbulent years of the early twenty-first century" (p. 601). We take this to mean that concepts of efficiency and effectiveness, albeit key to public service, must not be the only measures where vulnerable populations are concerned—particularly when working with Spanish-speaking and Spanish-surnamed immigrants who may be caught up in drug trafficking—innocent or not.

In other words, careful attention must be given to providing needed services, and services must be delivered ethically and responsibly. One way to help curb temptations to abuse vulnerable populations is to make sure that they are being served by people who have insight and influence in their affinity group. Ethnic group representation needs to be part and parcel of recruiting new employees to prevent the possibility of administrative evil—all the while enhancing and improving representative bureaucracy. Long ago, Rivlin (1971) suggested, "As a necessary first step to more effective services, all kinds of people should be encouraged to try out new ways of delivering services" (p. 306). In sum, Latinos residing in border communities should be encouraged to add their ideas to important trade policies and programs that cope with narcotics trafficking in border states. In the next section, we turn to a review of the narcotics trafficking literature.

A Review of Narcotics Trafficking Literature

Research shows that organized crime has become more complex and poses a myriad of challenges for U.S. federal law enforcement. Mexican traffickers carry out their illegal business professionally, effectively, efficiently, and with proven ability to widen their capacity for continuous operations. Organized cartels hire lawyers and accountants and utilize high technology to help them with their illegal operations. In *Mexico and the United States: Neighbors Confront Drug Trafficking*, Finckenauer et al. (2007) articulate that annual incomes of crime organizations figure in the tens of billions of dollars. By way of comparison, they estimate that the entire country of Mexico had a nominal gross domestic product (GDP) of $557 billion in recent years. In sum, financial incentives are enormous for drug cartels to continue illegal operations.

Because drug trafficking has become a billion dollar business, money laundering has become a necessity. In their article *Organized Crime: An Evolving Challenge for U.S. Law Enforcement*, Bjelopera and Finklea (2012) reported "Making ill-gotten gains appear legitimate is critical to the success of organized criminals. For many criminals, the movement of money—either as bulk cash or digital transactions—across international borders plays an integral role in this process. They use many techniques to launder money, often exploiting legitimate financial structures to mask the illegal origins of their profits" (p. 9). They also reported that the United States suffers from two directions—those operating abroad adroitly exploit U.S. banking structures to launder money while domestic operations launder illegal profits abroad in an effort to avoid prosecution by U.S. law enforcement.

In his testimony to the U.S. House of Representatives, in hearings before the subcommittee on Criminal Justice, Drug Policy, and Human Resources, Ledwith (2000) testified that even though drug lords are well-known to major law enforcement agencies in Mexico and the United States, they skillfully avoid arrest and extradition. Analyses of drug violence in Mexico documented by the Trans-Border Institute (TBI) concluded, in part, that:

- U.S.–Mexico counter-drug collaboration remains strong, with room for improvement. Nearly $2 billion in U.S. aid to help fund Mexican and Central American counter-narcotics initiatives has boosted regional cooperation. However, numerous human rights violations have surfaced in Mexico, while U.S. investigations allowed guns and cash to flow into the hands of organized crime groups in Mexico. Greater oversight and coordination are needed, as well as a clear commitment to bilateral cooperation beyond the 2012 presidential elections.
- Mexico urgently needs to implement police and judicial sector reforms. To the extent that the federal government has previously relied on large force deployments to restore order in areas where violence is highly concentrated, the tendency toward widely dispersed, mass violence presents a significant challenge. The authors recommend a greater focus of resources and attention to the challenges of local police reform, state-level judicial reforms, and penitentiary reform at all levels (Duran-Martinez et al., 2010).

We agree with the TBI authors that greater collaboration and greater attention to police reform (policies and practices), state-level judicial reforms, and local incarceration and penitentiary reforms are needed. The TBI report (2012) also suggests that there is a need to reevaluate strategies that prioritize success in counter-drug efforts over the basic security of ordinary citizens. They further recommend that in view of the growing "… criticism of the war on drugs, and increasing public support for drug legalization, both countries should work with other partners in the international community to examine the potential costs, benefits, and public health implications of legal drug consumption" (p. 29). It is time to reevaluate U.S. strategies implemented to combat the war on drugs to determine if accepted practices, policies, and programs that are currently in place are working.

Relevant new questions have become: From where will new ideas and new personnel come? Who will write new perspectives, new policies, new reforms, and new procedures? Who will conduct the requisite evaluations of programs, policies, and procedures? In the United States, perhaps it is time to review the need for the professional development, education, and training of the next generation of Latino leaders who may help combat the war on drugs—before it is too late. These questions bring us full-circle to the two research questions that will be explored in this chapter.

Restating Research Questions in the Context of U.S.–Mexico Drug Trafficking

This research asks two questions: (1) Are Hispanics graduating from colleges at comparable rates as Whites and Blacks, and (2) are Hispanics employed in management positions within border state governments? To answer these questions, college graduation rates and EEO employment demographics from the States of Arizona, California, and Texas are examined. These states are proximal to "ground zero" for drug trafficking and illegal immigration and provide data supporting our concern that there is a crisis in college graduation rates of Hispanics. If we are not educating Latinos for public service, then the United States is leaving untapped a significant group of young people, and mid-level managers, who may offer culturally competent, professional advice to help combat illegal immigration and drug cartel problems.

Educational Attainment by Hispanics

Are Hispanics graduating from colleges and universities at the same rates as Whites and Blacks? Table 8.1 illustrates differences among the number of degrees conferred by race/ethnicity and gender. Even though they are the largest ethnic minority group in the United States, the figures show that Hispanics lag behind Whites and Blacks at all levels of college degrees: bachelor's, master's, and doctoral degrees. Between the two ethnic groups—Blacks and Hispanics—Latino/Hispanics also lag behind.

Table 8.1 Degrees Conferred by Sex and Race/Ethnicity

	Educational Attainment		
	Bachelor's	Master's	Doctoral
Men	573,079	211,381 (41%)	24,341 (53%)
Women	775,424	301,264 (59%)	21,683 (47%)
White, Non-Hispanic	943,745 (70%)	309,055 (60%)	25,863 (56%)
Hispanic	84,333 (6%)	22,560 (4%)	1457 (3%)
Black	117,774 (9%)	40,046 (8%)	2362 (5%)

Source: Adapted from U.S. Department of Education, National Center for Education Statistics, 2007; Adapted from U.S. Department of Education, National Center for Education Statistics. 2012. The Condition of Education 2012 (NCES 2012-045), Indicator 47. http://nces.ed.gov/fastfacts/display.asp?id=72; Adapted from U.S. Department of Education, National Center for Education Statistics. (2011). Digest of Education Statistics, 2010 (NCES 2011-015), Chapter 3. http://nces.ed.gov/fastfacts/display.asp?id=61.

These figures show that Whites earned 70% of all bachelor's degrees, while Latino/Hispanics and Blacks earned significantly fewer bachelor's degrees with only 6% and 9%, respectively. The table also shows that with respect to gender, men earned 41% of all master's degrees and women earned 59%. Looking at master's degrees, 60% were awarded to Whites while 4% and 8% were awarded to Hispanics and Blacks, respectively. Men also outstripped women and ethnic minorities by earning 53% of all doctoral degrees, while women earned 47%. Among those earning doctoral degrees, Whites earned 56% of all doctoral degrees, Hispanics and Blacks have been conferred with significantly fewer doctoral degrees earning only 3% and 5%, respectively. Latino/Hispanics lag behind the numbers of Blacks earning doctorates.

Population and Employment Demographics for the State of Arizona

Table 8.2 shows 2012 U.S. Census information for the State of Arizona. Hispanics comprise 30% of the population in Arizona, and Blacks total 4%. In the City of Phoenix, Arizona's largest city, the Hispanic population is 41% and 8% are Black. Latino/Hispanics are the dominant minority group in Arizona's border cities—largely because of the proximity to Mexico.

In the City of Tucson, Arizona's second largest city, the population is 42% Hispanic and 6% Black. In Maricopa County, where Phoenix is located, the population is 30% Hispanic and 6% Black. In Pima County, where Tucson is located, the population is 35% Hispanic, 5% Black. This table shows that Hispanics are the

Table 8.2 Arizona

	Total Population	Total Hispanic	Total Black
Arizona	6,392,017	1,895,149 (30%)	259,008 (4%)
Phoenix	1,445,632	589,877 (41%)	109,544 (8%)
Tucson	520,116	216,308 (42%)	32,361 (6%)
Maricopa County	3,817,117	1,128,714 (30%)	229,981 (6%)
Pima County	980,263	338,802 (35%)	44,332 (5%)

Source: Adapted from U.S. Census Bureau, 2010 Demographic Highlights: Arizona. http://www.census.gov/2010census/popmap/ipmtext.php?fl=06.

dominant population throughout Arizona. In the next section, college graduation rates are compared to public sector employment in border states where Latino/Hispanic populations are the largest.

In prior tables, as well as the following tables, for Arizona, Texas, and California it is evident that Latino/Hispanics are the dominant minority group; however, even though they are the dominant minority group, the data show that they hold fewer jobs in the Equal Employment Opportunity Commission's (EEOC) top management category, officials and managers, then Whites and Blacks. They also hold the fewest number of positions in the second highest EEOC professionals category. Table 8.3 illustrates Arizona employment figures for EEOC's two highest level occupations, officials and managers and professionals.

Table 8.3 shows that White men in Arizona hold 16% of the positions in the top management category—officials and managers, while another 20% hold positions in the second highest category—professionals. Out of all working White women in

Table 8.3 Arizona

	Occupation		
	Total Employment	Officials and Managers	Professionals
White men	274,576	42,753 (16%)	54,007 (20%)
White women	250,881	25,240 (10%)	55,083 (22%)
Hispanic men	115,450	6055 (5%)	5836 (5%)
Hispanic women	87,862	3481 (4%)	6567 (7%)
Black men	22,459	1525 (7%)	2255 (10%)
Black women	21,013	1193 (6%)	2856 (14%)

Source: Adapted from United States Equal Employment Opportunity Commission, 2006. 2006 EEO-1 AGGREGATE REPORT Arizona: http://www.eeoc.gov/eeoc/statistics/employment/jobpat-eeo1/2006/state/4.html.

Arizona, 10% hold positions as officials and managers, while 22% hold positions as professionals. Combining figures for White men and White women, Table 8.3 shows that 68% hold the majority of white-collar jobs in the highest level EEOC categories—officials and managers and professionals.

Out of all working Hispanic men in Arizona, 5% hold positions as officials and managers, while 5% hold positions as professionals. Out of all working Hispanic women in Arizona, 4% hold positions as officials and managers, while 7% hold positions as professionals. Combining Hispanic men and women, Table 8.3 shows that only 21% hold positions in the categories of officials and managers and professionals. In the State of Arizona, Black men hold 7% of the jobs in the category of officials and managers, while 10% hold positions as professionals. Out of all working Black women in Arizona, 6% hold positions as officials and managers, while 14% hold positions as professionals. Combining the figures for Black men and Black women, Table 8.3 shows that 37% of Blacks hold positions in the combined top categories of officials and managers and professionals.

These figures suggest there is a need to educate, recruit, retain, and promote Latino/Hispanics to assume positions in the highest level categories of officials and managers and professionals. Clearly, Latino/Hispanics are not garnering their fair share of professional—leadership positions in the State of Arizona.

Table 8.4 presents population demographics for the State of Texas.

It shows that Latino/Hispanics are the largest ethnic population in the State of Texas. In the State of Texas, the population is comprised of 37% Hispanics, 12% Black, and the rest are White, Asian, and other groups. In cities like San Antonio, closer to the Mexican border, the population is 59% Hispanic and 6% Black. Table 8.5 shows ethnic distributions of Whites, Blacks, and Hispanics in Texas employment in the top two EEOC categories, officials/managers and professionals.

Table 8.5 shows the same pattern of under-employment in high-level employment positions remains constant in the state of Texas for Latino/Hispanics in the officials/managers and professionals categories. These figures are similar to those found in the state of Arizona where Latino/Hispanics clearly lag behind all other groups in the top EEOC employment categories even though they are the largest ethnic group. This lack of Latino/Hispanic representation demonstrates that

Table 8.4 Texas

	State and City Population Figures		
	Total Population	Total Hispanic	Total Black
Texas	24,311,891	8,917,477 (37%)	2,864,666 (12%)
San Antonio	1,359,758	805,870 (59%)	87,301 (6%)

Source: Adapted from U.S. Census Bureau, Census 2010 Demographic Highlights: Texas.

Table 8.5 Texas

	Occupation		
	Total Employment	Officials and Managers	Professionals
White men	1,004,058	195,289 (19%)	218,003 (22%)
White women	748,096	87,109 (12%)	175,408 (23%)
Hispanic men	524,384	32,272 (6%)	28,273 (5%)
Hispanic women	397,430	17,332 (4%)	30,853 (8%)
Black men	225,828	14,270 (6%)	16,967 (8%)
Black women	272,715	12,396 (5%)	31,706 (12%)

Source: Adapted from United States Equal Employment Opportunity Commission, 2006.

there is a concomitant lack of representative bureaucracy in the states of Arizona and Texas.

Table 8.5 shows that, in Texas, White men fill 19% of all positions within the officials and managers category and another 22% fill professional positions, while 12% of White women fill officials and manager senior management positions and another 23% of them are categorized as professionals. Combining figures for White men and White women, these figures show that 76% of White men and White women hold the majority of officials/managers and professional positions. Out of all working Black men in Texas, 6% hold positions as officials and managers while 8% hold positions in the professional category. The same figures show that out of all working Black women in Texas, 5% hold positions as officials and managers while another 12% hold positions as professionals. Combining Black men and women, these figures show that 31% of all Blacks hold positions as officials and managers and professionals.

Figures for Hispanic men indicate 6% hold positions as officials and managers, and another 5% are in the professional category. Out of all working Hispanic women in Texas, 4% hold positions as officials and managers, while 8% hold positions in the professional category. Combining Table 8.5 figures for Hispanic men and women, these figures show only 23% of all Hispanics in the state of Texas hold positions within the officials/managers and professionals categories. These figures show that the same pattern that was found in Arizona also is true for Texas—Latino/Hispanics fall dramatically behind in all management positions even though they are the largest ethnic minority group in each state. Now, we will examine population and employment demographics for the state of California. Table 8.6 illustrates population demographics for the state of California.

Table 8.6 California

	State and City Population Figures		
	Total Population	Total Hispanic	Total Black
California	36,637,290	13,456,157 (37%)	2,580,672 (7%)
San Diego	1,307,402	376,020 (29%)	87,949 (7%)
National City	58,582	36,911 (63%)	3024 (5%)

Source: Adapted from U.S. Census Bureau, Census 2010, Demographic Highlights: California. http://www.census.gov/acs/www/Downloads/data_documentation/pums/Estimates/pums_estimates06-10.lst.

Population and Employment Demographics for the State of California

Table 8.6 shows population demographics for the state of California. Similar to the population in Arizona and Texas, Latino/Hispanics are the dominant ethnic group in California.

Because the state of California borders Mexico, it is not surprising that Latinos are the largest minority group in the state. Table 8.6 shows that Hispanics comprise 37% of the state's population, and Blacks comprise 7% of the population. The remainder of the population consists of Whites, Asians, and other groups. In the City of San Diego, a major metropolitan city close to the Mexican border, the population is 29% Hispanic, 7% Black, and the remainder are White, Asian, and other groups. A city even closer to the Mexican border than San Diego is the City of National City, California. It is located only 5 miles south of downtown San Diego, and 10 miles north of Baja California, Mexico. National City's population is 58,582 and is made up of 63% Hispanics—Mexican Americans and Mexican nationals are the dominant group (City of National City, 2010). The closer a city is to the Mexican border, the larger the population of Latinos/Hispanics, and the more likely that drug trafficking issues will rise to the top of local agendas. Table 8.7 presents a picture of where Hispanics residing in California are likely to be found in EEOC official occupational categories: officials/managers and professionals.

EEOC employment figures for the state of California show that 20% of working White men in California hold positions as officials and managers, and another 24% hold positions in the professional category. Out of all working White women in California, 13% hold positions as officials and managers, and 25% hold positions as professionals. Out of all working Hispanic men in California, 6% hold positions as officials and managers while 5% hold positions as professionals. Out of all working Hispanic women in California, 4% hold positions as officials and managers, and 7% hold positions as professionals. Out

Table 8.7 California

	Occupation		
	Total Employment	Officials and Managers	Professionals
White men	1,164,171	236,435 (20%)	274,995 (24%)
White women	958,031	129,278 (13%)	240,875 (25%)
Hispanic men	800,679	45,153 (6%)	36,662 (5%)
Hispanic women	577,205	24,411 (4%)	42,563 (7%)
Black men	169,491	13,255 (8%)	16,310 (9%)
Black women	176,464	11,652 (7%)	25,259 (14%)

Source: Adapted from United States Equal Employment Opportunity Commission, 2006.

of all working Black men in California, 8% hold positions as officials and managers, and 9% hold positions as professionals. Out of all working Black women in California, 7% hold positions as officials and managers while 14% hold positions as professionals. Combining both management categories, officials/managers and professionals, it is clear that White men and women dominate the California work force (82%), and Blacks hold more positions in both categories (38%) than do the dominant ethnic minority—Hispanics. Combining Hispanic men and women in both categories shows that Hispanics hold only 22% of jobs within the EEOC top-level employment categories of officials and managers and professionals.

Population and employment figures for the state of California reveal that even though Hispanics are the dominant ethnic population (37%), they are not proportionally represented in state bureaucracies. Only 22% of all Hispanic women and men are employed in the top EEOC categories of officials and managers and professionals. An examination of figures for Blacks in the State of California indicates that they are 7% of the population, but have garnered 38% of all jobs in the top two EEOC categories.

Return on Investment

There is a strong link between investments in human capital and economic growth. The rate of ROIs in education may be costly but will pay off over time as employees become more efficient, more effective, and even more productive. Arellamo and Fullerton (2005) point out that "widespread international recognition exists for the positive correlation between education and income, recognizing that education leads to improved human capital" (p. 242). In Table 8.8, comparative measures

Table 8.8 Comparative Economic Statistics for Mexico and the United States

	Year	Mexico	United States
Gross domestic product (GDP)[a]	2011	$1.667 trillion	$15.080 trillion
Education expenditures (% of GDP)	2007	4.80%	5.50%
Unemployment (15–24 labor age)	2009	10%	17.6%
Population growth rate (estimate/1000)	2012	1.86%	.90%
Distribution of family income (Gini Index)	2008/2007	51.7	45.0
Population below poverty	2010	51.3%	15.1%

Source: Adapted from Central Intelligence Agency 2012. *The World Factbook for Mexico and United States*. Retrieved from https://www.cia.gov/library/publications/the-world-factbook/.

[a] Purchasing Power Parity.

show educational and economic indicators for Mexico and the United States, the two countries significantly affected by illicit drug trafficking. The table shows the gross domestic product (GDP) in the United States is more than 10 times that of Mexico. At first glance, educational expenses between the two countries seem comparable. However, when we consider trillions in GDP differences and inequity in family income, we begin to understand the impoverished conditions of Mexico. Mexico's population living below poverty level is more than three times greater than those living below poverty in the United States. Nonetheless, both countries struggle equally with the persistent issues of supply and demand for illicit drugs manufactured in Mexico and smuggled into the United States.

Thinking about how we invest in human capital makes good economic sense for both countries. Training and developing future employees who have the requisite knowledge, skills, abilities, attitudes, and awareness to competently address complex societal challenges produce long-term economic benefits for each country. In the United States, many public agencies under the auspices of the Office of Personnel Management (OPM) continue to rely on effective human capital practices to recruit a diverse workforce that reflects America's society, create an inclusive workplace that embraces all Federal employees and sustain efforts to institutionalize diversity and inclusion in compliance with Executive Order 13171 (U.S. Office of Personnel Management, 2011).

Some of the most effective human capital practices to recruit, retain, and promote Hispanic leaders throughout the public sector can be found in American public agencies. In recent years, the Federal Trade Commission (FTC) conducted community outreach with Hispanic professional associations and hired Hispanic liaison specialists to increase agency awareness within the Hispanic community. The Federal Bureau of Investigation (FBI) as part of the Department of Justice (DOJ) also created an Honors Internship Program to recruit outstanding Hispanic students to intern with the FBI. The Department of Agriculture (USDA) created a Hispanic-serving Institution (HSI) Liaison Officer Program to strategically recruit graduates from the top colleges and universities awarding degrees to Hispanics in Florida, New Mexico, Texas, and California and to create internship opportunities for Hispanic students. Within the Hispanic workforce, OPM also promoted the Federal Executive Institute and Management Development Centers as an effective approach to train and diversify leaders in the public sector. While each one of these programs can position an agency to recruit, train, and retain a skilled diverse workforce, the most effective strategy for Federal departments and agencies is the approach that holds leaders and managers accountable for creating an inclusive environment and rewards them through the performance management system (U.S. Office of Personnel Management, 2006).

The drug conflict in Mexican–U.S. border threatens important university collaborations and halts longstanding student exchange programs. In 2010, for example, a local chapter of Engineers Without Borders at New Mexico State University was unable to finish building a water well because the U.S. State Department issued a travel advisory warning for Mexican borders states (Boulard, 2010). In the interest of safety, Boulard (2010) reported that the University Texas system, the Michigan State University, the University of Wisconsin at Eau Claire, and Northwestern University also halted student exchange programs amidst the growing threat of violence. For those living and working in border states, the threat of violence is immediate. In Texas, the Department of Public Safety (2013) in collaboration with law enforcement and homeland security agencies identified the Mexican cartel as the number one crime threat to Texans. The Texas Department of Public Safety acknowledges that their ability to "share information, intelligence, and capabilities to effectively address public safety threats" is paramount to protecting citizens from transnational threats of drug trafficking and other illegal activities (Texas Public Safety Threat Overview, 2013, p. 7). Universities and governments have been collaborating for several decades, but the rise of transnational threats has intensified the need for strategic partnerships that extend beyond traditional outreach and recruitment activities. From education to job promotion, our ability to transform the government workforce into an inclusive environment for the Hispanic community will result in an efficient and effective way to address the transnational threats.

Importance of Early Career Challenges, Management Trainee Programs, Education, and Mentoring to Job Success

An early longitudinal study of Bell System employees (Howard and Bray, 1988) found that challenging assignments offered *early* in a male's career results in later job success. Rosenbaum (1979) also found that managers receiving early promotions are more likely to reach mid-management positions within 13 years. Similarly, Sheridan and colleagues (1990) confirm the importance of entering a company through a management trainee program and beginning a job in departments perceived as "powerful." Management trainee programs and being part of powerful departments enhance chances for upward career mobility. The Bell System study also confirms the importance of education to job promotion.

Mentoring Influences on Careers

Roche (1979) and Knouse et al. (1992) examine the relationship of mentoring to career advancement. A "mentor" is an individual who is usually older and established in an organization. Mentors provide younger employees with advice, counseling, coaching, social support, serve as sponsors, and provide entry to top management. The career of the protégé/protégée or "mentee" is enhanced because he or she becomes identified with a respected member of the corporation (Collins, 1983; Fagenson, 1988; Ragins, 1989; Forbes and Piercy, 1991; Knouse et al., 1992). A mentor may recommend the mentee for promotion or identify opportunities leading to promotion. Results of Roche's (1979) study of upper-level managers underscore the role mentors can play. Managers in the study reported having one or more mentors helped their careers.

Hispanics in Mentoring Relationships

A study that looks specifically at Hispanics in mentoring relationships is "The Mentoring Process for Hispanics," Knouse et al. (1992). The study describes advantages and disadvantages of Hispanics serving as mentors for other Hispanics. Also described are advantages and disadvantages of Anglos serving as mentors for Hispanics.

One advantage of Hispanics mentoring other Hispanics is cultural identification. Awareness of special needs, serving as role models, and assisting in socialization processes are other advantages. A disadvantage is Hispanic mentors are perceived as less powerful—having only recently made it into top-management positions. New managers have less influence and prestige to share. Upper-level Hispanics are also inundated with requests to mentor—a disadvantage to Hispanics who need them.

Advantages of Anglo/Hispanic mentoring relationships include the perception that Anglos are more powerful; Anglo managers socialize newcomers by modeling accepted behavior; and Anglo executives have a network of high-profile friends to share. Disadvantages involve difficulty in relating to Hispanic employees and initiating mentoring relationships. Companies with Hispanic mentoring programs are AT&T, Johnson & Johnson, Merrill Lynch, Federal Express, and the Ore-Ida company. The FBI and the Internal Revenue Service (IRS) also have formal Hispanic mentoring programs (Knouse et al., 1992).

Knouse and colleagues describe successful mentoring programs as those having "well-defined and communicated goals, commitment of mentors, and continuous monitoring and adjustment of the program" (p. 145). Once a program begins, mentors should be trained in how to mentor Hispanics. Second, program implementers should know that, given the scarcity of Hispanic mentors and disadvantages associated with Anglo/Hispanic mentoring relationships, identifying mentor alternates is essential for program longevity. Knouse et al. suggest the need for formal Hispanic mentoring programs will increase as more Hispanics enter white-collar positions.

Conclusions

Hispanics are the largest ethnic group in the United States and graduating them from colleges and universities must become a national priority. A well-educated workforce is an efficient and effective way of meeting narcotrafficking challenges currently facing border states. It is also a way to add Latino voices to important trade discussions between the United States and Mexico. This research posed two questions: (1) Are Hispanics graduating from colleges at comparable rates as Whites and Blacks? (2) Are Latino/Hispanics employed in management positions within border state governments where they can make a difference in policies and programs?

Throughout this chapter, the thesis has been that the United States must place a high priority on educating, training, and graduating Latinos from colleges and universities if they are to take their rightful places in public service agencies responsible for securing U.S. borders. This study examined college graduation rates of Whites, Blacks, and Latinos. It also examined employment figures in Arizona, Texas, and California for the two highest EEOC categories, (1) officials and managers and (2) professionals to determine where Whites, Blacks, and Latinos are employed within border state governments. Comparisons were made to determine if Hispanics are garnering a proportional share of high-level positions within state bureaucracies.

U.S. Census, education, and employment figures provide ample documentation illustrating that Hispanics are not graduating from colleges at the same rate as the two comparison groups, and they are not proportionately represented in high-level administrative positions in any of the three states. Latinos, therefore, are not representatively filling decision-making positions important to their social, political, and economic security. This also means that border state governments are losing the opportunity to tap into Latino perspectives on critically important issues such as drug trafficking, illegal immigration, and newly emerging U.S./Mexico trade issues.

The data show that theories of representative bureaucracy are not working for Latinos in Arizona, Texas, and California. This may be attributable, in part, to a failure to educate, recruit, and train Latino/Hispanics to prepare them for administrative positions. This, in turn, means that the United States lacks the administrative capacity to effectively place Latinos in leadership and decision-making positions. If Latino/Hispanics are not trained in the efficient, effective, responsive, and responsible delivery of critically important public goods and services, how can we expect to tap into their perspectives and special knowledge of social and political issues? The data show that the states of Arizona, Texas, and California have not hired a proportionally representative number of Latinos in top-level executive positions. If obligations mandated by theories of representative bureaucracy are to be fulfilled, then the United States must accept the responsibility of educating, recruiting, and training greater numbers of Latino/Hispanics for the public service. Research on the return on diversity investment in public service is essential if we are to account for the strong link between education, employment, and improvement in human capital. The ability of the public sector to recruit, train, and retain a cultural and experiential public sector workforce yields positive benefits for the public good. The formal mentoring of Hispanics sets the stage to retain and promote Hispanics into leadership positions.

Future Studies

U.S. Census facts and figures illustrate that Latino/Hispanics are the new majority minority in the United States. Future studies may seek to examine population demographics and EEOC employment statistics for other American states having high numbers of Latino/Hispanics in the population such as Florida, New York, New Mexico, Colorado, and Nevada to determine if there is a national trend toward under-education and concomitant under-employment of Latino/Hispanics in executive, that is, decision-making, positions throughout the United States. It is important that we learn more about the growing Latino population, especially where important decisions are made that impact the economic future and welfare and safety of the country's largest minority population—one that is still growing.

Another area for future research may lie in the realm of comparing progress, successes, and EEOC differences made by groups like the National Association for the Advancement of Colored People (NAACP). Latinos may be able to use the best practices of the NAACP as models to help them gain needed advancements in the public service, especially in border state government employment where they are the largest minority population. Latinos have cultural organizations in place such as the League of Latin American Citizens (LULAC) and the National Council of La Raza. Researchers may identify ways in which these organizations may benefit from examining successful NAACP practices to help shape future policies and programs important to Latino populations. Both future studies we have proposed may result in greater numbers of Hispanics taking their rightful—representational—places in American bureaucracies. Only then can we say that Latinos have benefitted from ideas espoused by early proponents of representative bureaucracy.

References

Adams, G. and Balfour, D. 2012. Unmasking administrative evil. In: J. Shafritz and A. Hyde (Eds.), *Classics of Public Administration*. Boston: Wadsworth Cengage, pp. 598–609.

Associated Press. 2013. Illegal immigrant identities pose challenge for large Arizona border morgue. Retrieved from http://www.foxnews.com/us/2013/03/07/at-arizona-border-morgue-bodies-keep-coming-despite-drop-in-illegal-traffic/.

Arellamo, A. and Fullerton, T. 2005. Educational attainment of regional economic performance in Mexico. *International Advances in Economic Research*, 11, 231–242.

Berry-James, R. M. 2010. Managing diversity: Moving beyond organizational conflict. In: M. E. Rice (Ed.), *Diversity and Public Administration: Theory, Issues, and Perspectives*. New York: M. E. Sharpe, pp. 61–80.

Bjelopera, J. P. and Finklea, K. 2012. Organized crime: An evolving challenge for U.S. law enforcement. *In Congressional Research Service Report for Congress*. CRS, 7–5700. Retrieved from www.crs.gov (R41547).

Boulard, G. 2010. Mexican drug conflict threatens U.S. college study abroad programs. *Diverse Issues in Higher Education*. Retrieved at www.diverseeducation.com/article.14180/.

Central Intelligence Agency. 2012. *The World Factbook for Mexico and United States*. Retrieved from https://www.cia.gov/library/publications/the-world-factbook/.

City of National City. 2010. Retrieved from http://www.ci.national-city.ca.us/.

Collins, N. 1983. *Professional Women and their Managers*. Englewood Cliffs, NJ: Prentice-Hall.

Duran-Martínez, A., Hazard, G., and Ríos, V. 2010. *2010 Mid-Year Report on Drug Violence in Mexico: A Justice in Mexico Project*. Trans-Border Institute, University of San Diego.

Fagenson, E. A. 1988. The power of a mentor: Protégés' and non-protégés' perceptions of their own power in organizations. *Group and Organizational Studies*, 13, 182–194.

Finckenauer, J. O., Fuentes, J. R., and Ward, G. L. 2007, December 6. Mexico and the United States: Neighbors confronting drug trafficking. *United Nations Activities. NJI Publication*. Retrieved from https://www.ncjrs.gov/pdffiles1/nij/218561.pdf.

Forbes, B. J. and Piercy, J. E. 1991. *Corporate Mobility and Paths to the Top*. New York: Quorum Books.

Fox News. 2010. *Border States Deal With More Illegal Immigrant Crime than Most Data Suggest*. Retrieved from http://www.foxnews.com/politics/2010/04/29/border-states-deal-with-more-illegal-immigrant-crime-than-most-data-suggest.

Howard, A. and Bray, D. W. (eds.) 1988. *Academy of Management Review*. New York, NY: Gilford.

Hyde, A. C. and Hopkins, A. 2004. Diversity climates in human service agencies. *Journal of Ethnic and Cultural Diversity in Social Work*, 13(2), 25–43.

Jeszeck, C. 2011. *Criminal Alien Statistics: Information on Incarcerations, Arrests, and Costs*. Retrieved from http://www.gao.gov/products/GAO-11-187.

Kaufman, H. 2012. Administrative decentralization and political power. In: J. M. Shafritz and A. C. Hyde (eds.), *Classics of Public Administration*. Boston: Wadsworth Cengage, pp. 264–276.

Kingsley, D. 1944. *Representative Bureaucracy*. Yellow Springs, OH: Antioch Press.

Klingner, D. 2000. South of the Border—Progress and problems in implementing new public management reforms in Mexico today. *American Review of Public Administration*, 30(4), 365–373.

Klingner, D. and Pallavicini Campos, V. 2002. Building public HRM capacity in Latin America and the Caribbean: What works and what doesn't. *Public Organization Review, 2*, 349–364.

Knouse, S. B., Rosenfeld, P., and Culbertson, A. L. (eds.). 1992. *Hispanics in the Workplace*. Newbury Park, CA: Sage Publications.

Krislov, S. 1974. Representative bureaucracy. In: J. M. Shafritz and A. C. Hyde (Eds.), *Classics of Public Administration*. Boston, MA: Wadsworth Cengage, pp. 328–332.

Ledwith, W. E. 2000. Testimony to the U.S. House of Representatives. Hearings before The Subcommittee on Criminal Justice, Drug Policy, and Human Resources, of the House Committee on Government Reform, *U.S./Mexico Counternarcotics Efforts*; 106 Congress, 2nd Session 2000. Retrieved from http://www.gao.gov/archive/1998/ns98129t.pdf.

Luce, E. 2012. Mexico is forgotten story of US election. *The Financial Times Limited*. Retrieved from http://mexicoinstitute.wordpress.com/2012/10/15/mexico-is-forgotten-story-of-us-election/.

Molzahn, C., Rios, V., and Shirk, D. 2012, March. *Drug Violence in Mexico: Data and Analysis through 2011. A Special Report*. San Diego, CA: Trans-Border Institute, University of San Diego.

Mosher, F. C. 1968/1982. *Democracy and the Public Service*. New York: Oxford University Press.

Ortega, R. 1999. Affirmative action policies and workplace discrimination: Perceived effects on the careers of Mexican Americans in municipal administration. *Review of Public Personnel Administration, 6*(3), 49–57.

Ortega, R. 2001. Mexican American professionals in municipal administration: Do they really lag behind in terms of education, seniority, and on-the-job-training? *Public Personnel Management, 30*(2), 197–210.

Ospina, S. 1996. Realizing the promise of diversity. In: J. L. Perry (Ed.), *Handbook of Public Administration*. San Francisco: Jossey-Bass, pp. 441–459.

Ragins, B. R. 1989. Barriers to mentoring: The female manager's dilemma. *Human Relations, 42*, 1–22.

Rhys, A., Boyne, G., Meier, K., O'Toole, L., and Walker, R. 2005. Representative bureaucracy, organizational strategy, and public service performance: An empirical analysis of English local government. *Journal of Public Administration Research and Theory, 15*(4), 489–504.

Rivlin, A. 1971. Systematic thinking for social action. In: J. M. Shafritz and A. C. Hyde (eds.), *Classics of Public Administration*. Boston: Wadsworth Cengage, pp. 306–316.

Roche, G. R. 1979. Much ado about mentors. *Harvard Business Review, 57*(1), 14–28.

Rosenbaum, J. E. 1979. Tournament mobility: Career patterns in a corporation. *Administrative Science Quarterly, 24*, 220–241.

Rosenbaum, J. E. 1984. *Career Mobility in a Corporate Hierarchy*. Orlando, FL: Academic Press.

Serrano, M. 2012. *Justice in Mexico: U.S. Anti-Drug Policy Transitions away from Military Funding, toward Justice Reform*. Retrieved from: http://justiceinmexico.org/2012/09/19/u-s-anti-drug-policy-transitions-away-from-military-funding-toward-justice-reform/.

Sheridan, J. E., Slocum, J. W., Buda, R., and Thompson, R. 1990. Effects of corporate sponsorship and departmental power on career tournaments. *Academy of Management Journal, 33*, 578–602.

Smith, J. W. and Joseph, S. E. 2010. Workplace challenges in corporate America: Differences in black and white. *Equality, Diversity and Inclusion: An International Journal, 29*(8), 743–765.

Texas Department of Public Safety. 2013. *Texas Public Safety Threat Overview*. Retrieved from http://www.txdps.state.tx.us/director_staff/media_and_communications/threatoverview.pdf.

United States Equal Employment Opportunity Commission 2006. 2006 EEO-1 AGGREGATE REPORT Arizona: http://www.eeoc.gov/eeoc/statistics/employment/jobpat-eeo1/2006/state/4.html.

United States Office of Personnel Management. 2006. *Fifth Annual Report on Hispanic Employment in the Federal Government*. Washington, DC. Retrieved from http://www.opm.gov/policy-data-oversight/diversity-and-inclusion/reports/hispanic_feb2006.pdf.

United States Office of Personnel Management. 2011. *Government-Wide Diversity and Inclusion Strategic Plan*. Washington, DC. Retrieved from http://www.opm.gov/policy-data-oversight/diversity-and-inclusion/reports/governmentwidedistrategicplan.pdf.

U.S. Border Patrol Statistics. Retrieved from http://www.cbp.gov/xp/cgov/border_security/border_patrol/usb.

U.S. Census Bureau. 2010. Demographic Highlights: Arizona. http://www.census.gov/2010 census/popmap/ipmtext.php?fl=06.

U.S. Department of Education, National Center for Education Statistics. 2007.

U.S. Department of Education, National Center for Education Statistics. 2011. Digest of Education Statistics, 2010 (NCES 2011-015), Chapter 3. http://nces.ed.gov/fastfacts/display.asp?id=61.

U.S. Department of Education, National Center for Education Statistics. 2012. The Condition of Education 2012 (NCES 2012-045), Indicator 47. http://nces.ed.gov/fastfacts/display.asp?id=72.

Wagner, D. 2010. Violence is not up on Arizona border despite Mexican drug war—Mexico crime flares, but here, only flickers. *The Arizona Republic*. Retrieved from http://www.azcentral.com/news/articles/2010/05/02/20100502arizona-border-violence-mexico.html.

Chapter 9

The Frontier of Knowledge
Between Life and Death

Adriana Plasencia Diaz

Contents

Introduction 141
¡Vámonos pal Norti! (Let's Go North!) 142
A Team of Rivals 145
Mexican Federalism and Its Consequences for the Border Region 146
Education on the Line 149
Are We All Juárez? 154
Conclusion 157
References 159

Introduction

Thinking about the border from within the Mexican heartland does not do justice to this region's potentialities in a global context. In reality, this area has become the focus of great opportunities to boost regional development and to make Mexican federalism a reality. This is because the border region epitomizes two critical conceptual variables—unity and diversity, sovereignty and autonomy (Plasencia, 2010).

The purpose of this chapter is to recognize some indicators for assessing educational achievement in states situated along the northern border of the country. Determining the current educational level of the region will allow us to take advantage of the "perfect storm" represented by drug trafficking to recommend changes in primary (and other levels of) education in order to promote the scientific, technological, and cultural development of that region. In addition, we will assess the effectiveness of a strategy designed during President Calderón's administration (i.e., "Todos Somos Juárez" [TSJ], or "We all are Juárez") to improve educational achievement in one of the most dynamic and lively municipalities of the northern frontier by moving it under the control of the national government. We will use two conceptual variables—that is, the continuum between unity and diversity, and the one between autonomy and sovereignty—to evaluate the effectiveness of the TSJ strategy to mitigate the conditions of underdevelopment and insecurity that affect the City of Juárez.

¡Vámonos pal Norti! (Let's Go North!)

During the nineteenth century, Mexico's northern frontier was seen as an inhospitable place, distant from Mexico City and isolated from the rapid growth that was occurring in the United States. Meanwhile, Mexico responded to American expansionism—notably the independence of Texas and its subsequent admission to U.S. statehood—by initiating a war against the "great country" in 1847 (Davies, 1972). The disastrous effects of this war and the subsequent Treaty of Guadalupe-Hidalgo resulted in Mexico ceding vast amounts of territory (i.e., what is now California, Arizona, New Mexico, Colorado and Texas) to the United States. They also contributed to the creation of a collective image of the United States in which the "gringo" was despised and despicable. Also, the road to the north, though fascinating for some, was primarily viewed as leading to a barbaric country.

Considered historically, the borders in the world are zones of confrontation between countries, political institutions, cultures, belief systems, and people. In the case of Mexico, the infamous boundary between Mexico and the United States separates development from underdevelopment, order from disorder, legality from illegality, and functionality from dysfunctionality. The population located on the Mexican side of the border considers itself threatened and discriminated against by the "giant neighbor." Also, people in Mexico City and other urban areas in the central highlands of Mexico tend to devaluate and belittle them, categorizing them as "chicanos, ayankados, pochos, cholos and chundos." Under these conditions, it is not surprising that residents of border area cities like Tijuana, Ensenada, and Mexicali in Northern Baja California do not share the same patriotic vision as those who live in the rest of the country. Why should they? They are isolated from the rest of Mexico, forced to cross into the United States in order to reach the mainland of their own country on the east side of the Sea of Cortes. Their local brands, local clothing, local customs, and local attitudes mark their isolation from the rest of Mexico. Is it any wonder that other Mexicans consider them "ayankado" (i.e., exotic, related to "Yankees")? (Gamio, 1991, 1993).

Despite this mixed view of the border and those Mexicans who live along it, the reality is that Mexicans have always moved back and forth across the border as a personal response to comparative politics. While the U.S. census of 1910 reported a foreign population of about 100,000 people across the country, it also reported that about 250,000 Mexicans lived there (McCaa, 1993). By 1920, the figure had almost doubled to 486,000 Mexicans; and by 1930, one of every 10 foreigners in the country was a Mexican (De la Peña, 1950) and our migration to North America had only been limited by the critical economic conditions in that country (Alba et al., 2010).

By contrast, the economic contraction represented by the Great Depression of 1929 in the United States led that country to "repatriate" 300,000 migrants to Mexico (Carreras Velasco, 1974). The era of Prohibition in the United States caused a shift of the centers of production and distribution of liquor south across the Mexican border, which caused the relocation of other businesses such as brothels, casinos, gambling, and other illegal activities. But northern Mexico also became an industrial development area linked with U.S. capital markets, industrial production, and supplies of precious metals and other raw materials. During both World Wars I and II, Mexico and the border region in particular became the supply center of agriculture, livestock, and timber. Mexican labor was needed to exploit the agricultural and pastoral areas of the southern United States, and to build the railroads that continue to mobilize people and goods throughout the region (Aboites, 2010).

Railroad construction was critical to the growth of cities like Monterrey, where people took advantage of both changing market conditions and their proximity to the border to redesign the city's industrial plant and invest in education so that they could offer competitive goods and services in U.S. markets. Northern businessmen and politicians soon gained national influence. That wave of prosperity required skilled labor and reliable employees, domestic and foreign alike. Between 1870 and 1910, the northern population grew faster than in any other region of Mexico, as seen well in Table 9.1. In the north, the employment picture was characterized mainly by the great demand for labor, shortage of labor and, consequently, for higher wages (Aboites, 2010). Thanks to this growth, urban areas (e.g., Lerdo, Gómez Palacio, Ensenada, Torreon, Mexicali, San Luis Rio Colorado, Nogales, Cananea, Tijuana, Madero, Cuauhtémoc, and Los Mochis) became and remain important to economic growth in this region. Later other cities such as Reynosa, Matamoros, and Ciudad Juárez were included in this process.

Currently, the importance of the northern border area of the country is undeniable. It is the beginning and the end of the country, and an area vitally concerned with national and public security. The U.S.–Mexico border is the one with the largest number of legal crossings in the world, with 50.23 million pedestrian crossings since 2002. It is also the site of the most illegal border crossings in the world (Cornelius, 2008), with almost 12 million in 2007 (NIH, 2008). About 250 deaths are reported along the border each year. Most are Mexican, followed by those from Central and South America, the Caribbean, and Asia (NIH, 2008). But despite the long history of regional migration and regional economic development represented

Table 9.1 Population Distribution by Regions, 1870–1930

Year	North	South	North-Center	Center
1870	12.2	14.7	31.5	41.5
1890	13.7	13.9	30.0	42.4
1910	16.5	13.9	26.4	43.1
1930	17.5	14.0	23.4	45

Source: Adapted from McCaa, R. 1993. El poblamiento del México decimonónico: Escrutinio crítico de un siglo censurado. In: J. Gómez de León Cruces y C. R. Romero (Eds.). *El Poblamiento de México. Una Visión Histórico-Demográfica.* Colegio de México. México, Vol. III, pp. 33–77. Table 1; Inegi-Inah, 1990: I, Table 1.2.

Note: North, south, north-center, and center refer to the regions that integrate the Mexican states located in those regions.

by the border region, and in spite of its importance to a range of "intermestic" issues between the United States and Mexico, it is still considered mainly from the limited perspective of migration.

Thus, despite the unbalanced nature of Mexican federalism (i.e., the fact that both Mexico's northern and southern borders have been forgotten and discriminated against), the northern border has regained its place in the national agenda on its own merits and through the capacity of its people, and because of the strategic significance of the international context in which it operates, particularly since the signing of NAFTA in 1994. It is true that because the boundary delimits the political and territorial boundary between the United States and Mexico (Emerich, 2013), people on one side of the line are Mexicans and those on the other are Americans.

Yet despite inflammatory political rhetoric and the existence of anti-immigrant groups like the Minute Men in Arizona and other states along the border, people along the border live and work together in the course of their daily lives. In 2003, the U.S. Census Bureau reported that Latinos were the largest minority group in the United States (Kincannon, 2008). The Latino population grew nearly 60% from 1990 to 2000, adding more than 12 million people to the "American family." Currently, there are over 40 million Latinos in the United States; this figure is projected to increase from 47 to 133 million people between 2008 and 2050, representing an increase from 15% to 30% of the total U.S. population (Kincannon, 2008) (Figure 9.1).

The Mexican side of the border has experienced rapid population growth, even greater than that observed throughout the Republic and comparable only to that in Mexico's metropolitan areas during their periods of greatest expansion. This is a result of a high birth rate—especially during the 1960s—as well as of internal migration (Corona, 1991). Additionally, at least until the recent U.S. recession that began in 2008, Mexican migration to the United States was the largest bilateral migration nexus of the world (Castles and Miller, 1998; Ramírez Ceballos, 2001).

■ Series 1

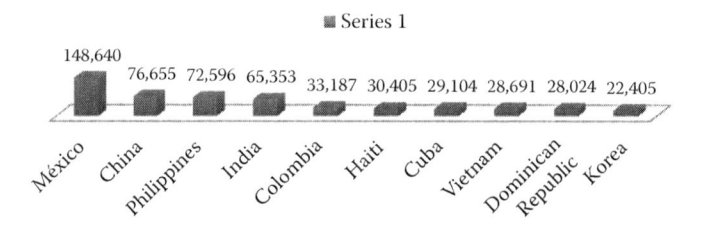

148,640 — México
76,655 — China
72,596 — Philippines
65,353 — India
33,187 — Colombia
30,405 — Haiti
29,104 — Cuba
28,691 — Vietnam
28,024 — Dominican Republic
22,405 — Korea

Figure 9.1 Flow of permanent legal residents by country of birth. (Adapted from the U.S. Department of Homeland Security, Computer Linked Application Information Management System (CLAIMS), Legal Immigrant Data, 2007.)

There is no contemporary stream between two countries as large and as long as the Mexican historical tradition (Tuirán and Avila, 2010; Gibson and Jung, 2006).

Durand and Massey suggest that every 20 or 22 years, the pendulum swings in politics and migration patterns result in "… opening the border and recruiting on one hand, and partial closure of the border, border control and deportation on the other" (Durand and Massey, 2003). This approach led to three identifiable phases of migration between 1942 and the present: the Bracero Program (1942–1964), the prevalence of illegal immigration (1965–1986), and the Reform Act and the Immigration Control (1987–present), characterized by a marked concern for U.S. national security.

A Team of Rivals

The border between the United States and Mexico extends more than 3100 km (2000 miles) from the Gulf of Mexico to the Pacific Ocean and 100 km (62.5 miles) on each side of the international boundary. The region includes large deserts, mountain ranges, rivers, wetlands, estuaries, and shared aquifers. The region has a variety of climatic zones and a remarkable biodiversity, including many rare and endemic species, national parks, and protected areas.

During the past 20 years, the border population has grown rapidly to more than 11.8 million inhabitants, of whom 6.5 million live on the American side and 5.5 on the Mexican side. It is estimated that this will increase to 19.4 million by 2020 (Inmigration National Statistics, 2008). Rapid population growth in urban areas has resulted in unplanned development, greater demand for land and power, increasing roadway congestion, increased waste generation, treatment and disposal infrastructure being overburdened or unavailable, and increased incidence of environmental contamination. Residents of rural areas suffer from exposure to dust, pesticide use, insufficient water supply, and lack of infrastructure for waste treatment. The border residents suffer significantly from other environmental health problems, including diseases caused by water pollution and respiratory problems (Environmental Program: Mexico–United States, 2012). Also, the indigenous peoples inhabiting the border area share common problems such as illegal dumping, discharge of agricultural wastes, and degradation of natural resources and ecosystems (SEMARNAT, 2012). Native American tribes are recognized by the federal government of the United States and seven Mexican indigenous groups: Papago, Kikapúes, Cochimí, Cocopah, Kiliwa, Kumiai, and Pai Pai, according to the National Indian Institute (SEMARNAT, 2012).

While its people share natural resources like air and water, the border region is marked by several contrasts, particularly in socioeconomic terms. Ninety percent of the border population resides in 14 interdependent pairs of "sister cities," so-called because they share municipal-level agreements designed to strengthen ties, deepen understanding between their communities and therefore knowledge between nations, and bring them closer together in cultural, social, and economic terms. While it is true that the border region shares historical, cultural, social, and even family ties, the economic, scientific or technological development of these "sister cities" has been asymmetric. Though the Mexican side of the border region is marked by many contrasts, the sister cities on the Mexican side of the border share one common characteristic—they are less developed than their U.S. counterparts. The five states and 35 municipalities along the Mexican border zone have recorded significant growth, but this has not been reflected equally in the levels of prosperity in the area. Growth has exceeded the management and governance capabilities of state and local governments having a dramatic impact on the lives of its inhabitants (Table 9.2).

Mexican Federalism and Its Consequences for the Border Region

Unlike its U.S. counterpart, Mexican federalism (Leví, 1985) is distinguished by a "disconnect" between the shared authority stipulated by the Mexican constitution and national laws and the tendency toward political and administrative centralism that is embedded in Mexico's political culture. The country's vast geography and the lack of an active nongovernmental network of community-based organizations have led to the centralization of power, emphasizing the debate about the powers that correspond to each level of government. Mexico is thus entering the twenty-first century with an emergent democracy marked by political and electoral competition. But the basic institutional design (Caminal, 2002) in which we have been working for more than 90 years is no longer an effective mechanism for mobilizing consensus and building government capacity. The institutional design presuming the existence of a single nation, a homogeneous population, a single political tradition, and even a single religious tradition corresponds to an idealized historical and social reality, not to current circumstances (Monsiváis, 2000).

In the Mexican case, federalism was built from the top down. The omnipotent, omniscient, and omnipresent national government hindered the development in practice of other levels of government and community-based organizations. This explains the

Table 9.2 Sister Cities in Mexico and the United States

México	The United States
Tijuana	San Diego
Mexicali	Calexico
San Luis Río Colorado	Yuma
Nogales	Nogales
Naco	Naco
Agua Prieta	Douglas
Puerto Palomas	Columbus
Ciudad Juárez	El Paso
Ojinaga	Presidio
Ciudad Acuña	Del Rio
Piedras Negras	Eagle Pass
Nuevo Laredo	Laredo
Rio Bravo	Weslaco
Reynosa	McAllen
Matamoros	Brownsville

Source: Developed by the author based on Castro Castro, L. J. 1994. Programa de 100 Ciudades: Una Estrategia de Desarrollo Urbano Regional Sustentable y Concertado. Available online at: http://148.206.107.15/biblioteca_digital/capitulos/270-4153cxx.pdf. Accessed March 17, 2013.

institutional weakness (Blanco and Gomá, 2003) of the five states along the northern border. The institutional weakness of Mexican municipalities can be largely explained by the institutional design of Mexican federalism, under which key decisions affecting people in remote areas were made by the President. Hence, there was a failure to strengthen state and local governments by developing their managerial, technical and political capacity, professionalizing public servants, or strengthening public policy networks (Cabrero, 1999). As things now stand, the governments of the five border states and their corresponding municipalities face specific problems relating to health, education, and social development with funds mainly from federal grants (SHCP, 2012), so their ability to define or direct the application of these resources is also limited.

The lack of a legal structure and institutional design that could strengthen states and municipalities plays a significant role in the political and administrative underdevelopment of these levels of government. While municipal government should be the foundation on which Mexican government capacity is built, it does not have the reputation or resources to support this performance expectation. Mexicans perceive local government as an extension of national politics and political structures, and view it as highly corrupt and either ineffective or minimally effective in terms of management capability and public service delivery (Editorial, 2003; Merino, 2013).

In 1983, during the administration of President Miguel de la Madrid Hurtado, the national government reformed Article 115 of the Constitution to spark the radical transformation of municipalities so that they might assume new roles as stewards of urban and social development, choosing to define a municipality with sufficient autonomy and capacity of its own. Previously, since the revolutionary period a century ago, mayors functioned as intermediaries between the people and the governors, solving local problems control through patronage, the discretionary allocation of public resources and favors or privileges to certain social sectors. There are numerous accounts in the literature (Revueltas, 1944; Valadés, 1955) and film (Estrada, 1999) that exemplify how life developed under this model of municipal governance. This meant that service as a mayor was widely regarded as a testing ground for potential governors. But under a strongly centralized administrative system, both mayors and governors functioned as local or regional political bosses ("caciques"). Their accountability was only upward to the president and the dominant political party, not to the public. They were responsible for everything and nothing, managing public finances in their desk drawers, dispensing funds to meet local needs and solidify political support, and staffing state and local governments through a corrupt system of political and personal patronage.

The demographic revolution of the late 1960s led to urbanization throughout Mexico, with urban areas growing significantly. Since 1970, Mexico has largely become an urban country: while it still has 280 municipalities with fewer than 10,000 inhabitants, it has 55 cities with over 1 million inhabitants. Therefore, local governments require a major transformation to provide basic infrastructure services. The central government developed the "100 Cities Program," which includes practically all border towns, to provide basic infrastructure in these areas (Castro, 1994).

A series of federal legislative reform measures from 1983 to the end of the last century elevated the legal status and rights of municipalities in Mexico. However, while municipalities now have greater autonomy, they still lack the resources or the institutional capacity required to address urban growth, public safety, and other issues (Merino, 2013). The development of communities along the Mexican side of the border is the natural result of attracting a migrant population that chooses to settle near the border because it is unable to cross to the "other side."

With increasing migration and population growth, the border municipalities are unable to provide basic services to their people. Since they lack sufficient financial resources, municipalities nationwide, mainly urban, resort to public borrowing. Currently, state and municipal debt has increased to 396 billion pesos. Of this total, 44 billion pesos is owed by 22 municipalities, including some of the cities along the border (Merino, 2013). On the other hand, the current tax code only provides for municipal revenues through property taxes, water fees, licenses and permits. Major revenue comes from property taxes and the collection of urban service fees, whose rates are politically contentious and not well accepted by citizens. Major revenue sources like the VAT (value added tax) and income taxes are outside the scope of municipal finance, as are other potentially productive sources like dedicated investment revenues. Thus, even when municipalities wish to manage their finances more productively, they cannot, pending agreement on a more rational and effective tax structure (Merino, 2013).

While a redesigned national tax structure would undoubtedly help municipalities face their ongoing responsibilities (particularly public safety), their constitutional powers are only administrative and their financial resources are always scarce. They have few incentives to spend money well, and many to increase spending. According to the latest report of the Auditor General, municipal entities and municipalities continue to borrow beyond reasonable expectations of future revenue, and to commit financial irregularities (Portal, 2013).

Even though the growth rate among the border municipalities facing this administrative and political financial crisis exceeds that of the rest of the country, this economic condition is not reflected in the prosperity of their inhabitants. Meanwhile, high rates of violence and public insecurity have become a national and international concern. Mexico still aspires to a true federalism, one that transcends current legislative and administrative realities.

Education on the Line

The title refers to the educational system prevailing in the border area, in villages near the international line drawn to mark the Mexican territory, rather than to "online education." In this area, the educational system of each state benefited from the Agreement for the Modernization of Basic and Normal Education that was approved in the 1990s (Plasencia, 2010) in that it initiated the development of educational innovations that moved the educational systems of Nuevo León and Baja California up to par with the rest of the country. The states of Chihuahua, Coahuila, Sonora, and Tamaulipas have educational indicators below the national average, particularly in the case of the PISA (Program for International Student Assessment) developed by the OECD (Organization for Economic Cooperation and Development).

For the OECD, PISA assessments measure not only school system performance, but also that of the entire society. If the results for a country are unsatisfactory, young people will not be able to develop certain abilities and capabilities, to the necessary extent, which are identified as important for life in contemporary societies. The results of the PISA-standardized tests are not the average scores of all subjects of the population, but are estimated from the results obtained by the members of the sample. The distribution of reagents for each area in PISA 2009 is 19% math, 28% in science, and 53% in reading (PISA, 2012).

In PISA 2003, Mexico scored on average 385 points placing mathematical competence at level 1; it scored 419 points in 2009, but rose 34 points, remaining on the border of level 1. This means that there is a large proportion of students (51%) who are only able to answer reagents involving familiar contexts, clearly defined questions and solve direct instructions in explicit situations, performing actions that are obvious. Reading and science are in a similar situation (Table 9.3).

The states that form the border reflect test performance close to the national average. Nuevo Leon and Chihuahua are above the national average and even the average for Latin America. In both cases, the results have been increasing regarding the above applications, as well as the other entities in the area. Baja California is below the national average in mathematics and science but in reading it is four points above. According to OECD estimates, it is considered that every 40 points equals one year of education, so that overall the northern border states of the country would be two educational cycles average of the OECD countries (Table 9.4).

According to the latest census by the National Institute of Geography and Statistics, the border states have educational indicators above the national average. The actions of the national education system to achieve total incorporation and retention of children with 6–14 years of basic education, which is reflected in all states of the country, over 90% of girls and boys are in school. All six border states have an attendance rate of 95 percent or above. The rate of illiteracy among the population aged 15 and older is only 3.6 percent—3.3 percent less than the national average. Although this represents but a small percentage of the population, it still indicates the need to design educational programs that can offer formal education to everyone, even as adults (Figure 9.2).

One of the basic indicators of the educational profile of the population and its potential for progress toward better conditions is the level of education of its people. Average schooling refers to the number of completed years of people aged 15 and over within the national education system. Nuevo Leon exceeds 1.2 years of schooling more than the national average of 8.6 years of school, while the rest of the entities are also above the national average (Table 9.5).

Table 9.3 PISA Results for Mexico

Competencies	2000	2003	2006	2009	2012
Math	387	385	406	419	435
Sciences	422	405	410	416	
Reading	422	400	410	425	435

Source: Program for International Student Assessment (PISA) 2012. *Resultados de PISA-México, 2012.* http://www.pisa.sep.gob.mx/pisa_en_mexico.html.

Table 9.4 PISA Results for North Border States in Mexico

State	Mathematics	Sciences	Reading
Baja California	416	415	429
Coahuila	368	412	428
Chihuahua	440	442	449
Nuevo León	445	443	450
Sonora	410	405	415
Tamaulipas	405	406	417
Nacional	419	416	425
Average OCDE	501	496	493
Average Latin America	405	398	408

Source: Program for International Student Assessment (PISA) 2013. *Resultados de PISA-México, 2013.* http://www.pisa.sep.gob.mx/pisa_en_mexico.html.

Dropping out is a phenomenon linked to several factors such as migration, economic status, and, more recently, public safety. These circumstances appear to be present in the border area; however, elementary school dropout levels are below the national average except in the states of Chihuahua and Tamaulipas. High school dropout rates are increasing and are above average (5.3) in the region, although they are below average in Nuevo León (4.1) and Sonora (5.2).

Dropout rates rise as the educational level increases. There are many reasons for this, ranging from complex academic issues to persons' needs to be incorporated into the productive economy, whether in the formal or informal sector. We must also include malnutrition and lack of incentives to stay in school, factors that the International Labor Organization (ILO) classifies as "job quality" or Social Security issues. The increase in educational dropout rates among border states is not uniform: Tamaulipas and Coahuila achieve a higher retention level in technical and professional programs but Chihuahua, Sonora, and Baja California are between 3 and 4 percentage points above average. Nuevo Leon is almost double the percentage of dropouts (39.7%).

At the high school level, attrition is reduced with respect to technical vocational education but increases considerably with respect to basic education. Tamaulipas and Sonora manage to retain almost 90% of its population in high school and the other states exceed the national average (Table 9.6).

According to the data analyzed, the states of the northern border state of education reflect a reasonably good level compared to the rest of the country. These are

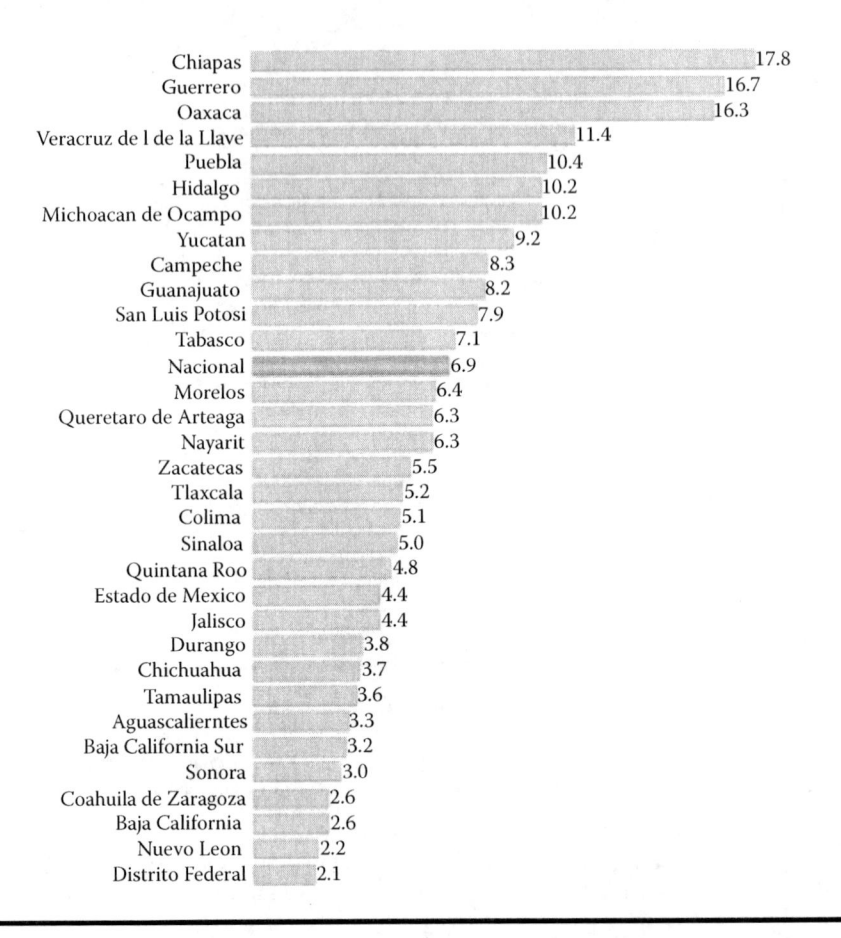

152 ■ *Using the "Narcotrafico" Threat to Build Public Administration*

State	%
Chiapas	17.8
Guerrero	16.7
Oaxaca	16.3
Veracruz de l de la Llave	11.4
Puebla	10.4
Hidalgo	10.2
Michoacan de Ocampo	10.2
Yucatan	9.2
Campeche	8.3
Guanajuato	8.2
San Luis Potosi	7.9
Tabasco	7.1
Nacional	6.9
Morelos	6.4
Queretaro de Arteaga	6.3
Nayarit	6.3
Zacatecas	5.5
Tlaxcala	5.2
Colima	5.1
Sinaloa	5.0
Quintana Roo	4.8
Estado de Mexico	4.4
Jalisco	4.4
Durango	3.8
Chichuahua	3.7
Tamaulipas	3.6
Aguascalierntes	3.3
Baja California Sur	3.2
Sonora	3.0
Coahuila de Zaragoza	2.6
Baja California	2.6
Nuevo Leon	2.2
Distrito Federal	2.1

Figure 9.2 Percentage of illiteracy (age 15 and over) by state, 2010. (Adapted from INEGI, Censo de Población y Vivienda 2010.)

states with solid-state educational systems, both active and proactive. The system of trade unions is relatively stable and well coordinated with educational systems. The end result is that education "along the line" in the border states is not bad, but could do a better job of customizing educational policies to more exactly suit individualized needs in different communities, including not only economic aspects, but also cultural development and community service. Educational policies must incorporate culture, but also sports science and technology. They must promote the development of the area for the benefit of its inhabitants, taking advantage of the extraordinary opportunities represented by the border states' geographical location. This will result in better educated citizens who are more equipped to cope with abuses by officials and businessmen. To combat the "perfect storm" represented by drug trafficking, we can minimize the impunity and lawlessness in which the

Table 9.5 Educative Indicators in the Border States (2010)

State/Indicator	Attendance[a]	Illiteracy[b]	Number of Years[c]
Baja California	95.4	2.6	9.3
Coahuila	95.8	2.6	9.5
Chihuahua	94.0	3.7	8.8
Nuevo León	95.8	2.2	9.8
Sonora	96.2	3.0	9.4
Tamaulipas	95.0	3.6	9.1
National	94.7	6.9	8.6

Source: Based on data from Instituto Nacional de Estadística, Geografía e Informática (INEGI) 2010. *Censo de Población y Vivienda.* México: INEGI.

[a] Percent of population aged 6–14 years attending the school.
[b] Average illiteracy of population 15 years and over.
[c] Average number of years of schooling for population 15 years of age or older.

Table 9.6 Dropout Rate by State and Level of Education (School Year 2011–2012)

State	Primary	Secondary	Technical and Professional	High School
Baja California	0.2	5.4	25.1	14.7
Coahuila	0.2	7.9	18.1	16.7
Chihuahua	0.9	5.6	24.5	16.1
Nuevo León	0.3	4.1	39.7	18.2
Sonora	0.5	5.2	24.5	12.3
Tamaulipas	1.1	6.5	16.6	12.2
National	0.7	5.3	21.6	13.7

Source: Adapted from Secretaria de Educación Pública (SEP) 2012. *Sistema Educativo de los Estados Unidos Mexicanos. Principales Cifras, Ciclo Escolar 2011/2012.* Available online at: www.sep.gob.mx.http://www.sep.gob.mx/work/models/sep1/Resource/1899/2/images/principales_cifras_2011_2012.pdf. Accessed January 9, 2013.

maquiladoras now constitute the main source of work, and transform the border area into an industrial area of scientific and technological innovation. We can take advantage of the opportunities offered by a new presidential administration (2012–2018) to consolidate educational reform proposals in science, technology, engineering and mathematics (STEM). It is not enough that we increase investment in these areas. Our investment in education must also be guided by national objectives that incorporate the demographic bonus into educational programs that are beneficial to individuals and have a positive impact on their immediate social environment.

The idyllic vision in which foreign direct investment (FDI) promotes national development is just one of the false promises of neoliberalism. In reality, foreign capital can result in positive FDI, but once dividend payments are subtracted, little is left in the developing country. Karl Marx's dictum that "capital has no national interest" is still valid, and can easily be confirmed by cross-border development marked by large international hotel chains that that profit from geographic advantages such as comparatively lower wage scales and tax rates. However, the municipalities where they are located do not receive many direct benefits, though they do contribute much to the narrowly defined economic interests of transnational companies. The same applies to the inhabitants of those regions who accept the crumbs of transnational corporations—low-wage jobs without fringe benefits—in addition to addressing the social problems generated by these companies authorities under irresponsible, inappropriate, and corrupt models of development.

National development is promoted only by recognizing the binomial unity–diversity and the possibilities that this entails in a country like ours, in a region like the northern border of the nation. Historically, government programs aimed at "development" of the region have been limited by ignorance of the potential of the area. It is not about more resources but more creativity to design strategies to contain and strengthen society and the boost to higher levels of human development.*

Are We All Juárez?

Obviously not everyone is Juárez, although the idea refers to the solidarity that should prevail in a nation with each and every one of their locations, the fact is that the political disdain and lack of opportunity to meet the town, had as Consequently a number of events that reflected the increasing violence in the

---

* The Human Development Index (HDI) is an indicator of human development by country, prepared by the United Nations Development Program (UNDP). It relies on a statistical social indicator that consists of three parameters: a long and healthy life, education, and standard of living, designed by the economist Amartya Sen.

city. "We are all Juárez" is the product of one of the most despicable crimes in recent history.* So far, as presented to the media, the lawlessness prevailing in the region did not seem to merit the solidarity and responsibility of the federal government in what had been happening for decades in one of the most dynamic populations of the border between Chihuahua and Texas: Ciudad Juárez. For two decades, Juárez was placed in the global context for the wave of feminicide occurring, but no response came from the municipal, state, or federal authorities. For two decades, Juárez has been a "hot spot" for crimes against women, without any meaningful response by municipal, state, or federal officials. Border towns throughout the world are characterized by high rates of crime, particularly prostitution, human trafficking and other types of smuggling. This has been true for "El Paso del Norte," now renamed "Ciudad Juarez" and "El Paso," throughout its history (Galeana, 2006).

Its geographical location made Juárez vulnerable from the beginning. It is situated in a large valley nestled in the desert, along the Rio Grande. In the colonial era, the Franciscan missions gave way to military prisons, due to the attacks of the Apaches, which was the capital of New Mexico. Their isolation led to impunity for the criminals who came there (Galeana, 2006). In 1866, President Benito Juárez relied on this area to support the Mexican Republic during the struggle against French intervention (Piñó, 2006). In 1885, El Paso became a "free zone" to encourage economic development. World famous casinos such as Casino Hotel, Diamond Electric Keno, The Tivoli, located here, and brothels proliferated (Pérez López, 2006). El Paso and Ciudad Juárez was renamed in honor of the Father of the Americas (Benito Juarez). Although its status as an economic free zone ended in 1905, the casinos and other related businesses continue to operate. Years later during Prohibition in the United States, US businessmen ("bootleggers") used the location's advantages to produce and smuggle distilled spirits into the US.

Three factors contributed to the development of the city beginning in the 1960s, and particularly during the Echevarria and Lopez Portilla administrations: population growth, urban concentration, and border revitalization programs. Thus,

---

* Shots fired at those invited to a party southeast of the city killed 14 people and injured 14 more, two of whom later died. The attack occurred early Sunday inside and outside three houses on Villa de la Paloma Street in the community of Villas Salvárca, where nine students from a local technical institute were celebrating the birthday of one of the teens. Three of the victims were killed outside house number 1306, three in 1308, and four in 1310. Four more died on the way to hospitals. According to the State Attorney's Office, the dead included 10 high school students, one college student from the Autonomous University of Chihuahua, and three adults. Some of the dead were found in backyards where they had been shot trying to escape. An unidentified spokesperson for the authorities said the attackers had been looking for an unidentified individual, presumably someone "linked to drug trafficking and organized crime." http://www.eluniversal.com.mx/estados/74607.html, 21/02/2013.

Juárez recorded the highest increase of population engaged in industrial activity, was established as the state's most dynamic boom following the maquiladora program, with a majority of the female population. There are numerous studies that account for the abuses to which women are subjected to in the maquiladoras who are victims of bullying are high employment and rivals in economic and political importance to the state capital of Chihuahua but today a city with extremely high levels of violence not only on the country but in the world. Feminicide began in 1993, although it is likely that since the nineteenth century violence against women involved in prostitution existed but ignored his condition. Currently, the prevailing gender crimes have increased significantly under the municipal, state, and federal authorities. Today Juárez is a town, a city struck down by violence not only against women but against the general population, so we believe that, until now, "we are all Juárez" is only part of the official rhetoric and the strategy comes late to address a situation that has long gestated.

The strategy by Todos Somos Juárez (Gobierno de la República, 2010) in Rebuilding the City is a comprehensive action program of the Federal Government with the participation of Chihuahua State:

1. *Citizen participation.* The Federal Government recognized that citizens of Juarez best understand their City's situation, and therefore organized workshops with representative citizens for their opinions and developed specific proposals to address the problems of Ciudad Juárez. In these working groups were discussed over 15 specific topics, including housing, health, education, culture, sports, security, poverty and employment, among others, and had a wide participation of academics, organizations of civil society, employers, workers, youth, and many other interested citizens to contribute to the search for solutions. From these workshops emerged the commitments contained in this document and further defined to representative citizens who, through Citizens Advice, continuously follow up and monitor the progress of commitments. In sum, the citizenship of Ciudad Juárez plays a fundamental role in the design, implementation, and monitoring of all actions of the Strategy Todos Somos Juárez.
2. *Comprehensiveness of public policy.* The current situation requires solutions for Juárez. While the lack of security is a problem that plagues the daily lives of Juárez, there are other economic and social problems that fuel insecurity and threaten the quality of life of the city. Therefore, the Todos Somos Juárez Strategy includes actions not only on the issue of public safety, but also includes specific commitments on issues of economy, employment, health, education, and social development. Implementing a coordinated action of these six policy areas is expected to generate additional synergies for the benefit of the entire population of Ciudad Juárez.
3. *Responsibility and participation of the three levels of government.* The "Todos Somos Juárez" ("We are all Juarez") strategy calls for effective coordination of the three branches of government. In this regard, the agencies and

departments of the federal government work with state and local counterparts to ensure that the actions and commitments of the Todos Somos Juárez Strategy are comprehensive, have a high impact, and address the problematic background of the city (Government of the Republic, 2010)*.

Of these commitments, 70 correspond to the educational, athletic, and cultural sectors. Some of the "commitments" corresponded to the annual operating program of the SEP, or the state or municipal administration but we have to recognize that it was an attempted binomial form of unity–diversity, recognizing the unique characteristics of the city and the municipality and establishing direct communication channels between the authorities at all levels and the population that wishes to participate in the preparation of the strategy. The approximate total cost of the strategy reached 3300 million pesos, historic for Ciudad Juárez and of these, $800 million was allocated for education, culture, and sports. The Government of the Republic established a period of 100 days to fully realize each of the commitments made to the people of Ciudad Juárez. According to government reports, at the end of three months, the achievement of goals recorded an increase of 70% and at the end of the fiscal year 95% of the shares were executed and some goals exceeded.

The strategy met all the requirements for an effective, comprehensive public policy except that many of the goals were not met by the previously established time deadlines. Also, the emphasis on accomplishing these goals in a short time frame (100 days) meant that the situation in Juárez soon reverted to the previous status quo. High rates of violence and apparent impunity continued. What is required is not only the recognition that "We are all Juárez", but also the permanent steady and forceful application of administrative pressure by public safety agencies, but also the creation of an effective legal framework to enable local authorities to have the institutional capacity to meet their constitutional responsibilities. This means "hands-on" management and real administrative federalism, present and active.

Conclusion

The materials presented in this chapter allow us to reach some general conclusions and recommendations for action:

- The border is an area of opportunity that must be analyzed from the unique perspective of the border region.
- Mexico should build an administrative federalism in which networked governance prevails across different levels of government.

---

* A list of the 160 commitments that authorities and citizens in Ciudad Juarez have pledged to to follow through on can be found at http://todossomosJuárez.gob.mx/estrategia/index.html

- Public policies and government programs must be designed that are suited to the characteristics and conditions of each municipality.
- Policy making must take advantage of the border to develop activities that generate direct and timely welfare for its citizens.
- Investing in education means investing in multiple factors; education spending should be directed transparently to meeting its goals.
- We should build an education system from the classroom up, with the participation of the different stakeholders, but mainly by strengthening the role of teachers.
- We should develop specific performance standards for educational systems in the border states and municipalities.
- Educational performance should be slightly better than the national average in the states of Coahuila, Chihuahua, and Tamaulipas and remarkably better in Baja California, Nuevo Leon, and Sonora, with respect to both basic and secondary education.
- We should identify the reasons for dropouts at any level.
- We should create economic incentives and provide scholarships so that children and young people stay in school.
- The school must represent an integral transformation for individuals as well as facilitating their insertion into the labor market. If there are no jobs, education also fails.
- Schools should emphasize prevention programs against violence and addictions.
- Schools should revitalize their connection to the community through social outreach and community-based programs.
- Schools should develop specialized programs based on the economic orientation of each municipality and border town to promote the development of the region.
- Relying on other nations for technological and scientific advances is a threat to national sovereignty, growth, and development.
- We should replicate the "We are all Juárez" strategy throughout the region, focusing on infrastructure and educational programs including culture and sports, and adapting the program to local needs and priorities.
- Plan on education is a daily exercise for those facing classroom teachers. It is also an indispensable process in the administration of education.
- Managing education will require sufficient resources to be made available (e.g., human, financial, and material), in a fashion that strategically links school-based planning, performance, and evaluation.
- School-based projects should inform and guide the operation of administrative and educational reforms nationwide.
- Educational reforms will be successful if they are data-driven, strategic, and designed with students, teachers, and administrators in mind. This is more important than imprisoning administrative reformers and teachers' leaders for political reasons.

References

Aboites Aguilar, L. 2010. Movimientos de población, 1870–1930: La reanimación del centro y el crecimiento del norte forman un nuevo país. In: F. Alba, M. A. Castillo, and V. Gustavo (eds.). *Los grandes problemas de México. Tomo III*. Colegio de México, México, pp. 65–92.

Alba, F., M. Á. Castillo, and V. Gustavo 2010. *Migraciones Internacionales* en Los grandes problemas de México. Tomo III. Colegio de México, México.

Blanco, I. and R. Gomá, June 2003. Gobiernos locales y redes participativas: Retos e innovaciones. *Reforma y Democracia, 26*. Caracas: CLAD.

Cabrero, E. (ed.) 1999. *Políticas Descentralizadoras en México 1983–1993. Logros y Desencantos*. Mexico: CIDE.

Caminal, M. 2002. *El Federalismo Pluralista: Del Federalismo Nacional al Federalismo Plurinacional*. Barcelona: Paidós.

Carreras Velasco, M. 1974. *Los Mexicanos que Devolvió la Crisis, 1929–1932*. México: Secretaría de Relaciones Exteriores.

Castles, S. and M. J. Miller 1998. *The Age of Migration. International Population Movements in the Modern World*. New York: The Guilford Press.

Castro Castro, L. J. 1994. *Programa de 100 Ciudades: Una Estrategia de Desarrollo Urbano Regional Sustentable y Concertado*. Available online at: http://148.206.107.15/biblioteca_digital/capitulos/270-4153cxx.pdf. Accessed March 17, 2013.

Cornelius, W. A. 2008. *Controlling Unauthorized Immigration from Mexico: The Failure of Prevention through Deterrence and the Need for Comprehensive Reform*. San Diego: Mexican Field Research Program, Center for Comparative Immigration Studies, University of California San Diego.

Corona, R. 2000. Estimación del número de emigrantes permanentes de México a Estados Unidos, 1850–1990. In: R. Tuirán (ed.). *Migración México-Estados Unidos, Continuidad y Cambio*. Mexico: Consejo Nacional de Población.

Corona Vázquez, R. 1991. *Principales Características Demográficas de la Zona Fronteriza*. Available online at: http://www2.colef.mx/fronteranorte/articulos/FN5/7-f5_Caracteriztricas_demograficas_fronteri.pdf. Accessed January 17, 2013.

Davies, K. A. 1972. Tendencias Demográficas Urbanas Durante el Siglo XIX en México. *Historia Mexicana. Siglo XXI, México*.

De la Peña, M. 1950. Problemas demográficos y agrarios, *Problemas Agrícolas e Industriales de México* II (3–4): 9–327.

Editorial. 2003. *El Universal*. Available online at: http://www.eluniversal.com.mx/estados/74607.html. Accessed February 21, 2013.

Emerich, G. Available online at: http://www.redalyc.org/redalyc/pdf/136/13602901.pdf. Accessed January 3, 2013.

Estrada, L. 1999. *La Ley de Herodes*. México: Bandido Films. 123´.

Galeana, P. 2006. *Historia de un Feminicidio. Las Muertas de Juárez*. Available online at: juridicas.unam.mx/sisjur/internac/pdf/10-466s.pdf. Accessed February 10, 2013.

Gamio, M. 1991. Número, procedencia y distribución geográfica de los inmigrantes mexicanos en Estados Unidos. In: J. Durand (ed.). (Taken from M. Gamio 1930. *Mexican Immigration into the US*. Chicago: The University of Chicago Press), pp. 19–33.

Gamio, M. 1993. *Mexican Immigration to the United States*. Illinois: The University of Chicago Press.

Gibson, C. and K. Jung 2006. *Historical Census Statistics on the Foreign Born Population of the United States: 1850–2000*. Washington, DC: U.S. Bureau of the Census, Working paper no. 81.

Gobierno de la República 2010. *Todos Somos Juárez*. México. Available online at: http://todossomosJuárez.gob.mx/estrategia/index.html Accessed February 10, 11, and 23, 2013.

Immigration National Statistics 2008. *Building an Americanization Movement for the twenty first century.* Available online at: http://www.uscis.gov/files/nativedocuments/M-708.pdf. Accessed December 24, 2012.

INEGI-INAH 1990. Estadísticas históricas de México, 2 vols. México, Instituto Nacional de Estadística, Geografía e Informática-Instituto Nacional de Antropología e Historia.

Instituto Nacional de Estadística, Geografía e Informática (INEGI) 2010. *Censo de Población y Vivienda*. México: INEGI.

Kincannon, L. 2008. *United States Census Bureau.* Available online at: http://iipdigital.usembassy.gov/st/english/texttrans/2005/05/20050516170242liameruoy0.133526.html#ixzz2IG6JQloM. Accessed January 22, 2013.

Leví, L. 1985. Federalismo. In: N. Bobbio and N. Matteucci (eds.). *Diccionario de Política*. México: Siglo XXI, pp. 627–639.

McCaa, R. 1993. El poblamiento del México decimonónico: Escrutinio crítico de un siglo censurado. In: J. Gómez de León Cruces y C. R. Romero (eds.). *El Poblamiento de México. Una Visión Histórico-Demográfica*. Colegio de México. México, Vol. III, pp. 33–77.

Merino, M. 2013 entrevista en *El Mañanero*. Forotv. México. Available online at: http://noticierostelevisa.esmas.com/economia/559677/condonaran-isr-estados-y-municipios/, 04/02/2013.

Monsiváis, C. June 4, 2000. Multiculturalismo y diversidad. *Diario El Norte*. Monterrey, México, p. 8.

National Institute of Health 2008. http://iipdigital.usembassy.gov/st/english/texttrans/2005/05/20050516170242liameruoy0.133526.html#ixzz2IG6JQloM, 01/22/2013.

Peréz López, D. 2006. Casinos en el Desierto en: Al margen, periodismo de investigación, medios y literatura, México, www.almargen.com.mx.

Piñó, A. 2006. *Con la República bajo el brazo*. México: Tecolote.

Plasencia Díaz, A. 2010. La federalización de la educación básica en el D.F. Una tarea pendiente.

Portal, J. M. 2013. *Informe del Resultado de la Fiscalización Superior de la Cuenta Pública 2011*. Auditoría Superior de la Federación. Available online at: http://www.asf.gob.mx/Trans/Informes/IR2011i/indice.htm. Accessed February 19, 2013.

Program for International Student Assessment (PISA). 2012. *Resultados de PISA-México, 2012*. Available online at: http://www.pisa.sep.gob.mx/pisa_en_mexico.html, Accessed January 10, 2013.

Program for International Student Assessment (PISA). 2013. *Resultados de PISA-México, 2013*. Available online at: http://www.pisa.sep.gob.mx/pisa_en_mexico.html. Accessed January 26, 2013.

Ramírez Ceballos, M. (Ed.) 2001. *Encuentro en la Frontera: Mexicanos y Norteamericanos en un Espacio Común*. Mexico: El Colegio de México-El Colegio de la Frontera Norte-Universidad Autónoma de Tamaulipas.

Revueltas, J. 1944/1996. Dios en la tierra. In: C. Monsiváis (ed.). 1996. *Lo Fugitivo Permanece: 21 Cuentos Mexicanos*. Mexico: SEP. Biblioteca para la actualización del maestro.

Secretaria de Educación Pública (SEP). 2012. *Sistema Educativo de los Estados Unidos Mexicanos. Principales Cifras, Ciclo Escolar 2011/2012*. Available online at: www.sep.gob.mx.http://www.sep.gob.mx/work/models/sep1/Resource/1899/2/images/principales_cifras_2011_2012.pdf. Accessed January 9, 2013.

Secretaría de Hacienda y Crédito Público (SHCP) 2012. *Presupuesto de Egresos de la Federación (PEF)*. Available online at: www.shcp.gob.mx

Secretaría de Medio Ambiente y Recursos Naturales (SEMARNAT). 2012. *Frontera 2012*. http://www.semarnat.gob.mx/temas/internacional/frontera2012/Documents/1_Programa_Frontera_2012_esp.pdf. Accessed January 17, 2013.

Tuirán, R. and J. L. Ávila 2010. La migración México-Estados Unidos, 1940–2010 en *Los Grandes Problemas de México*. Colegio de México, México, Tomo III, pp. 94–134.

U.S. Bureau of the Census 2003. *Government Census*. Available at: http://www.census.gov.gov/population/www/documentation/twps0081.pdf. Accessed February 10, 2013.

U.S. Department of Homeland Security, Computer Linked Application Information Management System (CLAIMS), Legal Immigrant Data, 2007.

Valadés, E. 1955/1996. *La Muerte Tiene Permiso*. In: C. Monsiváis (Ed.). *Lo Fugitivo Permanece: 21 Cuentos Mexicanos*. Mexico: SEP. Biblioteca para la actualización del maestro.

Chapter 10

How Cartel Violence Is Affecting Cross-Border Collaboration

Espiridion ("Al") Borrego

Contents

Introduction 163
Background 164
University of Texas Pan American 166
Hidalgo County, Texas, Health and Human Services Department ... 169
City of Mission, Texas Sister Cities Program 171
Conclusion and Recommendations 174
    Public Administration Learning Community 176
References 177

Introduction

Much of the discussion of policy initiatives on narcotrafficking is aimed at the national level. The intent of this chapter is to provide a local perspective and view from Hidalgo County, Texas, which is across the border from cities such as Reynosa and Rio Bravo, Tamaulipas, Mexico. This is one county along an almost 2,000 mile border, separating the United States from Mexico. National issues important to both the United States and Mexico converge on the border. Immigration, border security, cartel violence, drug smuggling, human trafficking, environmental concerns, pandemic outbreaks, and other health issues are cross-border issues. Cartel violence is affecting binational, and in this case, cross-border relationships and collaborative efforts among binational government agencies and universities. The local institutions are adapting to the changing conditions and these adaptations may be helpful to the other counties along the border, as well as adding a local perspective to the national dialogue.

Background

Hidalgo County and the cities of northern Tamaulipas, Mexico across from Hidalgo County, have a long history of cross-border collaborations between local and state governments. There is a common history and culture among the people on both sides of the border. There are many Mexican citizens who are day-workers, who cross the border to do a variety of jobs in Hidalgo, County. Many clean houses and then return to Mexico. There are U.S. citizens who find living in Reynosa cheaper and more convenient. There are families with family members on both sides of the border. The local university has students from Reynosa, who want to complete their university education in the United States. Hidalgo County is about 85% Hispanic/Latino. There are many cross-border agreements and relationships among cross-border communities. For example, when there is a disaster close to the border, such as a large explosion or fire, firefighting units from the United States respond and provide assistance. Those agreements have existed for many years.

The U.S.–Mexico border is almost 2000 miles long. The U.S. counties along the border have many commonalities. They are among the poorest counties in the United States. Many of the residents are from the lower socioeconomic strata. Approximately one-third of U.S. residents are at or below the poverty level. This is much higher than the rest of the United States. Texas has over 400,000 residents along the border who live in semi-rural areas called colonias. Many colonias do not have running water or paved roads. In Texas, counties along the border, about 40% of the adults and 8% of the children were born outside the United States. About one-half of the residents are bi-lingual. Half of the households receive some form of public assistance. The counties of Hidalgo and Cameron counties had the highest rates of households receiving public assistance (United States Centers for Disease Control and Prevention, 2001).

Cartel violence across the border from Hidalgo County in Reynosa has increased dramatically. On August 24, 2010, the Borderland Beat (Reporting on the Mexican Drug Cartel Drug War) reported that on the Mexican side of the U.S.–Mexico border the area known as Frontera Chica is being depopulated due to the cartel violence (Borderland reporter Bernardo). Barletti (2010) reported that Reynosa is a gateway for the flow of drugs into the United States and the drug cartels are fighting to keep it that way. These are just two of a continuing stream of media stories describing the violence in Reynosa across the border from Hidalgo

County. On August 14, 2012, the local television station KRGV reported that a wave of violence was gripping Reynosa (KRGV, 2012).

Reynosa is not the only city across the U.S.–Mexico border that is suffering cartel violence. Rio Bravo is the east of Reynosa on the Mexican side of the recently completed international crossing. The City of Donna in Hidalgo County is on the U.S. side of the international crossing. On September 28, 2012, Reuters reported that the cartel member responsible for drug operations in Rio Bravo was convicted (Taylor, 2012). On June 29, 2012, *The Daily News* reported on videos of cartel members beheading rivals from a competing cartel (Roberts, 2012). There is continuing violence across the border from Hidalgo County.

The cartel violence also affects governance in Mexico, especially in the northern states. Hale (2011) sees the possibility of Tamaulipas becoming a failed state with resulting anarchy. He comments that Tamaulipas has declared itself as ungovernable. He further comments that six mayors from Tamaulipas have moved to the U.S. side and conduct their business by telephone with occasional travel to their communities in Mexico. He includes the comments of Dr. Tony Payan who reviewed his paper as saying that the failure of the State of Tamaulipas is the failure to fight crime and that the cartels have established a parallel government.

There is also a diaspora of students and people fleeing the northern states due to the violence. Hale (2011) cites Mexican media reports that claim that there are 14,000 homes and houses abandoned due to the violence in Nuevo Laredo, Tamaulipas, Mexico. He cites the threat by the cartels to the residents of the city of Miguel Aleman, Tamaulipas to leave or to be killed. He includes the Municipal Planning Institute's reports of up to 116,000 empty homes in Juarez in 2010. Many students are leaving universities that are located close to incidents of violence.

The U.S. Department of State foreign travel warnings list the State of Tamaulipas as having armed robberies and carjackings on state highways in Tamaulipas. There are no highway routes in Tamaulipas that are considered safe. Since 2010, U.S. Government employees and their families are prohibited from driving from the U.S.–Mexico border into the interior. The employees are also prohibited from personal travel into these areas. Travel for official reasons should be conducted with extensive security precautions (U.S. Department of State, 2012).

The violence has been on the Mexican side of the border. The cities on the U.S. side tend to be some of the safest cities. A *USA Today* analysis of the violence in the cities on the U.S. side of the border showed that they were safer than other cities in their state (Gomez et al., 2011). It did not matter if the cities were 30, 50, or 100 miles from the border.

The U.S. side of the border has also benefited from the increased investment in border security. The number of U.S. Border Patrol agents on the border has more than doubled from 2000 to 2010. Homeland Security has provided $5 billion for increased border security (Gomez et al., 2011). The increased number of personnel along the U.S. border benefits communities. The housing requirements, education of their children, and local purchases contribute to the local economies of the cities along the border.

One of the effects of the cartel violence is an outright prohibition of official travel to Mexico. The University of Texas Pan American (UTPA) faculty and students are prohibited from traveling to Mexico for official purposes. These restrictions apply to Hidalgo County officials as well. Cities are also affected, but respond in different ways than the university and Hidalgo County. How UTPA, the Hidalgo County Health and Human Services Department, and the City of Mission are adapting will be discussed.

University of Texas Pan American

About 2006, the Vice Consul of the Mexican Consulate in McAllen, Texas approached the Masters of Public Administration (MPA) Program at UTPA. The Vice Consul was conveying the Consul's request for a collaborative relationship between the Mexican Consulate and the UTPA MPA Program. The Consul is a sociologist and was very interested in having faculty and students conduct research in Mexico. This was before cartel violence became an issue. The Vice Consul was asked to speak to MPA classes about international relationships, international protocols, and diplomatic skills. Latino/Hispanic students are about 85% of the students at UTPA. Most are fluent in Spanish and English. Students learned that being fluent in a foreign language and having similar cultural backgrounds were not enough to be successful in working internationally (Borrego and Johnson, 2011).

The Mexican Consulate would invite high-ranking delegations from Mexico to meet with Hidalgo County and local government officials. Many of the local government officials were not familiar with Mexican diplomatic protocols and did not possess international diplomatic skills. There were unintentional breaches of diplomatic protocols. This left Mexican officials unhappy. As a result of these unintentional mistakes, the Consul decided that many of the local government officials needed diplomatic training. The Consul wanted the training to be done at UTPA.

A Memorandum of Understanding (MOU) for a collaborative relationship was negotiated between the Mexican Consulate in McAllen and the College of Social and Behavioral Sciences at UTPA. A group of students were actively involved in the development of the MOU and the training programs under faculty guidance. The students attended the meetings at the Mexican Consulate and took notes of the meeting in Spanish and English. They learned to prepare agendas for the meetings and to practice their diplomatic skills in interacting with the officials of the Mexican Consulate.

A mutual decision between the Mexican Consulate and the College of Social and Behavioral Sciences was made to sign the MOU at the diplomatic training. The local U.S. Congressman was invited to officiate at the signing of the MOU and to open the training session. The students developed the agenda for the event.

They handled the registration for the event, welcomed the U.S. Congressman and the officials from the Mexican Consulate. They learned the diplomatic etiquette to welcome and host an international event and how to meet a U.S. congressman and brief each official and escort them to their location. A student was translating from English to Spanish as the Congressman welcomed the officials from the Mexican Consulate, the participants, and the Dean of the College of Social and Behavioral Sciences, UTPA. The Congressman presided over the signing of the Memorandum of Understanding between the Mexican Consulate and the College of Social and Behavioral Sciences, UTPA. There were between 60 and 70 local government officials at the Diplomatic Protocol training. The students created Certificates of Completion signed by the Mexican Consul and the Dean of the College of Social and Behavioral Sciences. The students prepared press releases and sent them to the local media, television, and print. They met the local media and directed them to interviews with the Mexican Consul and the Congressman. It was a very successful endeavor and all participants were very satisfied with the results. The Consul of the Mexican Consulate sent pictures of the ceremony and a report of the MOU to his superiors in Mexico for which he was highly commended.

The MOU between the Mexican Consulate and the College of Social and Behavioral Sciences allowed students to remain involved in cross-border activities. The Mexican Consul would invite the students and their faculty sponsor to attend meetings with visiting Mexican government officials. The students would officially greet the visiting Mexican delegation and take notes. The students were also invited to lunches with the Mexican officials hosted by the Mexican Consulate. At these lunches, the students learned that when working with Mexican officials, developing close personal relationships, led to better professional relationships (Borrego and Johnson, 2011).

The students were included in meetings and lunches with a delegation of officials from Ciudad Valles, San Luis Potosi, Mexico. At one of the lunches, the delegation from Ciudad Valles mentioned that they were interested in having solar panels installed in the rural areas of Ciudad Valles. It is helpful to view Ciudad Valles as more like a U.S. county than a U.S. city. The officials from the Mexican Consulate and the visiting delegation from Ciudad Valles looked at the faculty member overseeing the students. The faculty member looked at the UTPA students and said: "What do you think, would you like to help?" The students unanimously responded: "Yes."

The students discovered that many residents of Ciudad Valles would use car batteries to provide electricity to light their homes. They would pay to have the batteries recharged. The cost of solar panels was actually lower than the costs of recharging the car batteries over the course of a year. The problem was that solar panels required the full amount at one time. Recharging car batteries required much less costs weekly and most families did not have the money to purchase solar panels.

During the semester, the Ciudad Valles official responsible for public relations visited the students. The students would present informal reports on the progress of their research. There would be a discussion of the progress. The Presidente Municipal de Ciudad Valles visited the class. The students developed the agenda, welcomed the Presidente Municipal, and practiced translating as he spoke. The students briefed the Presidente Municipal on their research. By this time, the students had included information on the best solar panels for use in Ciudad Valles. They also included information on nongovernmental organizations (NGOs) that would provide funding for the solar panels and offered assistance in preparing grants to the NGOs for funding of the solar panels. Their report on the solar panels was presented to the Presidente Municipal of Ciudad Valles and the Consul of the Mexican Consulate. Ciudad Valles provided solar panels for some of their residents.

The Consul of the American Consulate in Reynosa, Tamaulipas, Mexico learned of the work the students were doing and drove to the Edinburg, Texas campus of the University of Texas Pan American. This was a trip for her of over 160 miles round-trip. The students presented and gave the Consul the results of their research. She complimented the students on the importance and quality of the research. It was information that she needed and found useful.

The students were invited to make a presentation of their research to a group of NGOs in San Miguel de Allende, Guanajuato, Mexico. The NGOs included Mexican NGOs and NGOs run by Americans living in San Miguel de Allende. A smaller group of students traveled to San Miguel for these presentations. They carpooled and drove from Edinburg, Texas to San Miguel de Allende. The students created a PowerPoint presentation with each slide having the same information in both Spanish and English. The students' presentations were well received and they already knew that in whatever language the question was asked the question and answer had to be translated to the other language. The students were asked many questions that they answered with the confidence of individuals who were prepared and professional. The presidents/directors of the NGOs had intense discussions among themselves about how they could use the research and research techniques to enhance the capacity of their nonprofits.

Other departments in the UTPA College of Behavioral and Social Sciences and other colleges at UTPA were conducting binational and cross-border research and working with the Mexican Consulate in McAllen. UTPA had developed a presence in San Miguel de Allende that also included the College of Arts and Humanities. Their students could go to San Miguel de Allende to learn about the local arts and music. The local population could learn about the work UTPA College of Arts and Humanities were doing.

It was shortly thereafter that the cartel violence in Mexico started to increase making ground travel into Mexico difficult and dangerous. UTPA instituted a prohibition for any UTPA employee or student to officially travel to Mexico. The presence that UTPA and especially the College of Arts and Humanities had in San Miguel was moved to the State of New Mexico. These opportunities ended.

At the time, it all seemed so ordinary and common, because it was. In retrospect, and examining what the cartel violence has prevented, it was very important to binational government officials, university faculty, and students. The UTPA students learned to use their research skills to solve issues in other countries. They also learned that in traveling to another country, they were representing the University of Texas Pan American and the United States and not just students. In the process of conducting binational and cross-border research, they transitioned from being students to being professionals. The work the students performed became part of their professional experience in their resumes. The students that were applying for employment opportunities reported that it was this part of their professional experience that employers wanted to know more about in their interviews. Academic work became professional experience.

The students/professionals became ambassadors from UTPA and the United States. They were able to disseminate accurate information about the United States and UTPA and in some cases change perceptions about the United States, its people and customs. They gained a greater understanding about Mexico, its people, and customs. In effect, they also became ambassadors for Mexico. Where there are misperceptions about Mexico, they will correct those misperceptions with accurate information. They along with their faculty advisor developed lifelong professional and personal relationships with government officials in Mexico. These relationships will serve both countries well in the future.

The government officials, university officials, and students also gained much from the mutual binational and cross-border collaborations. Ciudad Valles was able to provide solar panels for some of their residents who had been using car batteries to provide electricity to provide lighting for their homes (Borrego, 2006–2008).

Hidalgo County, Texas, Health and Human Services Department

The 1983 La Paz Agreement defined the border area between the United States and Mexico as extending 100 km into each country as measured from the international boundary (U.S. Department of the Interior). This created an identity for the border region. Although the La Paz Agreement is more commonly used for environmental purposes, it is also a useful way to examine cross-border health issues. In that case, it provides a geographic description of what a border area is. It is useful to understand that the border is larger than the immediate border area.

It is only the federal government that negotiates treaties with other countries. Local governments can negotiate memorandums of understanding (MOU) and cooperative agreements with foreign local governments. Counties are created by the state and do not have the flexibility that many municipal governments do. In Texas, home rule cities are basically those with populations over 5000. City charters that are approved by the city residents create these cities. In Texas, cities that are designated as home rule cities have any powers that are not denied to them by the state constitution. In many aspects, the counties administer state programs, many times through pass-through grants from the federal government.

Monitoring the spread of infectious diseases such as tuberculosis relies on knowing who is infected. The State of Texas can issue statewide press releases asking medical professionals to look for various diseases. In areas without medical laboratories, the alert may be to have medical personnel be on the lookout for symptoms such as high fever with a rash. Sharing infectious disease information is beneficial to both sides of the border. The sharing of information is driven by grassroots efforts and mutual interests. The State of Texas Border Health contracted with Hidalgo County Department of Health to build an Early Warning Infectious Disease Surveillance (EWIDS) (Borrego 2012c). Even in areas of benefits to residents of both sides of the border, there may be political sensitivities. An increase of infectious diseases on either or both sides of the border could inhibit tourism and people from Mexico coming to Hidalgo County to shop. There are many Winter Texans (snowbirds) from northern states that winter over in Hidalgo County. There would be fewer of them coming if there was a large increase in infectious diseases. It would affect local economies on both sides of the border. The cartel violence makes this a one-way flow. Mexican government officials can travel to the U.S. State and Hidalgo County officials are prohibited from traveling to Mexico because of the cartel violence. Technology is emerging to facilitate binational meetings. The Texas State Border Health has been using Blackboard Collaborate, which has teleconferencing capabilities, to hold binational meetings.

Those counties such as Hidalgo County that are on the U.S.–Mexico border must adapt to the changing conditions created by cartel violence. These counties face the micro versions of national issues such as immigration, the economy, epidemics, and binational relations. For county officials and their counterparts in Mexico, these are not abstract concepts, but practical issues. Their responsibilities remain as conditions change. The chief administrative officer of the Hidalgo County of Department of Health pointed out that there are six international crossings in Hidalgo County and 16 international crossings from Laredo, Texas to Brownsville, Texas. This is only part of the border between Texas and Mexico.

The Hidalgo County Health and Human Services Department is responsible for binational program including: the Secretary of Health, State of Tamaulipas, Mexico; Jurisdicción de Salud número III & IV; and U.S./Mexico Border Health Commission. The Hidalgo County Health and Human Services Department also works closely with the Texas Department of State Health Services, Office of Border Health. The County Health and Human Services Department is on the Office of Border Health Binational Hidalgo County—Reynosa, Tamaulipas Council. In 2008, the Binational Health Councils (BHC) held a strategic planning workshop in San Antonio, Texas. The conference emphasized a collaborative approach to cross-border health issues (Office of Border Health, Texas State Department of Health Services, 2008).

Health care is also an issue. In Hidalgo County, 45% of the population is uninsured or underinsured. In all, 25–30% are uninsured (statistics provided by

Hidalgo County Health Department). There are high rates of obesity and diabetes. The County Health Department must be vigilant about infectious diseases on both sides of the border. Across the border, Mexico uses a clinical approach to diagnosing diseases. A doctor diagnoses the disease based on the symptoms. On the U.S. side, a further step is taken. Samples are taken to a laboratory. There, it becomes a laboratory-based diagnosis. There are currently no official ways to deliver biological samples from Mexico to the United States. There are unofficial methods to accomplish this. These methods are best left not described to maintain their effectiveness.

Hidalgo County is also turning to technology to hold binational meetings. Their first attempt was using the free web-conferencing tool anymeeting.com. This is not meeting their needs. They are in the process of moving toward using Adobe Connect under the auspices of the Texas Association of Local Health Officials. This is not free, but it does contain the capabilities that Hidalgo County Department of Health requires. The technology is used for conference calls, developing binational protocols, and table-top exercises. Social media is also emerging as a communication tool. Texting and twitter are increasingly being used, especially when emergency operations centers (EOC) are needed.

Hidalgo County Health and Human Services is working with Secretaría de Salud-Tamaulipas, Jurisdicción Sanitaria No. IV-Reynosa to develop local binational communication protocols for a variety of public health events. The events would include before, during, and after surveillance investigations of binational cases, the importation and exportation of specimens, public health infectious disease outbreak events, natural/man-made disasters, and exercises/drills. The objectives of the draft agreement are:

- Maintain binational health collaborations
- Serve public health needs along the border
- Respond to binational cases, public health infectious diseases outbreaks, natural and manmade disasters, exercises, and drills
- Draft local binational communication protocol document provided by Hidalgo County Health Department

The document designates the binational contacts and the means of communication. The means of communication are landline phones and web-based conferencing. As cross-border travel becomes more dangerous, cross-border officials are adapting to the new conditions by adding Internet-based communications (Borrego, 2012b).

City of Mission, Texas Sister Cities Program

The City of Mission was chosen because of their active and collaborative relationships they have created through this program. The City of Mission's Mayor and city officials have created an innovative program that fosters international relationships in a way that strengthens city capabilities on both sides. Mission officials are adapting to the challenges that the cartel violence is creating. They currently have 12 sister cities.

The City of Mission has also been affected by the danger and difficulty of traveling on the Mexican side of the border. Before the increase in violence, it was common to move equipment, vehicles, and material that cities in Mexico might need. After clearing customs, city staff could drive the vehicles or equipment through Mexico. For the last two-and-half years, there has been no local travel. In an ironic twist, it is easier to visit sister cities that are further away in Mexico and which have airports. City staff can fly and not have to drive through the dangerous roadways near the border.

The fact that the City of Mission has expanded their sister city agreements with other cities in Mexico is a testimony to the benefits this program provides both communities. One aspect of Mexican culture is that business relationships arise out of personal relationships (Borrego and Johnson, 2011). As the Civil Service Director, Jesse Lerma, Jr. and Deputy City Manager Aida Lerma phrased it: "We get to know the Mexican officials and their families. Some of them stay at our home. We form life-long relationships and friendships. We exchange cultures and traditions."

One example of a cultural exchange is having officials from their Mexican sister cities create Dia de los Muertos (Day of the Dead) altars as they would in their cities. Celebrating Dia de los Muertos arose out of pre-Hispanic and Spanish customs in Mexico and Central America. People remember and commemorate the lives of departed family members and friends and welcome the return of their spirits (Smithsonian Latino Virtual Museum). Families may set up Dia de los Muertos altars in their homes. These altars will have pictures of those who have departed. There are many mementos of their lives and it is common to provide food and other offerings. Candles are lit and there may be skeletons and skulls made of sugar or candy. While Dia de los Muertos began in Mexico and Central America, celebration in the United States is increasing. Officials from the Mexican sister cities create the altars according to their customs, which vary from locality to locality in Mexico. Cultural understanding is enhanced among the participants.

This may seem to be just a cultural exchange. In reality, it is cultural competence. Respect for and understanding each other's culture is a management skill that is increasingly required of government officials in the United States and other countries. Globalization is increasing the interaction among government and business professional from different countries. Demographic changes in the United States are leading to more diversity where it is projected that Whites will not be the majority race sometimes in the 2040s. Professionals will have to be culturally competent to be effective and successful in this increasingly multicultural and more complex environment. Programs such as this have elements that are part of being culturally competent. The first is respect for and understanding another's culture. Programs, like the sister cities, create common ground or a shared culture. Culture refers to an ethnic and a professional culture that facilitate collaborative projects. There is a sense of inclusiveness that creates a professional environment of one working team instead of two separate groups (Borrego and Johnson, 2011). This is one of several ways that the professional capabilities of officials from both cities are enhanced.

The Sister City relationship between Laredo, Texas and Nuevo Laredo, Tamaulipas, Mexico is credited with the success of the international trade economy and the highly integrated economies of both cities. The social and cultural bonds led to a tighter integration of the cross-border economies. And similar to Mission there are shared celebrations of binational holidays and events. The Sister City relationship is a critical element of this economic integration (Mariñez and Vivas, 2011).

One of the reasons the City of Mission's Sister Cities program was chosen is that the program is expanding under the leadership of Mayor Norberto Salinas. It is very active and there are many collaborative efforts that are continuing. A sister cities agreement between the City of Mission and a sister city in Mexico provides the legal framework for carrying out cooperative activities. The City of Mission provided a copy of their agreement with city of Casimiro Castillo, Jalisco, Mexico as an example. The agreement and resulting relationships strengthen governance for both cities. Article III specifies the purpose of the agreement is for interchanging technologies, experiences, and professional teaching, and economic development benefiting both parties.

The sister city activities are implemented without any cost to the City of Mission except for the cost of staff working on specific activities. There is a considerable donation of materials and vehicles to many of the Mexican cities such as equipment or protective clothing that has been damaged and can no longer be used by the City of Mission Firefighters. This equipment and protective clothing can be repaired and still be useful to their Mexican counterparts.

Some examples of firefighting equipment that have been transferred are: Jaws of Life and spreaders, ladders, firefighting protective clothing, and hoses. The transfer of equipment and protective clothing are also accompanied by extensive training. Puerto Vallarta, Jalisco has a population of about 400,000. They have one fire station that protects the entire city. Their trucks did not have hoses. Since many homes have cinder block construction, in many cases it was easier to let the houses burn. By contrast, the City of Mission with a population of approximately 50,000 has five fire stations. The City of Mission provided fire hoses to Puerto Vallarta to enhance their firefighting capability. On September 25, 2012, Alcalde Municipal, Efrain De León León of Valle Hermoso, Tamaulipas recognized the relationships of the respective government institutions that led to the donation of a jaws of life by the City of Mission (Hoy Tamaulipas/Valle Hermoso, 2012). With the equipment and training, many lives can now be saved. There have been many donations that come from local school districts, and neighboring cities throughout Texas that have been given to Mission's sister cities. Officials are always looking for equipment that is in good working condition that can be donated to the City of Mission then donated even further to its respective sister cities and communities in Mexico that have such needs. Additionally, "friends" of the Mission Sister City Committee make personal contributions to support the acquisitions of supplies when needed.

In the pre-violence days, transporting the equipment and protective clothing was relatively simple. Civil Service Director Jesse Lerma, Jr. showed pictures of the truck he used with a trailer to transport equipment and materiel to the Mexican side after U.S. Customs paperwork was completed. It was driven there. The cartel violence is ending the simplicity of the transfer of material. It is dangerous and unwise for U.S. municipal employees to travel through the border regions of Mexico. As happens when the usual way of doing business cannot be officially done, informal and innovative ways emerge. Given the situation, these informal and innovative methods are best not discussed. Describing them can create dangerous situations for those involved, although it is a testament to the human spirit that these methods emerge (Borrego, 2012a).

It is common when there is an emergency immediately across the border to have U.S. local governments provide assistance. On September 18, 2012, there was a fire at a PEMEX gas facility on the outskirts of Reynosa, a city across the border from McAllen and Mission in Hidalgo County, Texas. At least 26 people were killed (CNN wire staff, 2012). The City of Mission was ready to have their firefighters respond in providing assistance. The author was talking to the city manager of another city close to the Mission. He said that he had received a call for assistance, but had decided not send his city's firefighters—another sign of the insidious way that cartel violence is diminishing the quality of relationships between cross-border cities and their ability to provide mutual assistance.

Conclusion and Recommendations

The border regions between the United States and Mexico have much to contribute to the national dialogue. The border regions have long histories of cross-border and binational collaborations and relationships. Many national issues such as immigration, bio-terrorism, pandemics, and infectious issues involve the border regions. Local governments benefit from cross-border agreements, which provide mutual aid and assistance in cases of fires or natural disasters. The cartel violence has led to the prohibition of U.S. officials traveling into Mexico. This makes the flow of government officials one-way; Mexico to the U.S. Technology is emerging as a way to continue meetings without U.S. officials physically having to travel to Mexico.

Slack et al. (2012) see the restrictions on traveling in northern Mexico creating a need for communication technology. They discuss their use of communication and social media in collaborative binational migrant border crossing research. The research team used Skype, Facebook, Twitter, and geographic information systems for binational communication. These are useful and very helpful tools. There is a new tool that can revolutionize binational research, collaboration, and increased governing capacity. Massive Online Open Courses (MOOCs) are receiving much media attention and funding. MOOCs are still at the experimental stage, but many universities are beginning to develop ways to use these capabilities.

MOOCs can be used as a technological method of having the cross-border interactions and relationships that had been so prevalent along the U.S.–Mexico border available to binational participants located far from the border. Policy is commonly framed in legislative terms. However, interested groups of informed and engaged individuals with well thought out proposals can have a considerable influence on the policy process. MOOCs can become learning communities where individuals can research and develop proposals.

Riddle (2012) describes MOOCs as being capable of being started at any time and be of any length. The audience is worldwide and many of the classes are free, although universities are exploring charging money for certificates of completion. Riddle (2012) sees a role for professional development where MOOCs include a certificate that is recognized by many employers.

Along with the increase in MOOCS is the rise of consortiums using MOOCs. One consortium is edX, which is a $60 million partnership between Massachusetts Institute of Technology (MIT) and Harvard. Other universities are joining this partnership. Coursera is a consortium of 30 universities, including Stanford, Michigan, Princeton, and others. MOOCs are generally free. The consortiums usually do not offer degrees, but certificates of completion can be issued. Over 1 million students from almost 200 countries have taken classes from Coursera (McCormick and Groll, 2012). MOOCs seem to be the wave of the future and undoubtedly universities will find a successful business model. For the purposes of this chapter, it is the communication tools in the technology, which allow the creation of Public Administration Learning Communities (PALC) that are useful.

The technology or platform for the MOOCs contains very useful communication tools. Participants have access to an in-class email system, wikis, blogs, journals, discussion boards, and teleconferencing equipment. The classes can be of any length and can be accessed anywhere in the world that there is an Internet connection. The University of Texas Pan American has joined edX. The author discussed the implications with the university people responsible for online classes. The author was told that since the online technology is owned by edX and not by UTPA, it is okay to use it for individuals who are not UTPA students. This opens a door into a new world. The UTPA Center for Online Learning, Teaching and Technology (COLTT) is interested in using edX for innovative programs. It may be assumed that other universities are interested as well.

MOOCs allow the duplication of the UTPA collaboration with the Mexican Consulate in McAllen without the travel restrictions and distance limitations. The MOOC technology creates a communication environment that lends itself to binational, as well as international efforts. An international public administration learning community can be easily created. All that is needed is interested binational and international faculty, students, and binational and international government officials with an email address and access to the Internet. It is helpful if one thinks of a MOOC as a collaborative learning community with wonderful communication tools instead of just as a class. These online classes are available 24 hours every day that the class is open. Participants can access it at any time. Only the teleconferencing feature requires everyone to be online at the same time. Collaborate; the teleconferencing tool, can be used to record the sessions. Participants log on and view the discussion and write comments or questions.

The public administration learning community (PALC) is developed and scheduled. The public administration learning community can be open to everyone or closed where only a preselected group can access the class. The faculty of record has control of the design and can select the communication tools that will be used. The communication tools that are available on the online platforms are discussion boards, wikis, blogs, an internal mail system, journals, and collaborate (a videoconferencing tool). Discussion boards allow communication threads in response to a question. Wikis allow participants to create a joint document. Blogs allow participants to have their own individual blogs. The email system is internal and includes all participants. Participants can maintain their own journals. Blackboard Collaborate allows videoconferencing among all or groups of the participants. PowerPoints and videos can be uploaded to the PALC. All the communication tools are there. All that is missing is the purpose.

Public Administration Learning Community

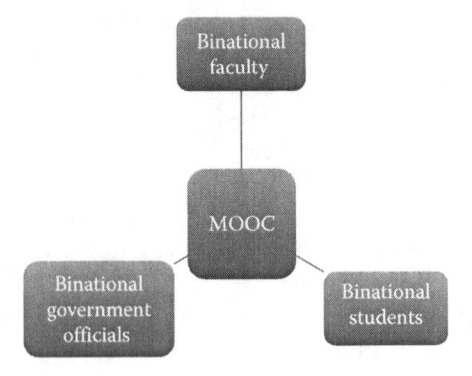

The PALC allows binational research, classes, and training. For example, three to four faculty members from three to four universities in the United States and Mexico can agree to be facilitators or professors for a PALC that is researching a particular issue for a Mexican municipality. This can be similar to the work that the UTPA students conducted for Ciudad Valles. Willing students at all the universities where the faculty members are residing can recruit students. The students can be grouped into binational teams. Government officials can be invited to participate. Where appropriate, Mexican Consulates, local members of Congress interested in U.S.–Mexico issues, and local governments are willing to help. The communication tools allow faculty, students, and government officials to participate in the process. Discussion is in both languages. Videos and audio recording can be uploaded. The final product is the set of recommendations presented to the faculty and government officials. All of this can be accomplished without physically having to cross the border.

Projects such as this allow students to use academic projects as professional experiences. Learning how to represent their universities and countries is a useful career skill. One of the lessons learned in the UTPA–Mexican Consulate collaboration is the importance of personal relationships in the development and strengthening of professional relationships. Personal and professional relationships can be developed with the communication tools in the MOOCs. Then where appropriate, participants can use professional organizations such as the American Society for Public Administration's (ASPA) National Conference to meet and present their results. Several projects such as this can become a U.S.–Mexico program.

Current online technology has vast communication resources where learning communities can be initiated. Most of the effort for online classes is on using the technology as an alternative to face-to-face classes. There have been little or no efforts toward using the technology to establish binational and international learning communities. Using the examples in this chapter makes it the perfect time to develop models for this technology.

References

Barletti, D. 2010. Reynosa, Mexico where the drug cartels rule, *Los Angeles Times*, downloaded November 18, 2012 from http://framework.latimes.com/2010/11/05/reynosa-mexico-where-the-cartels-rule/#/0.

Borrego, E. 2006–2008. Notes taken during University of Texas Pan American and Mexican Consulate in McAllen, Texas, Memorandum of Understanding for Collaboration.

Borrego, E. 2012a. Personal interviews and clarification emails, with City of Mission, Texas, Deputy City Manager Aida Lerma and Civil Service Director Jesse Lerma, Jr. conducted on October 22, 2012.

Borrego, E. 2012b. Personal interviews and clarification emails with Hidalgo County Health and Human Services Department Officials; Chief Administrative Officer Eduardo Olivarez and Lauren Garcia, binational coordinator, conducted October 26, 2012.

Borrego, E. 2012c. Phone interview and clarification emails with R.J. Dutton, Director Office of Border Health, Texas Department of State Health Services conducted on October 29, 2012.

Borrego, E. and Johnson, R. 2011. *Cultural Competence for Public Managers: Managing Diversity in Today's World*. CRC Press, Taylor & Francis Group, Boca Raton, FL.

Borderland Beat Reporter Bernardo. August 24, 2010. Reynosa, Tamaulipas: Urban Warfare 8/24/2010, Borderland Beat, Reporting on the Mexican Cartel Drug War, downloaded

on November 16, from http://www.borderlandbeat.com/2010/08/reynosa-tamaulipas-urban-warfare.html.
CNN Wire Staff. 2012. 26 killed in blaze at Mexican gas facility near border. Downloaded October 30, 2012 from http://www.cnn.com/2012/09/18/world/americas/mexico-refinery-explosion/index.html.
Gomez, A., Gillum, J., and Johnson, K. 2011. U.S. border cities prove havens from Mexico's drug violence, *USA Today*, downloaded November 18, 2012 from http://usatoday30.usatoday.com/news/washington/2011-07-15-border-violence-main_n.htm.
Hale, G. J. 2011. A "Failed State" in Mexico: Tamaulipas declares itself ungovernable, Nonresident Fellow in Drug Policy, James A. Baker, Institute for Public Policy, Rice University.
Hoy Tamaulipas/Valle Hermoso Staff. 2012. Donan equipo para el departamento de bomberos de Valle Hermoso, downloaded October 31, 2012 from http://www.hoy-tamaulipas.net/notas/53729/Donan-equipo-para-el-departamento-de-bomberos-de-Valle-Hermoso.html.
KRGV. August 14, 2012. Violence erupts in Reynosa, downloaded on November 16, from http://www.krgv.com/news/violence-erupts-in-reynosa/.
McCormick, T., and Groll, E. 2012. Rise of the MOOCs. Foreign Policy.com. downloaded November 20, 2012 from http://www.foreignpolicy.com/articles/2012/11/26/rise_of_the_moocs?page = 0,0.
Mariñez, F. and Vivas, L. 2011. Violence, governance, and economic development at the U.S.-Mexico border: The case of Nuevo Laredo and its lessons, *Puentes Consortium 2nd Annual on U.S.-Mexico Border Security*, Rice University Bioscience Research Collaborative, February 2011.
Office of Border Health, Texas State Department of Health Services. 2008. downloaded Nov. 2, 2012 http://www.dshs.state.tx.us/borderhealth/BHC.shtm.
Riddle, R. 2012. MOOCs: What do they have in higher education?, Duke Center for Instructional Technology, downloaded November 4, 2012 from http://cit.duke.edu/blog/2012/09/moocs-what-role-do-they-have-in-higher-education/.
Roberts, C. 2012. Drug cartel beheadings video surfaces, NYDailyNews.com, downloaded November 18, 2012 from http://articles.nydailynews.com/2012-06-29/news/32475737_1_gulf-cartel-drug-cartel-leader-zetas-cartel.
Slack, J., Whiteford, S., Zavala, S. B., and Lee, A. E. 2012. The use of social media as a tool for collaborative research on the U.S.–Mexico border, *The Puentes Consortium*.
Smithsonian Latino Virtual Museum. Smithsonian Dia de los Muertos Festival: A second life experience! Downloaded October 30, 2012 from http://latino.si.edu/education/LVMDayoftheDeadFestival.htm.
Taylor, J. 2012. U.S. jury convicts Mexico's Gulf Cartel manager in drug case, *Reuters* September 28, 2012, downloaded November 18, 2012 from http://www.reuters.com/article/2012/09/29/us-usa-mexico-drugs-idUSBRE88S02F20120929.
United States Centers for Disease Control and Prevention. 2001. Preventing and controlling tuberculosis along the U.S.–Mexico border: Work group report. *MMWR* 2001; 50 (No. RR-1).
United States Department of State. 2012. Downloaded Nov. 12, 2012 from http://travel.state.gov/visa/immigrants/types/types_5780.html#overview.

Chapter 11

The U.S.–Mexico Border in the Making of Bilateral Policy

Oscar Mauricio Covarrubias

Contents

Introduction 179
Problems without Borders 180
Interdependence in the Federal System 183
Interdependence between Mexico and the United States 185
The Border: Under Pressure for Action 186
Conclusion 190
References 190

Introduction

Increasingly public administration practitioners, scholars, and students must deal with issues that do not respect established political boundaries. A new generation of complex and interconnected issues requires improvements not only in decision-making processes within countries, but also between them. The resolution of the problems that affect Mexico and the United States demands comprehensive and coordinated policies at national and binational levels. Their problems are far too complex to presume that they can be solved unilaterally or through actions based solely on the border region. What we need is leadership and reasonable compromise on both sides of the border so that we can arrive at the right mix of policies in both countries. Until this happens, we will not progress.

This chapter deals with the U.S.–Mexico border in the context of the complex interdependence between the two countries. This shared border is arguably the region that most clearly reveals this bilateral interdependence. Severely affected and under pressure for action, the border tends to be the main reference point around which both governments build their responses. However, a more comprehensive approach is needed because border issues are an expression of broader social, economic, and political phenomena.

As neighboring nations, Mexico and the United States confront a common set of problems—for example, immigration, drug trafficking, organized crime, environmental degradation, water shortages, natural disasters, and infectious diseases. All these issues fall into the category of problems that no nation can tackle alone. They are too complex, and their solution requires a new, holistic approach that properly reflects these problems' nature and interrelationships.

The risks associated with the bilateral problems challenge the self-sufficiency of boundaries and national agendas, and provide motivation for both countries' governments to build alliances. Threatened common areas demand a shared responsibility and joint action. Unilateral actions and based predominantly on the border are more expensive, while actions based on a comprehensive approach and cooperation can lead to more effective and lasting solutions. This represents a major challenge to the national governments of the United States and Mexico because forging national and bilateral solutions implies empowering government at all levels (including state and local), and substantially improving coordination within and between the two countries based on a strategic and shared vision of the problems they want to solve.

The chapter covers four points. First, it gives an overview of the general nature of problems without borders. Second, it examines growing interdependencies in federal systems. Third, it analyzes the interdependence between Mexico and the United States. Finally, it examines the specific pressures for action along the U.S.–Mexico border.

Problems without Borders

In many ways, the complex issues of the twenty-first century are problems without borders. They do not respect not only geographical limits, but also functional and temporal boundaries that have traditionally guided the study and practice of public administration. The types of problems that government faces today cannot be addressed effectively through traditional bureaucracies (McGuire, 2006). Solving seemingly intractable problems such as poverty, health care, and natural disasters requires mechanisms that are more flexible, more inclusive, more adaptable, and more responsive (Alter and Hage, 1993) than those favored by conventional government organizations. These challenges—often referred to as "wicked problems"—have no clear solutions, only temporary and imperfect resolutions (Harmon and Mayer, 1986).

Figure 11.1 shows a three-axis graph. Each axis represents the different dimensions along which problems may escalate in terms of space, the number of causes or factors involved, and of time.

In the first case, these challenges transcend territorial boundaries affecting more places, more people and more deeply than ever. As Jieli Li (2001) notes, demography is also a territorial variable because population and territoriality are inseparable in terms of economic production and political organization. Second, since they are the result of many interrelated factors, their solution therefore involves different sectors of the public administration. Third, because these types of structural challenges demand long-term solutions, they require public policies that transcend the life of particular government administrations. In short, crosscutting or cross-border issues have a significant impact on policy making, and are more complex issues in terms of scope, intensity, and connectivity. They cut across traditional policy boundaries, and are affected by the interrelated factors that characterize political boundary areas. Therefore, we need a comprehensive and systemic approach to identify and resolve them.

Because of this, existing political and administrative divisions are not particularly useful for understanding and even less so for tackling complex issues that have a very complicated geography. The maps of underlying common factors (such as public insecurity, drug trafficking, unemployment, social exclusion, migration, urbanization, environmental degradation, and public health emergencies) overlap and intermingle, resulting in complex cartographic overlays. They are also interconnected problems whose origins, in a globalized world, are linked to the processes that originate far from the places where they become manifest. Because national issues interact with international ones, and with what is happening locally, global

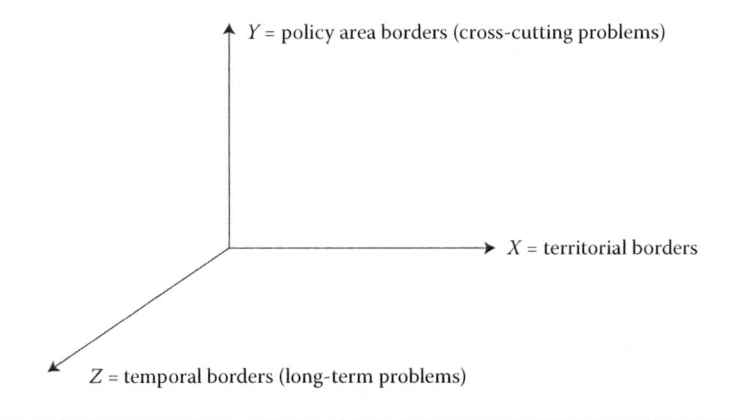

Y = policy area borders (cross-cutting problems)

X = territorial borders

Z = temporal borders (long-term problems)

Figure 11.1 Problems without borders.

interconnectivity has serious implications for public policy. Interdependence means that each participant and each point in the social process are affected by the context in which they are framed (Lasswell, 1968).

According to Harrop (1992), the international environment strongly influences the context in which national policies are formulated. Decision makers in each country share a political environment shaped by the international economic cycle of prosperity, recession, depression, and recovery. Therefore, while the same problems arise in different societies, common problems do not mean common solutions: that is, "interdependence does not mean convergence." In any event, the domestic public policy agenda becomes more international.

Interdependence means not only interaction but also the effects of one party over another in terms of benefits and vulnerability. This vulnerability—understood as the cost to a state of offsetting the negative effects of changes emanating from abroad—compromises prosperity, autonomy, and sovereignty (D'Anieri, 1999). As Streeten (2001) notes, interdependence exists when one country by unilateral action can inflict harm on (or provide benefits to) other countries. Common examples are competitive protectionism, devaluation, deflation, or pollution of the air and sea beyond national boundaries. Barber (2010) notes,

> In the last 50 to 75 years we have entered an era of interdependence. All the challenges we face are interdependent; AIDS, drugs, prostitution, weapons of mass destruction, global immigration, labor markets, you name it, but all the solutions are still wrapped up inside the territory of the nation state. We have states and citizens with borders, but problems without borders. How are we going to deal with that unless we find some form of citizens without borders, of democracy without borders?

Similarly, Barber (2009) notes that:

> The primary reality that has dominated history and our politics has been the reality of interdependence: the challenge of global crises in climate, health, crime, weapons, terrorism and markets that are global in nature and do not respond to the political solutions devised by traditional nation-states.

In a world with problems without borders, we rely on solutions within borders. Because we are confronting twenty-first century interdependencies via a nineteenth century architecture of sovereign nation states, the asymmetry between problems and solutions is the biggest crisis of all. If we have problems without borders, we need to have solutions without borders, because humanity is very keen to have human security, to have human development (Valle, 2011). Once we recognize that organized crime crosses borders, we must formulate transnational policies against it if we are to secure development and security for all involved.

Because of this, foreign policy is in many ways an extension of domestic politics (Ingram and Fiederlein, 1988). Internal political concerns are likely to trump international considerations when the policy issues at stake weigh heavily upon domestic political interests and institutions: "The study of foreign policy making so far has been only partially informed by the insights of the students of domestic public policy." This gap is unfortunate, for it hampers our understanding of foreign policies with strong domestic implications, particularly binational problems arising between nations with a shared boundary.

Interdependence in the Federal System

Interdependence can be conceptualized as a two-way process characterized by the extent to which government units located on different levels are invited or pressed to operate in a coordinated fashion. A certain level of interdependence is inevitable in any federal system; complete exclusivity of authority is also impossible. Federal systems vary in the extent to which their institutional design invites interaction between levels of government and the nature of this interaction (Bolleyer and Thorlakson, 2012). According to Covarrubias (2011), interdependence is the degree to which institutions that belong to different governments on the same or different levels must work together to achieve a common goal. The level of interdependence characterizing any particular social problem influences the capacity of a given government to solve the problem. Interdependence and coordination are closely related concepts.

Coordination, in turn, can be defined as the recognition of interdependence and ways of coping with it (Alexander, 1995). Coordination becomes a deliberate intervention that makes participants recognize their interdependence and that puts in place arrangements to harmonize their actions and decisions (Tuite, 1972). From this perspective, the effectiveness of the decision-making process in a federal system depends largely on the quality of interactions and negotiations between and within governments. As Peters (2005) argues, the political requirement of coordination means that more interdependent problems are likely to be more difficult to resolve. Governmental coordination as a complex political task, both formal and informal, that is essential for joint action by governments. It is related to environmental sensing, policy articulation, and organizational action interspersed with the reconciliation of interests, compatibility, autonomy, and harmonization of methods of action, as well as the management of interdependencies within and between different spheres of governmental activity. In other words, coordination is within and between institutions, sectors, levels, and branches of government and involves interaction with social actors and institutions of international character.

A direct consequence of the "problems without borders" is the reduction of threshold for the unilateral action. In other words, areas of responsibility are expanded. O'Toole (1997) indicates that policies dealing with complex issues will increasingly require collaborative structures for execution. This increase of the scope of joint decision-making has profound implications for the functioning of federal system, because the achievement of greater coherence and effectiveness requires increased coordination. Growing interdependence makes the task of government more complex and action more difficult, increasing both inefficiencies and conflicts (Covarrubias, 2011).

Elazar's (1985) definition of federalism—expressed by the formula *Federalism = Self-rule (self-government) + Shared rule (shared government)*—is a useful starting point for exploring how the nature of political organization has changed in societies governed by its principles due to the increased level of interdependence. Federalism involves the combination of self-rule and shared rule, an arrangement where two or more peoples or polities find it necessary and desirable to live together within some kind of constitutional framework that will allow all the parties to preserve their respective integrities while securing peace and stability through power sharing in those spheres where it is necessary. The diversity of arrangements is such that the synthesis of self-rule and shared rule, the basic elements in any federal arrangement, can be achieved in a number of different ways.

There is a defined relationship between the degree of interdependence and the level of self and/or shared governance. The proportion of each one is in direct ratio to the degree to which institutions belonging to different governments, of the same or different levels, must work together to achieve a common goal. This means that the

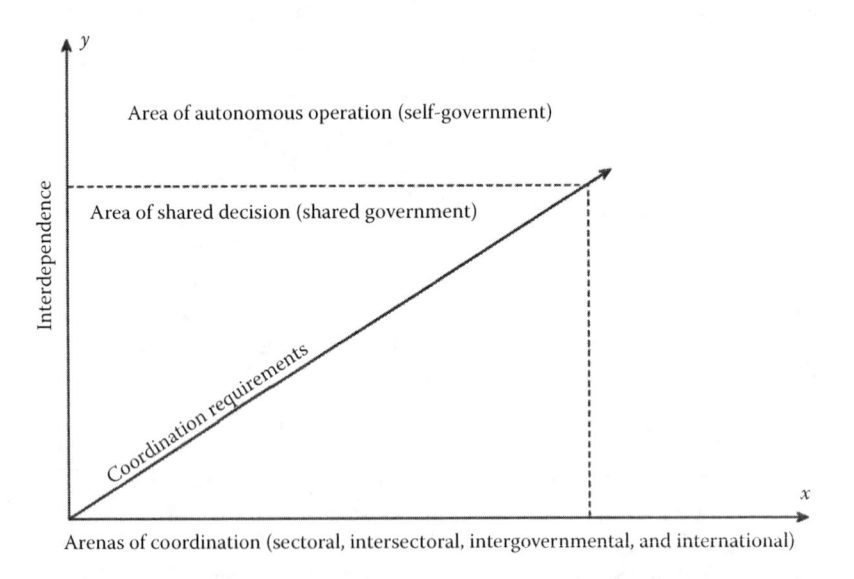

Figure 11.2 Interdependence and the expansion of shared decision making in the federal model. (Adapted from Covarrubias, M. 2011. The challenges of interdependence and coordination in the bilateral Agenda: Mexico and the United States. In J. W. Meek and K. Thurmaier Eds. *Networked Governance: The Future of Intergovernmental Management*. Washington, DC: Sage Publications.)

relations of governments are crucial in the implementation of policies concerning the treatment of problems or issues of a crosscutting nature which cannot be solved except in a coordinated manner. Figure 11.2 shows this relationship graphically.

At least three points can be inferred from the model. First, by their crosscutting and complex nature, current public problems increase beyond jurisdictions and political and administrative capabilities, expanding areas of common decision. Second, the need for cooperation is unavoidable because, despite the fact that in federalism the distribution of formal competencies encourages independent government performance, the reality is that mixed jurisdictions and zones of interaction are growing in importance. Third, the efficiency and effectiveness of government performance in a federal system increasingly depends on the level of coordination that enables joint work based on the strengthening of self-government, and simultaneously in the development of mechanisms of co-government from a comprehensive perspective. With respect to the third point, Chemerinsky (2008) argues that it is important to recognize federalism as empowering government at all levels, including state and local, to deal with society's urgent needs: "Federalism should focus on how to empower each level of government with the necessary authority to deal with the complex problems of the twenty-first century."

Interdependence between Mexico and the United States

These inferences also apply to international relations, where areas of shared responsibility grow among countries. This especially includes the case of Mexico and the United States, two federal republics that share a geographical border over 3000 km long and face a common set of problems—immigration, drug trafficking, organized crime, arms trafficking, and environmental degradation. Arturo Sarukhan, Mexican ambassador of Mexico to the United States, defined this critical bilateral relationship (2007): "… no country has such a direct profound impact on Mexico as the United States. No country has such a profound and direct impact on the well-being of the United States as Mexico."

The challenges facing Mexico and the United States as neighboring nations are a complex set of problems whose solution is beyond the ability of a federalist system centered on the principle of separation of powers where the key question is, "Which government has the responsibility to tackle the problem?" On the contrary, the intensification of interdependence should lead us to ask a more relevant question: "Which combination of governments is needed to address the problem?" Although one of the most important aspects of the federal system is the recognition that different types of issues require policies and institutions located in different levels of government, there are public problems for which it is difficult to devise solutions that do not involve the joint action by organizations belonging to different governments. Because the need for coordination will be higher, what is needed to deal effectively with bilateral problems is a type of coordination that can only come from a comprehensive approach. In this context, two things are imperative. First, we must recognize that the responsibility and management of the critical issues overwhelm governments within each federation; and second, we must extend this premise to the relationship between the two countries.

There are no shortcuts to binational coordination, because the decision-making authority and the political will to implement binational solutions are still rooted in each country. This means that the effectiveness of actions between Mexico and the United States will depend on the existence of comprehensive policies on both sides of the border, which can only be achieved through systemic action based on the principles of federalism. Given their level of interdependence, and accepting that national policies are largely a matter of foreign policy, the need for coordination within each country must be considered together with the need for coordination between the two federations. As the scope of common domestic policy decision making within both countries expands, greater coordination is needed among levels of government within each country, and between them. As two neighboring countries organized under the principle of federalism, interdependence means that although the agenda of public policies can become more binational, the modalities of implementation continue to be local.

The Border: Under Pressure for Action

Historically, the border has been a source of tension and disputes, the locale where uncoordinated national policies collide, and where the difficulties faced by states to control their territory and to fight against threats new and old crystallize (De Villepin, 2003). Given the complex and contradictory history of foreign relations between the United States and Mexico, their shared border is a psycho-social barrier that also epitomizes actual and imaginary rejection and exclusion, sometimes through violence.

In current political discourse, the unity of the nation-state is achieved in and through the invocation of a border: "… the border functions in this register as the very object of imagination around which (national) identity is created and recreated" (Golder et al., 2009). The border is the site where the state determines the limits of its own territory and arrogates to itself the right to determine who is to be included and who is to be excluded. However, when the boundaries that outline the geometry of a political principle are challenged by the differing geography of a public problem, this represents a serious challenge to governments that are accustomed to acting in a more unilateral and compartmentalized fashion.

Neilson (2010) argues that international borders tend to no longer exist as lines passing between territories but rather function as shifting zones of conflict that reorganize space and time in ways that can undermine the political unity and territorial integrity they were originally established to protect. This tension implies that borders are at once spaces of control and spaces of excess, at once sites for the restriction of mobility and sites of struggle. Second, borders are social institutions involved in producing the very conditions required for governance.

In the case of Mexico and the United States, the high degree of interdependence is a result of sharing one of the most complex and dynamic borders of the world, one that registers over 250 million crossings every year. From San Diego–Tijuana on the Pacific to Matamoros–Brownsville on the Gulf of Mexico, the boundary that separates and unites them is of paramount importance to the bilateral relationship. Therefore, any discrepancy in the definition of bilateral issues, and consequently in how to deal with them, affects the trans-border area not only within each country, but also between them.

The cases of Arizona and California are representative of this point. In 2004, the National Conference of Governors of Mexico (CONAGO, 2004) responded to an Arizona State policy:

> The Mexican governors gathered at the National Conference of Governors wish to express our dissatisfaction at the Proposition 200 of the State of Arizona, entitled Act to protect citizens and the taxpayers of Arizona, because the content of the proposal is a violation of human rights and inhibits access to education and health care of Mexican immigrants in the United States. It is important to mention that our countrymen contribute significantly to developing the economy of Arizona and the United States. (Conferencia Nacional de Gobernadores [CONAGO] 2004).

When former governor of California Arnold Schwarzenegger expressed support for the "Minuteman Project," a civilian group that carries out actions against migrant workers to achieve its objective of "sealing the border," Mexican governors warned Schwarzenegger that his support of armed groups taking action outside institutional channels did not contribute to a solution to the migration problem, but instead made it worse (CONAGO, 2005).

By contrast, the State of New Mexico views immigration differently. In addition to saying that walls between countries were ineffective, the then-governor Bill Richardson said:

> I have to basically state that we have dealt with the immigration issue in New Mexico differently than our three other border states. Our attitude is that immigration is a reality and the best thing to do with the undocumented workers that come into New Mexico …. is by integrating them in the society, by bringing them out of the shadows, that's more effective (2008).

It should be noted that each year about 400,000 immigrants cross the border into the United States and that only a fraction, 60,000–70,000, comes through New Mexico.

Reflecting the concerns of those living with the border problems affecting both countries, in August 2005, both Janet Napolitano (in Arizona) and Bill Richardson (in New Mexico) declared states of emergency in their border counties. One of the arguments made by Napolitano, when she declared the state of emergency in the counties of Cochise, Pima, Santa Cruz, and Yuma, was that the lack of action by the federal government to protect the U.S. border with Mexico allowed the entry of a large number of undocumented immigrants who endangered public safety. This criticism of the U.S. government came after Governor Richardson had a few days earlier declared a state of emergency in the New Mexican counties of Dona Ana, Luna, Grant, and Hidalgo, which he said had been devastated by the terrors of human smuggling, drug trafficking, kidnappings, assassinations, destruction of property, and cattle deaths. However, Texas declined to declare a state of emergency along its border with Mexico; according to Robert Black, spokesman for Texas Governor Rick Perry, border security is a federal issue and not a state one.

As neighboring nations and as federal countries, the common border is a crucial stage in the Mexico–United States relationship. However, the complex issues arising from the geographical proximity affect first the adjacent communities, but are far from being exclusively border problems. Bill Richardson (2008) indicated that the border governors from both sides have been forced to address the problems but they have done it without resources and without the federal leadership. He emphasized the need to have policies in place that address bilateral issues. Richardson also thinks that immigration could be effectively dealt with by comprehensive immigration reform, securing borders, a legalization plan, and a stronger relationship with Mexico. Because most of these problems are rooted in economic conditions and disparities, this means finding ways to identify and punish U.S. employers who knowingly hire illegal workers, and at the same time to address the need for seasoned and educated workers by policy reform of legal immigration: "I believe if the country deals with this as it should, on a national comprehensive basis instead of piecemeal, states like mine, and border states, and your state, would benefit."

Arizona, located at the crossroads of the integration of cultures and economies in the Americas, passed a law that allows police to detain people if there is "reasonable suspicion" that they are in the country as illegal immigrants (Kaplan, 2010). The law known as SB 1070 also requires that foreigners carry documents that prove the legality of their presence in the country. Arizona State Governor Jan Brewer defended the law by arguing that it was needed to respond to illegal immigration that was beyond the capacity of their state to resolve, and that Washington had failed to solve. As Arizona is one of the states with the highest population density of Latinos in the United States, the new law is disturbing for residents of Latin origin, and to neighboring countries where most of these people originate. Some of these governments protested against the law. President Barack Obama criticized it, and urged lawmakers to approve comprehensive national immigration reform law as soon as possible to avoid "irresponsibility by others."

The lack of a national U.S. migration policy has led some states to try to ignore the federal authority over immigration and create their own models to deal with those who are undocumented. However, U.S. courts have overturned state laws that violate Constitutional rights of undocumented immigrants. The rejected provisions were parts of two laws—H.B. 56 in Alabama and H.B. 87 in Georgia—that sponsors had openly acknowledged were designed to root out and punish illegal immigrants, making it impossible for them to live there. Following a recent Supreme Court ruling on Arizona's sweeping immigration law, the 11th Circuit Court of Appeals found that the statutes had unlawfully intruded on the carefully drawn system of federal immigration laws. The court rejected Georgia's effort to criminalize transporting and harboring illegal immigrants and to make it illegal to "induce or entice" them to enter the state—a crime unparalleled in federal law. It also blocked Section 28 of Alabama's law, which requires schools to collect information about students' immigration status. The court sensibly said this would deter children from entering school, violating the Supreme Court's 1982 ruling in *Plyler v. Doe* that guaranteed all children the right to an elementary education. However, the Court upheld the sections of laws in both states that allowed police officers to check the immigration papers of people they stop. Such provisions invite racial profiling. But as the Supreme Court had done in its Arizona ruling, it left open the possibility of future challenges on civil rights or due-process grounds. A recent *New York Times* editorial (2012) criticized Republicans in Congress for blocking proposed immigration reform, which would have laid the legal groundwork to prevent state attempts to legislate on the matter: "They set the stage for an ugly mess, with states rushing to erect their own rogue laws, which then have to be dismantled by the courts piece by piece."

According to Loaeza (2012), Latin America does not figure prominently on the agenda of President Obama. Not even Mexico or the Caribbean, whose geographical position would seem to justify their being treated as policy priorities by Washington, receives special attention. This lack of interest from the White House has a cost for the solution of bilateral problems such as drugs or migration that have been left to border governments, or specialized agencies of the U.S. national government. The difficulty with this displacement of bilateral issues between Mexico and the United States is that state governments do not view immigration or border security in light of the broader context of U.S. foreign policy. Within this general framework, Mexico would have more tools to negotiate with Washington that it has with the state governments of Arizona or New Mexico. However, with President Obama concentrating his foreign policy efforts on the Middle East and Asia, Mexico cannot expect much to change during his second term.

Even under these unsatisfactory conditions for bilateral policy making, we must not lose sight of the fact that we need a broad and comprehensive vision if we are to resolve the problems that are the most intense in border communities. Boundary-based solutions are out of sync with twenty-first-century problems. Addressing bilateral issues like border security requires concerted action by many agencies in different functional areas. A comprehensive strategy is needed to generate coherence between them.

Conclusion

Given the growing and irreversible interdependence that characterizes the contemporary world, and the intense pattern of government interactions that is its most direct consequence, we must conclude that coordination will increase over the next decade. The most indispensable coordination will come not just from incremental actions to improve government operations, but only from a comprehensive vision. Comprehensive vision is needed to

- Guide, integrate, and synchronize the operation of the agencies involved in solving the same or similar issues;
- Reduce mission fragmentation and program overlap and generate coherence;
- Identify vulnerabilities, threats, and consequences but also potentially beneficial synergies and relationships; and
- Develop crosscutting agendas.

An emerging set of complex and interconnected issues makes it necessary to improve decision-making processes not only within countries, but also between them. Resolving the common problems that afflict Mexico and the United States demands articulated policies at national and binational level. Although interdependencies within each country lead politicians to advocate comprehensive national policies, their reluctance to accept that this phenomenon also occurs bilaterally hampers the day-to-day activities of many government agencies on each side of the border—as evidenced by conflicts over immigration in U.S. state governments. And when there is no meaning and coherence at national level, it is difficult to find them bilaterally. The inescapable conclusion is that the development of comprehensive policies in each country is a prerequisite for arriving at effective binational policies. In the absence of this, each unit of government does what it can as it can, frequently without the necessary skills and resources.

References

Alexander, E. 1995. *How Organizations Act Together: Interorganizational Coordination in Theory and Practice.* Amsterdam: Overseas Publishers.

Alter, C. and J. Hage. 1993. *Organizations Working Together.* Newbury Park, CA: Sage Publications.

Barber, B. 2009. History is not over, but!.... A need for global governance" video. *Conference "Towards 'the Dignity of Difference': Neither 'the Clash of Civilizations' nor 'the End of History'",* University of Alberta, Edmonton. http://www.dofdifference.org/Dignity_of_Difference/Benjamin_R._Barber.html.

Barber, B. 2010. We need citizens without frontiers (A video-interview). Reset-Dialogues on Civilizations (Reset-DoC). http://www.resetdoc.org/story/00000021145.

Bolleyer, N. and L. Thorlakson. 2012. Beyond decentralization. The comparative study of interdependence in federal systems. *Publius: The Journal of Federalism*, 4(42): 566–591.

Chemerinsky, E. 2008. *Enhancing Government*. Federalism for the 21st Century Stanford, CA: Stanford University Press.

CONAGO. 2004. *Carta dirigida a la Sra. Janet Napolitano, Gobernadora del Estado de Arizona*. Hermosillo: Conferencia Nacional de Gobernadores.

CONAGO. 2005. *Carta dirigida al Sr. Arnold Schwarzenegger, Gobernador del Estado de California*. Aguascalientes: Conferencia Nacional de Gobernadores.

Covarrubias, M. 2011. The challenges of interdependence and coordination in the bilateral Agenda: Mexico and the United States. In J. W. Meek and K. Thurmaier Eds. *Networked Governance: The Future of Intergovernmental Management*. Washington, DC: SAGE Publications.

D'Anieri, P. 1999. *Economic Interdependence in Ukrainian-Russian Relations*. New York: SUNY Press.

De Villepin, D. 2003. Nuevo Espíritu de la Frontera. *Foreign Affairs*, en Español, 3(4): 22–35.

Elazar, D., ed. 1985. *Self-Rule/Shared Rule*. Lanham: Jerusalem Center for Public Affairs and University Press of America.

Golder, B., Ridler, V. and W. Illan Rua. 2009. The politics of the border/the borders of the political. *Law & Critique*, 20: 105–111.

Harmon, M. and R. Mayer. 1986. *Organization Theory for Public Administration*. Glenview, IL: Scott, Foresman.

Harrop, M., ed. 1992. *Power in Liberal Democracies*. Cambridge: Cambridge University Press.

Ingram, H. and S. Fiederlein. 1988. Traversing boundaries: A public policy approach to the analysis of foreign policy. *The Western Political Quarterly*, 41(4): 725–745.

Kaplan, E. 2010. Una ley forjada en la desesperación. *The Wall Street Journal* (Spanish) May 3. http://online.wsj.com/article/SB127258232553984435.html?mod=WSJS_inicio_MiddleTop.

Lasswell, H. 1968. The policy sciences. In *The Encyclopedia of the Social Sciences*, Vol. 12. Nueva York: Macmillan/Free Press.

Li, J. 2002. State fragmentation: Toward a theoretical understanding of the territorial power of the state. *Sociological Theory*, 20(2): 139–156.

Loaeza, S. 2012. Transcript of an editorial at the Noticiero, López Dóriga December 12. Television.

McGuire, M. 2006. Collaborative public management: Assessing what we know and how we know it. *Public Administration Review*, December, Special Issue.

Neilson, B. 2010. Borderscape: Between governance and sovereignty—Remaking the borderscape to Australia's North. *Local-Global: Identity, Security, Community*, 8: 124–140.

Peters, G. 2005. The problem of policy problems. *Journal of Comparative Policy Analysis: Research and Practice*, 7(4): 349–370.

Richardson, B. 2008. *Meeting with Governor Bill Richardson*. Transcript of a presentation at the Council on Foreign Relations, New York, June 18.

Sarukhan, A. 2007. The U.S. and Mexico: Challenges & opportunities. Transcript of a presentation at the Commonwealth Club of California, San Francisco, September 10.

Streeten, P. 2001. Integration, interdependence and globalization. *Finance and Development*, 38: 34–37.
The New York Times. 2012. Setback for Rogue Immigration Laws, Editorial, *The New York Times*, August 21. http://www.nytimes.com/2012/08/22/opinion/setback-for-rogue-immigration-laws-in-georgia-and-alabama.html?_r=0
Tuite, M. 1972. Towards a theory of joint decision making. In M. Tuite, R. Chisholm, and M. Radner Eds. *Interorganizational Decision Making*, pp. 12–20. Chicago: Aldine Press.

Chapter 12

Civil Service
A Critical Feature of Stability for Reducing Corruption in a Country Such as Mexico?

David Arellano Gault and Enrique Cabrero Mendoza

Contents

Introduction 193
Corruption, Citizens, and Government in Mexico 195
The Political Nature of Civil Service Systems 201
Civil Service and Corruption 203
Final Reflections 206
References 208

Introduction

Corruption elicits many conflicting feelings, and is extremely difficult to study because of its hidden, illegal nature. Also, despite the existence of laws and regulations, empirical studies show that a very high percentage of people accused of corruption does not consider that they have committed a corrupt act (De Graaf, 2007). Therefore, studying it as a phenomenon requires viewing it as a "normal" social activity that has existed in all societies over time, at various levels and in different manifestations. This pragmatic perspective has advantages. Because it avoids thinking that corruption is a matter of "rotten apples" or a war between "good guys and bad guys," it enables one to understand that systematic efforts, policies, and decisions are required, rather than only an individualistic moral or legal approach.

Corruption is a highly complex and deeply embedded social phenomenon. Those involved in it vary, and are found in various legal and institutional contexts where they create a pattern of institutionalized behaviors. Corruption involves relationships among various actors who are continuously able to establish transactions that may be considered improper. It may be defined as the violation of a positional duty (Malen Seña, 2003). The gravity of the problem is highlighted when these violations occur systematically, in other words, through social relationships that are relatively constant, repetitive, and stable. Systemic, corrupt relationships may even incorporate specialized strategies and stratagems to avoid being detected. In the real world, methods available for controlling corruption are both limited and costly (Arellano, 2012). Since corruption is a social phenomenon that also occurs as a hidden, illegal activity (at least in formal terms), understanding it and reducing it requires intelligently balancing not only its costs and benefits, but also considering the unintended consequences of efforts to control it. Because systemic corruption usually indicates the existence of embedded social relationships, some researchers have even proposed it represents an example of Nash's equilibrium,* in that none of the groups involved (citizens, public servants, or politicians) have any incentive to change (Vertiz, 2000).

Since it is so deeply embedded, systemic corruption is difficult to reduce and control through regulatory efforts or legal frameworks that address this phenomenon as an isolated phenomenon resulting from decisions by a few dysfunctional individuals (i.e., the "rotten apples" in a barrel). Systemic corruption can be so widespread that many find it difficult to avoid participating in some areas or at some times in their lives. The imposition of credible deterrents against acts of corruption is undoubtedly an important tool, but it is unlikely to be an effective strategy when applied against a strong, culturally embedded network of shared relationships, agreements, understandings, and symbols. In fact, efforts to eliminate corruption at an operational level often end by trapping relatively blameless citizens or consumers of public services without touching the underlying problem; this happens in virtually every city in Mexico with traffic police or other "street level" public servants.

Since corruption is an aspect of social relationships, it can become commonplace in relationships between governments and business, between elected or appointed officials and public servants, and of course between public employees and citizens. In Mexico, interlocking organizations, individuals, and structures

---

* A Nash equilibrium is a theoretical game situation where two noncooperative actors achieve such an equilibrium in their strategies that none of them have any incentive to change them. In the case of corruption, both the public official or politician and the citizen have reached an equilibrium in the corrupt game so neither one of them actually gains something trying not to play such a corrupted game.

take advantage of their institutionally interrelated positions to evade surveillance, standards, and audits, thereby maintaining their profits. Because corruption is considered "normal," actors become trapped in corrupt relationships if, for example, they know that traffic police may accept bribes, that health inspectors expect companies to offer them additional "compensation," and that administrative procedures are typically "streamlined" (greased) with money. People generally regard this as undesirable and objectionable, but also to a certain extent as normal. Trying to do something about it, at least as an individual citizen, entrepreneur, or public servant, seems like a losing battle.

Though there are a few Mexican politicians who deny this, Mexico is a country with high levels of corruption.* Paradoxically, given that as a country Mexicans are experts on corruption, the phenomenon has barely been explored, measured, or studied. However, this is gradually changing. Aside from some recent empirical studies (e.g., Arellano, 2012), the Mexican Informatics, Geography, and Statistics Institute (Instituto Nacional de Estadística, Geografía e Informática INEGI), the institution in charge of official statistics in the country, has undertaken the first National Government Quality and Impact Survey (ENCIG) in 2011. This survey contains a number of data and references to corruption that are worth studying (INEGI, 2011). A brief analysis of these initial data reveals a paradox. People in Mexico are concerned about corruption, yet apparently satisfied with government services. This insight may enable us to better understand the relationship between corruption and citizens and the government.

Corruption, Citizens, and Government in Mexico

According to the 2011 ENCIG, corruption is perceived as one of the most serious problems in our society, second only to insecurity, at almost the same level as unemployment and even above poverty (Figure 12.1).

Looking more deeply at the disaggregated data, the same survey shows that there is not much variation in the perception of the phenomenon by level of government. That is, over 8 out of 10 respondents believe that corruption occurs very frequently or frequently, with 84%, 85%, and 84% at the municipal, state, and federal levels, respectively (Figures 12.2 through 12.4).

In addition, respondents said that punishing corrupt public servants would be the action that would most improve the provision of procedures and services, confirming the perception of corruption as a serious problem that must be treated at the three levels of government (Figure 12.5).

However, and somewhat surprisingly, the same study indicated that citizens are generally very positive about the quality of public services provided at all three levels of government. Seventy-one percent felt that public service provision was "good"

---

* Mexico is 105 in the rank of Transparency International (2012).

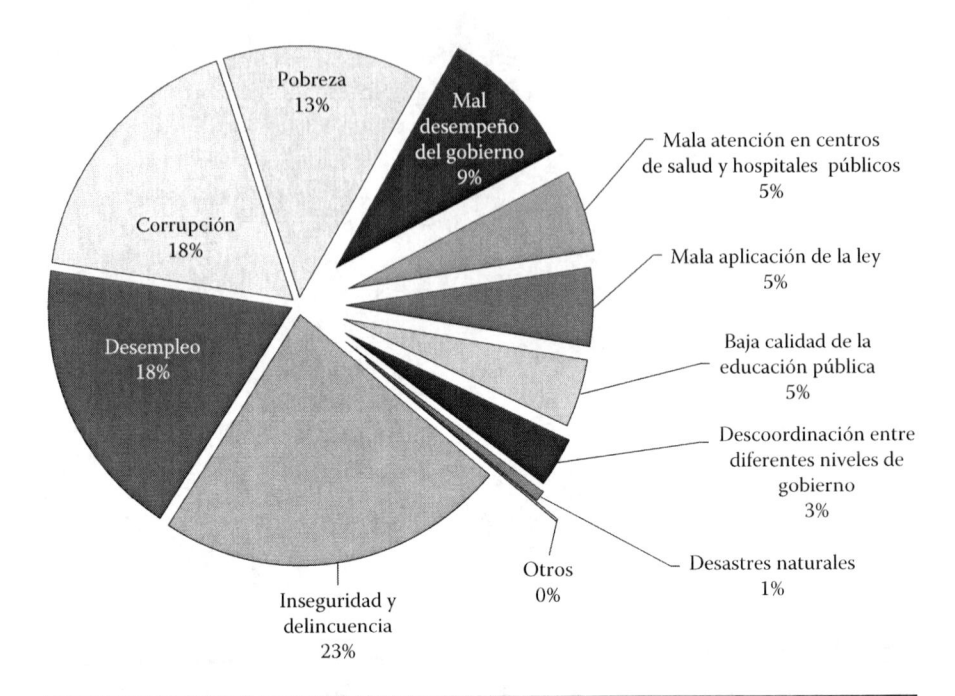

196 ■ *Using the "Narcotrafico" Threat to Build Public Administration*

Figure 12.1 Major social problems.[*] (All graphs produced by the author based on ENCIG, 2011.) Labels for pie chart, clockwise from the top: Poverty, governmental underperformance, low quality attention in health services and public hospitals, wrong enforcement of law, low quality of public education, uncoordinated relations among different levels of government, natural disasters, others, public insecurity and delinquency, unemployment, corruption.

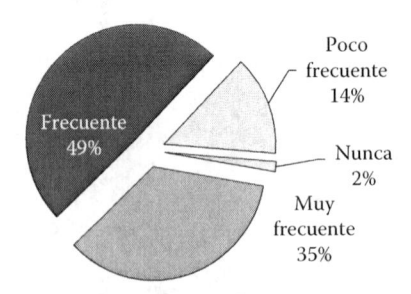

Figure 12.2 Perception of municipal corruption. Labels for pie chart, clockwise from top: Frequently, not very frequently, never, very frequently.

---

[*] We would like to thank Felipe Blanco and Emilio Zamudio for their assistance in compiling the INEGI survey data and producing the graphs (Figures 12.1–12.9).

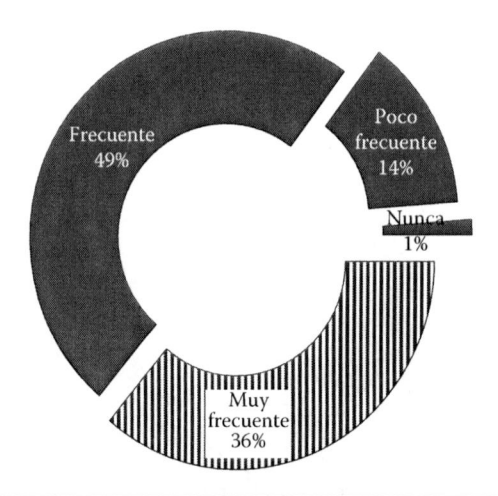

Figure 12.3 Perception of state-level corruption. Labels for pie chart, clockwise from top: Frequently, not very frequently, never, very frequently.

or "very good" at the state or municipal level, and 63% said the same at the federal level (Figures 12.6 through 12.8).

This widespread approval was corroborated by similarly high levels of satisfaction with the treatment received when undertaking a procedure or requesting a public service: nine out of 10 respondents rated the quality of service as extremely adequate or adequate (Figure 12.9).

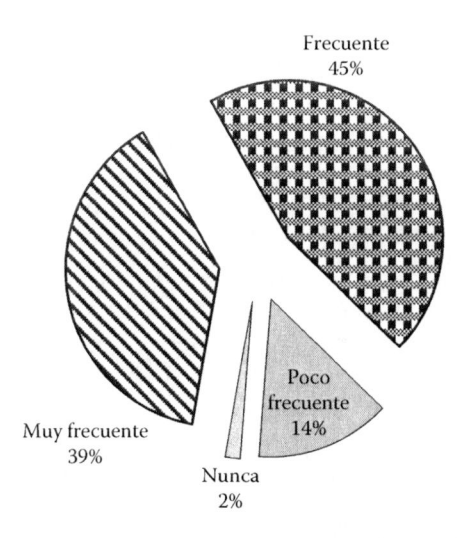

Figure 12.4 Perception of federal level corruption. Labels for pie chart, clockwise from top: Frequently, not very frequently, never, very frequently.

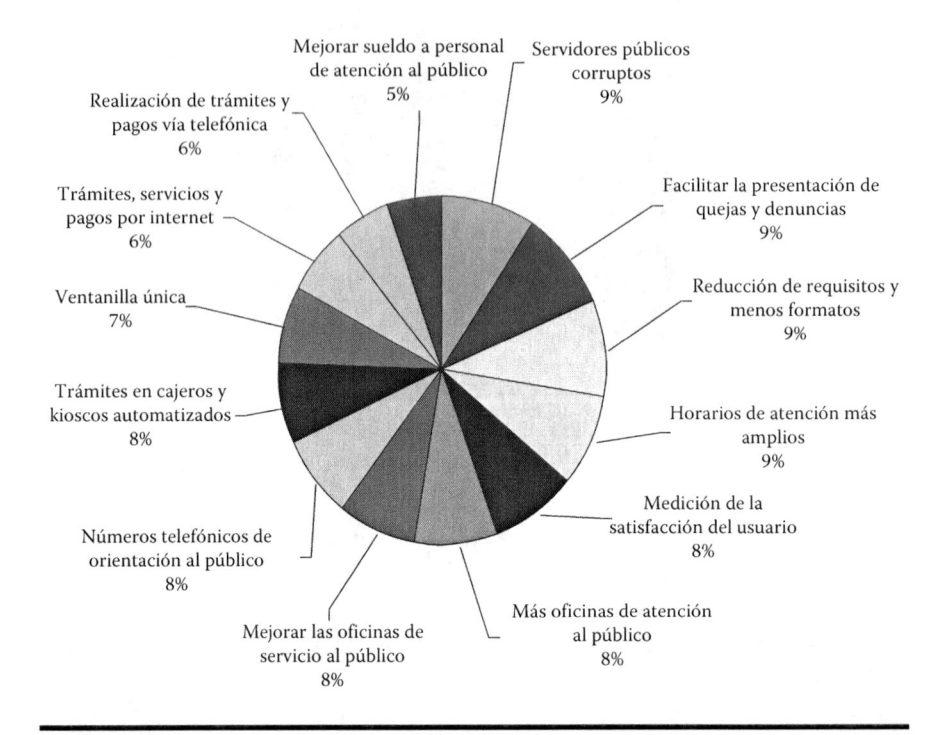

Figure 12.5 Perception of public regarding what actions might help improve public services delivery. Labels for pie chart, clockwise from top: Improving the salaries of public servants, punishing corrupt public servants, facilitate presentation of inquiries and complaints, better time schedules to offer services, hours of opening morebroad, measurement of public satisfaction with services, more public offices available, better office attendance schedules, telephonic help, use of automated systems to present papers and documents, single-all-purpose offices for services, using of Internet, payments through telephone.

The ENCIG data therefore highlight an apparent paradox—the existence and severity of corruption as an abstract phenomenon is broadly accepted, but it is not regarded as a negative factor in government performance, defined in this case by evaluating the procedures and public services public agencies routinely offer. How can this be explained?

One possible hypothesis is that once corruption has become deeply embedded in a society, it is viewed as part of a utilitarian relationship between society and government. In other words, corruption is a concern only to the extent that citizens and businesses are unable to undertake their activities. If services, procedures, and regulations can be "effectively" resolved, citizens and entrepreneurs are unconcerned. If they have to deal corruptly with their authorities but can receive effective services by doing so, it is less of a serious social or ethical concern than a

Civil Service ■ 199

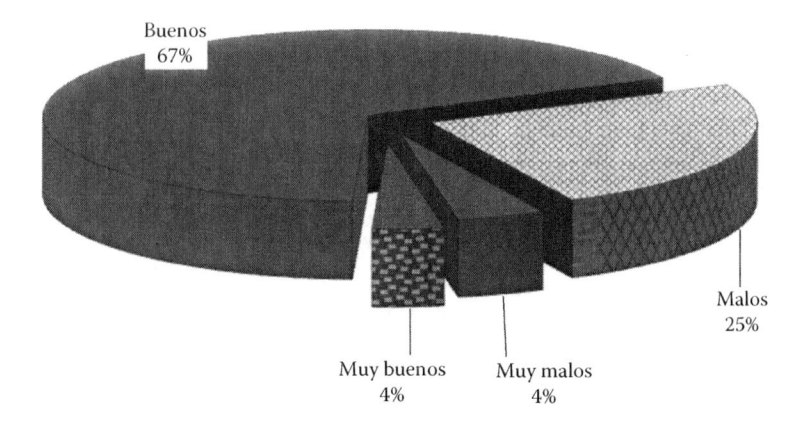

Buenos 67%
Malos 25%
Muy buenos 4%
Muy malos 4%

Figure 12.6 Perceived quality of municipal public services. Labels for the pie chart, clockwise from top: Good, bad, very bad, very good.

practical consideration. Corruption in the abstract may be "bad," but still be considered a socially accepted means of "problem-solving" or "speeding things up" in the daily course of events. While some studies do attempt to show that, at least in the long run, corruption tends to produce worse results for societies (Stapenhurst and Kpundeh, 1999), our intent here is not to engage in this (sometimes idle) regulatory discussion. Rather, we are suggesting a rational explanation for citizens' counterintuitive and paradoxical responses to this phenomenon.

Regardless, these data certainly are cause for concern. A society with systemic corruption such as that suffered by Mexico will not improve through purely instrumentalist or rational ideals, much less through ineffective moralizing. But a pragmatic approach can help. While corruption cannot be eliminated, it can be reduced

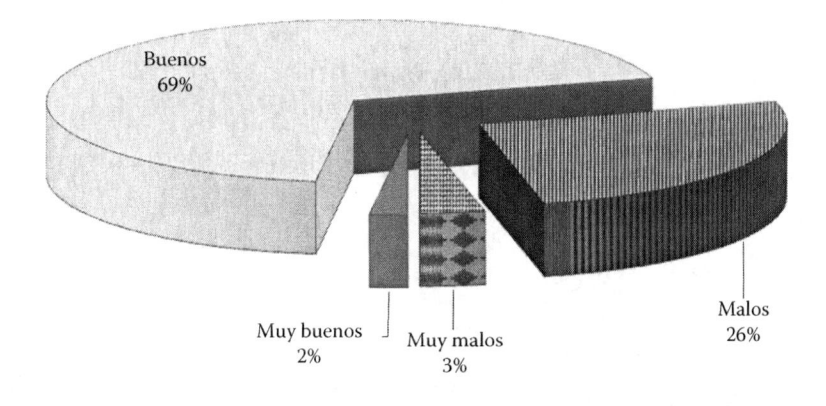

Buenos 69%
Malos 26%
Muy buenos 2%
Muy malos 3%

Figure 12.7 Perceived quality of state-level public services. Labels for the pie chart, clockwise from top: Good, bad, very bad, very good.

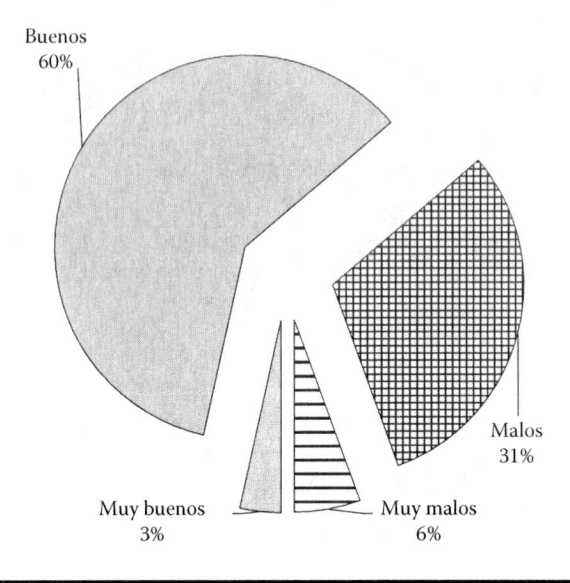

200 ■ *Using the "Narcotrafico" Threat to Build Public Administration*

Figure 12.8 Perceived quality of federal-level public services. Labels for the pie chart, clockwise from top: Good, bad, very bad, very good.

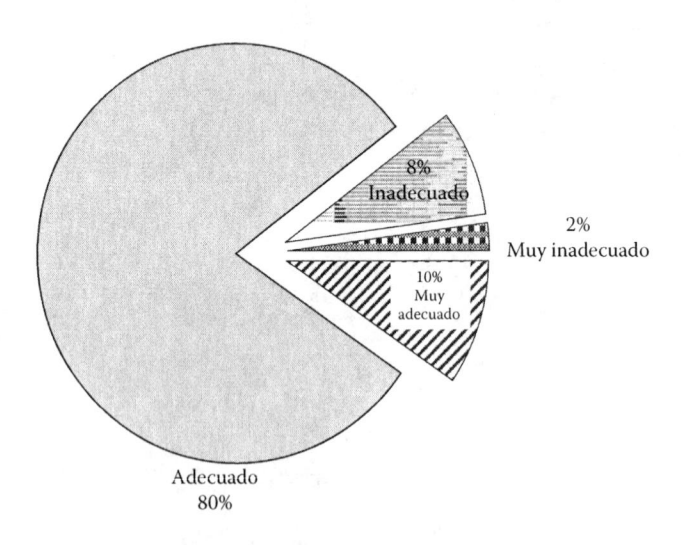

Figure 12.9 Citizen's perceived satisfaction with service provided by governmental offices. Labels for the pie chart, clockwise from top: Adequate, inadequate, very inadequate, very adequate.

and controlled once policy-makers understand that it is not only a question of laws, rules, and punishments, but also of transforming the underlying norms and values comprising the relationship between society and government. No single "magic bullet" will eliminate corruption. Tackling corruption requires constructing multiple actions, rules, norms, and values. Institutions, rules, and standards must be created from a broad perspective that will observe the actual or net effect of such instruments. Good intentions do not suffice; instruments can fail and above all can easily be circumvented when corruption has become systemic.

Many instruments are for doing this are available (Arellano, 2012). In this chapter, we want to emphasize one not originally intended to attack corruption directly, but which in practice has substantial unintended positive effects. In many countries, the civil service is a determinant of the relationship constructed between citizens and public servants and the government in action, for better and for worse. A rigged, rigid, and clientelistic civil service will mark its relationship with its society in all these ways. An effective, meritocratic civil service, constructed on an ethos of impartiality and professionalism, will also mark the government's relationship with society in this respect.

In this context, linking the civil service to the fight against corruption makes a great deal of sense. A civil service is a highly important political institution, one whose existence undeniably transforms political relations at all levels. It also radically affects how elected governments deal with administrative structures. In the presence of a good civil service, administrative agencies and administrators are no longer dependent on political or electoral ups and downs.

However, as a political institution, civil service has very high costs and creates substantive new issues. The expectation, then, is that the benefits of a civil service (e.g., long-term stability of public policies) will exceed their inevitable costs (e.g., the difficulty of assessing the performance of public servants to prevent their inflexibility or bureaucratization). The question, then, is in what sense civil services become a critical political institution for controlling and reducing corruption as a social relationship.

The Political Nature of Civil Service Systems

A civil service system is first and foremost a political construct. Its main function is to artificially isolate administrative structures from the interests and decisions of elected and appointed politicians. It is this fundamental characteristic that provides its essential stability in the long run. In many countries including Mexico, civil service has often been confused with professional service (Arellano, 2008). In other words, it assumes that all that is needed is to professionalize public servants' behavior in order to achieve effective, efficient behavior in public administration. Actually, the latter is but a by-product of the political nature of a civil service (Klingner and Nalbandian, 1998). The key is to construct an institution capable of defending itself from the vagaries of normal power switching in a democracy. It is intended to prevent the perpetuation of a "spoils system" whereby elected and appointed politicians place their political allies into public office so they can control decision making in the government's administrative apparatus.

However, the primary objective of civil service systems objective is to make the administrative apparatus professionally loyal to elected politicians by basing selection and advancement on merit and experience rather than political loyalty. Institutionalizing an effective civil service is clearly not only a matter of rules, laws, and professionalization, but also of a critical political understanding that results in the establishment of an institution able to defend itself against the fluctuations and political pressures it will inevitably suffer. Political agents will always seek different ways of influencing and affecting civil service rules; this is a "normal" situation in any democracy. But the existence and stability of the civil service will depend on the ability of its members to defend and stabilize it. This dynamic, in turn, may cause civil service systems to become a serious problem in a democracy—they can quickly become a stakeholder that defends its interests rather than those of citizens or of the elected officials to whom they are supposed to be professionally responsive.

Because of this fundamental distinction, civil service systems are political institutions that entail significant costs and risks. Attempting to isolate the administrative apparatus is a substantial medium- and long-term innovation that makes it possible to achieve long-term political stability. However, for a civil service system to achieve this level of stability requires that it be able to defend itself against the attempts of elected and appointed politicians to intervene. This is a common struggle in any democracy, where elected politicians seek to alter the rules to make them more flexible and therefore more amenable to situational intervention, while civil service advocates seek to stiffen these rules to prevent interference from elected or appointed officials. In any democracy, this is a constant battle. The ideal, according to Wildavsky (1993), will be achieved when the civil service is able to "speak truth to power," and at the same time when the exercise of this ability is not a constraint on sustaining the principle of substantive professional loyalty. In other words, for example, a civil service system enables career public servants to explain that policies being currently considered have already been attempted and have failed in the past. They will even be able to show them data, evidence, and elements to support this conclusion. If the elected or appointed official decides to implement the policy anyway, a civil service should then always attempt to implement the established policy in the most professional and loyal way possible according to their abilities and knowledge. This balance of political will and professional administrative implementation is the balance that a civil service system gives democracy in the long term. However, it is clear that it also involves the risk that a civil service system may seek stability (at least for itself and its members) over the long-term viability of the policy solutions it is professionally and legally required to implement. Once elected and appointed officials seek to circumvent this as an expression of self-interest rather than of the public interest, the civil servants' logical response is to defend civil service rules and make them increasingly less liable to be affected by politicians' decisions. Herein lies the danger that a civil service system will stagnate—in the battle to defend itself, it may create the conditions for defining itself politically as a bureaucratic interest group, and acting based on this definition political group. In short, a civil service system must be perceived primarily as a political institution and secondarily as a system for human resource management. It is the stability of civil service that permits professionalization rather than the other way around.

In any event, the establishment of a civil service system as a political institution inevitably leads to the development of *esprit de corps* among civil servants. Esprit de corps is indeed the construction of what Weber called the ethics of the office or the office as a vocation (Du Gay, 2011). As a bureaucratic principle, it is crucial in a democracy that public servants maintain a substantive distance from political interests, in order to ensure the fair, effective registration of the various interests at stake or in competition. All this must take place without their being substantively affected by the de facto powers of political factions, due to the differences in religion, gender, or race. The esprit de corps of a civil service is therefore critical to constructing a government action of due process as an essential tool that guarantees fair, equal treatment to individuals when they confront or relate to the state.

Esprit de corps, this vocation of bureaucracy, as Weber called it, is certainly also a source of problems—among them bureaucracy, the impersonalization of treatment between rulers and the ruled, the formalization of any relationship through procedures and records. In any democracy, this duality exists and must be confronted contextually and practically. Because in the last analysis, without esprit de corps it is impossible to construct a stable civil service, capable of defending itself from political vagaries and the manipulative efforts of elected politicians. Without this esprit de corps, there is no possibility of speaking truth to power. Nor, given the substantive legitimacy of elected politicians granted by votes in the polls, would there be any possibility of professional loyalty by the civil service. But at the same time, an esprit de corps creates the possibilities of a process of inflexibility, of creating a faction that ends up defending itself as an apparatus of power rather than as a political institution that can provide long-term stability in an emergent democracy.

Civil Service and Corruption

Let us therefore link these two lines of investigation. On the one hand, there is corruption as a social phenomenon, a complex social relationship that produces a web of links between various government and nongovernment sectors, creating the systematic possibility of the violation of a positional duty. And on the other, there is the civil service as a political institution, which is fundamental and indispensable to the long-term stability of a democracy, but which also embodies the potential to become a partisan, bureaucratic, rigid political force in its own right.

Systemic corruption leads to a sequence of linked events from a variety of actors. It constitutes a sort of social fabric that is constantly reproduced, which can even become an institutionalized practice. That is why it is difficult to tackle this type of corruption with good intentions alone, with laws and general rules that attempt to attack it as if it were a decision by people or individuals (Rose-Ackermann, 2011). These persons or individuals may be systematically embedded in a network of relationships, as a result of which their individual decisions are unimportant. Moreover, the instruments created to combat corruption must in turn affect a social reality. In other words, tools must be implemented; it is in implementation that costs and benefits, the unexpected and unwanted effects of the action, systematically emerge. Indeed, the instruments available for fighting corruption are all costly and limited.

Some scholars (e.g., Arellano and Zamudio, 2011; Arellano et al., 2012) have analyzed three instruments for fighting corruption, in terms of these constraints, costs and complex processes are involved in their implementation. By this we mean the regulations of conflicts of interest, sanctions, and the implementation of the whistle-blower. Through studies in various countries and their organizational structures, we can see how the instruments available for tackling corruption have significant constraints and associated costs that must be taken into account as part of a complex process of implementation and involvement of a phenomenon such as corruption as a social relationship.

In the case of conflicts of interest, the substantive problem observed in the international literature is that of the complexity of identifying such conflicts. Since conflict of interest is a perennial possibility, the problem arises when this conflict of interest becomes a reality and develops in a negative way, with a negative effect on public interest. Conflict of interest is defined as the moment when the decision by a public servant is adversely affected by related private interests (OCDE, 2005). However, in practice, public servants always have private interests. According to the definition, the problem arises when private interests negatively affect the effective performance of their duties. The question is when and how one can measure and know that a decision by a public servant has been negatively affected.

In many countries, it is even acknowledged that a public servant may not realize he is entering an arena of potential conflict of interest. Trying to use regulatory or organizational mechanisms to control each of the possibilities every time a public servant may experience a conflict of interest is impractical, costly, and probably futile. In many countries, progress has been made toward a perspective that sees conflict of interest as an opportunity for education and training: public servants must be warned and trained to locate possible and potential conflicts of interest, and it is the responsibility of public servants themselves to point out and take action on the matter. In other words, a preventive rather than a punitive approach is suggested. This approach shifts responsibility to the public servant to identify these opportunities and warn of the need to take action. In practical terms, handling conflicts of interest will always be a fairly complex, expensive action. The gray areas of definition of the spheres of conflict of interest exist on a daily basis and are normal. That is why their implementation requires the participation of public servants in a constant process of education and prevention. A stable civil service with a strong esprit de corps is essential for dealing with the gray areas of conflicts of interest. The civil service must be jointly responsible in this regard, involving public servants in practices, knowledge, examples, and training to avoid conflicts of interest in practice. Coming from the civil service, public servants themselves will perceive the importance of prevention over punishment.

The same is true of sanctions. In practice, a public servant is forced to understand numerous regulations and standards to make decisions and at the same time to be accountable. This is a normal logic in any democracy: decision makers in public service must constantly balance the need to make decisions effectively and efficiently yet at the same time in such a way that they can constantly be accountable for their actions. Achieving a balance between these two criteria (efficiency/effectiveness and accountability) is a constant task in the life of a public servant in a democracy. A critical tool for achieving this balance is to establish sanctions for those who deviate from these criteria. The issue lies in the viability of the actions needed to create and implement these sanctions in practice. Who should be entrusted to implement and oversee them, and what criteria should be used to systematically apply them, thus become key elements for achieving the desired objectives in practice.

Sanctions are ultimately threats to public officials to prevent them from deviating from norms. But the rules are many, heterogeneous, and varied. Fulfilling them all may be simply impossible, knowing about them all impractical. Some sanctions are due to administrative or procedural failures, others will be for creating opportunities for corruption. Agencies or groups tasked with oversight are at the same time individuals and groups, organizations that need practical criteria to act and in turn are being watched or pressured to obtain results (which for these people are often reduced to locating procedural flaws or opportunities for corruption by any means).

It is therefore plausible to think that the implementation of sanctions for public servants due to regulatory deviations or actions that could address corruption requires the constant involvement of public servants in various organizations and agencies. Again, the importance of a civil service and of an esprit de corps is present, given the complexity involved in implementing the various instruments to fight corruption.

Our last example is that of whistle-blowers. Given that whistle-blowers are both organizational deviants and protectors of the public interest, the regulations needed to protect them must deal with various complexities. How does one protect whistle-blowers? Who should have the burden of proof? How does one (the authority and the complainant himself) ensure that a report on a possible act of corruption is valid and reliable? What effects does the possibility of allowing or encouraging "whistleblowing" have on the organizational environment? How and whom must a whistle-blower respond when an act of corruption appears to be systematic (i.e., occurs with the assent or complicity of senior agency officials?) How can one be sure that what is observed is real and how does someone accused by a whistle-blower know that this accusation is fair and justified? The implementation of protection for whistle-blowers is full of details and complexities. Some regulations make it an obligation or a crime not to report corruption. But placing the burden of proof on a public servant makes this an extremely risky, undesirable activity. At the other extreme, in the absence of clear rules, anyone can report on others without being sure that what has been observed is an act of corruption. If corruption is systemic, the complexity of the act of denunciation may require discretion, time, intelligence, and specialized support. Last but not least are the consequences for the organizational environment: the dynamics of internal reporting may be detrimental to the organizational environment when surveillance becomes a weapon used by certain groups or simply creates an oppressive, demotivating environment of systematic distrust.

Once again, the existence of a civil service with an esprit de corps would be substantive for implementing the figure of a whistle blower, which requires close collaboration and broad communication so that this figure is not distorted and is implemented in a way that is clearly communicated and specified in the various agencies that intervene, implement, and monitor.

Final Reflections

The two dilemmas we have presented here can be extremely important for a country such as Mexico that is plagued by very high levels of systemic corruption and at the same time, suffers not from the lack of an esprit de corps in the civil service but from the lack of a civil service *per se*.

Indeed, corruption is undoubtedly a stable social relationship and one that has been well established in the political system and in the relationship between business and government, politicians and public servants, and the latter and citizens. It is apparently necessary to evaluate the ineffectiveness of current instruments that may be good intentions and even good ideas, but when it comes to implementing them, they certainly face enormous challenges that require more practical visions and constant adjustments regarding strategies.

On the other hand, the civil service is still in its infancy in Mexico. The federal civil service only covers certain middle and senior managers. There is no hope in the short term of involving the majority of the public servants trapped in Mexico's historical paradigm of corporate, clientilist trade union politics. Article 78 of the Federal Act on State Workers, which establishes the status of the State Workers' Federation (FSTSE) as an official monopoly, is an anachronistic example of political system's unwillingness to advance meaningfully toward comprehensive reform of the relationship between the government apparatus and citizens.

According to the 2007 report on the professional career service (SFP, 2007)—there have not been any reports since, although the brief minutes of the Advisory

Council (SFP, 2010) refer to unspecified data available for 2010—of the 36,812 positions identified within the service structure, only 8342 public servants had been certified. The 30,000 odd public servants who can belong to the civil service are currently facing a system designed more to professionalize human resource management than to endow it with legitimacy and credibility as a political institution. Public servants who are already certified will have to deal with the temptations and adjustments that elected politicians always attempt to offer in order to weaken a civil service. Since they do not participate in technical and professionalization committees, or in advisory boards, they do not have the opportunity to defend the civil service. Nor are they currently organized in such a way that they can begin to constitute a structure that is able to "speak truth to power." At least at present, it does not therefore appear to be a strategic body through which the systemic fight against corruption can develop. Without a civil service with an esprit de corps, fighting corruption will probably continue to be a series of good intentions, implemented in isolated regulatory frameworks, and relatively ineffective.

Two reforms appear to be necessary and possible. First, the country's anti-corruption mechanisms must be thoroughly reviewed and amended. Their clear incorporation into a law will make it possible to examine all these instruments together, define them clearly, and establish specific objectives. This will make it possible to evaluate them in terms of their effectiveness, making it possible to understand the costs of these instruments, and adjust them according to their results. In other words, reducing corruption requires instruments, all of which are costly and have limits, and it would therefore be better if they were incorporated into a single regulatory framework, and constantly evaluated in a transparent public fashion, with a comprehensive, accessible information system for citizens and scholars.

In terms of a civil service, it will be necessary to shift from a perspective of professional service to one of civil service, seeking to legitimize a political institution, not just a human resource system. Seeking the legitimacy and credibility of the federal civil service is substantive: its certified members must participate in selection and professionalization committees precisely in order to protect the logical, fair implementation of rules. They must participate on advisory boards precisely to permit the adjustment and strengthening of the rules that make the civil service stable and professional. With these measures, certified public servants will probably start constructing the esprit de corps, which is essential to creating an apparatus that speaks the truth to power and which is professionally (not politically) loyal to elected politicians, and its legitimate immediate superiors. The transformation of the corporate unionist logic in which the vast majority of federal public servants (and those the states) are immersed is another topic of debate: without a more integral civil service and one that incorporates other operating levels, it will be difficult to speak of a civil service capable of supporting, as we have proposed in this chapter, the battle against corruption.

References

Arellano, D. 2008. La implementación de un servicio civil meritocrático: un asunto técnico? El caso de México in F. Longo and C. Ramió (Eds). *La profesionalización del empleo público en América Latina.* Barcelona: CIDOB.

Arellano, D. 2012. *Podemos reducir la corrupción en México? Límites y posibilidades de los instrumentos a nuestro alcance.* México: CIDE.

Arellano, D., A. Medina, and R. Rodríguez. 2012. Instrumentado una política de informantes internos (whistleblowers): mecanismo viable en México para atacar la corrupción? *Foro Internacional* LII(1), 38–91.

Arellano, D. and L. Zamudio. 2011. Organizational and institutional dilemmas in minimizing conflicts of interests in a democracy: Canada, the United States and Mexico. In Sandoval, Irma. *Contemporary Debates on Corruption and Transparency.* Mexico: UNAM.

De Graaf, G. 2007. Causes of corruption: Towards a contextual theory of corruption. *Public Administration Quarterly* 31(1/2), 39–86.

Du Gay, P. 2011. Without regard to persons: Problems of involvement and attachment in 'post-bureaucratic' public management. Stewart Clegg et al. (eds). *Managing Modernity. Beyond Bureaucracy?* Oxford: Oxford University Press.

INEGI. 2011. ENCIG 2011. Available online at: http://www.inegi.org.mx/est/contenidos/Proyectos/encuestas/hogares/especiales/encig/2011/presentacion.aspx

Klingner, D. and J. Nalbandian. 1998. *Public Personnel Management.* New Jersey: Prentice-Hall.

Malen Seña, J. 2002. *La corrupción. Aspectos éticos, económicos, políticos y jurídicos.* Barcelona: Gedisa.

OCDE. 2005. *Guidelines for Managing Conflict of Interests in the Public Service.* Paris: OCDE.

Rose-Ackermann, S. 2011. The political economy of corruption: Research and Policy, in Sandoval, Irma. *Contemporary Debates on Corruption and Transparency.* Mexico: UNAM.

SFP. Secretaría de la Función Pública México. 2010. Minutes to the Advisory Council for the Professional Career System. Mexico.

SFP. Secretaría de la Función Pública México. 2007. Informe Anual Servicio Profesional de Carrera. Mexico.

Stapenhurst, R. and S. Kpundeh. 1999. *Curbing Corruption.* Washington, DC: World Bank.

Transparency International. 2012. Annual Report. Berlin: Transparency International.

Vertiz, M. 2000. El combate a la corrupción en los trámites administrativos. Una aproximación teórica. In *Gestión y Política Pública.* IX (2).

Wildavsky, A. 1993. *Speaking Truth to Power.* California: Tavistock.

Chapter 13

Latin American States and the Imperatives of Unfinished Modernity
State Crisis and Public Security in Mexico

Miguel Moreno Plata

Contents

Introduction	210
Modernity: Approaches and Debates	210
The Failure of Modernity and the State Crisis in Latin America	210
The Dimensions of the Contemporary State	211
The Institutional Crisis of the Mexican State	212
Bureaucracy	212
Functional Legal Authority	213
Collective Identity and Defense of National Interests	217
Conclusion	218
References	220

Introduction

Societies and states in Latin America continue to suffer the effects of unfinished modernity, including the crisis of the State and its troubled relationship with society. Because Latin American modernization generally proceeded based on the premises of central state action and the building of homogeneous societies, it cannot proceed farther without addressing and reversing these false premises. The current crisis of society and State in Mexico illustrates this situation.

The contemporary manifestations of this unfinished modernity include a general lack of state capacity, particularly the inability to develop institutions capable of realizing the public interest and common good. With this assertion as the theoretical starting point, we analyze the current status of the Mexican state, particularly with respect to public security, organized crime, and the emergence of community self-defense groups in various regions of the country. Next, we analyze the functionality of Mexican public administration using evidence related to bureaucratic effectiveness in general and law enforcement in particular.

Modernity: Approaches and Debates

The term "modern" implies consciousness of an historical transition from the old to the new. In Europe, modernity is understood as opposition between tradition and the present (Habermas, 2001). It refers to ways of social life or organization that emerged in Europe in the seventeenth century, and whose influence has spread to most of the world via globalization (Giddens, 2008).

The state is the quintessential political form of modernity. It replaces existing traditions, customs, and laws with a culture and a legal order integrated within a territorial unit. However, the link between the state and modernity is more complex and contradictory in Latin America and other regions that have different cultural traditions and trajectories than the Western world. To understand the characteristics and scope of modernity in non-Western regions, we must analyze the development of capitalism and the nation-state from varied cultural, social, and political perspectives.

The Failure of Modernity and the State Crisis in Latin America

Modernization is a process of social secularization that implies the predominance of collective action grounded in instrumental rationality, the institutionalization of change in relation to this rationality, and increasing differentiation and specialization of roles and institutions (Calderón, 1995). Because culture is related to social mobilization and economic development (Huntington, 1996), modernization also involves the struggle for social order, defined in several different ways (i.e., technical/

instrumental rationality achieved through technical and social division of labor) and normative rationality achieved through hierarchies and other organizational principles of communication, coordination, and control. The former relates to modernization and the latter to modernity (Medellín Torres, 1996).

Recent conflicts in the developing world, particularly in the Middle East, illustrate the failure to synthesize traditional cultures and modernization (Ottone, 2000; Mansilla Blanco, 2012; Abu-Tarbush, 2012; Gutierrez de Terán Gómez, 2012; Cruz, 2013). Having developed a model of elite leadership perceived as separate from society rather than democratic participation, they share a common lack of capacity for economic and social inclusiveness (Ottone, 2000).

Because Latin American countries originated in a mercantilist era, their economic development was predicated on exporting raw materials to Europe and importing manufactured goods from Europe. As colonies became independent, the structural characteristics of their social, political, and economic order did not change. Societies remained hierarchical, polarized, and rigid, with a strong concentration of wealth and power in elite oligarchies. Through the exercise of coercive power through political systems—what Kaplan termed the "Creole Leviathan" (1989)—the ruling elite monopolized the means of societal decision making, direction, and control. Thus, Latin America today epitomizes an instrumentally rational form of globalization with respect to "modern" technology, communications, and economic structure. With the assistance of external consultants and international development organizations, the prototypical Latin American state emerged during the transition to participatory democracy and market capitalism that began in the mid-1980s. Institutional restructuring was part of an externally imposed order within which "… democracy and a democratic transition was proclaimed as the new strategic center of modernization: all that the market cannot discipline, democracy will" (Medellín Torres, 1996).

The Dimensions of the Contemporary State

Since the crisis between modernization and modernity leads to weaknesses in State capacity, it may also be useful to explore the dimensions of the contemporary state. According to O'Donnell (2004, 2008), the state can be viewed as (a) a set of complex bureaucratic organizations with legal responsibilities to perform and to protect the public interest, (b) a regulatory system (i.e., the administrative state) that permeates and determines numerous social relations, (c) a collective identity related to the emergence and consolidation of nationalism, and (d) a regulator of the different degrees of openness or penetrability of its spaces and borders by agents operating on the State's population from outside its territory.

These four factors can be used as to assess a state's capacity. With some exceptions, Latin American states have low scores on these items. Because of the fundamental conflict between instrumental modernization and normative modernity

(Medellín Torres, 1996), modernization in most Latin American countries reflects deep tensions and conflict over the appropriate role of the state as it cedes institutional authority to other nongovernmental actors in an era of privatization and social mobilization (Medellín Torres, 1996). States continue to struggle with incapability to integrate hierarchical systems of authority and responsibility with the imperatives of networked governance.

This crisis manifests itself in their inability to control territory and institutionalize state order within their geographic borders. This leads to the existence of "brown zones," vast geographic regions and segments of society where rules are not really set by the state, but instead dictated by various mafias and other vested interests (O'Donnell, 2008). For example, various substitutes for institutional state power (e.g., self-defense brigades and drug cartels) have emerged throughout Latin America. Also, the growth of informal economies and widespread tax evasion illustrate the gulf between the formal economy and informal activities that are anchored to traditional social norms and structures that diminish the state's regulatory capabilities.

The Institutional Crisis of the Mexican State

These same four criteria (i.e., bureaucracy, legal system, collective identity, and filtering function) can be used to describe and analyze the social and institutional crisis in Mexico.

Bureaucracy

The 70 years of hegemony of the Institutional Revolutionary Party (PRI) over Mexican politics ended with the election of PAN candidate Vicente Fox Quesada to the presidency in 2000. This brought about the passage of laws and the implementation of administrative reforms designed to modernize and transform government bureaucracy by improving public access and accountability. These included the Federal Law of Transparency and Access to Public Government Information (DOF, 2002) and the General Law on Governmental Accountability (DOF, 2008). While some agencies (e.g., the Federal Electoral Institute, the Mexican Foreign Service, and technical areas of the Ministry of Finance and Public Credit) had operated under specialized civil service systems, there was no general law to support implementation of a professional public service until the Law on the Professional Career Service in the Federal Public Administration was approved (DOF, 2003). This system now operates in 15 units and 62 decentralized agencies of the centralized national government. According to the latest available data (SFP, 2007), the professional career service system includes 41,765 positions from officer to general director. It filled 812 positions in 36 agencies and opened 1828 vacancies for public competition, for a total of 8342 public servants with appointments.

The Mexican government has also instituted legal and bureaucratic reforms to professionalize and improve the performance of national, state, and local public security agencies. In 2009, Congress passed a general law establishing a national public security system based on professionalization and performance across all three levels of government (LGSNSP, DOF, 2012). A key element of this system was the creation or strengthening of internal evaluation and control standards via the creation of a Center for Research and National Security (CISEN) responsible for evaluating and certifying law enforcement professionals (SESNSP, 2012). From January 2010 through December 2012, CISEN reported that it had conducted evaluations of 332,497 of 424,860 state and municipal public safety employees (78%). Of the total over the total universe, CISEN evaluated 220,657 of 270,062 state police (81%), of whom 31,264 were certified; and 111,840 of 154,798 municipal police (72%), of whom only 819 were certified (SESNSP, 2012). During the same period, CISEN also evaluated 80,619 applicants for police positions—70,258 state and 10,361—and approved 30,948 (38%) of them (SESNSP, 2012). These national laws are paralleled by similar legislation in the states of Veracruz (Law of Public Service Career in Centralized Public Administration (2003), Quintana Roo (LSPCQR, 2002), and Mexico City (LSPCAPDF, 2008).

Functional Legal Authority

While substantial efforts have taken place to improve the administrative performance of public safety institutions at the federal, state, and municipal levels, the Mexican government has arguably been much less effective at establishing functional legal authority throughout the country. Southwest Mexico (e.g., Michoacán, Guerrero, Oaxaca, and Chiapas) has always been considered different from the rest of Mexico, in fact if not in law, due to a culture of political instability, rural chiefdom, political repression, social violence, rural and urban guerrilla activity, and a tradition of strong local control through community-based indigenous organizations (Bartra, 2000; Rodriguez Wallenius, 2005).

This situation is illustrated by the emergence of community-level vigilante groups in parts of the States of Guerrero and Michoacán. Beginning in 1995, indigenous Mixtec and Tlapanecos from several municipalities in Guerrero formed a Regional Community Authority (RCCA) to address the wave of violence and insecurity that had afflicted the region. Despite being considered illegal, this community police agency did achieve a significant reduction in insecurity and violence, and built a regional justice system based on community law. State public security agencies have thus far failed to dismantle it, despite several attempts to do so.

The increasing militarization of the fight against drug trafficking undertaken by the Mexican government, particularly during the presidency of Felipe Calderón, highlighted long-standing disputes over the cultural identity and legal rights of indigenous people vis-á-vis the national government (Sierra, 2010). The extreme poverty of the Montaña and Costa Chica areas in Guerrero has led to enduring patterns of social injustice, structural violence, and military repression. Because of racist institutions and actions, the State has not only failed to provide basic services to the population, but also failed to protect the indigenous population against human rights violations by civil and military authorities (Gasparello, 2009). The racism, corruption, and arbitrariness in the local justice system, especially in criminal matters, instigated the emergence of a second grass-roots organization in Guerrero, the Community Security and Justice System (SSJC), an "… autonomous institution that maintains security and imparts justice at a regional level, promoting collective community security, providing free services, and reintegration prisoners into society" (Gasparello, 2009). But because Article 2 of the Mexican Constitution is insufficient with respect to the rights and autonomy of indigenous people (López Sollano, 2010), the Mexican state still does not recognize the legality of community-based organizations that provide police security and administer justice (Hale, 2004).

A third example is the institutional and economic crisis in the State of Michoacán, caused by drug trafficking and the war against it. State government sources admit that organized criminal organizations have infiltrated 85 of the State's 113 municipalities (Fuentes-Salinas, 2013), with the most severe cases being municipalities located in the region of Tierra Caliente. The case of La Ruana, Buena Vista Township Tomatlán is paradigmatic. According to news reports, this town was besieged by a drug cartel known as the "Knights Templar." Out of gas, and with little food and medicine, the community organized a self-defense group with its Tepalcatepec neighbors, although they are also suspected of receiving support of a rival gang, the "Jalisco New Generation Cartel." So far, at least 20 have died (Becerra-Acosta, 2013).

The lack of governability in Tierra Caliente is due to the combined effects of strong criminal organizations and weak government. Michoacán is in many ways a social laboratory of organized crime as a "shadow" government, beginning a decade ago with the Zetas and "La Familia Michoacana." In addition to their other revenue sources, TCOs extort money from the community, especially businessmen engaged in trade and agriculture (Valdés Castellanos, 2013). They are able to do so with impunity due to wholesale corruption of state and local police agencies, abetted by high-ranking State and local officials. Among the most notorious examples are Julio Cesar Godoy, who was member of the PRD Chamber of Deputies and is currently a fugitive. Saul Soliz, the alleged leader of the "Knights Templar" and the "La Familia Cartel," served as public security director of Turicato, Michoacán (2003–2005) and ran for Congress in 2009. He was captured in 2011 and is now in federal prison.

These TCOs use two strategies to infiltrate and control local governments in at least 20 municipalities in Michoacán. By controlling the allocation of public works contracts, they divert tax revenue to themselves; and by controlling the selection of local police chiefs, they obtain vital information about the movements and operation protocols of public security agencies, including the Mexican army, federal police, judicial police, and state police (Valdés Castellanos, 2013).

Clearly, under these circumstances, the State has lost—or surrendered to the cartels—the power of law in parts of Michoacán, principally in Tierra Caliente. Under this circumstance, many indigenous communities (e.g., the Municipality of Cherán) have opted for armed self-defense by hiring community guards as part of the system of "uses and customs" granted by the Constitution, as in the case. Other nonindigenous communities have done the same. In 2013, the Municipality of Buenavista (where the town of Felipe Carrillo Puerto, better known as the Ruana is located), Tepalcatepec and Coalcomán reported the emergence of community police (QUADRATIN, 2013). The new centralized national security strategy attempts to reassert government control through a "surge" of military units and federal policy, while maintaining intergovernmental coordination and control.

The basic function of the state is to maintain order and achieve predictable social relations among the population (O'Donnell, 2008). This means establishing the rule of law, based on four fundamental principles:

1. The government and its officials and agents as well as individuals and private entities are accountable under the law.
2. The laws are clear, publicized, stable, and just, are applied evenly, and protect fundamental rights, including the security of persons and property.
3. The process by which the laws are enacted, administered and enforced is accessible, fair, and efficient.
4. Justice is delivered timely by competent, ethical, and independent representatives and neutrals who are of sufficient number, have adequate resources, and reflected the makeup of the communities they serve" (Agrast et al., 2013).

Derived from these principles, the rule of law index is composed of nine basic dimensions: limited government powers, absence of corruption, order and security, fundamental rights, open government, regulatory enforcement, civil justice, criminal justice, and informal justice. These nine factors are further disaggregated into 48 specific indicators (Agrast et al., 2013). The third factor ("order and security") measures the extent to which society ensures the safety of people and property, as indicated by the absence of conventional crime, of political violence (including terrorism, armed conflict, and political unrest) and of violence as a socially acceptable means to redress personal grievances (Agrast et al., 2013). The WJP assumes that an effective system of criminal justice is a key aspect of the rule of law, the natural mechanism to resolve grievances and bring action against individuals for offenses against society. Thus, the factor "criminal justice" consists of seven indicators: the criminal investigation system is effective, criminal adjudication system is timely and effective, the correctional system is effective at reducing criminal behavior, the criminal system is impartial, the criminal system is free of corruption, "the criminal system is free of improper government influence," and due process of law and the rights of the accused are protected (Agrast et al., 2013).

According to the WJP:

> Mexico has a long constitutional tradition with an independent judiciary and strong protection for free speech and freedom of religion. Mexico stands out among in Latin American countries for effective checks on government power (ranking sixth in the region) and open government (ranking thirty second globally and fifth within the region). Corruption is a serious problem in all branches of government (ranking seventy-four), and Mexico's police forces struggle to guarantee the security of its citizens against crime and violence (ranking ninety-first). The criminal justice system also ranks ninety-first, mainly because of weakness in the criminal investigation and adjudication systems, prevalent discrimination against vulnerable groups, corruption among judges and law enforcement officials, and violations of due process of law and the rights of the accused. (Agrast et al., 2013)

Another important and complementary source is the National Survey on Victimization and Perception of Public Security (ENVIPE) conducted by the National Institute of Statistics and Geography (INEGI) since 2010. The most recent ENVIPE (INEGI, 2012a) indicates that:

- An estimated 18,675,004 persons (24.5% of those over 18) were crime victims in 2011; there is no significant statistical difference between the rate in 2010 and 2011.
- In both 2010 and 2011, 91.6% of crimes were not reported or did not result in even a preliminary investigation.
- When asked their reasons for not reporting crimes, 63% of respondents said this was due to lack of action by the authorities, loss of time, and distrust of criminal investigation and justice systems.
- With respect to corruption, traffic police are perceived as the most corrupt (83%), followed by municipal preventive police (71%). The authorities identified as the least corrupt are the Navy (15%) and the Army (22%).
- As a bright spot, perceived insecurity declined from 69.5% to 66.6% of the population.
- However, 50% of the population rated the institutional performance of authorities related with security, enforcement, and administration of justice as "poor." This varied by institution: while the performance of the Army or the Navy was rated over 80% "effective," judges (44%), and municipal preventive police (30%) were considered much less so.

The National Survey on Victimization of Business 2012 (ENVE) estimates the extent to which victimization of representative common law crimes harms the private sector. The main results of the ENVE (INEGI, 2012b) are

- Prevalence: crime affects 3,737 of every 10,000 businesses (37.4%). The most frequently noted crimes are corruption, theft (of merchandise, money, supplies or goods), and extortion.
- Reporting: 88% of crime was not reported or did not result in a preliminary investigation.
- Public insecurity: 76% of economic units perceived insecurity in their environment and activities.
- Institutional performance: Army (86%), Navy (85%), judges (49%), state police (44%), public prosecutors (37%), and municipal preventive police (37%).
- Seriousness: 59% of businesses consider insecurity and crime as their biggest problem.
- Economic cost: 115.2 billion pesos annually.

According to the Failed States Index (FFP, 2013), Mexico ranks 97th out of 178 countries, and it is in the "high warning" category. The Failed States Index (FSI) is not only an essential tool for evaluating the pressures on nation states in concrete terms, but also an important tool for the identification of these pressures that are leading a state to the brink of collapse. From the above, we can establish the fact that according to the basic indicators of rule of law, Mexico has serious problems of enforcement in areas related to public security, criminal investigation, and criminal justice systems. We note serious deficiencies in the functioning of institutions responsible for law enforcement, particularly at the state and municipal levels. The Mexican state has low levels of performance on key indicators related to the absence of crime, the effectiveness of the criminal investigation system, and the criminal justice system. Thus, at least based on O'Donnell's metrics (2008), Mexico seems closer to the definition of a "failed state" than to a democracy categorized by the rule of law.

Collective Identity and Defense of National Interests

While Mexicans do share a collective identity, they are also divided by race, gender, and indigenous cultures and languages (Shorris, 1992). Mexico's difficulties with enforcing the rule of law, achieving social equity, and providing public services among certain populations and in certain geographic areas undercut the ideal of a collective national identity. Also, among other issues, the international legal system is marked by the clash between the principles of modern law versus common law (i.e., human rights versus traditional legal systems and indigenous customs) (Grossi, 2003). For example, Eufrosina Cruz Mendoza was struck from a municipal ballot in Santa Maria Quiregolani (Oaxaca) for failing to meet a long-standing informal requirement (i.e., time of service to the community), despite having met all federal, state, and local laws for candidacy (CNDH, 2008). Globalization has negatively affected all countries' regulatory authority to defend their borders and their people against outside influences (Ocampo, 2004: 375). This affects national sovereignty and international law (Moreno Plata, 2011). It also has concrete operational effects on Mexico, as measured by various international economic treaties and agreements.

According to sources in the Ministry of Economy (SE, 2013), Mexico currently has 12 free trade agreements with 44 countries, 28 agreements for the promotion and reciprocal protection of investments, and nine partial and complementary economic agreements under the Latin American Integration Association (LAIA). Among the most significant of the free trade agreements is NAFTA (Mexico, Canada, and the United States) and the Mexico–European Free Trade Association. Within the LAIA framework, we note the ACE-55 between Mexico and the MERCOSUR and the ACE-53 agreement between Mexico and Brazil. These international treaties give us a first approximation of the openness of Mexican markets to the international economy. However, the internationalization process also covers matters relating to the environment and social development, whose international instruments also contribute to the porosity of the borders functional of the Mexican national state.

Finally, it must be noted that the transnational criminal organizations (TCOs) are an important aspect of globalization and the changing definition of national sovereignty. The processes of democratization and the policies of stabilization in Latin American economies occurred in a context of simultaneous explosion of international market of drugs such as cocaine, with a great demand in the United States (Gamarra, 2004). This is particularly significant in the case of countries such as Colombia, Mexico, Central America, and the Andean region. This leads us to point out the fact that an important part in the functioning of the current national security system and justice system depends on the consolidation of international systems of cooperation and an effective transnational governance, particularly in matters relating to terrorism, drug trafficking, organ trafficking, and trafficking in persons.

Conclusion

In developing countries, the crisis of modernity is manifested in the clash of two rationalities. On one hand, transnational agents of modernization—the consumption and production systems—are the main actors of instrumental rationality through the globalization of economics and technology. On the other, nation states remain the guardians of normative rationality, responsible for defending the social contract with citizens. In Latin America as elsewhere, conflicts between modernization and modernity arise from social and cultural particularities of the region.

In Latin America, the crisis of the state in Latin America is the crisis of unfinished modernity, as reflected by a lack of state capacity (measured in terms of bureaucratic effectiveness, legal authority, national identity, and border protection) in the exercise of institutional domain; crisis that crosses the central nerve of the state apparatus.

At a conceptual level, this requires review of the role of the state and a reconstruction of its relationship to other institutions in society (e.g., a review of the efficacy of state power, the effectiveness of the legal system, and the exercise of regulatory functions).

In the case of Mexico, the modernity conflict is manifested in the crisis of the state and society. The problems of public security and crime are the tip of the iceberg. The problem is actually much deeper, because it has to do directly with the inefficacy of the state to exercise its appropriate role (O'Donnell, 2004, 2008) in society. What we are left with is an inadequately professionalized bureaucracy, inadequate rule of law, lack of collective identity and inadequate protection of social and national interests. With respect to the bureaucracy, we can point to few signs of progress in implementing the public service career system as a *sine qua non*, for progress in developing an administrative state. Creation of the federal public service had some initial momentum during the second half of the presidency of Vicente Fox (2003–2006) government of Vicente Fox and the start of his successor Felipe Calderon's term (2006–2009), but this motivation seems to have slackened since. Effort seems eclipsed on the eve of the election of 2012 and start of the current government. There is some evidence to support the implementation of professional public administrative systems in state and municipal governments, particularly with respect to regulatory activities. The professionalization of public safety and criminal justice systems seem to parallel the trend. There is some progress at the federal level, but little or none at the state and municipal level.

The emergency of nongovernmental community self-defense groups in the face of minimally effective government and highly effective TCOs in the states of Guerrero and Michoacán seems to confirm this. By rights, municipal government should be the first line of defense and the first avenue for state action. But it is unfortunately also the weak link in the chain of institutions that operationalize government's capacity to protect citizens and reduce violence. Municipal governments have been relatively helpless against institutional assault by TCOs. Many have been but tools to maintain the private interests of local elites rather than protecting the public interest. Their dysfunctionality as instruments of the state is exemplified by their historical abandonment of people in regions such as Montaña and Costa Chica in Guerrero.

The only solution is to rely on public dissatisfaction with insecurity and extreme poverty to drive the formation of community-based groups that can pressure the political system toward a renovation and reengineering of the Mexican state. This means overcoming the disconnect between economic and technological modernization and normative modernity by working toward a society that is shared, inclusive, pluralistic, democratic, and federalist. At the same time, we must strengthen the state's institutional capacity with respect to bureaucratic effectiveness, the rule of law, preservation of national identity with cultural and regional diversity, and the defense of national interests and promoting sustainable development of regions and localities.

References

Abu-Tarbush, J. 2012. Las revueltas árabes responden a sus propias condiciones y peculiaridades. *Boletín de Arredalia*, 3: 6–10. Pontevedra, Spain: Instituto Gallego de Análisis y Documentación Internacional. Available online at: info@igadi.org.

Agrast, D., Botero, J. C., Martínez, J., Ponce, A., Pratt, C. 2013. *Rule of Law Index 2012–2013*. Washington: The World Justice Project.

Bartra, A. 2000. Sur profundo. En A. Bartra (ed.), *Crónicas del Sur. Utopías Campesinas en Guerrero*. México: ERA, pp. 13–74.

Becerra-Acosta, J. P. May 15, 2013. Dejaremos las armas solo si se retiran los Templarios. *El Milenio*. Available online at: http://sipse.com. Accessed May 15, 2013.

Calderón, F. G. 1995. Subjetividad y modernización en las sociedades contemporáneas: del clientelismo burocrático a la cultura democrática en América Latina. *Reforma y Democracia*, 3: 47–66.

Comisión Nacional de los Derechos Humanos (CNDH). March 2008. Informe especial de la Comisión Nacional de los Derechos Humanos sobre el caso de discriminación a la profesora Eufrosina Cruz Mendoza. *La Gaceta* 212.

Cruz, M. 2013. Dos Años Después de la Primavera árabe". Available online at: http://www.temas.cl. Accessed August 10, 2013.

Diario Oficial de la Federación (DOF). December 31, 2008. Ley General de Contabilidad Gubernamental.

Diario Oficial de la Federación (DOF). April 10, 2003. Ley del Servicio Profesional de Carrera en la Administración Pública Federal (LSPCAPF).

Diario Oficial de la Federación (DOF). June 11, 2002. Ley Federal de Transparencia y Acceso a la Información Pública Gubernamental.

Diario Oficial de la Federación (DOF). December 28, 2012. *Ley General del Sistema Nacional de Seguridad Pública* (LGSNSP).

Fund for Peace. 2013. *The Failed States Index*. Available online at: http://www.failedstatesindex.org, Accessed August 15, 2013.

Fuentes-Salinas, S. 2013. *Municipios infiltrados y la nueva estrategia contra el crimen organizado*. Available on line at: http://www.impactousa.com Accessed May 16, 2013.

Gamarra, E. 2004. La democracia y las drogas en América Latina y el Caribe. *La Democracia en América Latina. Hacia una Democracia de Ciudadanas y Ciudadanos*. Buenos Aires: PNUD.

Gasparello, G. 2009. Policía Comunitaria de Guerrero, investigación y autonomía. *Política y Cultura*, 32: 61–78.

Gobierno del Distrito Federal. October 8, 2008. Ley del Servicio Público de Carrera de la Administración Pública del Distrito Federal. *Gaceta Oficial del Distrito Federal*.

Gobierno del Estado de Quintana Roo. February 6, 2002. *Ley del Servicio Público de Carrera. Periódico Oficial del Estado de Quintana Roo*.

Gobierno del Estado de Veracruz. October 10, 2003. *Ley del Servicio Público de Carrera en la Administración Pública Centralizada. Gaceta Oficial del Estado de Veracruz* de fecha 10 de octubre de 2003.

Giddens, A. 2008. *Consecuencias de la modernidad*. Madrid: Alianza Editorial.

Grossi, P. 2003, *Mitología jurídica de la modernidad*. Madrid: Editorial Trotta.

Gutiérrez de Terán Gómez, Benita. 2012. Hay una clara tendencia en el seno de la sociedad árabe hacia la democratización. *Boletín de Arredalia, 3*: 11–14. (Instituto Gallego de Análisis y Documentación Internacional).

Habermas, J. 2001. *Más allá del Estado Nacional*. Madrid: Trotta.
Hale, C. 2004. Rethinking Indigenous Politics in the Era of the Indio Permitido, in *NACLA, Report of the Americas*. New York: NACLA, pp. 16–21.
Huntington, S. P. 1996. *El Orden Político en las Sociedades en Cambio*. Barcelona: Editorial Paidós.
Instituto Nacional de Estadística y Geografía (INEGI). 2012a. *Encuesta Nacional de Victimización y Percepción sobre Seguridad Pública 2012*. Available online at: http://www.inegi.org.mx Accessed August 13, 2013.
Instituto Nacional de Estadística y Geografía (INEGI). 2012b. *Encuesta Nacional de Victimización de Empresas 2012*. Available online at: http://www.inegi.org.mx Accessed August 13, 2013.
Kaplan, M. 1989. *Aspectos del Estado en América Latina*. México: Universidad Nacional Autónoma de México.
López Sollano, S. 2010. Campesinos, autonomía y otro desarrollo en el Guerrero de hoy. *VIII Congreso Latinoamericano de Sociología Rural*, Porto Galinhas, Brasil, noviembre de 2010.
Mansilla Blanco, R. 2012. Ano II da Primavera árabe: o inevitable 'peso da realidade.' *Boletín de Arredalia*, 3: 15–18. Instituto Gallego de Análisis y Documentación Internacional.
Medellín Torres, P. 1996. La modernización del Estado en América Latina: Entre la reestructuración y el reformismo. *Revista de Administración Pública*, 91: 89–138. México: Instituto Nacional de Administración Pública.
Moreno Plata, M. 2011. *La Ineficacia del Derecho Internacional Ambiental. Repensando los Límites de la Soberanía Nacional desde la Problemática Ambiental*. México: Universidad Autónoma de la Ciudad de México, y Plaza y Valdés.
Ocampo, J.A. 2004. Economía y democracia. In *La Democracia en América Latina. Hacia una democracia de ciudadanas y ciudadanos*. Buenos Aires: PNUD, Alfaguara.
O'Donnell, G. October 2008. Algunas reflexiones acerca de la democracia, el Estado y sus múltiples caras. *Reforma y Democracia*, 42. Caracas: Centro Latinoamericano de Administración para el Desarrollo (CLAD). Available online at: http://www.clad.org. Accessed August 11, 2013.
O'Donnell, G. 2004. Acerca del estado en América Latina contemporánea: diez tesis para discusión. In Alfaguara (ed.), *La Democracia en América Latina. Hacia una Democracia de Ciudadanas y Ciudadanos*. Buenos Aires: PNUD.
Ottone, E. 2000. *La modernidad problemática. Cuatro ensayos sobre el desarrollo latinoamericano*, México: Editorial Jus.
QUADRATIN. 2013. *Surgen Policías Comunitarias en Buenavista y Tepalcatepec*. Available online at: http://www.quadratin.com.mx. Accessed February 24, 2013.
Rodríguez Wallenius, C. 2005. *La Disputa por el Desarrollo Regional: Movimientos Sociales y Constitución de Poderes Locales en el Oriente de la Costa Chica de Guerrero*. México: Plaza y Valdés.
Secretaría de Economía. 2013. *Acuerdos y tratados comerciales suscritos por México*. Available online at: http://www.economia.gob.mx. Accessed August 14, 2013.
Secretaría de la Función Pública (SFP). 2007. *Informe anual de operación del Sistema del Servicio Profesional de Carrera*. México.
Secretariado Ejecutivo del Sistema Nacional de Seguridad Pública (SESNSP). 2012. *Informe de Actividades 2012*. Available online at: http://www.secretariadoejecutivosnsp.gob.mx. Accessed August 11, 2013.
Shorris, Earl. 1992. *Latinos*. New York: W.W. Norton.

Sierra, M. T. 2010. Construyendo seguridad y justicia en los márgenes del Estado: La experiencia de la policía comunitaria de Guerrero. Ponencia presentada en la Mesa Justicia comunitaria y retos actuales (violencia, seguridad, derechos humanos, género), *VII Congreso de la RELAJU*, Lima, Perú 4–6 de agosto del 2010.

Valdés Castellanos, G. May 15, 2013. Michoacán: Casa tomada. *El Milenio.* p. 16.

Chapter 14

Publicness and Governance

Ricardo Uvalle Berrones

Contents

Context 223
Rethinking State Action 226
The Strength of the Public Interest 227
The New Rules of the Game.. 228
Relationship between Public Oversight and Good Governance 230
Conclusion...233
Implications for Relations between Mexico and the United States 233
References 236

Context

Crises and change are contextual factors that influence both the role of the State and the development of public administration. With the rise of interventionist States from 1945 to 1975 in the context of the Cold War, public administrations occupied a central place in the economic, political, and social processes to stimulate the production and distribution of goods and services. After the period of economic and financial adjustment that States experienced during the 1980s to correct problems of debt and fiscal deficit, public administration has been recovering its position and prestige in the public eye as a recognized institution that reflects commitment to collective goals. Moreover, with the fall of the Berlin Wall and the political regimes in Eastern Europe, global geopolitics and the acceleration of globalization are modified, changing the life of institutions including the market, the State and public administration, forcing review of the roles they played.

In the past, public administration was responsible for core tasks in the pursuit of economic and social development, using plans and strategies aimed at the development of wealth and capital and the distribution of social benefits. Within this perspective, the relationship between society and the welfare state (Luhmann, 1981) is built in implementing activities related to the planning, scheduling, and control, subject to significant administrative hierarchy relationships that ensure uniformity of tasks to fulfill. The end of the Cold War and of the era of State intervention in the 1980s, combined with the pressures of globalization, discredited administration, and bureaucracy, in that the public service was no longer considered a reliable vehicle for relating political leaders to those they governed. The failures of the Interventionist State led to adoption of market-driven development mechanisms (e.g., privatization and deregulation) aimed at curbing administrative and bureaucratic excesses. At the same time, the loss of responsiveness and the risks of lawlessness (Crozier et al., 1975) alerted political leaders of the need to strengthen the essential functions of the State, and of the need for corrective measures to prevent further disruptions in government.

Even after market mechanisms replaced direct State intervention in the economy, the failure of State operations continued to negatively impact the development of the market economy and its ability to achieve the tangible benefits people demanded. This failure was due to pronounced asymmetry between revenues and expenditures, and to the continued autonomy of administrative entities in the face of actual results and actual economic systems. The rise of industrial-age bureaucracies (Weber, 1973) resulted in economic surpluses that were nonetheless insufficient to support the operating expenses of the State. In addition, political pressures led to legislative gridlock that perpetuated deficit financing of public services, which led to continued reliance on an unsustainable model of public finances.

In this context of political and economic uncertainty, public agencies faced their own internal crises. In previous eras, bureaucracies had calibrated their responses to political pressure by first calculating political costs and benefits and then designing program monitoring and evaluation systems that catered to the groups and organizations that require the intervention of the authority in collective matters. But given the underlying mistrust of interventionist government policies, their accustomed responses, based on measuring program efficiency and effectiveness, were no longer adequate. However, despite the preferences of adherents to market models and mechanisms, this did not obviate the need for public administration. In the end, some sort of effective and responsive public bureaucracy is required if elected and appointed officials are to implement policies and programs that address collective issues. The functionality of administrative institutions is based on their ability to implement legislative and administrative policy decisions related to the control of the government agenda, the use of budgets, and the production of information that is intended for public decision making.

Politicians and top-level administrators have the advantage of being able to deal directly with the many stakeholders who seek to influence the government. In contrast, career bureaucrats are restricted to implementing existing laws based on current budgets, plans, and political directives, in a political environment in which business and labor leaders strive to seize the opportunity to build institutional and personal relationships with administrative agencies and officials. These stakeholders constantly attempt to influence not only the technical details of program implementation, but also to "capture" the administrative agency's processes of communication and engagement with societal stakeholders, thus allowing them to directly enter into the sphere of political decisions over proposed programs, policies, and budgets. Thus, despite the ideological dominance of market values and mechanisms, the context of political negotiations, understandings, and agreements that characterized bureaucracies during the era of the Interventionist State remains alive and well. It is in fact crucial to the effective operation of a political system, both with respect to administrative decisions and to the more extensive network of relationships with nongovernmental organizations and the fabric of society as a whole.

But because information means power, career bureaucrats have their own advantages in dealing with elected and appointed officials. Their greater ability to collect fragmented and dispersed (i.e., asymmetric) information (Ayala, 2000) gives them an advantage over politicians, despite the fact that administrative agencies are supposedly accountable to politicians is either elected or appointed. This asymmetry of information influences the treatment and fate of government policies, since bureaucratic entities can link with other bureaucracies to create a "shadow government" with its own administrative structures and objectives.

In the end, and despite the ideological shift from an interventionist State to market values and mechanisms, contemporary government still relies upon the relationship between elected and appointed officials and public administrators to establish program priorities and allocate resources so that the benefits of government action are distributed equitably among actors and stakeholders. This intensifies patronage and clientelism, thereby ultimately affecting the availability of public financial resources.

Nonetheless, the global trend in favor of discrediting public administration (Prats, 2005) continues to support the view that public agencies do not comprise a set of capabilities that support shared benefits, but instead are to be viewed as a harmful burden that devours economic surpluses and consumes public resources without effective controls. According to this logic, public administration itself has been discredited as a disciplinary guide to those who seek to use State action as a tool for societal development. In many countries and regions (e.g., Australia, Canada, Scandinavia, the United States, the United Kingdom, and New Zealand), the dominant political discourse continued to critique their performance unfavorably. Without a doubt, the financial cost of public administration—at least as it was practiced during the era of the Interventionist State—increased transaction costs and thus negatively impacted the implementation of government policies designed to benefit citizens and society.

When the Interventionist State finds itself in an era of constant crisis management because of negative popular sentiments and its own internal inefficiencies (Barzelay, 2003), it loses its ability to respond to these critiques because the indicated faults are not only administrative, but also relate to more fundamental understandings of the meaning of bureaucratic power and functions in the generalized scheme of centralized bureaucratic governance. This means that we need a new model of government that restores its systemic capabilities of the State within the limits delineated by civil society and markets. This is not a question of correcting administrative inefficiencies (e.g., formalism and delays in policy and program implementation), but rather the need to formulate a viable model of political–administrative relationships—including the many contractors involved in third-party governance via principal–agent theory—that accentuate information asymmetry, which in turn affects the performance of existing administrative agencies facing exponential demands and scarce resources, the political tendency to create new agencies rather than relying on existing ones to ensure the effectiveness of newly authorized policies and programs, the inability to reconcile conflicting demands for due process and the reduction of red tape, and the inability to consistently evaluate public agency performance in the face of constantly increasing demand, without assessing the capacity of public administration to process and respond to them.

Maximizing bureaucratic advantage within this political context affects the behavior of managers and politicians. Absent external controls to evaluate their performance in a systematic and unbiased way, maximizing revenues within the context of the budget consideration and approval process thus becomes an exercise in political calculation that mobilizes and intensifies internal bureaucratic power. In Europe, the OECD (Organization for Economic Cooperation and Development) has the authority through its Committee and Secretariat on Public Management (PUMA) to review and transform the patterns of bureaucratic management in ways that positively affect public management (Barzelay, 2003). Both Mexico and the United States lack this institutional capability.

Rethinking State Action

Thus, currently we exist in a temporary and unsustainable situation that balances the assumptions and mechanisms of the Interventionist State with demands for a more fundamental review of government's role in an era of globalization market by increased competition and insurgency in markets and civil society. The previous model of hierarchical governance and bureaucratic implementation long ago reached its limits (Aguilar, 2006), to the point where internal administrative reforms cannot restore its functionality. This means that public administration is now facing a structural management crisis that can only be resolved by defining and establishing a new relationship between society and the State.

Crisis management thus constitutes not only solutions to specific policy issues, but solutions to a crisis of governance. This means that public administration, at least as it is currently defined, has also reached the limit of its effectiveness in the application and enforcement of unproductive management patterns that in the end have only led to decreases in productivity and disruptions of the market economy. It is therefore necessary to roll the film backwards so that we may understand the causes and reverse the effects of the Interventionist State, in order to transform existing institutional patterns of governance in light of the new tasks confronting public administration. The factors that affect the transformation of the State and its administrative institutions, and thus impede the creation of a more active, responsive, and effective public administration, include (1) the strength of the public interest, (2) the new rules of political game, (3) the professionalization of public service, (4) processes for ensuring political responsiveness, monitoring results; accountability; transparency and public evaluation.

The Strength of the Public Interest

One positive consequence of the negative costs of the Interventionist State is that it tends to strengthen public awareness and engenders the formation of community-based organizations (e.g., the emergence of the Solidarity Trade Union movement in Poland, the fall of Berlin Wall, and the end of authoritarian regimes in Eastern Europe). Such movements initiate when citizens demand rights and participation in the management of public affairs, and mark the start of a new dynamic in civil society. In States formerly accustomed to authoritarian rule, this signifies that the initiative to participate in communal life is no longer the exclusive domain of government, but of civil society. Once government no longer can claim a monopoly on the collective public affairs agenda, it becomes an exercise in community interaction and responsibility, thus creating a climate where increasingly diverse interest groups can emerge.

The increased diversity of the public interest (Rabonikof, 2005) is a decisive factor in expanding and broadening societal benefits when varied groups contribute in setting the social, economic, and political agenda. Their ability to participate is closely tied to the expansion of minority civil rights (e.g., homosexuals, racial and ethnic minorities, persons with disabilities, and other formerly marginalized groups). So the extension of the third sector—neither markets nor the State is comprised of individuals and nonprofit organizations with an interest to collaborating to address shared problems. The economic agenda encompasses issues related to the need to encourage and protect entrepreneurial freedom so that public monopolies do not disrupt free market actors. These include collaborative production of goods and services, the development of more open and responsive forms of business organization, and public–private partnerships, privatization, public services concession, franchise, and commercial delegation of tasks to groups of society.

This increased emphasis on cross-sectoral cooperation and incentives characterizes public policy making because of demands for participation in building and implementing collective decisions. The necessary conditions for effective interaction and coordination are defined and formalized through intergroup agreements. The public space within society thus becomes the locus for the expression of collective energy, self-management and solidarity, especially in context where resources are scarce. Once it begins, the expansion of public space is unstoppable because the newly empowered citizens and community-based organizations are reluctant to cede the initiative back to the interventionist state. For example, upheavals in Egypt since the overthrow of Mubarak in 2011 represent continued pressure to overthrow an authoritarian regime and to limit excessive statism in favor of a more open and representative government.

Society can thus take advantage of the capabilities unleashed by the replacement of the interventionist state by more participative, community-based forms of social organization. A dynamic public space (Rabonikof, 2005) is feasible once citizens become active, informed, and organized. This implies that the State, despite its history of more authoritarian and interventionist tendencies, comes to recognize that a society based on shared power and metacentric relationships enhances the response capabilities of effective systems. Because the emergent model of a community-based society has greater support, government itself is likely to be more participative, flexible, and supported by society.

The New Rules of the Game

Faced with the exhaustion of hierarchical authority and interventionist policymaking, the noninterventionist state is free to develop a more contemporary model of decision making based on the tenets of organizational learning that characterize our globalized and increasingly knowledge-based society. This means that the public management crisis that originally led to the social and economic bankruptcy of the welfare state, and to citizen disenchantment with politicians and public administrators alike, has only begun. At a managerial level, it requires that we evaluate state activity to determine and change outmoded management strategies that inflate public costs. This means not only the structure and function of public agencies in general, but their operational enforcement of rules, regulations, and procedures throughout society. This review of what the state does and what it can really do is the cardinal point that guides the transition from an Interventionist State to a Regulatory State (Majone and Spina, 1993). It means moving from a State that rows to one that steers via regulation and mobilization of forces within society through the application of stimuli, incentives, sanctions, penalties to markets; and through the encouragement of social networks and partnerships to encourage or correct their performance. It highlights the importance of institutional change (Majone, 1998) involving politicians, bureaucrats, citizens, interest groups, and organizations, understood broadly as systems of collective action. This requires that we recognize and confront the constraints and opportunities that characterize the new order of relationships between state, market, and society (Majone, 1998).

One additional consequence of the new rules of the game is to recognize that state failures predominantly occur at the intersection of the economy and public agencies (North, 1993), and involve stagnation and wasted resources due to the potential failure of institutions in a market economy. Consequently, even after effectively implemented privatization policies have eliminated the excesses, abuses, and negative costs associated with interventionist policies, the State still has a critical regulatory role to ensure the effective operation of open markets (i.e., the norms, rules, and procedures that authorize and restrict both individual and collective behaviors, particularly at a regional level, to ensure social and productive cooperation [Cassese, 2003]). The paradigm of producing and distributing the benefits of social democracy via Keynesian economic policies and mechanisms is replaced by the imperative to establish, define, and apply the new rules of the game in order to strengthen the certainty and predictability with which society and markets operate (Hayek, 1993), based on a new paradigm of enhanced economic freedom and reduced bureaucratic meddling.

In this case, public policy related to regulation becomes central to the relationship between society, markets, business leaders, citizens, and state agencies. The new objective—high-quality regulation—requires that the State, as both regulator and promoter, must consider and then transparently define such key variables as property rights, transaction costs, and information asymmetries in ways that ensure institutional certainty. Once property rights (e.g., ownership, land titles, contracts, and the use of eminent domain to expropriate private property for public purposes) are defined consistently and supported effectively by State agencies, the uncertainties caused by unclear rules or sudden changes are reduced. When these transaction costs decline, production of goods and service expands; this in turn increases investment, rewards risk, and stimulates capital formation and wealth production. In addition, this gives both capitalists and public administrators an incentive to collaborate in streamlining bureaucratic rules, processes, and procedures so that they are not onerous or costly.

Under these new rules, administrative institutions should support economic growth, not impede or block it. Similarly, private businesses should recognize that the State has a vital responsibility to avoid information asymmetries, thus guarding against the danger that monopolies and oligopolies do not produce benefits and privileges that alter the performance of economic exchange. Markets, as a system of institutions (North, 1993), need reliable and timely information to prevent the rise in transaction costs, and the development of practices that generate uncertainty among market participants. The types of information required include investment opportunities, openings, expansion, restructuring, new developments or market closures, the development of production and service lines; the operation of stock markets and private equity portfolios, the geographical movement of capital, goods, and technologies; regional or sectoral economic development; and oversight over stock exchanges and other business investment mechanisms; and other types of information needed to ensure the free operation of competitive markets. Thus, reforming the State's administrative and bureaucratic practices to ensure the open flow of information is crucial to accomplishing its responsibility to support economic competitiveness in our increasingly globalized world.

Relationship between Public Oversight and Good Governance

Governance concerns the process of collective life by which governments work with other stakeholders to address and resolve complexity public problems. The core of governance relates to governments' ability to lead, convene, and encourage civil society and its agencies to discuss and reach agreements to ensure stability, efficiency, and productivity as part of a more extensive political process of consultation and public responsibility. Therefore, governments are subject to greater demands and oversight from citizens, and the effectiveness of the public policies they develop is evaluated with the involvement of organizations in civil society, as part of the general process of shared governance responsibility that characterizes contemporary democracies.

This means that public administrators and appointed and elected officials must work together to develop new patterns of governance, understood as the networked pattern of interaction by governmental and nongovernmental stakeholders in undertaking actions that affect society as a whole. This new model of governance includes new actors, requires more agile responses, and more public management innovation to break cultural inertia and bureaucratic routines. Hierarchical decision making, resource allocation, and distribution of benefits only confirm the persistence of authoritarian practices and exclusive relationships that perpetuate social and political inequality.

The acceleration of globalization, the wider distribution of authority power, and the increased role of nongovernmental organizations as actors in civil society with respect to both the debate over and in the implementation of solutions to public problems have made political systems both more democratic and more inclusive (Luhmann, 1981). The ineffectiveness of administrative pyramids, combined with the rise of civil society, implies the emergence of polycentric networks of interest that in turn give rise to sociocentric networks of policy networks to carry out action on collective governance issues. These community-based organizations give life to the general concept of social action and communitarianism (Bresser and Cunill, 1998) by fighting for civil rights, cooperative public service efforts comprised of organizations fighting for civil rights, altruistic and cooperative organizations, and the development of social capital. This model comprises the new model of governance based on autonomy, cooperation, and the network of organizations to carry out the design and implementation of public and social objectives. This means that compliance with collective goals is based not only on traditional government authority, but based on community-based organizations' sense of identity and commitment.

Community-based organizations tend to be the vehicle for advancing general issues related to public welfare (e.g., ecology, environment, and minority rights) because they arise out of community ideals and needs (Vieira, 1998) rather than more particular or private interests based on corporatist relationships, political party affiliations or shared marketing agreements or trade to fulfill their public tasks. They earn a place in the public space as a result of the processes of democratization, which are nourished by the culture of citizenship, increasing social practices, and the advent of new forms of collective action. In this sense, they are reactive to the tasks undertaken by the authorities; and in any case, constitute a demand for a seat at the table where the public affairs agenda is defined and implemented.

Therefore, the collective solution of the problems is the angle that characterizes the new dynamics of the processes of social and public responsibility. In this case, the authority does not abdicate its responsibility or duty, but serves as a focal point of effort, skills, and resources that can be used to give effect to the fulfillment of public interest. Thus tasks related to education, health, production, and delivery of public services can be in the hands of organizations in civil society, without waiving the authority to carry out the functions entrusted to it by constitutional and legal mandates. Within the vision of the new governance represented by cooperation among government, markets, and civil society, public administration's latest role is as the entity responsible for stimulating and coordinating decentralized initiatives by individual and networked organizations. These include societal interest aggregation, participatory budgeting, social evaluation committees, citizen audits, citizen councils, and citizen observers or ombudsmen (Aguilar, 2007). These neither undermine nor replace the program planning, management, and evaluation activities, but represent a new way of articulating interests, organizing activities, and evaluating performance of collective action from multiple—including non-state—arenas of civil society.

Consequently, public administration is now more public and social. Its task is more specific (i.e., to develop the institutional arrangements required by political authorities and nongovernmental partners to fulfill collective goals). In this sense, public administration is increasingly involved in the dynamics of public policy networks (Cabrero, 2005) in order to stimulate the production of wealth, employment, safety, health, social security, and protection for vulnerable groups. This model of public administration demands that managers and employees develop the ability to respond more effectively to demands for regulation. The increased domination of public policy making by networks rather than hierarchies gives public administration greater connection to the public interest, defined in terms of social action by community-based organizations.

Networked governance gives public administrators the dual responsibility of representing citizens and monitoring the performance of networked organizations. This in turn requires better performance measurement instruments and greater awareness of how to integrate performance issues into the public agenda. This also demands the response of better instruments and a more public exercise in the way it is integrated the public affairs agenda. In this case, further highlights the regulatory side of the state in relation to society by emphasizing public administrators' role in helping to design and put into place a post-bureaucratic paradigm (Barzelay, 1998) that brings autonomy, adaptability, performance agreements, administrative freedom, flexibility, performance measurement, impact assessment, intensive use of technology and regulatory reform to encourage the responsiveness of administrative institutions. In this environment of greater flexibility and adaptation, public administrators interact more with contemporary society in the public arena, and focus less on the formal responsibilities of their jobs. Public agencies become part of the process by which the public interest is articulated in society, based on their interaction with individuals and entities in business and community-based organizations.

Public administration's ability to affect how government programs are structured and carried out (through agencies, budgets, policies, programs, and activities) is fundamental to the development of community life. Together, public administration and government provide the activity by which the State fulfills its responsibility by meeting public goals and objectives in specific areas (Subirats, 2005). Consequently, performance measurement and evaluation is a high priority task of administrative institutions in the context of public policy: What contextual variables are important?; what skills are required?; what results are achieved relative to initial objectives?; with what costs and benefits?; and with what degree of acceptance by citizens?; and with what long-term contribution to the growth of a market economy and a civil society that are more productive, efficient, and entrepreneurial? Policy evaluation in this sense involves not only the application of technical criteria, but open discussion and societal learning (Subirats, 1995) as part of a continuous process of knowledge management and organizational learning that leads to constant self-correction and self-improvement.

In this model of more intense collaboration between public administration and organized community life, expanding the public space requires greater horizontally focused coordination, cooperation, and incentives to produce institutional efforts that are more creative, visionary, and efficient. Because civil society is also responsive to this logic of coordination and incentives, evaluation is required to measure and assess how resources are used in public life, connecting the organizational capacity of businesses and civil organizations with that of the State (Zapico, 2005). Public administration must refine public policy assessment instruments (Majone, 1998) to include measures of the contributions of collaborating nongovernmental organizations (Guerrero, 1995). Similarly, it is essential that the evaluation effectively assesses the costs, benefits, and impacts associated with the activities of administrative institutions (Majone, 1998). From another perspective, administrative institutions are responsible for creating public value by addressing and solving community needs, taking into consideration the underlying characteristics of the political and community structures with which they work.

Because government administration is the first contact between agencies and citizens, the quality of administrative service provision and treatment of citizens' requests is another indicator of stress in the evaluation process. The appropriate focus of evaluation is the quality of services provided based on the policy formulation and implementation process, not administrative inputs or processes. The fact that multiple actors are now involved in addressing social problems and performing public functions related to the production and distribution of goods and services means that the perspectives and contributions of social organizations must be assessed in terms of efficiency, effectiveness, and responsiveness to the public interest. Accountability requires that administrative institutions should be transparent, and that the comparative effect of programs on different groups of citizens be carefully measured. Multifaceted evaluation (i.e., benchmarking) is required because different stakeholders use different outcome criteria and effectiveness measures. Evaluation based on one set of outcome variables, or on internal administrative processes, increases the risk of inaccurate or invalid program assessments.

Conclusion

Contemporary governance requires that political institutions and public agencies work together with market- and community-based organizations. Networked governance requires a new set of administrative tools more related to communication and coordination, and less to the exercise of hierarchical authority or legal control. Not only does the shift from government to governance mean that a larger and more complex set of institutions are involved in the policy-making, implementation, and evaluation process, but also the fundamental change in the definition of citizens from subjects of the state to its co-owners means fundamental changes in the nature of political and bureaucratic institutions, including administrative agencies.

Implications for Relations between Mexico and the United States

Border governance is a consequence of the changes induced by the processes of globalization, which includes a new relationship between space and time, open borders, technological innovation, market integration, intergovernmental coordination, increased human migration, and the previously discussed changes in the role of the State, changes in public institutions, a more extensive public space occupied by a more varied network of interacting institutions, and new models of social interaction, organizational behavior, and stewardship in democratic societies.

Border governance is thus the result of global changes, including the intensification of global interactions and interdependencies and the consequent intensification of public demands for good governance. The bipolar structure of international relationships that characterized the world from the end of World War II to the fall of the former Soviet Union shifted fundamentally to an era of plurality and diversity. In relations between states as well as within them, centralized systems are being replaced by horizontal processes, including political decentralization. This model of "local regionalization" (Vigil and Fernández, 2012) based on interaction, trust, shared responsibility, and an enhanced role for community-based organizations means that a new model of civil society and governance must be applied to the traditional field of international relations and diplomacy among sovereign nation states.

Thus, border governance is linked to the general restructuring of power relationships in society toward forms of organization that are less centralized and bureaucratic. The formation of the European Union, the development of Asian nations along the Pacific Rim, and the North American Free Trade Agreement (NAFTA) are examples to the new order of institutional rules for cooperative development in border regions. Viewed as a general conceptual model, they indicate that our ways of structuring incentives, sanctions, opportunities, and constraints are focused toward increasing competition, technological innovation, digital information, and the development of open markets for trade and finance, which sets an environment of interdependence and cooperation from the perspective of institutional change (Aboussi and Garcia-Quero, 2012).

Viewed in this light, trans-boundary governance is a form of regional governance (Vigil and Fernández, 2012) that results from changes in institutional power relations in the face of imperatives to enhance governance capabilities in the face of globalization's imperatives. Information and business innovations occur in a world moving rapidly beyond the scope of national governments, particularly in countries characterized by shared borders and economic and social interdependence. This certainly applies to the relations between Mexico and the United States, since these countries have unarguably entered a new phase of border governance that befits their status not as distant or hostile neighbors, but as next door neighbors with a shared history, culture, economics, politics, trade and—in many crucial respects— shared policy agendas.

Because the relationship between Mexico and the United States is increasingly broad and complex broader and therefore more complex, their shared cooperative policy agenda includes issues related to the fight against organized crime, the containment of drug markets, the treatment of migrants, regulation of imports and exports, border security, military cooperation, and economic development. One of the most sensitive issues is immigration reform. Given the current political climate in the United States, this includes not only immigrants, but popular acceptance of Hispanics as U.S. citizens and residents in key states such as California, Texas,

New York, Illinois, and Florida. Of the 312 million people now living in the United States, 35 million are of Mexican origin. In 2012, they paid over $50 million in taxes and contributed 8% of the country's GDP, indicating that Mexicans contribute significantly to the U.S. economy. During 2012, Mexican's living in the United States sent over $22 million to in remittances (Section Money, 2013).

The State of California is home to 11 million of Mexican immigrants and has the fourth largest economy in the U.S. ranks in terms of GDP. In agricultural areas of the state, Mexicans comprise over 90% of the population. Moreover, Mexican migrants are consumers of goods and services in the economy, and also pay taxes that support the U.S. economy. They buy cars and houses, and spend on leisure and other consumer goods and services. However, the uncertain status of undocumented migrants produces distortions in the market economy, and reduces their ability to contribute to economic development through the production, distribution, and consumption of goods.

Hence, immigration reform must be understood not only as crucial to migration, but as directly related to the rights and political participation of Mexicans living in the United States. It is the key to their equitable involvement as stakeholders in formulating and implementing public policy on health, education and other public services, loans and mortgages, competitive salaries, welfare, and social security. On the other hand, attitudes toward immigration reform are also framed by fear of transnational criminal organizations (TCOs), since they focus popular attention on insecurity, human trafficking and prostitution, extortion, drug trafficking, violence, and death (Heredia, 2012). The involvement of TCOs in money laundering (Heredia, 2012), organ trafficking, and illegal arms traffic increases the complexity and scale of the immigration issues. The immigration problems between the United States and Mexico tend to be complex because the underlying policy agenda comprises issues related to employment, wages, remittances, taxes, civil rights, education, public health, demographic shifts, economic growth, social inequality, comparative birth rates, labor market conditions, unemployment, and human trafficking.

The overwhelming long-run advantage of democracies is that they are centered on the interests of the individuals and on their inclusion in government. With the approval of public policies that reinforce the principles of equality and reduce large-scale inequities among groups and individuals, they can avoid the economic and social conditions that lead to different lifestyles and policy outcomes in spite of individual initiative. With respect to the issues addressed in this chapter, it's important to design policies that include migrant workers within U.S. society regardless of their national origin, ethnic identity, or location. The effectiveness of an advanced Western nation like the United States in accommodating itself to globalization and modernity can best be demonstrated by achieving a social consensus that expands migrants' socioeconomic benefits by recognizing their formal legal status as citizens or residents, and thus permits them to take their place as valued members of their communities.

References

Aboussi, M., and F. Garcia-Quero. 2012. Una aproximación institucional al emprendimiento de los inmigrantes. *Revista Reforma y Democracia,* 53: 97–130. [Caracas, Venezuela, Centro Latinoamericano de Administración para el Desarrollo].
Aguilar, V. and F. Luis. 2006 *Gobernanza y gestión pública.* México, Fondo de Cultura Económica.
Aguilar, V. and F. Luis. 2007. El aporte de la Política Pública y la Nueva Gestión Pública a la gobernanza. *Revista Reforma y Democracia,* 39: 5–32.
Ayala Espino, J. 2000. *Instituciones y economía. Una introducción al neoinstitucionalismo económico,* México, Fondo de Cultura Económica.
Barzelay, M. 1998. *Atravesando la burocracia. Una nueva perspectiva de la Administración Pública,* México, Colegio Nacional de Ciencias Políticas y Sociales y Fondo de Cultura Económica.
Barzelay, M. 2003 *La nueva gestión pública. Un acercamiento a la investigación y al debate de las políticas.* México, Fondo de Cultura Económica.
Bresser, P., C. Luiz, and N.C. Grau. 1998. Entre el Estado y el mercado: Lo público no estatal, in L. Bresser Pereira and Nuria Cunill Grau (eds), *Lo público no estatal en la reforma del Estado.* Buenos Aires, Centro Latinoamericano de Administración para el Desarrollo (CLAD) and Editorial Paidós, pp. 25–56.
Cabrero, E. 2005. *Acción Pública y Desarrollo Local.* México, Fondo de Cultura Económica.
Cassese, S. 2003. *La Globalización Jurídica.* Madrid, Instituto Nacional de Administración Pública.
Crozier, M., S. Huntington, and J. Watanuki. 1975. *The Crisis of Democracy.* New York, New York University Press.
Guerrero Amparán, J.P. 1995. La evaluación de políticas públicas: Enfoques teóricos y realidades en nueve países desarrollados, *Revista Política y Gestión Pública,* 41: 47–118.
Hayek, A. F. 1993. *Camino de Servidumbre.* Madrid, Alianza Editorial.
Heredia Z. C. 2012. Políticas públicas y migración en las Américas. *Revista de Administración Pública,* 128: 27–38. [México, Instituto Nacional de Administración Pública].
Luhmann, N. 1981. *Teoría Política del Estado de Bienestar.* Madrid, Alianza Editorial.
Majone, G. and A. la Spina. 1993. El Estado regulador. *Revista Política y Gestión Pública,* 22: 97–261.
Majone, G. 1998. *Evidencia, argumentación y persuasión en la formulación de políticas.* México, Colegio Nacional de Ciencias Políticas y Administración Pública y Fondo de Cultura Económica.
North, C. D. 1993 *Instituciones, Cambio Institucional y Desempeño Económico.* México, Fondo de Cultura Económica.
Prats Catalá, J. 2005. *De la Burocracia al Management, del Management a la Gobernanza.* Madrid, Ministerio de Administraciones Públicas.
Rabonikof, N. 2005. *En busca de un lugar común. El espacio público en la teoría política contemporánea.* Mexico, Instituto de Investigaciones Filosóficas, UNAM.
Seccion Dinero [Business]. April 7, 2013. *Periódico Excelsior.*
Subirats, J. 1995. Los instrumentos de las políticas, el debate público y el proceso de evaluación. *Revista Gestión y Política Pública,* 4.1: 5–24.
Subirats, J. 2005. Podemos utilizar los instrumentos de evaluación como palanca de gobierno del sector público? en *Responsabilización y Evaluación de la Gestión Pública* (et al.), Caracas, Venezuela, Centro Latinoamericano de Administración para el Desarrollo,

Agencia Española de Cooperación Internacional Ministerio de Administraciones Públicas y Fundación Internacional y para Iberoamérica de Administración y Políticas Públicas, p. 48.

Vieira, L. 1998. Ciudadanía y control social, en Luiz Carlos Bresser Pereira y Nuria Cunill Grau (eds.), *Lo público no estatal en la reforma del Estado*. Buenos Aires, Centro Latinoamericano de Administración para el Desarrollo, y Editorial Paidós, pp. 215–255.

Vigil, J. I. and V. R. Fernández. 2012. Gobernanza y regiones en perspectiva crítica: un abordaje para la construcción de políticas públicas. *Revista Reforma y democracia*. Caracas, Venezuela, Centro Latinoamericano de Administración para el Desarrollo, núm. 53, pp. 21–60.

Weber, M. 1973. *El político y el científico*. Madrid, Alianza Editorial.

Zapico, E. 2005. Desarrollo integrado de la evaluación y el presupuesto por resultados: un camino largo y pedregoso con destino incierto. *Responsabilización y evaluación de la gestión pública*. Caracas, Venezuela: Centro Latinoamericano de Administración para el Desarrollo, Agencia Española de Cooperación Internacional, Ministerio de Administraciones Públicas, Fundación Internacional y para Iberoamérica de Administración y Políticas Públicas, p. 109.

Chapter 15

Analysis, Conclusions, and Final Considerations

Roberto Moreno Espinosa

Contents

Preface 239
Mexico–U.S. Relations 240
"Wicked Problems": Complex Issues in U.S.–Mexico Relations 242
Migratory Movements 242
Illegal Drug Trafficking 244
Policies Promoted by Mexico in the Fight against Drug Trafficking 244
Possible Solutions from the Perspective of Democratic Governance and
Bilateral Political Commitments 247
Final Reflections 248
References 250

Preface

Whether we are scholars, diplomats, statesmen, or interested public citizens, it is essential that we think about how to substantively improve relations between Mexico and the United States, and that we take steps to do so based on the multiple and almost unlimited benefits provided by our common diversity and shared status as neighbors. While there have been times in our common past that have historically been less than cooperative and even marked by open conflict, this is not an insurmountable obstacle. Just as people can learn and change, so countries can seek to define new relationships that take advantage of their complementarity, find common ground, and promote new solutions to old problems. For example, despite the economic and political crises that have recently emerged in some European Union (EU) countries (e.g., Greece, Spain, Portugal, and Italy), its general benefits still outweigh the perceived problems today. The most obvious example is that the two world wars of the previous century, which claimed millions of lives and billions in financial losses, have (with the noted exception of the Balkan conflict of the 1990s in the former Yugoslavia) not been repeated.

It's time to start a debate about viable ways to make the relationship more friendly, intelligent, productive, durable, and complementary. By building bridges that lead to more promising paths, we can improve our relationship in worthwhile ways. And unless we do this, we are doomed to indefinitely prolong old problems and worsen new ones, while the organized crime and drug trafficking that have caused such great harm to our respective societies continue to expand in more sophisticated ways.

We start by discussing and analyzing the fundamental economic and social links between Mexico and the United States that have led us to where we are today, a "perfect storm" of drugs, money, and firearms that has cost Mexico 60,000 deaths and nearly 27,000 missing persons in the last six years alone, as shown by the figures released by the government headed by President Enrique Peña Nieto. Many of these cases are the result of conflicts arising from the infighting of the cartels involved, and also as an unintended consequence of the strategy followed by the Mexican government to engage intensively with the cartels using the army and air force controlled by the Ministry of National Defense (SEDENA), and the Navy (SEMARNAT).

Another essential factor is the geopolitical connection between the United States and Mexico that has emerged because the United States is a large consumer of illegal drugs. While some are produced in Mexico, others are shipped through Mexico from Latin America and the Caribbean. Because migrants are sometimes used as drug traffickers, drug trafficking exacerbates long-standing disagreements between our two countries over how to handle migration and economic development in the border region. Some well-intentioned U.S. efforts to combat drug trafficking—like the ill-fated U.S. government operation (called "Fast and Furious") that allowed hundreds of U.S. firearms to cross into Mexico for subsequent use by the cartels—have had disastrous consequences for which the United States has not yet accepted responsibility. These are but a few examples of the complex and interrelated issues that must be addressed if our countries are to move forward together.

Mexico–U.S. Relations

Relations between the United States and Mexico are varied, diverse, complex, and often asymmetric. They are stories that have been branded into generations of

Mexicans and Americans for the past two centuries. Geographically, it is a story of a border between two countries that extends over 3000 km from the Pacific Ocean to the Gulf of Mexico. Politically, it is a story about U.S. conquest and domination, marked by U.S. annexation of Texas and the U.S. invasion and defeat of Mexico in 1846–1848, remembered forever by Mexicans for the doomed but heroic sacrifice by Mexican military cadets who died defending Chapultepec. This resulted in Mexico ceding (through purchase by the United States) large amounts of territory (i.e., California, Arizona, New Mexico, and southern Colorado), thereby enabling U.S. transcontinental expansion to the Pacific but also effectively foreclosing Mexico's own geopolitical ambitions.

It is the story of two neighbors with different characteristics and traditions with respect to ethnicity, language, culture, and political systems. Mexico's is highly centralized, bureaucratic, and—at least through the end of the last century—run by political elites in a culture based on absolute authority and clientelism. That culture is now changing, due to demands for increased citizen participation, government decentralization, and inroads on the constitutional power of institutionalized unions and other private interests. The U.S. political system is fundamentally decentralized, with a dynamic, participatory, and entrepreneurial tradition that inspired Alexis de Tocqueville to write one of the classics of nineteenth-century political sociology, *Democracy in America*. Its presidential system, marked by separation of powers (legislative, executive, and judicial) and the marvelous checks and balances designed primarily by James Madison, was itself a reaction against its own historical colonial relationship with Great Britain.

It is a story about 150 years of imperialism that resulted from the two countries' asymmetric political and economic conditions and from the long-standing U.S. tendency to either ignore Mexico or blatantly intervene in its internal affairs. U.S. and European investors have often dominated Mexican politics, including taking control over the port of Veracruz in the 1920s. The U.S. placed strong pressure on Mexico not to implement the constitutional provisions of the country's Third Federal Constitution (1917), in particular Article 27 of the Constitution, which gave rise to part of the contents of the Bucareli Agreements signed by both countries and Mexico that established conditions for diplomatic recognition by the government of the United States.

It is a story about interdependence. Millions of Mexicans have migrated to the United States in search of better economic and social conditions. Many remain in that country today without being U.S. citizens or legal residents. About 80% of Mexican exports go directly to the United States. In 2012, Mexicans living in the United States sent back over U.S. $20 billion in the form of remittances, the area of remittances from the North Country to Mexico, during 2012, exceeded U.S. $20 billion dollars. In the 20 years since the signing of NAFTA in 1994, the two countries' economies have become increasingly interconnected. The growth and profitability of international organized crime—including drug trafficking—is but one aspect of this.

"Wicked Problems": Complex Issues in U.S.–Mexico Relations

Wicked problems are complex, interrelated, and lacking obvious agreement on the nature of the problem and/or the desired solution. They thus result in a series of imperfect, piecemeal, and palliative solutions. In the case of Mexico–U.S. relations, each country has tended to address the problems it perceives independently of the other, and often in opposition to it. Sometimes, when the countries' interests have coincided, effective policies have been the result. In the case of migratory policy, the shortage of U.S. workers brought on by World War II resulted in the *Bracero* and the *Railroad* programs, which led to the presence of at least 50,000 agricultural and 75,000 railroad workers in the United States by 1945. However, these were short-term agreements brought on by wartime exigencies. In the early 1980s, the Simpson–Rodino Act promoted strengthening police forces in the border area, and also provided alternatives to legalize a number of immigrants.

The illegal drug trade is another "wicked problem." It is an extensive and highly profitable species of the genus known as international organized crime, involving many South and Central American countries as well as Mexico. The violence resulting from cartels competing for control of markets and smuggling routes in Mexico has threatened government authority in major areas of the country, and brought about the spread of violence (murder, kidnapping, rape, and "disappearances"), particularly in the border region.

Migratory Movements

At various times in recent history, a gamut of political, social, economic, and demographic conditions in Mexico have led to massive migration to the United States. In fact, Los Angeles (California) has the highest concentration of Mexicans of any city outside Mexico. During President Vicente Fox Quesada's administration (2000–2006), an average of at least 450,000 Mexicans migrated north each year. This mass migration was a consequence of Mexico's high birth rate during the period 1960–1980, and a labor surplus resulting from the depopulation of rural areas and the perceived lack of economic opportunities in Mexico. At one point shortly before the end of his term of office in 2006, President Fox remarked that he would rather that Mexicans stayed in Mexico and ate tacos instead of going to Los Angeles and eating hamburgers. While most Mexicans agreed with this sentiment, many privately concluded that they had no choice except to migrate due to the lack of economic opportunity in Mexico. In fact, several recent Mexican administrations have not yet dealt with the consequences of this vast migration, particularly the wholesale departure of working-age men (and some women) from the countryside.

One characteristic of the contemporary phase of globalization is diasporas, the complex movements of populations sparked by new forms of production, economic cycles, the population explosion, and violence (particularly ethnic, sectarian, or tribal) (Imaz, 2012).

These affect about 3% of the world population, and are one of the most important issues in the national and international agendas of many countries. This of course includes Mexico and the United States, which grew into a multiracial and multicultural nation as a result of successive waves of migrants from various countries, mainly European but also from Africa and the Americas. In this regard, the United States has a strong tradition of openness and has thus experienced major flows of immigration. It is the country with great variety and number of ethnic groups, defined in economic, social, and political terms. Since the 1970s, the national origin and racial composition of immigration to the United States ceased to be primarily European, as it had been previously. Between 1820 and 1960, roughly 82% of immigrants were of European origin. This share had fallen to 18% by the late 1970s, and had been replaced by significantly increased immigration from Mexico, the Caribbean, Central America, and parts of Asia. (Report of the Presidential term from 1982 to 1988, fourth year, available at: http://mmh.org.mx/nav/node/605, accessed 02-13-2013.)

The change in the composition and proportion of immigrants to the United States in the second half of the last century has had enormous effects on Mexico. Although there had already been a tradition since ancient times for Mexicans to migrate to their northern neighbor, its intensification fundamentally affected—and to this day continues to affect—various aspects of national life: economic, political, and social.

A good portion of these migrants noted in the quote above were in the country illegally. In some sectors of society and within the U.S. government, this generated concern, prompting the government to revise immigration policies. The main objection of various sectors of the American public opposed to this was that immigration reduced employment opportunities for Americans. Since 1980, these significant societal groups have fought for the establishment of legislation to curb illegal immigration. (Report of the Presidential term from 1982 to 1988, fourth year, available at: http://mmh.org.mx/nav/node/605, accessed 02-13-2013.)

Consequently, the United States approved legislation (the Simpson–Rodino Act) intended, among other objectives, to punish employers who hire illegal workers, exert greater border control, expel illegal immigrants, and increasingly regulate those who remained. As Imaz suggests,

"Migration is an issue that touches heartstrings, because it affects the cultural and national identity of the population, especially in the countries of destination. More developed regions require additional manpower, but refuse migrants permanent status and stigmatize them during times of high unemployment" (Imaz, 2012).

Because immigration varies as conditions change, and because it has profound implications for those who migrate as well as for their countries of origin and destination, it is necessary to address migration as a chronic policy issue, and to address the most pressing problems while working toward more permanent solutions.

Mexican migration to the United States started over 160 years ago, beginning with the division of the territory north of Mexico in 1848. It should be noted that the respective data 2010 census threw in both countries. The flow of Mexican migrants has since declined due to many factors, primarily demographic. The rate of population growth has declined significantly and large families are the exception. In the 1970s, Mexican families had an average of seven children, and could not support them. The result was emigration. Now that families have an average of two children, migration is not the only, or the best, option (Imaz, 2012, p. 40).

Migration from Mexico to the United States has solved problems in both countries, and has been an escape valve for Mexico's population, but at a high cost to Mexico in terms of the breakup of families and the loss of human capital, given that regardless of however low or high the migrants' qualifications, the costs are borne by Mexico, and the United States becomes the recipient of multiple benefits, including cheap, skilled labor among others.

Illegal Drug Trafficking

The illegal drug trade is perhaps the most complex of the problems that embody the "perfect storm" between the two countries, one that generates perverse links among different issues that are at stake: arms trafficking, money laundering, and the production, shipment and use of drugs and narcotics, which in turn provoke a set of social and personal issues that cause immeasurable damage in both countries.

The drug problem has resulted in a number of policy agreements defined or adopted by countries throughout the Americas, several of them crafted by policy makers in the United States. The Harrison Act, passed by the U.S. Congress in 1914, prohibited over-the-counter sale of opium, morphine, cocaine, and heroin. The results were counterproductive because it generated greater drug trafficking and illegal drug use, spurred the development of organized crime and catalyzed the production, distribution, and consumption of drugs throughout the Americas, particularly in the United States as the largest market for drug consumption. In sum, it is an "intermestic" problem that transcends the border between Mexico and the United States. Though the core of the problem is in this frontier area, the decisions these countries make and implement have implications that extend throughout the Western Hemisphere.

Policies Promoted by Mexico in the Fight against Drug Trafficking

Elaborating on the issue that concerns me, it is noteworthy that illegal drug trafficking has become a scourge not only for Mexico, but throughout the Hemisphere (particularly in South America) and other parts of the world. The problem is that the United States is the world's largest consumer of illegal drugs, and the main distribution routes go from South American countries (Bolivia, Peru, Colombia, and

Ecuador) through Central America and Mexico. As was with the case when alcohol was smuggled from Mexico, Canada, and the Caribbean into the United States during the 1920s, making drugs illegal did not stop their being produced, shipped, or consumed. It did make trafficking more lucrative, and it made the transnational criminal organizations (TCOs) that engage in drug trafficking much more violent. Astorga (2009), a major specialist in the field in Mexico, emphasizes that drug trafficking has always been linked to politics, but until the end of the last century it had been controlled and protected by the Federal Security Directorate, to the extent that its effects in Mexico were less visible and less violent.

The drug problem has gotten out of control and has become so serious mainly because of two factors. The first is economic, since this illegal activity generates more than U.S.$19 billion in Mexico alone, according to calculations based on data from the governments of Mexico and the United States (Aranda, 2009). To illustrate the magnitude of this amount, consider that it is about the same as the total annual amount of remittances that Mexicans in the United States send their countrymen back home and considerably larger than Mexico's annual income from international tourism. With this much money at stake (and available to distribute as bribes), TCOs find it relatively easy to corrupt the police, most of whom are poorly paid, low-skilled, and cannot depend on their own nation's security forces to protect them and their families from TCOs. Drug trafficking's profitability intensifies competition for control over production and distribution routes, which has caused the terrible wars between rival gangs that have left a toll of thousands of lives around the country.

What's worse, the civilian authorities responsible for public safety have no financial means or human or technical resources to deal with a problem of such magnitude. TCOs exercise *de facto* control over significant areas in Mexico, to the point where they pose a serious threat to the stability and permanence of democratic institutions in the country. It was at this point that the previous administration of President Felipe Calderon (2006–2012) ordered the Mexican military to join the fight against drug trafficking. But the armed forces lack the training to engage in a guerrilla war like the one in which they were ordered to intervene, and they were equally unprepared to act as civilian police.

The policies designed to contain the growth of organized crime in Mexico during the two most recent presidential terms, both won by candidates from the Partido de Accion Nacional (PAN), were merely palliative. President Vicente Fox (2000–2006) strengthened the recently created federal police so that it became the civilian agency charged with the fight against organized crime. But its effect was limited, as its staff numbered only a few thousand and its financial scope was minimal. When Felipe Calderon came to power (2006–2012), he needed a strategy that would demonstrate the power of the State, avoid the appearance of weakness, and increase popular support for his party and its administration.

One of his first actions he took during the start of his administration was to send contingents of soldiers and sailors to combat illegal drug trafficking, accompanied by a significant flood of pro-government media coverage, to spread the word that the President could and would act decisively against the threat posed by TCOs. To improve the quality of life for military personnel and prevent the mass desertion that had been experienced during the previous six years, he also increased the gross monthly salary in virtually 100% during the period between 2006 and 2009 (CNN Mexico, 2010).

President Calderon's strategy was to organize joint operations in states with high crime rates, starting with his own home state of Michoacán, where competing cartels like the Sinaloa cartel and "La Familia Michoacana" had gained a dangerous power that threatened to spread to neighboring states. He sent 4,260 troops from the Army and Navy of Mexico, supported by more than 200 vehicles (*El Universal*, 12/12/2006). This troop deployment, termed the Joint Operation Michoacán, was accompanied by an intense media campaign that publicized and magnified the work done by the troops. Popular support for this military action was overwhelmingly favorable (reaching 80% in the first quarter of 2007), and silenced critics (*El Universal*, 12/12/2006).

The effectiveness and popularity of this first joint operation led the government to extend the tactic to Tamaulipas, the "Gulf Cartel's" home ground, and to Nuevo Leon, where this criminal group sought to control drug trafficking. However, the military's lack of experience with guerilla warfare led it to confront the drug cartels directly, as if they were fighting a conventional war against uniformed combatants. But direct confrontation proved to be ineffective against an enemy that was embedded in the population, and did not withdraw in the face of the military presence. Also, increased security in the border areas resulted in the TCOs initiating a fierce struggle to control the remaining available areas they could still use to introduce drugs into the United States.

The result was the most violent six-year period in living memory (2006–2012), a frenzy of indiscriminate murder, kidnap, assault, and extortion that left at least 60,000 dead, 26,000 more "disappeared," and much of the civilian population traumatized by the fear and insecurity that resulted from being caught in the middle between the drug gangs and the military that was supposedly there to protect them. The lesson learned was a costly one. While confrontation was inevitable, the use of troops against the cartels should have been integrated with other strategies proven effective against this kind of enemy, starting with the construction of an intelligence capability that would have allowed the government to launch precision attacks, capturing or killing the TCOs' leaders and leaving the organizations weakened and leaderless (at least temporarily), and avoiding the high social cost of flooding the streets with soldiers and police, as in a conventional military operation.

Financially, expenses for security agencies and the military skyrocketed, diverting resources that could have been sent to high priority sectors such as health, education, or employment generation. As Table 15.1 shows, the total resources allocated to public safety almost doubled in just four years, and tripled in the Ministry of Public Security.

Table 15.1 Resources Allocated to Public Safety in the Draft Budgets of Federal Expenditures from 2006 to 2010 (Millions of Pesos)

Unit	Ministry or Agency	PPEF 2006	PPEF 2007	PPEF 2008	PPEF 2009	PPEF 2010
4	Interior	4737	5083	6736	9594	8640
7	National Defense	26,031	32,200	34,861	43,623	42,531
13	Marina	9163	10,951	13,382	16,059	15,887
17	Attorney General's Office	9550	9216	9307	12,309	12,090
36	Public Safety	9274	13,664	19,711	32,916	31,802
	Total	58,755	71,114	83,997	114,501	110,950

Fighting the drug wars as if they were a direct confrontation with a foreign enemy not only resulted in loss of life for thousands of Mexican citizens, but also used resources that could have been channeled to fund the creation of more universities or public hospitals. In a country like Mexico—without a recent history of military confrontations or external enemies, it was not a profitable investment in the medium and long term. Security policies focused only on military-police action, and put aside the preventive work that could have helped to save the lives of thousands of citizens, as a decisive boost to education through scholarship and financial aid, growing the economy by investing in infrastructure that would allow the creation of thousands of jobs for young Mexicans to avoid them falling into the hands of organized crime.

Possible Solutions from the Perspective of Democratic Governance and Bilateral Political Commitments

The issues related to illegal drug trafficking and migratory movements, among others, are complex and intractable "wicked problems" that comprise a genuine "perfect storm." To resolve them, we must look for more—and more effective— long-term strategies and tactics on the part of both Mexico and the United States, strategies first defined separately and then coordinated. These strategies must first be defined by each of the countries involved and then jointly, with an emphasis on facing underlying issues as well as immediate threats, and treating the civilian population as if it were comprised of citizens—which it is—rather than enemy combatants or a hostile enemy. Here are some policy suggestions for the Mexican government to consider:

- To improve internal policy coordination and continuity, develop and refine a long-term (i.e., more than one 6-year presidential term) policy oriented

toward fighting organized crime in all its forms, in which the several federal agencies involved would align mission, vision, policies, and programs (i.e., the Ministries of the Interior, Foreign Affairs, Education, and specific elements of the Mexican military).
- To discourage emigration to North America and reduce the attractiveness of organized crime as a source of income or a viable career option, enhance job creation efforts among the most vulnerable sectors of the population. The United States and Canada can both contribute by increasing investment in Mexico, a policy which will also do much to strengthen the NAFTA economy that increasingly competes with China as a center for manufacturing and export.
- To realize the full potential of NAFTA to promote concerted economic, social, and political development throughout the Northern Hemisphere, work with the United States to define a migration policy that provides immigrants to the United States with legal status, thus enabling them to contribute to the U.S. economy without enduring the social, economic, and political inequality that result from continuing to apply the current ineffective, inefficient, and unfair U.S. immigration control system.

The "perfect storm" (Klingner, 2012) is a "wicked problem" because it comprises a number of complex and interrelated policy issues—migration, money laundering, and trafficking in firearms and illegal drugs (Klingner, 2012). It is also a self-inflicted injury brought on by the governments of two neighboring countries that have stubbornly insisted on following uncoordinated and unilateral policies. By first intensifying the quality of the bilateral policy debate, and then aligning policies and resources to achieve greater complementarity, both countries can create and maintain the political will needed to tackle these tough issues. Because each country confronts a range of "intermestic" issues, this enhanced political and administrative capacity could be profitably extended to other heretofore intractable policy issues involving other countries and regions.

Final Reflections

At first glance, the idea of writing a book on the drug trafficking crisis between the United States and Mexico as an unrecognized opportunity to improve relations between these two countries seems preposterous. Why write about such a problem that has caused such great damage to both countries, with no end in sight? Why tackle such a difficult set of policy issues (e.g., migration, drugs, guns, and money laundering) when many other safer and more manageable topics are available? Yet in fact, all of our contributing authors accepted the idea with enthusiasm and followed through with commitment. In less than a year, each chapter was outlined, drafted, completed in either English or Spanish, translated into the other language, and edited to ensure uniform standards of clarity and documentation.

Understanding why this happened is important. First, globalization has affected higher education in general and public administration in particular by expanding its focus from individual countries to global trends and issues. The editors and contributing authors all have extensive international experience in the United States, Mexico, and other countries. Regardless of their country of origin, they have studied, taught, and consulted throughout the world. They have been widely exposed to international scholarship in public policy and management, learned from it, and applied these insights into their own work.

Second, professional expectations have become more international and multidisciplinary. Within both Mexico and the United States, there is increasing recognition that the most valuable work is now being done across national, linguistic, and cultural boundaries, and in the interstices between academic disciplines such as public administration, political science, law, economics, business, and sociology. For many years, it has been accepted that those who wish to be considered for—much less promoted into—top positions in the world of business and finance will have international experience, because the organizations they work for require it. This increasingly applies not only to academics and consultants, but to practicing public administrators as well. Although politics is focused on local, regional, or national geographic jurisdictions, worldwide movement of people guarantees that even administrators who do not themselves work internationally need to be comfortable with those who have immigrated from other countries. This means that the field of public administration is increasingly defined in terms that are multilingual, multicultural, and multinational.

Third, the colleagues who accepted the challenge of writing on such a complex and intractable topic did so because they felt it was important to do so. We have each invested the time and taken the risks required to gain international experience, and have earned the credibility that comes from having worked effectively with colleagues in other countries. We have each benefitted professionally and personally from it. One consequence of becoming an international scholar is that once you have looked at it from an outsider's perspective, there are times when no country seems as strange to you as your own. So like border crossers everywhere, we have learned things that others may not know, things we think and feel are applicable to the "intermestic" (i.e., "international" and "domestic") policy issues our countries face. If we do not apply our experiences and understanding in an effort to resolve this important policy issue, one that has had such a terrible effect on both Mexico and the United States, who do we expect will do it, and when, and how?

Fourth, a project of this scope and significance requires a great deal of mutual respect and trust. The editors and contributing authors have all worked together for many years in university venues and professional associations. We have done research together, written books and articles together, been on conference panels together, and worked as consultants for many of the same international development organizations. We know each other's qualifications, and we have learned to respect each other's intelligence, insights, and motivation. Put another way, we have worked together long enough, hard enough, and well enough to have developed the social capital required for a shared undertaking like this project. If not, it wouldn't have happened.

So I'd like to close by thanking each of the contributing authors from Mexico, Canada, and the United States for the opportunity to work together on this book, for all they have taught me about what the "border area" means as a physical space and a psychological concept that both divides and unites our countries, how the "perfect storm" represented by drug trafficking between Mexico and the United States has affected each country, and how we might work together to resolve it. This includes, but is not limited to: Donald E. Klingner, Denis Proulx, Angélica Pérez Ordaz, José Luis Cisneros, José Antonio Rosique Cañas and Gloria Rosique Cedillo, Kurt Johnson and Michael A. Noll, Mario Rivera and Sofía Alejandra Solís Cobos, Ramona Ortega-Liston and RaJade M. Berry-James, Adriana Plasencia Díaz, Espiridion ("Al") Borrego, Oscar Mauricio Covarrubias, David Arellano Gault and Enrique Cabrero Mendoza, Miguel Moreno Plata, and Ricardo Uvalle Berrones.

References

Astorga, L. 2009. *México, transición democrática, organizaciones de traficantes e inseguridad*. *Razón Pública*. Bogotá: Fundación Razón Pública.
Astorga, L. 2010. El tráfico de armas de Estados Unidos hacia México. Responsabilidades diferentes. *Informe de Política del International Drug Policy Consortium*. Available online at: http://www.seguridadcondemocracia.org/oco-im/documentos-de-analisis/el-trafico-de-armas-de-estados-unidos-hacia-mexico.-responsabilidades-diferentes.htmlAccessedJuly3, 2013.
Bonnin, C.-J. 2004. *Principios de Administración Pública*. Compilación y estudio introductorio de Omar Guerrero. México: FCE.
Comisión Intersecretarial para la Prevención Social de la Violencia y la Delincuencia (CIPSVD). 2013. *Bases del Programa Nacional para la Prevención Social de la Violencia y la Delincuencia*. Mexico: Gobierno de la República.
Covarrubias, M., O. Mauricio. 2006. *El problema de la coordinación en el gobierno contemporáneo. Hacia un estado federal coordinado*. México: IAPEM.
Covarrubias, M., O. Mauricio. 2011. The challenges of interdependence and coordination in the bilateral agenda: Mexico and the United States. In J. W. Meek and K. Thurmaier (eds.). *Networked Governance: The Future of Intergovernmental Management*. Washington, DC: Sage Publications.
Crónica del Sexenio 1982–1988, cuarto año, http://mmh.org.mx/nav/node/605.
Diario, *El Universal*, 12/12/2006.
Diario, *La Jornada*, 11/08/13.
Ganster, P., (ed.) 2001. *Cooperation, Environment, and Sustainability in Border Regions*. San Diego: San Diego State University Press, Institute for Regional Studies of the Californias.
Hobbes, T. 1651. *El Leviatán*.
Ley General del Sistema Nacional de Seguridad Pública (LGSNSP). 2009. Cámara de Diputados del H. Congreso de la Unión, México.

Ley General para la Prevención Social de la Violencia y la Delincuencia (LGPSVD). 2012. Congreso General de los Estados Unidos Mexicanos, México.
Morales y Gómez, J.M., R. M. Espinosa (eds.). 2011. *Democracia y gestión pública. Fundamentos para la Reforma del Estado en México*. México: UAEM, Miguel Ángel Porrúa.
Moreno Espinosa, R. et al. 1996. *La administración pública estatal y municipal en el Estado de México en los procesos de globalización, apertura e intercambio*. México: IAPEM.
Observatorio Nacional Ciudadano Seguridad, Justicia y Legalidad. 2012. *Reporte Periódico de Monitoreo sobre Delitos de Alto Impacto, Mayo-Agosto de 2012*. Mexico: Observatorio Nacional Ciudadano Seguridad, Justicia y Legalidad.
Revista de Administración Pública. 2012. Las políticas públicas sobre migraciones, México, D. F., XLVII(2), (mayo–agosto, 2012).
Revista *Buen Gobierno*, No. 11 semestral, Jul–Dic, 2011.
Revista *Buen Gobierno*, No. 13 semestral, Jul–Dic, 2013.
Revista del CLAD *Reforma y Democracia*, No. 53, Jun. 2012, pp. 97–130.
Secretaría de Seguridad Pública. 2008. *Programa Nacional de Seguridad Pública, 2008–2012*. Mexico: Gobierno Federal, Secretaría de Seguridad Pública Federal.
Subsecretaría de Prevención y Participación Ciudadana. 2012. *Modelo de Prevención Social del Delito*. Mexico: Gobierno Federal, Secretaría de Seguridad Pública.
Uvalle Berrones, Ricardo (ed.) 2005. *Perfil contemporáneo de la administración pública*. México: IAPEM.

Index

A

Administrative evil, 124
Affirmative action, 123
Almada brothers, 52
American Council on Education (ACE), 12
American Management Association (AMA), 12
American Planning Association (APA), 12
American Political Science Association (APSA), 12
American Society for Public Administration (ASPA), 12
    Good Governance website, 12–13
    National Conference, 177
"Anthrax, The", 55
Arizona, 188
    Arizona State policy, 187
    population and employment demographics, 127–129
Armed forces
    Mexican, 84
    mobilization, 99
    permanent, 98
    respecting IACHR decision, 91
    roles for, 90
Arturo Beltran Leyva, staged execution of, 52
ASPA, *see* American Society for Public Administration (ASPA)
Association for Public Policy and Management (APPAM), 12
Association for Research on Nonprofit Organizations and Volunteer Agencies (ARNOVA), 12
Autodefensas Unidas de Colombia (AUC), 25

B

Bilateral political commitment, 247–248
Binational comprehensive legal migration solution, 9
Binational health council (BHC), 170
Binational law enforcement model, 9
Border management, 9
Brazil, drug trafficking in, 22–23
Brown zones, 212
Bureaucracy, 212–213
    inadequately professionalized, 219
    representative, 121, 122

C

Cartel violence, 164
    affecting governance in Mexico, 165
    City of Mission, 171–173
    health care issue, 170–171
    Hidalgo County, 164–165, 170, 171
    issues in Texas, 169–170
    outright prohibition of official travel, 166
    potential against media and journalists, 67, 68
    Texas Sister Cities program, 173–174
    UTPA, 166–169
CENCOS, *see* National Center of Social Communication (CENCOS)
Center for Investigation and Security, *see* Centro de Investigacióny Seguridad (CISEN)
Centro de Investigacióny Seguridad (CISEN), 100, 213
CIFA, *see* Customs inspection (CIFA)
Citizen participation, 156

254 ■ Index

City charters, 169
City of Mission
    cartel violence, 171–172
    cultural competence, 172–173
    cultural exchange, 172
Ciudad Juarez, 154; *see also* Education on line
    development factors of city, 155–156
    strategies in Rebuilding City, 156–157
Civil service system, 193; *see also* Federal system
    conflict of interest, 204
    corruption, 193, 194, 195
    federal level corruption, 197, 200
    involving public servant, 205
    "magic bullet", 201
    municipal corruption, 196, 199
    as political institution, 203
    political nature, 201–203
    public service, 198
    service by governmental office, 200
    social problem, 196
    state-level corruption, 197, 199
    whistle-blower, 206
Civil society, 107, 232
    ineffectiveness of administrative pyramids, 230
    new model of, 234
CLAIMS, *see* Computer Linked Application Information Management System (CLAIMS)
Cockroach effect, 21
Collateral victims, 28
Colombia, drug trafficking in, 23–25
Colonias, 164
Commission of investigation (CPI), 20
Community Security and Justice System (SSJC), 214
Community-based organization, 230–231
    centralization of power, 146
    federalism, 146, 147
    public space, 228
Computer Linked Application Information Management System (CLAIMS), 145
Conferencia Nacional de Gobernadores (CONAGO), 187
Conflict of interest, 204
Contemporary state dimensions, 211–212
Corruption, 14, 89, 193–194
    in Colombia, 24
    criminal system, 215
    as domestic policy issue, 8
    ENCIG data, 198
    federal-level public service, quality of, 199
    federal level, 197
    involving public servant, 205
    IPC, 66
    "magic bullet", 201
    in Mexico, 65, 195
    municipal, 196
    municipal public services, quality of, 199
    perception of public, 198
    sequence of linked events, 204
    state-level, 197
    state-level public service, quality of, 199
    systemic, 194
    in West Africa, 21–22
    whistle-blower, 206
Counterintelligence, 89–90
CPI, *see* Commission of investigation (CPI)
Cristero War, *see* Time of Cristeros
Cross-border collaboration, 164; *see also* Cartel violence
CSN, *see* National Security Council (CSN)
Cultural competence, 122, 172
Customs inspection (CIFA), 106

D

DEA, *see* U.S. Drug Enforcement Agency (DEA)
Department of Justice (DOJ), 82, 134
Dream Act, 40, 41
Dropout rate, 151, 153
Drug addiction, negative consequences of, 30
Drug production, 29
    Colombia's role in, 24
    U.S. efforts to control, 3
Drug trafficking, 18; *see also* U.S.–Mexico drug trafficking
    Brazil, 22–23
    collateral victims, 28
    Colombia, 23–25
    CPI, 20
    drug addiction, consequences of, 30
    drug production, 29
    drug victims, 28
    FARC and AUC, 25–27
    global drug markets, 20–21
    in Mexico, 31–32
    from Mexico to Central America, 21
    PA, 18, 19
    weakness of governance, 19
    West Africa, 21–22
Drug victims, 28
Durango, execution in, 53

E

Early Warning Infectious Disease Surveillance (EWIDS), 170
Education on line; *see also* ¡Vámonos pal Norti!
  average schooling, 150
  dropout rate, 153
  dropping out, 151
  idyllic vision, 154
  indicators in border states, 153
  national development, 154
  percentage of illiteracy, 152
  PISA assessments, 149–150, 151
El Paso del Norte, *see* Ciudad Juarez
Emergency operations centers (EOC), 171
Enemies of society, 49
Equal Employment Opportunity Commission (EEOC), 121, 128
  employment categories, 129, 131
Estrategia Nacional de Prevención del Delito y Combate a la Delincuencia (ENPDyCD), 108
European Union (EU), 240
EWIDS, *see* Early Warning Infectious Disease Surveillance (EWIDS)

F

Failed States Index (FSI), 217
FARC, *see* Fuerzas Armadas Revolucionarias de Colombia (FARC)
"Fast and Furious" program, 2, 240
FBI, *see* US Federal Bureau of Investigation (FBI)
FDI, *see* Foreign direct investment (FDI)
Federalism, 184, 185; *see also* Mexican federalism
Federal level corruption, 197
Federal system, 183
  coordination, 183
  federalism, 184
  inferred points, 185
  interdependence in, 183, 184
  shared decision making, 184
Federal Trade Commission (FTC), 133
FIP, *see* International Press Federation (FIP)
Foreign direct investment (FDI), 154
Frontera Chica, 164
Frontier of knowledge, 141
  education on line, 149–154
  Juárez, 154–157
  Mexican federalism, 146
  team of rivals, 145–146
  ¡Vámonos pal Norti!, 142–145
FSI, *see* Failed States Index (FSI)
FTC, *see* Federal Trade Commission (FTC)
Fuero militar, 91
Fuerzas Armadas Revolucionarias de Colombia (FARC), 25, 26, 29, 31
Functional legal authority, 213; *see also* Bureaucracy
  ENVIPE, 216
  FSI, 217
  "Knights Templar", 214
  principles, 215

G

Governance, 223; *see also* "Perfect storm"
  border, 234
  cartel violence effect, 165
  centralized bureaucratic, 226
  drug trafficking and, 19
  networked, 232
  options for bolstering, 94–95
  relationship with public oversight, 230–233
  rethinking state action, 226–227
  in West Africa, 22
Gross domestic product (GDP), 38, 125, 133

H

Hidalgo County, 164
  cartel violence, 164–165, 170
  Health and Human Services Department, 170
  health care issue in, 170–171
  objectives of draft agreement, 171
  and U.S.–Mexico border, 164, 170
High-risk profession, 61; *see also* Journalism under attack
  anomie concept, 63
  IPC, 66
  National Commission of Human Rights, 62
  organized crime, 63, 67
  risk factor for organized criminality, 63–64
  sociological model, 65
  State's ability, 64–65
  violence, 64
Hispanic-serving Institution (HSI), 134
Hispanics, 39, 120, 132
  decision-making positions, 121
  educational attainment by, 126–127
  in mentoring relationship, 135–136

Home rule cities, 169
Homeland defense activity, 92
HSI, *see* Hispanic-serving Institution (HSI)
Human Development Index (HDI), 154
Human resource (HR), 122
Human service department, 170–171

I

IACHR, *see* Inter-American Commission on Human Rights (IACHR)
ICE, *see* Immigration and Customs Enforcement agency (ICE)
ICESI, *see* Institute Studies Citizen Insecurity (ICESI)
ICMA, *see* International City/County Management Association (ICMA)
ICTs, *see* Information and communications technologies (ICTs)
Idyllic vision, 154
Illegal drug trafficking, 244
ILO, *see* International Labor Organization (ILO)
Immigration agents (INM), 106
Immigration and Customs Enforcement agency (ICE), 10
Immigration and Naturalization Service (INS), 122
INAP, *see* National Institute of Public Administration (INAP)
INEGI, *see* Instituto Nacional de Estadística, Geografía e Informática (INEGI)
Information and communications technologies (ICTs), 36
INM, *see* Immigration agents (INM)
INS, *see* Immigration and Naturalization Service (INS)
Institute Studies Citizen Insecurity (ICESI), 67
Institutional Revolutionary Party (PRI), 212
Instituto Nacional de Estadística, Geografía e Informática (INEGI), 65, 195
Intelligence, 89–90, 100
Intelligent management, 9
Inter-American Commission on Human Rights (IACHR), 91
Inter-American Press Society (SIP), 73
Interdependence, 182
  in federal system, 183–185
  between Mexico and U.S., 185–186, 187
Internal Revenue Service (IRS), 135
International City/County Management Association (ICMA), 12
International Labor Organization (ILO), 151
International organized crime, 83, 241, 242
International Press Federation (FIP), 73
International Public Management Association for Human Resources (IPMA-HR), 12
IPC, *see* Perceptions Index of Corruption (IPC)
IRS, *see* Internal Revenue Service (IRS)

J

Journalism under attack, 67; *see also* High-risk profession
  IPC, 66
  murder of Manuel Buendía, 66
  murders and disappearances, 69
  principles of, 62
  protection in Mexico, 61, 72–74
  reflections and recommendations, 74–75
  socio-economic context, 65
  violent cities in World, 68
Journalists, 62
  dead and missing/kidnapped persons, 71, 72
  murders and disappearances of, 69, 70
  protection, 72–74
  violence against, 74
Juarez, *see* Ciudad Juarez

K

Kingpin strategy, 94
"Knights Templar", 56, 214

L

La Paz Agreement, 169
Latin American Integration Association (LAIA), 218
Latin American States, 210; *see also* Mexican state institutional crisis
  dimensions of contemporary state, 211–212
  failure of modernity, 210, 211
  modernity, 210
  state crisis in, 210, 211

M

"Magic bullet", 201
Masters of Public Administration (MPA), 166
Memorandum of Understanding (MOU), 166, 167, 169
Mexican federalism, 146
  current tax code, 149

PISA result, 150
urban country, 148
weakness of municipalities, 147
Mexican state institutional crisis, 212; *see also* Latin American States
  bureaucracy, 212–213
  collective identity, 217–218
  defense of national interest, 217–218
  functional legal authority, 213–217
Mexico
  AFI, 106
  climate and topography, 67
  federal police role, 103–104
  federal public administration, 100
  institutional systems, 105, 107
  legal and institutional frameworks in, 98
  legal framework, 104
  marijuana, 3
  Mexico–U.S. relation, 240–241
  military operations, 86–87
  military transformation, 88–89
  national security, 99
  National security system, 101, 111
  new institutionalism, 109
  organized crime, 99
  Peña Nieto administration, 102
  police operations, 106–107
  policy, 247–248
  public safety, 108
  SSyE, 110
  trans-territorial effort, 107
Migration, 243
Migratory movement, 242
  change in composition and proportion, 243
  diasporas, 242–243
  Mexican migration to U.S., 243–244
Military in Homeland, 79
  border control, 91–92
  civil support mission, 81
  counterintelligence, 89–90
  Department of Defense, 82
  as enabler, 94–95
  human rights issue, 90–91
  intelligence, 89–90
  limitations on use of, 83–84
  Mexican military operations, 86–87
  Mexican military transformation, 88–89
  military affairs, 84
  SEDENA, 84–86
  SEMAR, 84–86
  US and Mexican militaries, 80
  US military on border, 93–94

Modernity
  approaches and debates, 210
  failure of, 210–211
  unfinished, 210
Modernization, 210–211, 212
MOU, *see* Memorandum of Understanding (MOU)
MPA, *see* Masters of Public Administration (MPA)
Municipal corruption, 196

N

NAFTA, *see* North American Free Trade Agreement (NAFTA)
Narcotics trafficking literature, 124–125
  analyses of drug violence, 125
  drug trafficking, 125
  TBI report, 126
Nash equilibrium, 194
National Center of Social Communication (CENCOS), 73
National Conference of Governors of Mexico (CONAGO), *see* Conferencia Nacional de Gobernadores (CONAGO)
National Guard troops, 91, 92
National Institute of Public Administration (INAP), 12
National Institute of Statistics and Geography (INEGI), *see* Instituto Nacional de Estadística, Geografía e Informática (INEGI)
National security, 99
  drug trafficking effect, 98
  Federal Police role, 103, 104
  law enforcement or defense, 81–83
National Security Council (CSN), 100, 101
National Security System, 101
National Strategy for the Prevention of Crime and Combating of Delinquency, *see* Estrategia Nacional de Prevención del Delito y Combate a la Delincuencia (ENPDyCD)
National System for Democratic Planning (SNPD), 109
National System of Public Security (SNSP), 66
Networked governance, 232
New institutionalism (*nueva institucionalidad*), 109
New York Times (NYT), 189

Index

NGO, *see* Nongovernmental organization (NGO)
Nongovernmental organization (NGO), 168
   role in civil society, 230
   in United States and Mexico, 94–95
North American Free Trade Agreement (NAFTA), 3, 37
NYT, *see New York Times* (NYT)

O

Office personnel management (OPM), 133
Operation Condor, 21
Organization for Economic Cooperation and Development (OECD), 149, 226
Organized crime, 18, 65, 99, 111
   conditions, 63
   effect on Mexican entities, 70
   federal government propaganda, 51
   geography of violence, 49
   international, 83, 241, 242

P

PA, *see* Public administration (PA)
Partido de Accion Nacional (PAN), 245
Peña Nieto administration, 102, 114
Perceptions Index of Corruption (IPC), 66
"Perfect storm", 1, 2, 152, 154, 240, 248
   ASPA, 12–13
   border management, 9
   complexity of relations, 6
   drug trafficking in Mexico, 2
   governance capacity, 8
   long-term foreign policy initiative, 10
   Merida initiative, 4
   Mexico's traditional political culture, 5
   policy innovations, 11
   professional associations, 12
   strategic research exchanges, 11–12
   between two countries, 244
   United States, 7
   war on drugs, 3, 5
PFP, *see* Policía Federal Preventiva (PFP)
PGR, *see* Procuraduría General de la República (PGR)
PISA, *see* Program for International Student Assessment (PISA)
Plan Nacional de Desarrollo (PND), 108
Planeación Estratégica mechanism, 109
Policía Federal Preventiva (PFP), 106
Policies against drug trafficking, 244, 246
   draft budgets of federal expenditure, 247
   drug problem, 245
   TCOs, 245
Posse Comitatus Act, 83, 92
PRI, *see* Institutional Revolutionary Party (PRI)
Procuraduría General de la República (PGR), 67, 104
Program for International Student Assessment (PISA), 149, 150
   results for Mexico, 150
   results for North Border States, 151
Public administration (PA), 18
   criminal economies, 27
   federal, 100
   money laundering, 28
Public education systems, 42
Public management (PUMA), 226
Publicness, 223
   game rules, 228–230
   OECD, 226
   public administration, 224
   relationship between governance, 230–233
   shadow government, 225
   strength of public interest, 227–228
Public policy
   comprehensiveness, 156
   in Mexico and U.S., 3
   performance measurement and evaluation, 232
   related to regulation, 229
Public safety, 108
   civilian authorities responsibility for, 245
   resources allocation to, 247
PUMA, *see* Public management (PUMA)

R

Regional Community Authority (RCCA), 213
Representative bureaucracy, 121
   concomitant lack of, 130
   role and place, 121
Rethinking state action, 226–227
Return on investment (ROI), 123, 132
   career challenge, 134–135
   economic statistics for Mexico and U.S., 133
   Hispanics in mentoring relationship, 135–136
   mentoring influences on career, 135
Reynosa, 164–165
Rio Bravo, 165
ROI, *see* Return on investment (ROI)
Rondônia's miracle, 22

S

SB 1070 law, 188
Science, technology, engineering and mathematics (STEM), 154
Secretaría de la Defensa Nacional (*SEDENA*), 101
Section on Public Management Practice (SPMP), 12
Servicio de Carrera Policial (SCP), 108
Shared border, 180, 186
SIP, *see* Inter-American Press Society (SIP)
Sistema de Seguimiento y Evaluación (SSyE), 110
Sister cities, 146, 173
    in Mexico and U.S., 37, 147
        Texas Sister Cities Program, 171, 173–174
SNPD, *see* National System for Democratic Planning (SNPD)
SNSP, *see* National System of Public Security (SNSP)
Spoils system, 202
SSJC, *see* Community Security and Justice System (SSJC)
SSyE, *see Sistema de Seguimiento y Evaluación* (SSyE)
State-level corruption, 197

T

Team of rivals, 145–146
Texas Sister Cities program, 173–174
Time of Cristeros, 53
Tipping point, 81–82, 92
Todos Somos Juárez (TSJ), 142
Trans-Border Institute (TBI), 125, 126
Trans-border region, 39
    economic interdependence, 39
    education, 43
    knowledge-based society, 42
    New Mexico and Texas, 40
    social and political mobility, 41
Trans-boundary governance, 234
Transnational criminal organization (TCO), 2, 218, 245

U

Undocumented student, 40
United Nations Development Program (UNDP), 154
United States Mexico border region (US–Mexico border region), 36, 79, 141; *see also* Trans-border region
    coherent economic strategy for, 9
    contrasts in socioeconomic terms, 146
    demographic shifts, 38
    economic interdependence, 39
    Mexican federalism and consequences, 146–149
    native-born workers, 39
    new order of institutional rules, 234
    sister states and cities, 37
    undocumented student, 40
University Texas Pan American (UTPA), 166
    binational and cross-border research, 168
    disseminate accurate information, 169
    MOU between Mexican, 167
    MPA program, 166
U.S. Department of Agriculture (USDA), 134
U.S. Drug Enforcement Agency (DEA), 3
US Federal Bureau of Investigation (FBI), 65, 134
U.S.–Mexico border, 143, 179
    Arizona State policy, 187
    Barber note, 182
    interdependence, 183–186
    Mexican migration to U.S., 144
    pressure for action, 186
    problems without border, 180, 181
    SB 1070 law, 188
    team of rivals, 145–146
    U.S. migration policy, 189–190
U.S.–Mexico drug trafficking, 126
    educational attainment by Hispanics, 126–127
    employment demographics, 127–131, 132
    population, 127–131, 132
U.S. political system, 241
UTPA, *see* University Texas Pan American (UTPA)

V

Value added tax (VAT), 149
¡Vámonos pal Norti!, 142
    flow of permanent legal residents, 145
    population distribution by region, 144
    railroad construction, 143
    U.S.–Mexico border, 143

Violence, 48; *see also* Cartel violence
   Anthrax, 55
   Arturo Beltran Leyva, staged execution of, 52
   in banana-producing regions, 23
   conceptual categories, 50
   and criminal law, 64
   diminishing in Colombia, 29
   enemies of society, 49
   execution in Durango, 53
   Federal government propaganda, 51
   geography of crime, 48, 49
   instrument of control and dominance, 53
   Knights Templar, 56
   Mexican government, 50
   mutilated corpse, 55
   scenarios of, 56–58
   threat of, 54

W

"War on drugs", 5, 47
   general failure, 11, 29
   in U.S. and Mexico, 120
Washington Office on Latin America (WOLA), 28
West Africa, drug trafficking in, 21–22
Whistle-blower, 205, 206
"Wicked problems", 181, 242, 247

DATE DUE

**RETURN TO
LIBRARY
Room 1E41OHB
For Renewals Call
482-5647 or x 55647**

JUN 2 4 2014